Musical Creativities
in Practice

Musical Creativities in Practice

Pamela Burnard
Faculty of Education,
University of Cambridge,
Cambridge, UK

OXFORD
UNIVERSITY PRESS

HUMBER LIBRARIES LAKESHORE CAMPUS
3199 Lakeshore Blvd West
TORONTO, ON.   M8V 1K8

OXFORD

UNIVERSITY PRESS

Great Clarendon Street, Oxford OX2 6DP,
United Kingdom

Oxford University Press is a department of the University of Oxford.
It furthers the University's objective of excellence in research, scholarship,
and education by publishing worldwide. Oxford is a registered trade mark of
Oxford University Press in the UK and in certain other countries

British Library Cataloguing in Publication Data
Data available

Library of Congress Cataloguing in Publication Data
Library of Congress Control Number: 2012932684

ISBN 978–0–19–958394–2

Printed by CPI Group (UK) Ltd
Croydon, CR0 4YY

Whilst every effort has been made to ensure that the contents of this work
are as complete, accurate and-up-to-date as possible at the date of writing,
Oxford University Press is not able to give any guarantee or assurance that
such is the case. Readers are urged to take appropriately qualified medical
advice in all cases. The information in this work is intended to be useful to the
general reader, but should not be used as a means of self-diagnosis or for the
prescription of medication.

Links to third party websites are provided by Oxford in good faith and
for information only. Oxford disclaims any responsibility for the materials
contained in any third party website referenced in this work.

Dedication

To Brent

Acknowledgements

A number of people have helped me with this project. The 19 musicians who share their stories in this book are extraordinary people at various stages of exceptional careers. I wish to acknowledge their enormous generosity in accepting the challenges of interviews and emails, from inception to publication.

Thanks also to Anna Williams who contributed at the early stages of the research process and to Susan Barnard and Sue Conrad for their transcriptions. My thanks are also extended to colleagues at the University of Cambridge, especially Mike Younger, Paul Andrews, Morag Morrison, and Richard Hickman, for facilitating time to keep working on the book.

I wish to acknowledge the personal support given to me during the writing process by friends and colleagues. I am appreciative of the honesty, ideas, feedback, and advice given on various parts of the manuscript, at crucial times by Liz Tray, Cecilia Björk, Gary Spruce, Martin Fautley, Martin Cloonan, Leah Kardos, Garth Stahl, Michael Pearson, Glen Ladner, and Charlie Ford. Special thanks to Christine Yau, Anna Wong, Roberto Valente, and Christine Watts for playing key roles in the completion of this book.

I would also like to thank Martin Baum, Charlotte Green, and Abigail Stanley from Oxford University Press, as well as freelance employees Lotika Singha and Kim Stringer, whose long-standing support and enthusiasm has helped this text become a reality.

And lastly, but most importantly, I thank my own family for their love and my husband Brent, for his patience and belief in all I do.

Contents

List of figures

List of tables

Advance Praise for *Musical Creativities in Practice*

Pam Burnard is already internationally known for her work on creativity, and this book will not disappoint. Here she brings together, in elegant prose, an original appraisal of the social dimensions of musical creativity, or rather, as she argues, creativities. The discussion cuts across 'real world' processes in a range of contexts, to close with an illuminating application of the ideas to the fields of pedagogy and learning. This book will be on the core reading list of every music education course, and of everyone at all interested in the creative processes governing our diverse musical world, for many years to come.

Lucy Green, Professor of Music Education, London University Institute of Education

Pam Burnard has produced a remarkable book. It examines and analyzes a spectrum of practices of musical creativity. It is well grounded methodologically and supports a comprehensive set of empirically detailed studies of various musical creators with a theoretically sophisticated appraisal of that research material. The narratives of musical practices she engages with range from those of singer-songwriters through to DJ Culture, original bands, composed and improvised musics of the classical tradition, through to interactive audio design. She places each of these narratives against the fields of music pertinent to each and develops a view of creativity that situates it within social and cultural practices. Dismissing many of the myths surrounding musical creativity, this work is linked to a highly useful pedagogical and analytical framework that synthesizes the important work on creativity presented by both Mihaly Csikszentmihalyi and Pierre Bourdieu. Pam Burnard has created a work that will be an exemplar for those undertaking research of this type and will no doubt serve very well indeed those who have set out on the journey to teach and supervise these methods. This is a masterful realization of a major set of ideas. It sits at the cutting edge of research into musical creativity in its many forms and is a necessary addition to the growing body of literature in this area.

Phillip McIntyre, University of Newcastle, author of *Creativity and Cultural Production* (2012).

This is a wonderful book, lyrical in style as befits a book on musical creativities but also theoretically rich and conceptually polished. A real treat for anyone interested in learning more about music.

Professor Diane Reay, University of Cambridge

Burnard's *Musical Creativities in Practice* represents a major achievement in our contemporary understanding of creative music making. Building on mounting empirical and conceptual evidence of the importance of social context in understanding creativeness, this beautifully written and reasoned book presents not only a theoretical framework but also keenly rendered portraits of the creative lives of 19 musicians from a variety of music settings that back up the theory. A 'must read' for any music professional interested in what makes for creative achievement in today's complex world.

Peter R. Webster, Ph.D., John Beattie Professor of Music Education, Chair, Department of Music Studies, Henry and Leigh Bienen School of Music, Northwestern University, USA

For too long thinking about musical creativity has been dominated by the Beethoven myth. This book vividly shows how the everyday practices of musicians working in widely divergent genres embody equally divergent creativities, and explores the educational consequences of this. Never again will it be possible to talk glibly about 'musical creativity': Pam Burnard has let the genie out of the bottle.

> Nicholas Cook, FBA, 1684 Professor of Music, Unversity of Cambridge

The ambition and breadth of this book are astonishing. Burnard must have spent years completing these nineteen interviews with world-class professional musicians in Britain, Europe, and Australia—including originals bands, singer-songwriters, club DJs, contemporary classical composers, improvisational performers, and the interactive audio designers who create video game soundtracks. The best part of the book is reading the words of these articulate musicians as they describe their own creative practices. Burnard's insightful analysis captures the unique creative practices of each musician, and convincingly demonstrates that there is no one way to be musically creative today—instead, we must speak of 'musical creativities.' And yet, all of the musicians constantly refer to the collaborative and socially embedded nature of musical creativity. With the publication of this important book, it is no longer possible to believe in the 19th century Romantic myth of the composer as a lone genius.

> R. Keith Sawyer, Associate Professor of Education, Washington University in St. Louis, USA,
> author of *Group Genius* and *Explaining Creativity*

Pamela Burnard's new book offers a sociological account of how creativity emerges in music relating these to the classroom, challenging conventional assumptions and extending understandings. Well-crafted, thoroughly researched and written with the reader in mind, it will be a provocative and practical resource for those seeking to explore the social context to fostering musical creativities.

> Professor Anna Craft, University of Exeter and The Open University

Pam Burnard's important book takes its rightful place among a growing second generation literature seeking to expand our notions of the nature of creativity and its relationship to learning. Such literature unhooks creativity from 'artiness', individual genius and idiosyncrasy, and renders it team-based, observable and learnable. In doing so it insists that we can no longer step around creativity's challenge to traditional learning and teaching practice at all levels of music education.

The book provides readers with an authentic interrogation of the habitus of creative musical practice, shifting us from the romance of the remote, 'natural' genius who has no need of pedagogical engagement. In doing so, it allows a more important focus on creative ways of learning and performing that are observable and replicable processes and practices within our daily living, learning and earning. Always and inevitably complex, musical creativity becomes less mystical through her research. And once de-mystified, it can be engaged with intentionally as the outcome of real pedagogical work.

> Erica McWilliam, Adjunct Professor, ARC Centre of Excellence for Creative Industries and
> Innovation, Queensland University of Technology

By tackling the many myths surrounding children's music creativities this inspiring contribution fills a much needed gap in the literature. I particularly enjoyed the framework that is provided for understanding musical creativities and how this emerges from real practice across many different settings. Such innovative thinking provides a major advance in our awareness of creativity in music education and a theoretical position that will have enormous impact on the field in the years to come.

Professor Gary McPherson, Ormond Chair of Music and Director, Melbourne Conservatorium of Music, The University of Melbourne, Australia

Engaging, accessible, and well-grounded in conceptual discourses as well as practical examples, Burnard 'corrects' singular and overly individual preconceptions of creativity in Western contexts, presenting a framework that provides the foundation for music education to embrace multiple creativities in both design and practice.

Professor Huib Schippers, Queensland Conservatorium Research Centre, Griffith University, Australia

Introduction

I was a musician long before I was an educator, researcher, and author. My performances and interpretations of the Great Composers number in the hundreds. I know the works of the Great Composers as a musicologist knows music, as an ethnomusicologist knows culture, as a sociologist knows society, and as a psychologist knows the person behind the composer. Being involved with music from childhood has been about learning who I was, what I might hope for, and something about the kind of career trajectory that being a conservatoire-trained pianist helps construct. My role models were many from a long list of Great Composers and Great Performers, and I surrounded myself with their portraits and busts. The attention I devoted to Bach and Beethoven was huge compared with women composers, popular songwriters, or jazz musicians, who would later exert a powerful influence on me. These were precursors to my later practices, but were given little recognition in the development of my learning career.

During both school and university, I was taught to play and encouraged to perform, but not to compose or to forge links between my own creativity and self-discovery or self-realization as a musician. Performances of my own compositions can be counted on one hand. Yet, like all children and young people, I used to make up my own music at home. I even performed one of my compositions in an Eisteddfod. But it was one of the very few times that resulted in my going home as a disappointed non-prize winner. I quickly learned 'the rules' and the powerful and subjectively held opinions adopted hegemonically by institutions—the constructions of social taste that require us to pay attention.

I studied at a conservatoire for four years and I topped the final year by playing Beethoven's Emperor Concerto with an orchestra. However, composing or improvising was never a recognized factor of my achievements. As a child growing up in Australia, I attended country schools, and my abiding memory of music, its learning and teaching, is of graded examinations, successfully competing in Eisteddfods, networking, and visits to the 'big smoke' to play for celebrated international pianists giving special masterclasses at the conservatoire.

Everybody comes with a history or a past that continues to influence practices and attitudes in the present. My habits and disposition as a musician developed well before my creative identity when, several years after graduating from the conservatoire, feeling unprepared and frustrated as a professional musician, I joined a rock band and performed vocals on keyboards and synths. My immersion in popular music and new activities offered variety, independence, creativity, a sense of identity and a whole new perspective on my life in music. I loved the band dynamics, the interplay between music, audience, and media, and the collective creation of music. Having acquired a high level of technical skill and the versatility to work as a session musician in the world of popular music, I crossed over into a distinctly different musical world that included both rock and pop. It felt like I was celebrating my own creativity and that of others for the first time.

All the while, the conservatoire's high art status, either as a social institution in its own right, or in terms of the dominant knowledge forms of a conservatoire curriculum, initially precluded the possibility of developing an alternative to the privileging of Western classical music above all other musics. At the conservatoire, the canon of Western 'art' music, the cult of Beethoven and the fetishization of composition defined some of the rules of the music profession. The conservatoire preserved the canons of good taste through the emphasis on Great Composers.[1]

As I look back now, I am not surprised that my learning career led me to doctoral studies on children's musical creativities. I did not discover music through school. The unfortunate perception of music teachers as lesser beings and 'second rank' helps to form the hierarchy of music careers that still inhibits today's new graduates. My own music learning felt restricted to music history and aural training. It was only when I moved away from all this that I came to see, particularly when I started teaching music in schools, why children fear the act of creativity and creative failure. While some children (as was the case with me) silently disengage, withdraw, or seek simply to avoid creative expectations, others rail against the system, become disruptive, and challenge conventions. The experience of writing this book has shown me that researching musical creativity is no simple matter.

I have learned the importance of representing a variety of voices, of tracing the history of the field, of developing methods of enquiry that generate discussion and deep listening in ways that faithfully represent people's realities and experiences. I have gone to clubs, to jazz and rock subcultural concerts, gatherings, and scenes where, I have come to realize, that the hierarchy of music careers is mirrored in the positioning and status of specific genres. I am still learning how institutionally, we live and work in increasingly complex and competitive socio-cultural environments wherein the positions taken by particular genres and sub-genres require musicians to break down attitudinal and hierarchical barriers.

This book focuses on the real world practices of twenty music industry professionals who champion contemporary creative practices. It traces the changing meaning of musical creativity. It also attempts to expand the concept of musical creativity in the light of contemporary sociological, cultural, and psychological perspectives. By bringing a fresh new perspective to the social construction of musical creativity, it presents a diversity of creative practices that will help build bridges and partnerships between industry and education, artists and educators for the cultural development of both virtual and real communities. Whilst I am not a Bourdieu scholar, I will use his tools in a pluralistic way in the study of multiple creativities in music.

This book offers a powerful corrective to mythological and historical conceptions focused exclusively on notions of creation as a singular activity. It argues for the need for conceptual expansion of musical creativity, to become a plural expression of musical creativities as being distributed and relayed between subjects and objects across cultural-historical time. It builds on the work of Howard Becker (1984) and Michael Grenfell (2008), amongst others. It examines musical creativity in terms of its conceptual history and explores what, as producers and consumers, we believe and do about:

(i) the cult of the Romantic stereotypes of the creator as individual genius;

(ii) the fetishization[2] of composition, mythologized as a fixed thing, deeply rooted in its history;

---

[1] See S. Bennett (2010) for an excellent book on music tertiary institutions, and the dilemmas and opportunities in training and career preparation of classical musicians and the classical music profession. See also Perkins (2012), who has written a detailed analysis of conservatoire learning culture, and Triantafyllaki (2008), who has uncovered corroborating findings about conservatoire teaching and learning and the questions we need to ask about musicians' perceptions of their education and training in music tertiary institutions.

[2] See Goehr (1992), *The Imaginary Museum of Musical Works*, in which she sets out a strong argument for a 'work-based' practice that centres on the belief that musical works were perfectly formed as masterworks imbued with history and myth.

(iii) the canonization of high-status genres (or 'high art' orthodoxies), as evidenced in the hegemonic force of dominant Western, jazz, and popular music discourses,[3] the power of personal myth in the cultivation of public opinion, and the valorized view of composers as superior, even divinely gifted beings who enshrine discourses of originality.

Key questions include: What renders particular types of musical creativities distinctive? How do musical creativities help to define relations between production and consumption (whether these stem from elite or religious patronage, market exchange, public and subsidized cultural institutions, or late capitalism's multi-polar cultural economy)? While I acknowledge that 'music' is both a singular and plural noun, the singular conception of musical creativity does not reflect the plurality of the social production of musical creativities. In this book, I will describe a pluralist conception of musical creativities that has emerged over the past three centuries, and which feature in the most dominant and ubiquitous contemporary music practices.

This book offers a broadening of the concept of 'musical creativity'. It also offers a critical analysis of both the Romantic stereotypes of the creator as individual genius and the hegemonic force of dominant Western and popular music discourses. It provides an empirically based investigation of the principal ideas associated with multiple-categorized creativities in music that can form a basis for moving beyond entrenched positions in both theoretical understanding and empirical research. It attempts to demystify musical creativity, seeing it not as something that a person has or does not have, but rather as something that people do together.

This book strikes at the heart of traditional studies of Western music by asserting that there is no single musical creativity for all musics. Placed centre-stage are accounts of practices by contemporary musicians including digital musicians, video game sound designers, community musicians, singer-songwriters, record producers, originals bands, disc jockeys (DJs), performance artists, traditional musicians, and classical contemporary and avant-garde composers. These professional musicians share narrative accounts that enable us to move from speculation to the specification of multiple musical creativities. The book challenges the exclusive high-art orthodoxy that valorizes the individual Great Composer. It debunks residual misconceptions and myths associated with a notionally singular musical creativity. It argues for a closer examination of multiple musical creativities, which goes beyond taken-for-granted assumptions and stereotypical notions of the individual creative genius, while acknowledging the historical force and continuing appeal of such notions.

The book is organized into three parts. Part 1 focuses on a conceptual history of musical creativity, and traces the changing meaning of musical creativity; and it critiques the Romantic stereotype of the creator as individual genius. It uses Bourdieu's thinking tools—'habitus', 'field' and 'capital'—and by drawing on ideas from social realism, I show that 'official' musical creativity is not what it claims to be, but rather reflects the disguised interests and experiences of a dominant social group, and provide examples of the differences in the values accorded to some genres over others.

Part 2 makes use of Bourdieu's thinking tools of 'field', 'habitus', 'capital', and 'practice' to understand contemporary creative musical practices by nineteen musicians who champion a multiplicity of musical creativities. Sometimes their work resists easy classification in any one sector or particular industry. To understand these real world practices we are required to pay attention to how musicians think, act, and create; to understand what their practices are grounded in; and on what capital the processes and principles of their practices operate.

---

[3] See Blanning (2008), who examines how everything from the cult of the romantic to technology and travel all fed the inexorable rise of music in the West, making it the most dominant and ubiquitous art form.

Part 3 highlights the implications for teaching and learning music. I put forward a framework for understanding multiple musical creativities and the development of socially responsive teaching and learning practices. It explores how the field of music in education might relate a little closer to industry experience, at least in awareness of how musicians create in real world practices. Ways for operationalizing an expanded concept of musical creativity in the world of the Internet, e-learning, and virtual fields are discussed.

Appendix A (methodology and methods) and Appendix B (theory) will be of great interest to research students looking to the 'insider's' tale of the questions and dilemmas that emerged during these studies of music creativity. Appendix C provides supporting tables with summaries of creativities identified, and details of the participating musicians featured in the book. Appendix D attempts to debunk the top ten myths of children's musical creativities.

Most of this book's recent predecessors are concerned with explanations of musical creativity expressed in terms of entities such as personality traits, or compositional products arising from solitary endeavour, something which takes place in the realm of a single mind, working alone. Some are concerned with long-deceased Western art composers' biographies (John Sloboda's *Exploring The Musical Mind* (2005)) or creative process in music (Ann McCutchan's *The Music that Sings* (1999)); others are geared for an audience interested in the differently constituted worlds of jazz musicians (Paul Berliner's *Thinking in Jazz* (1994)), or the way that rock bands work to present us with a particular genre of musical creativity (as in Lucy Green's *How Popular Musicians Learn* (2002)), or cultural and contemporary practices (as in Andrew Ford's *Composer to Composer: Conversations about Contemporary Music* (1993) or William Duckworth's *Talking Music* (1995) or Anthony DeCurtis's *In Other Words: Artists Talk about Life and Work* (2005)); others, again, provide anecdotes about the long-gone individualized phenomenal world of composers (as in Anthony Storr's *The Dynamics of Creation* (1991)), or tell how we engage with improvisational and performance creativities (Keith Sawyer's *Creativity in Performance* (2006)).

Similarly, edited collections of multidisciplinary research studies specifically focus on how we can explain musical creativity from different scientific vantage points, such as psychology, cognitive science, artificial intelligence, computer modelling, and experimental psychology (Irene Deliège and Geraint Wiggins's *Musical Creativity* (2006)). Books, such as those edited by David Collins or by Oscar Odena, present a synthesis of the scientific study of the notionally singular term, 'musical creativity'. However, none of these explore the ways in which multiple musical creativities inhere in musicians' practices.

Another unifying feature of this book is the intention to give voice to innovative musical practices, such as collaborative, communal, and collective creativities. None of the non-domain-specific books (Keith Sawyer's *Explaining Creativity* (2006); Teresa Amabile's *Creativity in Context* (1996) or multiple intelligence theorist Howard Gardner's *Creating Minds* (1993; highlighting Stravinsky) or the Beethoven cult (as described by Erica McWilliam in *The Creative Workforce* (2008)) address musical creativity with the clarity and relevance that might attract the music specialist, music researcher, composer, songwriter, sound producer, and music educator. *Musical Creativities in Practice* is intended to help fill that gap.

This book attempts to put forward a sociology of multiple musical creativities, one which furthers understanding of the social scripting of creativities, of the ways we position ourselves in social groups, the strategies we use as individuals to maintain or improve our position in the field, as well as the power of individuals to define what constitutes highly valued activities. It moves beyond the individualistic view of musical creativity, of broadening the concept and, in doing so, comes to an understanding of the plurality of creative practices and distinctive features that constitute the multiple manifestations of music creativities.

Part 1

The field of music

Chapter 1

Conceptions

Introduction

Like all fields of human creativity, musical creativity arises in and as social practices. The field of music involves individuals, institutions, and social groupings, both large and small, all of which exist in structural relations to each other. These relations determine and reproduce musical practices in their multifarious forms. The coexistence of these practices allow us to objectify the field of music, which, in Bourdieu's sense, is a structured system of social relations at a micro and macro level,[1] so that we can make sense of what it is and how it works, the contexts in which it is operating, and the sorts of things that are at stake in musical creativities. Multiple manifestations of creativity arise across all music. They are contingent and socially constructed, durable, and inherited, as well as discontinuous and new, hard to pin down, and elusive.

For most of us, 'musical creativity' refers to a particular type of practice, perhaps that of the Great Composers, rather than to multiple possibilities. In other words, for most of us, the concept embodies a basic classification corresponding to an individualistic notion rather than a sense of multiple possibilities. If someone practices a song in a variety of ways, those ways demonstrate the process of performance creativity. In the global practices of young children, playground songs are composed collectively and are sung during their games at moments that lie beyond the creative intentions of their authors.[2] Similarly, the collective character of jazz improvisation is a continuum between graduated points of independence from a fixed musical form to a spontaneously free one shaped by spontaneous impulse. So this book is as much about expanding the concept of musical creativity as it is about how people decide who they are through it, how they express themselves through it, and how they think about the spectrum of possible practices that are at the centre of a multiplicity of practices.

There has been much debate in recent decades, although nothing approaching a consensus, about the concept of musical creativity. This debate has intensified as governments have pressurized the creative and cultural industries and other social institutions, particularly those involved with education, to articulate what constitutes the value of creativity, whether in terms of communication, or in relation to the global economy. Governments and industries are not only telling artists and educators what they should do but also prescribing the terms in which they should think and the ideals towards which they should aspire in their creativity practices.

We were first alerted to the coexistence of multiple musical creativities by Merker (2006), who made the key point that 'an infinite variety of musical forms are realizable in the multiple arenas of music as a performing art' (p. 36). Temporal acts of composition, real time performance-based forms, and musical improvisation across diverse musical traditions were differentiated in terms of 'whether there are musical constraints on musical creativity' (p. 32). However, the outmoded,

---

[1] See Grenfell and James (1998, p. 16 and Bourdieu (1993c)).

[2] For more discussion of the concept of 'musical creativity' see Berliner,1994; Burnard, 1999; Deliège and Wiggins, 2006; K. Marsh, 2008; Sawyer, 1997; Swanwick and Tillman, 1986. For considerations of elite arts or popular music professions, or as reflected in academic commentaries, see Blake, 2007; Deliège and Wiggins, 2006; Green, 2001.

notionally singular, phenomenon of 'musical creativity' remains to be defined in terms of practices corresponding to music's social and technological mediations: that is, how musical creativities produce their own varied social relations in performance, in musical associations and ensembles, in the musical division of labour and in social practices.

The ways in which musicians engage with local and global traditions of music-making involve new musical creativities that forge continuities with the past and a new vocabulary to go along with the expanding practices of the digital age. Furthermore, depending on whether one is allied to psychology, sociology, musicology, or ethnomusicology,[3] or to humanistic disciplines such as art history, aesthetics, or criticism, intellectual engagement with music starts from different premises. These various perspectives extend to the ways in which we formulate questions related to musical creativity: that is, how creativity is inscribed in all music is open to question. The presence of music is not a necessary condition for having creativity, but having creativity is a necessary condition for having music. Therefore, to understand music we need to understand what constitutes the changing nature of musical creativity. The purpose of this chapter is to illustrate the significance of the changing nature of musical creativity, and to explain why we think of it as a singular phenomenon rather than as multiple manifestations of distinctive and hybrid forms. It will deal with the contexts in which musical creativities arise. The composer immersed and at one with the act of composing, the arranger of jazz charts, the conductor of scores for music theatre or opera, the popular songwriter, the child in the playground, or the DJ in the club, all manifest distinct creativities. This chapter is not about the value of musical creativity, or about how it emerges in music, and neither is it about the mythologized forms of creative practice generally assumed to be realized by the individual artist as expressions of individual selfhood in specific social, historical, and cultural contexts. The argument in this chapter is about broadening the concept of musical creativity from its singular form, so as to let it embrace particular manifestations of multiple musical creativities.

Musical creativity in acts of composition by the Great Composers

Musical creativity remains deeply linked to the ideal of individual heroism, of the Great Composers' individual genius. Historically, composers are described as mystical, elusive, with inaccessible dispositions that bring new, reproducible pieces into existence. Mozart was one of the most famous composers to provide anecdotal evidence of the creative processes. He allegedly stated:

> When I am, as it were, completely myself, entirely alone, and of good cheer—say, travelling in a carriage, or walking after a good meal, or during the night when I cannot sleep; it is often on such occasions that my ideas flow best and most abundantly. When and how they come, I know not; nor can I force them . . . The committing to paper is done quickly enough, for everything is already finished; and it rarely differs on paper from what it was in my imagination.

(Mozart, cited in Ghiselin, 1952, p. 34)

In, fact it is established beyond doubt that this dubious quote was invented in the early nineteenth century by Johann Friedrich Rochlitz (see M. Solomon's 2008 article at http://ml.oxfordjournals.org/content/61/3-4/272.extract). Mozart was supposed to have composed without sketches because he imagined his music as ready-made, complete works. The belief that Mozart extemporized the majority of his compositions was based on the knowledge that he composed entire works using his imagination and memory. One could suggest that Mozart's creative approach was more

---

[3] Musicologists are concerned with Western classical music, while other musics, including Western popular and non-Western musics, are dealt with by ethnomusicologists.

improvisational than compositional in nature, although he allegedly rarely made any changes to melodic lines, and his themes show both completion and unity. As with Beethoven's claim about not making preliminary sketches of major works, such as string quartets and certain symphonies, many claims about composers' musical creativity have now been refuted. For instance, we are told that Mozart also talked about the 'wearisome labour' of composition (Einstein, 1945; Weisberg, 1993). Nonetheless, such idealized views are still being cited without qualification because they endorse our hero worship of Mozart.[4]

The Great Composers created works that were situated in and determined by a complex of social and ideological structures. Their writing sought to win favour economically or politically, whilst involving great inventiveness. The concept of 'originality' has dominated notions of musical creativity for centuries. In the nineteenth century, the demand for originality translated into a demand that each composer create from scratch. Goehr (1992), writing about the 'Beethoven Paradigm', tells how, when Mozart recomposed his Oboe Concerto in C major for another instrument, he was criticized for not having produced an original work. Whether composers expanded on newly conceived ideas, built on pre-composed ones, or absorbed successful improvisations into their larger storehouse of ideas, the ideal of originality had an impact on how composers viewed their compositional procedures, encouraging them, for example, to dispense with rule-following models.

All music in all cultures has involved 'remixing'. As individual composers underwent social emancipation from the extra musical demands of church and court, and experienced the freedom and vagaries of independence, professional organizations, private music societies, and new musical institutions emerged,[5] along with a concept of musical creativity embodying the new ideal of music autonomy, ownership, authorship, and authority. We have been offered a static and singular view of musical creativity in terms of the Western world's celebration of the Great Composer's individual accomplishments, a view that privileges a type of creativity that valorizes the individual as genius. The point is well illustrated by Beethoven's Third Symphony, the Eroica, which was performed in private for Prince Lobkowitz at his Vienna palace in the summer of 1804, and for the first time in public in January 1805. Twice as long as any symphony by Haydn or Mozart and sounding utterly different, the Eroica was recognized at once by friend and foe alike as an undoubted 'work of genius'. The roles of reviewers and publishers in the construction of the cult of genius are sufficient to show that actions and their effects are not discrete expressions of individual wills, but rather the outcomes of mediated practices. This can be seen in a report in the *Allgemeine Musikalische Zeitung* of Leipzig, the leading musical periodical of the day (as reported in Blanning, 2008, p. 101), which described the Eroica in the following language:

> This long, extremely difficult composition is actually a very long drawn out, daring and wild fantasy. There is no lack of striking and beautiful passages in which one must recognise the energetic and talented spirit of their creator; but very often it seems to lose itself in anarchy.

The Romantic legacy of Beethoven was to have a massive impact in securing the mythical cult of genius in which composers became enmeshed; and this expressive aesthetic of originality and authenticity has remained centre stage. It is this formulation of musical creativity that has become fixed in the musicological ideology of Western 'art' music. As musicians of renowned physical skill and inimitable artistic insight, the Great Composers have been viewed, typically, as either divinely inspired or as extraordinary mortals. The legendary performances of their own compositions set

---

4   See Boden (2005, p. 266); see also Blanning, 2008; Cook, 1998; De Nora, 2000.
5   Such as, in Britain, the Philharmonic Society in 1813 and the Royal Academy of Music in 1826 as discussed in Goehr (1992, p. 241).

an imperative for originality that persists to this day.[6] This privileging of originality in Western classical music above all others is a strange and contradictory phenomenon.[7]

In a comprehensive review of empirical studies on musical creativity, Deliège and Richelle (2006, pp. 1–2) described its concept as a 'spectrum' of activities, noting the dominance of 'the classical model' over the collective character of art worlds:

> Elucidating some of the many mysteries concerning the nature and origins of creative artefacts, which we do so much admire and enjoy though we still understand so little how they become part of our world . . . Creative behaviour takes place at all three levels . . . (someone has to play the piece of music to convey it from the composer to an audience) . . . we know the classical model of what is going on in creating, four successive phases are distinguished, viz., preparation, incubation, illumination and elaboration . . . the currently dominant cognitivist paradigm.

Yet this formulation of different conceptions of musical creativity, which seems set in the musicological ideology of the nineteenth century's Romantic tradition, has become a fact of music history. It plays up individualism and the innate nature of creative genius, and elevates the composer to the role of master genius. Reciprocally, it plays down musical creativity as a collective or collaborative activity, whilst presupposing a stable and unified subject. It allows for neither activity between domains nor for the radically creative challenge of interdisciplinary or cross-cultural exchanges of hybrid forms. Neither does it take cognizance of the fact that the really creative act may be ignored or dismissed by the broader institutional forces that could provide the basis of its production and reproduction.

As Finnegan (1989) has argued, although 'the one common form of musical creativity, is musical composition', for which 'this high-art model assumes a canon of accepted composers, notably the "greats" like Bach, Mozart, Beethoven or Chopin' (p. 160), there are a myriad of differing ways in which musicians at both ends of the high art and grass-roots spectrum are creative. What is more, the Western conception of musical creativity increasingly underpins the values and norms for measuring and standardizing the assessment of composition.

The sacred and fetishized concept of 'composition' is as far removed from most of the world's traditional music as it is from globally spatialized, internet forms,[8] both of which were not originated through formal acts of composition. In order to demythologize the scholarly rhetoric, we need to recognize that it is a human construction, a product of culture, and accordingly varies from time to time and from place to place. We need to ask what musical creativity means to us, and think how we might begin to situate creativity in music and music-making, and how it is mobilized in practice by social groups.

The idea of Great Performances of Great Works by Great Composers persists as a historically specific ideology, which has translated into a misleading view of the artist, and is in no sense representative of artists in other societies and those of earlier centuries in Western society either. The concept of the 'masterwork' celebrates a sacred and fetishized formal act of composition, set apart from music's social, technological, and temporal dimensions.

---

[6] See Willamson, et al. (2006, p. 161).

[7] Dalhaus (1983) tells us flatly and rather harshly that 'the subject matter of music is made up, primarily, of significant works of music that have outlived the culture of their age', and that the 'concept "work" and not "event" is the cornerstone of music history', and therefore the object of music creativity. See Lang (1941).

[8] Globally spatialized internet forms include digital and mobile music, their social networks, and the fluid roles of musicians, DJs and audiences in contemporary popular music.

Conceptualizing creativity in individual and collective improvisational performance

Even prior to the mid-1800s, improvisation was thought to be pivotal to the training of instrumentalists, since it enabled them to perform without notation (see McPherson, 1994). In the seventeenth century, composers' reputations rested on an amalgam of skills including improvisation; and documentation of the activities of Mozart, Beethoven, and Chopin indicates that improvisation was regarded as a viable alternative to the performance of compositions.[9] Indeed, whole pieces were improvised containing lavish embellishments, ornamentation, and cadenzas.

L. Solomon (1986) describes improvisation as 'the discovery and invention of original music spontaneously, while performing it, without preconceived formulation, scoring or context' (p. 224). Such a characterization suggests an independence from pre-existing styles so as to allow playing that more directly reflects immediate ideas through the motions and sensations of the improviser (Dobbins, 1980). This latter approach may liberate the improviser from the constraints of prior knowledge, and allow a freer approach. Alperson (1984) privileges the role of spontaneity in improvisation as follows:

> Musical improvisation can be, and, by experienced listeners, typically is, understood in terms of a kind of action, the particular shaping activity of the improviser who creates for us a musical utterance unmediated by another human being. It is as if the improviser's audience gains privileged access to a composer's mind at the moment of musical creation. (p. 24)

Huizinga (1970) advanced a notion of improvisation as arising in and as play, defining 'play-acts' as intrinsically creative, motivated, active, serious, structured, spontaneous, voluntary, and free of imposed rules. He situated human play as social creativity:

> An activity that proceeds within certain limits of time and space, in a visible order, according to rules freely accepted, and outside the sphere of necessity or material utility. The play-mood is one of rapture and enthusiasm and is sacred or festive in accordance with the occasion. A feeling of exaltation and tension accompanies the action, mirth and relaxation follow. (p. 154)

The conception of improvisation as being closely associated with play, experimentation, collective action, and spontaneity incorporates music's temporal and social dimensions. But does this imply some special power, granted only to the artistic elite? How can we be sure that musicians share similar understandings of what musical creativity is, and how it is practised in particular styles and genres? Without particularized practices, would musical creativity and its appreciation be impossible?

The way we think about musical creativity remains integrally tied to Western dominant conceptions of creative masterpieces and creative personalities. Unlike Mozart, who was thought to make few changes in his completed compositions, Beethoven never ceased improving his notated work. For example, he made no fewer than 12 versions of the Minor Quartet in C sharp minor, op. 131. He was also known to improvise for a half-hour on any theme, and even on themes thought to have been notated in their final form.

---

9 See Goehr (1992) and Cook (1998) for norms and expectations and behavioural patterns that have come to characterize classical musical practice. Zolberg (1990, p. 201) alerts us to the case of Theodor Adorno, who freely vented his scorn of certain kinds of musical works and art forms, and rejected all but the most limited sector of the arts in modern times. In addition to other 'commercial' music, his belittlement of jazz, which he considered a marginal ethnic form, won him the epithet of 'elitist'.

> For the uninitiated [Beethoven's improvising] was all the more interesting to notice how the music translated itself from the man's soul to his features . . . His facial muscles swelled and his veins stood out; the doubly wild eye rolled in twice as fine a frenzy, the mouth twitched, and Beethoven looked like a sorcerer who feels himself over-powered by the very spirits whom he has conjured up.
>
> (Schauffler, 1946, p. 379)

Paying attention, as this narrative does, to the Romantic notions of aesthetic struggle, inspiration and originality, privileges the creator as an absolute individual. Howard Becker has written extensively about 'the collective character of art worlds' and how works of art arise as collective action.[10] Additionally, there is confusion regarding the question of written versus oral forms of composition. There are numerous examples of musical creators (particularly if we look to composers from different cultures and the compositional styles of songwriters) to whom the compositional process is not defined by generative motives or structural frames but by the medium of a particular instrument. Instead, the compositional process becomes defined by instrumentally stylized patterns of movement that determine ideas to be developed (Baily, 1991). The instrument is construed as the main tool for composition by providing a 'framework for musical conceptualisation' (p. 151). The ethnomusicologist John Blacking (1955), commenting on a composition evolving from the physical movement of playing the instrument for which it was composed, states:

> A pianist who plays the Etudes of Chopin or many pieces by Liszt cannot help being conscious of the sheer physical pleasure of numerous passages, and noticing how the music grows out of physical movement . . . We find numerous examples of Western classical music, where the musical form is much influenced by the properties of the instrument for which it was written. (p. 52)

Additionally, we might ask when does the process of musical creativity transcend compositional modalities? Does notated, though improvisation-based, composition reflect the diversity of approaches that have contributed to the expansion of the concept of what it is to compose and to be a composer?

Accounts of the Shona people of Zimbabwe, in the absence of linear notated representations, describe the use of the mbira (m-bee-ra) in religious ceremonies in which ensemble members and participants can lead mbira players to expand upon newly conceived ideas or to abandon them.[11] Composers often emphasize the interplay of pre-composed ideas and those conceived in the moment, and the importance of sounding out and absorbing improvised ideas either vocally or instrumentally (Berleant, 1987). The genesis of a composition often involves improvisation, and improvisation often involves pre-composed ideas. So, how can a singular musical creativity be associated with all these temporal and social mediations, and embody this sense of multiple possibilities, when it is always so bound up in the changing institutional forces that provide the basis of its production and reproduction? Another ethnomusicologist, Bruno Nettl (1974), challenged the Western classical 'high art' view of improvisation by neither theorizing nor historicizing the term but by situating it in a collective, cultural context. He claimed that the culture influences the amount of improvisation employed during the course of a performance. This notion of a continuum of improvisational variation can be described in terms of graduated points of independence from a given musical model, which are, in turn, reflective of existing performative

---

[10] See Becker (1984; Becker et al., 2006), who argues that all creativity involves networks of interaction and organization.

[11] See Berliner (2006, p. 133), in which he gives detailed descriptions of how mbira players use pre-composed ideas and absorb successful improvisations into their larger storehouse of ideas to produce infinite ways of shaping improvised performances.

genres in various cultures. These ritualized genres are 'reproduced anew in each performance', involving 'component units—building blocks, stock phrases, and formulaic patterns—of a model piece' (Nettl, 1974, p. 13) which are recast, rearranged and renewed. These particularized genres can range from what Nettl (1974) described as 'ritualized' to 'improvisational' performances, depending on the degree of independence from the model. Similarly, Bruce Ellis Benson (2003) in *The Improvisation of Musical Dialogue: A Phenomenology of Music*, provides a kind of improvisatory conception of music, with reference to classical, jazz, and other genres, without imposing theories in which the lines between composition and performance are neatly defined. Benson reminds us that 'Baroque music functioned somewhat analogously to that of jazz today, so that a jazz "fake book", in which only the melody and chords are notated and the musician "fakes" the rest, is not so unlike the scores used by Baroque musicians. Essentially, then, Baroque performances were constantly in flux' (2003, p. 19).

Thus, there is a clear precedent for thinking about musical creativity as a broad and open concept. For example, what we know about the practices of creativity of Renaissance and Baroque music makes it clear that performance in those eras was heavily improvisational, and composers expected as much. Fuller characterizes Baroque music as follows: 'a large part of the music of the whole era was sketched rather than fully realized, and the performer had something of the responsibility of a child with a coloring book, to turn these sketches into rounded art-works' (1989, pp. 117–18).

There is no word equivalent to 'improvise' for classically trained Indian players. The two terms they use are '*upaj*' and '*vistar*', which mean 'to grow' and 'to spread out', respectively. Neither of these terms have 'spontaneous' connotations because much of Eastern music is predetermined and fixed in nature. The Indian *raga*, Javanese *gamelan*, Arabic and Turkish *maqam*, Persian *dastgah,* and African group drumming are examples of ritualized performance in which there is only limited opportunity for creative spontaneity. Subsequently, Nettl (1974) suggested that what we consider to be improvisation may in fact be culturally specified composition.

How do contemporary players conceive of musical creativity in performance? What effects do social aspects of performance have on musical creativity? How are we to understand the nature of music creativity in relation to practices of improvisation and composition in the age of multimedia wherein the elements of a 'transformative culture', of mashups and bastard pop, friendly record companies and the fan remix are proliferating technological mediations?[12]

Present time conceptions

So far, I have been considering some of the dominant historical and cultural conceptions of a singular understanding of music creativity, as one that is realized by the individual composer, focused on the organization of sounds, on human behaviour, on the act of creation, the composed work, its performance, or the composer's self. A good deal of aesthetics has proceeded on the basis of this assumption, which has resulted in a far too limited definition of creativity.

For new generations, commercial music, web space and the ever-expanding web world provide a dynamic and complex context wherein all kinds of creativity nestles in the nooks and crannies. So too does the ever-expanding sonic spectrum of net-radio stations, small labels, 'zines', and blogs, specializing in noise, drone, free folk, improv, and dozens more marginal and micro-genres from black metal to grime, indie, indie-bop, from German minimal techno to West African guitar-pop, hip hop, European deep house, techno and house, funk, punk, post-punk, pop, and teen-pop, to name just a few. We have witnessed a predominance of recycling in the 1990s and mix-and-matching elements from across the past couple of decades. Then there is the changing

---

12 For a detailed discussion see Black (2007).

sound of webbed connectivity, mainstream media supersaturation, and entrepreneurial activity in the making and selling of music for city-based mainstream or sub-mainstream scenes such as US street rap which refuses recording, or DIY mixtapes, recalling 1980s indie, or the post-rave electronic dance genres, which cater to a discerning niche market that runs in parallel with the mainstream but slightly elevated, or underground, music that is off the radar.

Against such a background, it is surprising that the concept of musical creativity, as with all creativity, has been too narrowly defined. Very often musical creativity uses a research focus that is based exclusively on observable phenomena, namely creators and their creative personalities and behaviours, and creative products or objects: the piece of jazz or classical music, and the solo singing performance and style that arise from composer or performer creativity.[13] But, as with jazz, Indian improvisations and DJ turntable compositions are also established systems with skill requirements, and the creativities these disciplines produce are invariably 'reproductive'. That is to say, they merely reproduce rather than test the creativity systems on which practice is based.

Many authors emphasize a collectivist perspective on music and art works. Becker (1984) argues that 'all artistic work, like all human activity, involves the joint activity of a number, often a large number of people' (p. 35). For Becker (1984), works of art are not the products of individual artists who possess a rare and special gift, but rather 'joint products of all the people who cooperate' as 'a network of people cooperating', all of whom will be part of the construction of objects and actions through 'collective activity' (p. 35). From this perspective, the context of musical creativity becomes a source of meaningful representations of objects and actions, representations which are socio-historical because they emerge from the historical experience of a social group situated in time and space. What is particularly telling, however, is that it is rock musicians who point out that it is the community, and a collective rather than the individual, that manifests creativity in music.[14]

The renewed importance of live music, and especially festivals, provides a whole other context wherein an audience has a sense of itself, potentially, at least as a community. Consider the hype surrounding Michael Jackson's final concert programming, or Take That's performance at the O2 arena with an elephant. Performances are events. You have to be there in person to experience the performer's presence and the collective activity of a super-select fan base that wants to share and own the music in a physical form. These are groups of people who belong to and radiate out from the social practices and industrial concentration on specific genres and media and entertainment conglomerates (DeNora, 2003). There are now musical worlds involving millions of people, and a sense of a hierarchy in terms of the medium via which you discover music, such as via MySpace, YouTube, and Facebook, or through a blog conversation, by which means useful contextual information may be drawn from shared past experiences, or from a broader cultural base of knowledge associated with a particular body of understandings embodied in common practices, in collective activity, and in frequently played music and gigs.

Whether the collective process flavours listening, collecting, downloading, sampling, performing, mashing, DJing, dancing, or 'style mixing' (see below) at an urban dance music club, the way we think about musical creativity falls far short of grasping the potential multiplicity of musical creativity today. Yet music needs an audience. Audiences engage in 'a collective experience', and are a part of, 'doing' music. Audiences seek both interpreters and interpretations of performances. Gell (1998, p. 252) takes the corpus of Maori meeting houses constructed between 1870 and 1930 as a collective instance of the extended mind, proposing that it represents a composite

---

[13] See the work of Davidson and Coulam (2006).

[14] See Benson (2003), Csikszentmihalyi (1996), and Sawyer (1997).

object distributed in space and time. He argued, 'Maori meeting houses may have been the collective production of many separate artists and builders, working in separate communities at different times, each striving to produce something distinctive; yet all are expressions of a common historical trajectory, a common cultural system, of common ideological and political purpose' (p. 252). They embody the 'physical expression of 'Maoridom' as a collective experience in this period. As an example, consider the field of expectations and collective experience that envelops the listeners in music-making as an outcome of the process of 'style mixing'.

At British urban dance clubs style mixing has generated a new participatory compositional style of creativity, which is derived from an outcome of the fluid roles between musicians, DJs, and audience. Style mixing is a form of composition/production in which the music created at urban dance music clubs is facilitated by state-of-the-art digital technology. The desire of the consumer to choose from and engage with a variety of different music has been enabled by using different rooms or floors to stage parallel events. Clubbing is thus regarded less as a singularly definable activity, and more as a series of fragmented, temporal experiences as the clubbers move between different dance floors and engage with different crowds.

The process of style mixing merges musical production and consumption in the blatant appropriation and reassembling of stylistically diffuse hooks, riffs, and melodic phrases, which are exchanged in, and contingent on, the dance, the bodies and sensibilities of the dance-goers, and its consumers. The music stands in a variety of relations to artists, DJs, and dancers. DJs are not considered to be solely responsible for the existence and characteristics of the music played, mashed, sampled, and remixed, but instead they become the vehicle of the agency of others. Gell (1998) makes explicit the ways in which it follows from this conceptual inclusion of audiences 'doing' music creativity 'that actions and their effects are similarly not discrete expressions of individual will, but rather the outcomes of mediated practices in which performers and audiences are implicated in complex ways' (p. 9).

Virtually all music consists of a three-way exchange between creators, performers, and audiences. Moreover, each of these is an active and essential participant (Jameson, 1991). Notes move from abstraction to sonorous form only when they are turned into sound by musicians (or machines in the case of a machine-based aesthetic) and are heard by listeners. Of course, much depends on the period, since the historical context determines the mix of the various elements that constitute music-making. But no one can think or talk about musical creativity for long without becoming involved in debates about whether the earlier divine sense of creation has given away to the human and secular origins of musical creativity, or whether only certain special people are innately creative in music, or whether some activities, cultures, and periods are more creative than others.

Traditional authority derives its legitimacy simply from having existed, because 'who says it, is what counts, not what is said' (Moore, 2010, p. 74).[15] Particularly in the case of the more complex forms of performing arts, legitimizing the process of musical production as an individual process supports misleading ideologies about creativity.

Musical creativities (i) comprise both the relational structures of concepts, with methods for relating these to the empirical world, *and* actors positioned within specific social and historical contexts; (ii) manifest multiple forms of authorship and mediating modalities; and (iii) are social

---

[15] Moore (2010) presents the basis for competing claims to status and material resources within education. These are strategic stances aimed at maximizing the actor's positions within a relationally structured field of struggles (cf. Bourdieu, 1988). At the same time, from a social realist perspective (see Chapter 1, same volume), the knowledge comprising these claims may be legitimate.

constructions[16] of musical production and consumption as they operate across and between genres. This tripartite model helps to distance the 'what' and 'how' of musical creativity from dominant ideologies and the mythical belief of the cult of the genius. From here we may come to understand that actions and their effects are similarly not discrete expressions of individual will, but rather the outcomes of mediated social and temporal practices. Whether as creative producers or creative consumers of music, whether by traditional or technological means, we are working with social mediations between artists and audiences, listeners and sound systems, musicians and instruments, composers and scores, conductors and orchestras, actions and venues, and social and cultural institutions.

Music creativities and social technologies

Working from the premise that, although as artists and audiences, producers, and consumers we are encouraged to think of ourselves as individuals, we work with social technologies.[17] Thus, the study of musical creativities surely needs to incorporate an understanding of music's social, temporal, and technological dimensions. Since the proliferation of digitized musics in the late 1980s and early 1990s, a new vocabulary of musical creativity has been facilitated by social technologies such as the Internet. The sites on which artists and fans create their own music, download playlists, remix music, and share files have a sense of a virtual community and collectiveness.

Not surprisingly, the Internet is allowing new musical creativities to emerge. This emergent communal music-making process, involving the appropriation and mixing of existing musical material, can be found in new or derived techno-communal innovations in digital media space. Virtual music-making is now presented in game form, through such computer games as *SingStar®* and *Guitar Hero®*. In addition to console games, there are a number of interactive loop mixing sites where players share and exchange loops and mixes, giving rise to new kinds of creative practices, such as relayed creativity or hybrid genres where pre-existing sources are 'blended'. 'Mash ups' blur the boundaries between production and reception.

The need for a conceptual expansion of the idea of musical creativities to embrace the world (or habitus) of the Internet is something of an imperative. How and where music is being created and creatively consumed may be valued differently in accordance with what is considered to be individually or historically novel. In the habitus[18] of the Internet there are 'virtual fields' on which to make digital music. Meanwhile social networking sites bring together musicians, DJs, and audiences. Most recently, an iPhone application called 'Street Orchestra' lets you play classical music with up to 200,000 synched iPhones. The notion of equally valued musical creativities is pertinent to the radical changes in the production and experience of music across the past 20 years.

The creativity from which music originates is evident in the interplay of myriad social and technological practices, and produces its own varied social relations in performance, in musical associations and ensembles, and in the musical division of labour. Cooperative categories of creativity can be perceived in the 'cooperative maxims' proposed by Benson's (2003) analysis of the

---

[16] Wolff (1993) argues that theories of artistic production and consumption need to be integrated but are rarely treated as such.

[17] See Collins (2008) for more discussion of these practices.

[18] 'Habitus' is a Bourdieuian (Maton, 2008) term denoting both a system of schemata for the production of practices and a system of perception and appreciation of practices which one has acquired, but which has become durably incorporated in the form of permanent dispositions and which implies knowing one's place but also having a sense of the place of others (i.e. the rules of the game).

improvisation of musical dialogues, or in the collective conversation of jazz performance.[19] The increased connectivity of producers and consumers is shaking up the music industry and the music-licensing sector (Wikström, 2009), with new business models being developed by music entrepreneurs. The rise of amateur creativity and increase of so-called 'user-generated content' are evidence of the changing conceptions of creativity in professional music-making. For professional musicians, whether their wildest ambitions are to be a scratcher, a digital composer, or rock megastar, like Trent Reznor, of pioneering industrial collective Nine Inch Nails, who have no recording contract, building online communities is a fundamental part of the social interaction of developing new creativities. In the field of new music production, the peculiar, ever-expanding web world is the medium through which musical culture increasingly organizes itself. These new musical networks challenge the individualist conception of creativity, and demand a much broader collective and plural definition.

One of the key concerns is how we come to engage in and with music as a digitally mediated creative practice. The idea that mass consumerism engages us in passively listening to and appreciating music is something sold to us by the advertisements of record companies. The idea of exceptional charismatic performers is sold to us by online distributors selling concert tickets. Yet audiences are an active and crucial component in decisions about what sort of space the music will be performed in, and what sort of people might be expected to form an audience.

Conclusion

The dilemmas posed by the concept of 'musical creativity' are twofold. First, at least in the past two or three decades most attempts to address the term have been reduced to particular standpoints: psychologists follow a reductive logic that polarizes dominant knowledge against absent or silent voices that it excludes; whereas sociologists have shown that locating creativity in the social world does not lead to the abandonment of truth and objectivity. Second, attempts to develop a sociology of the arts (as, for example, Zolberg, 1990) that give creativity a central place, easily slip back into the discredited, neo-conservative, traditionalist position that legitimizes their knowledge and excludes that of others.

It is necessary to find a way of resolving the dilemmas concerning musical creativity that arise from: (a) the attempt to explain the phenomena; and (b) the cultural contingency which acts as an enabling condition for the concept. The latter is beautifully described by Merker (2006) as 'the crest of a historical travelling wave of gradual change diversification of musical patterns for which the substance of tradition provides the moving mass and for which the innovative musical imagination supplies impulses for directional change' (pp. 36–7).

It is in addressing the question of the extent of the creativities that constitute music that I turn to what I refer to as a 'social realist' approach to the social production of musical creativity. The notion of 'practice' is particularly relevant here. Bourdieu looked at institutionalized social practices such as marriage and education, before he turned his attention to creative practices. His interest in what he calls 'the field of cultural production' led him to analyse the relationship between ways of understanding the world, and the principles behind creative works that are made in a particular place and time, and the meanings people attach to what he calls 'practices of distinction'. Bourdieu (1977) puts forward a theory of practice:

> The knowledge we shall call phenomenological . . . sets out to make explicit the truth of the primary experience of the social world . . . The knowledge we shall term objectivist . . . constructs the objective

---

[19] As described by Berliner (1994).

relations . . . which structure practice and representations of practice . . . and the theory of practice inscribed (in its practical state) in this mode of knowledge, that we can integrate the gains from it into an adequate science of practices. (p. 3)

This provides an interesting perspective on musical creativity as practice or practice as the locus of musical creativity. What might the practice of musical creativity in the popular music composition of an adolescent rock guitarist whose end-products are the result of an originals' band collective effort share with the contemporary classical composer whose creativity is embedded in improvisatory practices? What practices of 'composition' are inscribed when club DJs and crowds interact through records to create unique happenings? What practice of musical creativity is inscribed by DJs who legitimately claim to compose, arrange, improvise, and perform by combining new and remixed samples in a club, wherein interacting, mediating, and orchestrating the crowd establishes a collective musical creativity? How are we to understand the elasticity, slipperiness, and elusiveness of the term?

One of the most compelling questions concerns how myths of musical creativity play out in the production and reproduction of music. In the next chapter I shall first pose some pivotal questions about the myths of music creativity. This will sharpen the argument and reorient the debates that arise around a set of durable dispositions, which will help shape a framework for understanding how contexts give rise to different musical creativities in and as practice.

Chapter 2

Myths

Introduction

In this world, whether we aware of it or not, beliefs about musical creativity are ubiquitous. Our beliefs and self-perceptions often stem from myths about exceptional creators in the performing arts, who in some cultures and traditions form a small elite exemplifying distinctive creative talents in a particular form of music-making. Creative distinctiveness and segmentation may be downplayed in some societies, cultures, and communities, tending toward egalitarianism, such as with the Venda people, the ethnic group that lives mostly in the Limpopo province in South Africa, in whom creativity and competence is differentiated according to gender and age.[1] In other societies, the distinctiveness deriving from differentiation of creative activity, and myths of musical creativity are, as with myths of general creativity,[2] so widely believed that they become repositories of our deepest fears and desires. In some societies and communities, myths can be expressions of all the contradictory and incomprehensible elements that mediate the position and possibilities of musical creativity in our lives. For example, myths about the distribution of creativity amongst singers in gospel congregations can be linked to the marking and maintenance of social distinctions in particular communities. How and why have creative archetypes such as court musicians, the village musician, drummer, or folk singer developed in particular communities? We need to learn more about how myths are fostered and accommodated in specialized collectivities. Myths about the musical creativity of performers who distinguish themselves from all others through their own way of making music can become cultural and social goals in their own right for patrons, schools, religious sects, and teachers. Myths can also define the nature of the relationship between musicians, and those between musicians, consumers, and fans of music, and influence our thoughts about those who are considered to be musically creative.

The reasons why we think in these ways are deep-rooted. They are built into schools and universities and other institutions, and into the subtexts of books about music, most of which reflect the way music was portrayed in nineteenth-century Europe rather than the way it is today. The ways we think about music and the only music we think about represents what Nicholas Cook calls the 'credibility gap',[3] that is, the gap between the portrayal and practice of musical creativities

---

[1] For further ethnomusicological discussion see Brinner (1995) for exemplary work on how Javanese musicians recognize different kinds of multiple competences (and creativities) of players, the development of distinctive traditions as defined by cultural communities in Java, and the clear distinctions between facts, and going beyond the facts (i.e. myths) associated with performance practices of the Javanese *gamelan*; see Neuman (1980) for exemplary work on Hindustani musicians; and Campbell (2004) for exemplary work on composing and improvising across many cultures.

[2] For further discussion of general creativity myths, see Sawyer (2006) and R. Pope (2005).

[3] A term coined by Cook (1998), in which he explains the ways we think about music and each type of music comes with its own way of thinking about music, as if it was the only way of thinking about music (and the only music to think about).

that are integrally wrapped up in the hegemony of Western classical music. We can obtain some insight into how this has come about from numerous brilliant studies of classical musicians,[4] which show what musicians are, and what being a musician means. By way of example, prior to the first vinyl records hitting the market around 1950, the music business as we think of it today barely existed. Music was dancing, cabaret, sing-alongs, concerts, instrumental performances and eventually radio. People didn't 'own' music; they listened to it, experienced it, and shared it. Music was never played in exactly the same way since it was impossible to reproduce the exact circumstances of a performance. We need to remember that the score objectified music so that music could be 'owned', and that the creation of concert halls and subscription concerts was also a means of 'owning' music. The instruments and orchestration would change, as would the performers, their modes and audiences, their performance environments, and their interpretation of the music. Songs were performed as well as they could be at that moment, and composers worked hard to create a continuous flow of fresh music for fairs, operas, concerts, trade shows, ceremonies, theatres, rituals, and church services. The composers of the time, at the turn of the century, liberally borrowed material from one another, often adapting, updating, and improving the songs for the players and performances at hand. How times have changed! And how, too, has the perception and practice of musical creativity. If everyone is born musical and creative, then everyone's musical creativity is valid. That being so, why do we construct and reconstruct so many myths about musical creativity?

Myths about musical creativity fuelled my dreams about composers and improvisers. But, while free improvisation seems so fundamental to music, it was never mentioned in my entire Western classical training. Here, I do not wish to overly criticize my undergraduate training as being needlessly narrow. I cannot deny the overwhelming impact on me, both past and present, of the defining the limits of the disciplining of classically trained musicians to spend the greater percentage of time focused on preparing for a performance career coached in the musical canon of either jazz or classical music. For all of us, however, different and often overlapping discourses about multiple manifestations of musical creativity become more relevant with every day that we use the Internet, mp3s, share files, and progress into a digitally networked society.

In this chapter, I discuss what these myths are, why exploring the assumptions underpinning them is so important, and why, in doing so, one feels obliged to capitalize the 'Great Composers'.

Myths and mythmakers

Myths are of great significance to those in the music business and music education. Our thinking is guided by: the relationships and dynamics between artists, writers, and producers; those who market, deliver, and distribute music, such as the record companies and publishers; the consumers and fans of music, who ultimately pay for it all; and of course those of us who work in education, whose perceptions and assessments of musical creativity exemplify its complexity (see Odena and Welch, 2009).

Mythmaking and myth telling are deeply embedded forms of human behaviour. They can function in many ways. Myths can give legitimacy and support to a particular social group. Myths can be confirmatory. They can also be subversive. Myths can serve the interests of those wishing to maintain a certain order or change it. What we choose to believe or not is of great importance.

---

[4] See Spruce (1999), Cottrell (2004), and D. Bennett (2008), for discussion of the broadening of the discipline of music for professional musicians and their training.

Myths have always been a way for people to explain their societies, their belief systems, the lives they live and the lives of the artists we elevate to the status of heroes and celebrities. Consider, for example, Brian Wilson (an artist with a troubled past) and his exaltation in the following quote:

> You wonder if some god said, 'I'll create a being whose work will mean so much to so many people, a being whose work will enrich people, put sun in their lives, show them a way to express themselves, to understand themselves, to find their place in the world. And yet I'll make him suffer terribly. I'll remove him from his own gifts and I'll make the world he improved a foreboding cell for him.

> (Fusilli, *Pet Sounds*, quoted in Jones, 2008, p. 40)

One mythologizing story has it that Ludwig van Beethoven, the Romantic hero, made no fewer than 12 versions of the Minor Quartet in C sharp, op. 131. He was also known to improvise for half an hour on any theme—even for pieces supposedly notated in a final form. As for Brian Wilson, he is regarded as the rock hero primarily responsible for the iconic album *Pet Sounds*, one of the albums that set the pattern for later rock legends.

Stereotypically, when we think of a composer, we think of Wolfgang Amadeus Mozart, the famous composer and child prodigy; a classic instance of 'genius' and the object of many historical studies in that area (see Gardner, 1998). We all know the famous image of the child Mozart in formal dress seated at the harpsichord with his father looking over his shoulder. It conveys the message that Mozart was trained to excel as a well-schooled composer-musician who is a kind of divinely inspired paradigm on the one hand and a naturally spontaneous 'genius' on the other hand. These two views continue to have resonance in the debates of today about how far musical creativity is innate or taught. But to what extent is creativity innate? Can genius be learnt? What if musical creativity is not something that a person has or does not have but is something that people do together?

Most people think they are not very creative compared with the tiny minority who have profound artistic talent. The sociologist Lucy Green has discussed the myth that most people are 'not really very creative or musical':

> Classical music has in fact maintained a hegemonic position of cultural superiority ever since the Enlightenment. Ideology immanently ratifies and maintains the dominance of an elite musical institution that, along with its reified products, is made to seem superior: and it does so by propagating the appearance that there is a musical mass which, along with its profane products, is not really very musical. Hence a complex and multifarious division is created and maintained between elite and mass productive and receptive musical modes, and between the elite and mass musical styles to which these modes correspond. (1988, p. 2)

Is it because of mythmakers, or is it because of misconceptions, that most people consider themselves to be not really creative in comparison with a tiny minority who consider themselves to be 'composers' or jazz musicians, capable of expressing their own personal aesthetic vision? Adorno (1976 [1962]) raises some of the most important questions about the role of music in contemporary society from his focus on the sociology of music. He deals with the ubiquity of the middle-brow audience that has become the soul of high art concert performances. The large symphony orchestra has become subordinated to the patrons and the audience for the Top 40 classics—Mozart and Haydn, the Beethoven symphonies and concertos, the works of Chopin, Tchaikovsky and Brahms; and a sprinkling of twentieth-century music: the neoclassical Stravinsky and works influenced by the late Romantic era, or the nationalist phase of American music of the 1930s and 1940s. At the time of publication of Adorno's book on the sociology of music in 1976, the works of Schönberg, Berg, Webern and their followers were virtually absent from the classical repertoire, certainly among major US and European orchestras. Adorno took this fact to be one more empirical validation of the thesis that fashion governs the musical canon and forms middle-brow taste. The commodification of high culture has been amply demonstrated by cultural history since the end of the Second World War, but Adorno's claim that jazz is merely a 'perennial fashion' (1967) possessing little or no intrinsic aesthetic value (an Adorno preoccupation in the 1940s and 1950s) demonstrates the stylistic hierarchy of the ruling ideology and the hegemonic cultural superiority of Western classical art music (Aronowitz, 1994).

The repertory or classical *canon* has been an obstacle to looking at music and musical creativity from a wider perspective from the time of the cult of Beethoven (Cook, 1998), when the 'musical museum' came into existence and provided the conceptual framework within which music took its place in the cultural heritage. Similar myths exist in a number of musical traditions and musics positioned in 'World Music' wherein, as argued by Schippers (2010) in an insightful chapter on the myth of authentic traditions: 'the sheer ambiguity of the concepts involved and by the (often self-imposed) impossible demands of attempting to realise "authentic traditions in context"' has caused confusion (p. 41). Thus we see the power of personal mythmaking working through statements about artists, in the cultivation of public opinion. Mozart (cited in Ghiselin, 1952, p. 34) was claimed to say:

> Nor do I hear in my imagination the parts successively, I hear them all at once. What a delight this is! All this inventing, this producing, takes place in a pleasing, lively dream.

Unlike Beethoven, who is portrayed as having never ceased improvising upon his notated work, Mozart is thought to have made few changes to his completed compositions. Mozart was famous for mythologizing the creative processes, as the anecdotal evidence offered in Chapter 1 has shown. Even reputable dictionaries and theorists furnish us with conceptions of composing based on the mythical idea of 'imagined wholes'. In fact, Mozart extemporized the majority of his compositions, making preliminary sketches of his major works such as string quartets and certain symphonies (Weisberg, 1993).

Stephen Holden (1992) goes further, suggesting that such mythologizing is actually part of the creative process(es) of composition and song writing. Creativity myths, such as the view of the artist as a unique genius (Blanning, 2008), and other myths of compositional history[5] (such as the privileging of the paradigm of Western compositional logic), have proved so strong that they no longer act as an overt part of our musical consciousness, and contributed to the power and integrity of the 'autonomous vision' of the composer and singer-songwriter (Jones, 2008). For example Holden (1992) says that '[Van] Morrison (in his groundbreaking 1968 acoustic album *Astral Weeks*), and later Tom Waits, Rickie Lee Jones, and David Bowie were Romantic visionaries who mythologized their singer-songwriter experiences in often private stream-of-consciousness lyrics' (p. 301). Bob Dylan, through his roots in the folk music tradition, is regarded as the ultimate example of the authentic, autonomous singer and songwriter of rock:

> After Dylan, instead of a polished interpreter, the writer became the definitive exponent of his or her work. The recording medium, through which idiosyncratic voices could be distinctively showcased in custom-designed settings, also encouraged a greater intimacy in both song writing and performance.

> (Holden, 1992, p. 482)

This ideal of 'autonomous vision' is also played out in the central positioning and descriptions of the towering figures linked to the mythmaking of contemporary Western 'art' music. In a chapter entitled 'Summoning Up the Dead Composer', Small (1998) observed how myths are

---

5 See DeNora, 2003, pp. 26–7, writing on myths of Western compositional logic.

expressed through the dominant mode through which creativity is expressed in contemporary Western culture, and how they contribute to the negative mythologization of the exclusive clubs and canons of Western music literature. Concerning the social scripting of Western 'art' music concert programming, he observes:

> It is not surprising that concertgoers and musicians alike should feel a close, direct and personal relationship with those musicians of the past or that they should have an insatiable curiosity about their lives and personalities sufficient to keep alive a whole industry of composer biographies and critical studies . . . a great composer is almost by definition a dead composer, and no musician who is alive today, or even lived past the first two decades of the twentieth century, has the hold that dead composers have on the imagination of either listeners or performers in concert halls.

(Small, 1998, p. 87)

We see the origins of mythmaking in the late eighteenth century. Mozart and Haydn made massive contributions to raising both the status of music and the status of the musician by their demonstration of what could be achieved through the quality of their compositions. Their musical heir Beethoven built on their achievement. Whilst numerous studies have helped to unveil the strategies by which the musical canon and its hierarchy of 'masterworks' were constructed and institutionalized during the nineteenth century in Europe as an ideology for the furtherance of music as a profession, the fascination with 'high' music culture during the nineteenth century was simultaneously a vehicle for the construction of class and status group distinction. More specifically, the focus on the distinction between 'high' and 'low' musical forms has widened to include the investigation of how 'authenticity' itself is constructed and contested.

Musical creativity is most often reported as an adult-legitimated process conceived as an adult practice in recognizable 'high art' contexts. Yet the processes and practices of children's musical creativity, as documented by several authors[6] suggest that a distinction exists between adult and child modes of musical creativity. The idea that people and things are either creative or not creative in music is implicit in much of the thinking on musical creativity.

The need to move beyond the musical hegemony of Western art and jazz music is also present in cross-cultural practices of musical creativity. For example, traditional Chinese folk music contains no final immutable version of a musical piece. Where there is no final product, a continuous state of change through polishing and refinement occurs as part of performance creativity (Stock, 1991). This requires high levels of composition in performance which is regarded as part of the expertise of expressive performance behaviour. Similarly, in Vietnamese musical culture, composition involves an adaptive process of performing a traditional melody. This allows opportunity for the performer to elaborate new versions. The nature of invention in this composition–performance spectrum depends on the cultural context. In Western educational research it has been suggested that the degree of invention in musical performance depends on degrees of musical aptitudes and understandings, craftsmanship, and the aesthetic sensitivity of the player.[7] In popular music

---

[6] Kanellopoulos (1999), has explored improvisatory 'just playing' with eight-year-old Greek children, views on intentionality as a characteristic of improvisation, in terms of the authenticity of the children's experience, and allowing them to say it in their own way; on children's and young people's creative practices; see Banaji et al. (2006), M.S. Barrett (2006), Burnard (1999, 2002, 2004, 2006b,c), Burnard and Younker (2004, 2008), Stauffer (2001, 2002), and Folkestad (1998).

[7] Webster (1990) presents education research on the definition of performance as a creative activity and suggests that musical creativity is dependent on musical aptitudes (i.e. knowledge of tonal and rhythmic imagery, etc.), conceptual understanding (cognitive facts that constitute musical understanding), craftsmanship (the ability to apply factual knowledge in the service of the task), and aesthetic sensitivity

performance tradition, the defining features of creativity are illustrated through the socio-cultural elements of their presentation which communicate the inventiveness and individualism of personal style and sound.[8]

The composer, on the other hand, is often viewed as a kind of individual prophet, the score as his sacred text and the conductor as his priest. And yet musical creativity is rarely, if ever, a matter of the lone composer, or self, composing in isolation. Rather, it is a matter of composers working and playing with and with respect to others, intentionally or unintentionally. We have evidence that composers in modern Western society were not set apart from other musicians in a separate caste. The realm of musical creativity cannot be *re*-presented as a cast of characters engaged in a drama of competing, antagonistic interests, and struggles, but is rather socially constructed through an interaction between producers and audiences. Creativity is not the product of single individuals, but of social systems making judgements about individuals' products.

The Beethoven myth is one of the most consistent of these distortions. This is the claim that Beethoven was a misunderstood genius whose music was not valued in his own day. Critical accounts of the first performance of the Ninth Symphony, for example, constantly play down its considerable success, despite what appears to have been a fairly shambolic performance.[9] However, and crucially, whose voice is speaking? But, equally important is, who is hearing, or more accurately, reading? Because we only ever encounter 'voices' in texts. 'Voices are textual productions, or to be precise, recontextualizations' (Bernstein, 1990, p. 66). The rhetoric of vocal discourse disguises the fact that 'voice' is entirely a product of texts and is constituted by the principles whereby the text is written. The rhetoric that re-presents text as 'voice' suppresses precisely the syntax that generates the text and displaces its principle to the imaginary place occupied by the imaginary subject whose voice is invoked as author. Every description of the reality of musical creativity, every theoretical tendency, depicts the world in such a way that a certain community will recognize the description of the world 'as it really is'. The questions to address now are: How does the discourse of voice constitute its description of the world? How is the standpoint positively

---

(the shaping of sound structures to capture a 'feelingful' response). More recently, with new approaches to creative arts enquiry, a proliferation of new and emergent practices emphasizing strong collaborations and human arrangements between creativity researchers and industrial partners, including artists, are influencing the act of according value to performance creativity, the value of invention as the distinct focus of creative research, located neither after nor before the process of making but in the performance itself. The usual forms of classification—traditional definitions of roles, relationship, techniques, functions, and outcomes—are set aside for poetic principles of homology, convergence, disruption, and coincidence, in which the usual logic of combination is suspended. See E. Barrett and Bolt (2010).

[8] See Davidson and Coolam (2006) for further discussions on performance creativity.

[9] A story is told of Sir George Grove, who later talked to Fräulein Unger and gave the following account: 'The master, though placed in the midst of this confluence of music, heard nothing of it at all and was not even sensible of the applause of the audience at the end of his great work, but continued standing with his back to the audience, and beating the time, till Fräulein Unger turned to him, or induced him to turn around and face the people, who were still clapping their hands, and giving way to the greatest demonstrations of pleasure. His turning around, and the sudden conviction thereby forced on everybody that he had not done so before because he could not hear what was going on, acted like an electric shock on all present, and a volcanic explosion of sympathy and admiration followed, which was repeated again and again, and seemed as if it would never end.' Anton Schindler told Beethoven later, 'The whole audience was impressed, crushed by the greatness of your work.' (Grove, 2004. The anecdote (with footnote) is on page 335.)

constructed (from where is the description made) and correlatively, in relation to what is nega-tively characterized (against what is its distinctiveness constructed)?

A description of the world from a standpoint of inequality would be from the standpoint of the voice when it is established by means of a critique of the dominant knowledge-form.[10] For exam-ple, Kurkela and Väkevä, in their book *Decanonizing Music History*, show how different styles and traditions in music have formed their own canons. The goal is to deconstruct these canons, to describe, analyse and problematize them in all their variety. The de-canonizing refers to artistic crossover and cross-border encounters with the dominant knowledge forms of classical, jazz, and rock music that are central to the construction of the subordination of contemporary and sub-cultural genres. The question arises as to whether Western classical music is the dominant form these days. I suspect hegemony goes where the big money goes (that is marketing of superstars, starlets, and divas) giving rise to new mythologies (for example, the norm in twenty-first century chart pop, is for millions of fans of pop divas to identify powerfully with the 'uniqueness' of the Lady Gaga, Rihanna, or Britney Spears' brands; and yet we know that a communal conception of creativity, as opposed to the Western myth of individual genius is captured in their albums, where, in the studio, a kind of commodified team approach is the norm.[11] A description of the world in terms of the social relations of domination/subordination is transcribed as an epistemic relation that is then treated as the constitutive principle of the social relations. For example, women composers/conductors/songwriters are subordinated to men because the dominant forms of knowledge are male ('male' dress codes, 'male' history predominantly made up of men). Echoing the account of A. Bennett (1980), Finnegan (1989) describes seven musical worlds that she found in Milton Keynes between 1980 and 1984, in which she identified a number of different social institutions that support music and the organizations of the musical worlds, pointing to the importance of music to everyday life. Bands studied by Cohen (1991) found that female members of bands were systematically marginalized. But it was Bayton (1993) who identified some of the particular processes that affect women, such as the fact that they are more likely to join a band at an earlier stage of learning an instrument, and less likely to practise in the parental home. The all-women bands considered by Bayton tended to be more involved in writing original material. By mapping the constraints imposed on women musicians, Bayton was mapping the world from a standpoint that sees itself as subordinated.

Western education has traditionally reflected the myth that only a small proportion of children are 'musical', in the sense that they possess the particular abilities required of a capable performer, or are 'creative' in the sense that they possess what it takes to compose new music. This assump-tion is not made in other cultures, argues Blacking, nor is it particularly well founded in our own. Indeed the very existence of a professional, or even virtuoso, performer presupposes an audience who participate as listeners in the same musical culture. That is to say, for Blacking (1976), to be seen as musically creative in a culture, depends on the functions that music performs in a particu-lar society. For the Venda of southern Africa, with whom he lived for two years, 'the chief func-tion of music is to involve people in shared experiences within the framework of their cultural

---

[10] Taking the position of social realism, sociologists Maton and Moore (2010) put forward a persuasive case for a different form of critique that holds open the possibility of knowledge-building as that which works critically within a canonic tradition.

[11] For two reviews of 'Femme Fatale' by Britney Spears, both of which talk about collective and communal creativities in the creating of 'product' and 'brand', see issue 29, March 29 at NYDailyNews.com (Farber, 2011). Also for another album review in the *Los Angeles Times*, Pop and His Music Blog entitled album review, see 'Femme Fatale for Britney Spears' at http://latimesblogs.latimes.com/music_blog/2011/03/album-review-femme-fatale-by-britney-spears.html

experience' (p. 48); and there is no concept of a small group of particularly 'musical' people (unlike the Greek ideals of specialization as described by Plato). In contrast, modern Western societies, where the division of labour is advanced and there is an elaborate pattern of social stratification, do have such a concept, reinforcing the belief (or myth) that music, and certainly music education, may play a significant part in maintaining such hierarchical divisions. Like Bourdieu, Blacking views conventional assumptions about the distribution of musical abilities in general and musical creativity in particular as myths which serve to sustain and legitimize the existing pattern of inequality (1976).[12]

A number of familiar strands will illustrate my argument plainly and provocatively. First, there was the misleading depiction of the Great Composers and the privileging of the act of a single individual creator and its massive social hegemony. Second, there was the characterization of musical creativity in terms of a self-contained musical work, of one musical creativity for all musics. Combined with this was a view of the primacy of composition and its hierarchy of masterworks which came to emerge as 'facts' of music history; while all the time, Mozart, the epitome of the Great Genius, employed a range of different practices, not just one. Third, given the privileged status of such things as the composition, the fetishization of composition caused it to emerge as the act of all music acts. Fourth, in the relationship between composer and performer, assigning a subordinate status to the performer, and privileging the originators of the music—the authors—is misleading in its depiction of single individuals, and does not take into account the interactions between producers and the audience and social systems that make judgements about individuals' products.

Succinctly, in my view, the mythology of 'musical creativity' based on the idolization of the Great Composers and their masterworks is:

◆ misleading in its depiction of composers;

◆ mistaken in its view of the hegemonic position of composition within society;

◆ mistaken in its depiction of the position and hegemonic status of composers; and

◆ mistaken in its conclusion about its social consequences for subordinated groups such as performers and listeners/audiences.

Other myths of compositional history

In support of these arguments against the current hegemony of Western 'art' music and how the domination and subordination are constructed, the idea of the Romantic artist is one of the strongest elements uniting classical, jazz, and rock mythmakers.[13] The artists are celebrated as unique, and their masterworks or single albums that are at the top of the pop and rock genre list (such as the Beatles *Sgt Pepper*, and the Rolling Stones *Exile on Main Street*) stand as the greatest example of their kind. Each masterwork/album has its own associated genius or geniuses, and the man as myth—an enigmatic persona unique in classical, jazz, or popular music—contributes to the aura of the work, irrespective of style or genre. Typical characteristics of classical and rock canons feature 'man as myth', with the idea of 'truth' or legacy located in the masterwork or album as it relates to the identified author/genius. Greatness is attributed to the primary creators of each album, who are perceived as different or separate from those around them. This chapter

---

[12] With reference to the assumed distribution of 'musicality', see also Gordon (1987) quoted in Colwell (2002), Chapter 27.

[13] Jones (2008) and Kurkela and Väkevä (2009) offer critiques of the rock and jazz canons.

tells the story of how myths of musical creativity concern the composer/songwriter and his[14] self-contained masterworks and albums, which, as it will be shown, came to emerge as a 'fact' of music history.

Historically, composition has often been described as the mystical, unconscious, elusive, and inaccessible means by which composers bring new, reproducible pieces into existence over time. In this way, Mozart was one of the most famous and charismatic of composers to provide anecdotal evidence of the creative processes.

It is not difficult to see how Goehr's 'musical museum' (which, in the case of Western art music, provided the conceptual framework within which music took its place in the cultural heritage, the repertory or canon) came into existence, as described by Nicholas Cook in his book *Music: A Very Short Introduction* (1998):

> The term 'classical music' came into common currency. Borrowed from the 'classical' art of Greece and Rome, which was seen as the expression of universal standards of beauty, this term implied that similar standards had now been set in music, against which the production of all other times and places must be measured. (p. 30)

Behind the making of the masterworks of composers and albums by songwriters there lie a virtuosity of the imagination, exceptional technical skill, personal gifts, devotion, and self-confidence, amongst other qualities.

How does the myth survive? Moore (2010) reminds us of the importance of the dominant discourse to supporting its historical and social character and what authorities do to invoke support for their views. Thus, the implications of these masterworks and albums and the development of debates not only bears relationship to privileged positions from which to know, but also as explications of the 'rules of practice understood as their generative principles and conditions of existence' (p. 70) by which standards are measured. We will never know if Mozart's ideas were enabled by a spontaneous mode of thought before becoming a fixed product. It is ironic that differentiated types of musical creativity are responsible for creating an improvisation as the basis for musical compositions. Perhaps it is that the position-taking logic of the field of music that propels our assumptions, and overtly in serious debates concerning whether improvisation, is an outcome of the same kind of musical creativity as composition? For musicologist Nicholas Cook, the distinction between improvised and performed music, as characterized in the genres of free jazz improvisation and classical chamber music, is embodied in the same relational values and performative qualities as the socializing power of musical enactment. But does this argument operate as discursive positioning that revalorizes the social relations between groups? Theorist and researcher, Aranosian (1981) places a different emphasis on types of musical creativity, and the myths upheld by Western classical traditions:

> The difference between composing and improvising is based on whether or not the individual decides to retain, permanently, the phrases which are created. The composer makes something so that he/she may keep it and reuse it, while the improviser makes it only so that it will cause him/her to make something else. (p. 73)

But can a distinction between improvisation and composition be made only on a temporal basis? The practices of improvisation and composition do not look the same in all music. By their nature, they reflect what is known and who knows it, where voice and experience produces a

---

[14] Whilst it may be politically correct to write 'her' works, the historical fact is that for most of the nineteenth century composers were men, as is also the case in the rock canon.

result that is inherently unstable. For Mozart, who spoke of an auditory or mental image of the whole, it took Langer (1953) to mythologize this theoretical notion, legitimizing the concept of composition in which a category of 'total Gestalt' becomes specific as follows:

> The total Gestalt presents itself to him, [the composer] recognises the fundamental form of the piece . . . This form is the 'composition' which he feels called upon to develop . . . Once the essential musical form is found, a piece of music exists in embryo . . . One might call that original conception the commanding form of the work. (pp. 122–3)

With scholarly rhetoric, Langer (1953) describes the first stage of the creative practice that for a piece of music to come into being it must first be imagined. She said:

> The first stage is the process of conception that takes place entirely within the composer's mind (no matter what outside stimuli may start or support it), and issues in a more or less sudden recognition of the total form to be achieved. (p. 121)

My concern is within the sense of keeping alive the myth of the position-taking of composers, the production of an object and of issues relating to mass-producing a commodity, of contesting a dominant knowledge claim by differentiating it against all cultures and traditions, the claim being authorized by its own voice. It has been stated that the experience of composing may be the result of a collaboration between the composer and imagined or sounded out ideas. Whether the piece is preserved in the form of notation or not, it would appear that the composer identifies and values a piece as a result of the deconstruction of time and its reconstruction as a scored piece in time (Clifton, 1983; Goehr, 1992; Wolterstorff, 1994). How does the creation of music necessitate imagining anything? Do audio designers, who compose music to accompany games, use their time to compose music in this way? How long are the bits of music they write and how long do they spend writing them? Another myth that music is a product is the issue to which I next turn.

Composition as object

Ethnographers Campbell and Teicher (1997) reported on the distinctive forms of oral-aural traditions of musical creation in a variety of musical cultures, and described traditional Vietnamese music as 'compositions'. The festival-ritual music genre (*nhac le*), chamber music from the central (*nhac hue*) and southern regions (*nhac tai tu*), are 'fixed' traditional melodies which are preserved in partially notated forms but learnt using an aural tradition. The adaptive process of performing a traditional melody, with opportunity for the performers to elaborate their own versions, adheres to the Vietnamese musician's motto of 'learning a dead song (but) performing a live melody' (Campbell and Teicher, 1997, p. 36). The nature of the compositional process is characterized as follows:

> No part of the process of musical creation and performance predominates over the other: conceiving a musical idea and shaping it into a melodic form by the composer is no less important than the re-shaping and personal interpretation of it by the performer.
>
> (Campbell and Teicher, 1997, p. 36)

These cultural interpretations of composition inform us about the composer's experience and the identification of a piece as an object that is not bound to its maker. Additionally, a composition can exist as a fixed product or an evolving piece which is revitalized in and by each performance. This suggests that composition could be considered as a form of processual object continually redefined through performance. Clifton (1983) described it this way:

> By and large, a composer moved from a general understanding of what has to be done to a specific feeling which is the result, not the cause, of the actual production of the composition . . . The composition as

a complex object of 'feeling and knowledge' is understood by uncovering its sense . . . If we prefer not to simply confer significance onto a composition, the binding of feeling and understanding can help us remember the intuitive origins of implicit significations . . . [but just as] . . . the composition is presented by a performance . . . the composition is not reducible to the performance. (pp. 78–9)

Composition as fixed

Wolterstorff (1994) stated that composition was guided by the 'rules of completeness specifying what constitutes' a composed work for 'a complete playing' (p. 118). This view was echoed in the writings of Margolis (1977) and Goehr (1992), both of whom considered that a necessary pre-condition for composition was a work-concept which affected the way compositions were judged, valued, and received. According to Goehr (1992), a function of the composition is to produce an enduring artefact, which:

> . . . is not generally thought to be just any group of sounds, but a complex structure of sounds related in some important way to a composer, a score and a given class of performances. (p. 20)

Margolis (1977) emphasized that the explicit intention of a composer is to produce a musical manuscript or score as 'a record' of the creator's 'determination'. Margolis maintained that the process of composition incorporates the selection and rejection of ideas on the basis of the goals of composing, 'since in the course of composing a work he [*sic*] normally considers a great many more [ideas] . . . than he actually settles on' (p. 247). Margolis developed this notion to suggest that the composer's intention is not just to ensure a particular 'kind of performance' (for what is a performance without interpretation?) but that the nature of composition requires the composer to create a certain 'kind of sound-sequence-occurrence' (p. 244). Consequently, composition can be regarded not only as an adaptive process, revitalized in and by performance, but one based on attentiveness to creating a piece which is 'properly formed'. Similarly, Wolterstorff (1994) claimed that composing results in the production of identifiable kinds of pieces. For example, he described a 'norm-kind' which contains certain 'properties'. Certainly, a composition has an identity as an object of work as well as an object in and of itself.

Because the use of musical scores as permanent records was the standard practice in nineteenth-century Western music, the composer's ownership, through authorship of the music, enabled his or her music to be preserved. Performances in earlier centuries were often less notated and involved improvisatory practices in which performers embellished and elaborated on the score (Goehr, 1992). Goehr argued that composition is characterized by the fixed and repeatable score which identifies the piece as 'property'. Certainly there can be little doubt that composition is the domi-nant ideology in Western art music. These discourses, unsurprisingly, feature the towering central-ity of the Great Composers in the canons of Western art music. They are dominating and venerated figures. Their stories get mythologized in both the literature and the reception of classical music from the nineteenth century (as with twenty-first century singer-songwriters and their albums), and are located or positioned, and finally become 'hegemonic knowledge claims' repeated over time.

But what is also as significant as the perceived truth that underlies the myths is that the myths reflect the values and concerns of the mythmakers. Crucially, the rhetoric of 'myths' and 'myth-makers' has proved so strong that it is used to explain conventions and working practices within the production system, as if constituted by the principles and ideologies of music history. Myths are, however, mere constructions. This is made quite clear in relation to the first myth discussed earlier, illustrating the relationship of the composer or songwriter and his/her works or albums to the myths of compositional history, as Small (1998) argued:

> The myths of compositional history are as embedded in classical music history as they are in rock music history. They can be stories, naive misconceptions, and fictitious narratives, even simple

untruths embodying some popular idea concerning natural or historical phenomena, or a fictitious or imaginary person or event. The fact that reputable books perpetuate them, telling us how things came to be as they are more often presents the construction of a privileged viewpoint. Myths serve as stories we tell ourselves concerning how things came to be and therefore how they are. They thus place the past, whether real or imagined, at the service of the present. Importantly, their actual historical accuracy is irrelevant to their value. (p. 92)

Whose voice takes priority and why?

The key question to be asked about the branding of composers and other types of musicians as charismatic heroes and the field positioning of masterworks and albums in the canonic traditions of classical and rock music is not only who is speaking but also who is hearing, or, more accurately, whose voice is regarded as the author and by whose authority. In other words, who says what counts? Bourdieu explains this in terms of the concepts of cultural capital, and the relation between habitus and field, which authorizes it and invests it with authority (see the end of this chapter and Appendix B).

How can we determine the standpoint of musical creativity myths as well as their positioning strategy? That is, can we determine how their distinctive standpoint on musical creativity is constructed? Its positioning is complex and multifaceted. On the one hand, we have a model of genius creators who work alone and operate in a field that places some limits on the nature and extent of their creativity. On the other hand, we have notions of creativity expressed in musicians' desire to compose their own music, when a rock band or string quartet, for example, provides a setting for players to express their own personal aesthetic vision and, through their music, achieve a sense of controlling their values, destiny, and self-identity. (This recalls the themes raised by Becker in his account of jazz musicians, since the notion of self-expression in jazz repeats the idea of the artist, above commerce, and lies at the core of jazz musicians' beliefs.) Yet again, musical creativity is asserted as 'an enacted freedom' that always goes beyond, and never simply derives from, that which already is.

Thus, I welcome the view of Bernstein, who says: 'The voice of a social category (in this case musical creativity) is constructed by the degree of specialization of the discursive rules regulating and legitimizing the form of communication' (1990, p. 23, in Moore, 2010, p. 75). The possibility that music makes creativity manifest still privileges the notion of the creator as a 'person' (singular). As Moore (2010) states: 'If categories of either agents or discourse are specialised, then each category necessarily has its own specific identity and its own specific boundaries' (p. 75). The term 'musical creativity' makes creativity manifest as a singular term focused on single creators and on a distinctive set of masterworks (i.e. creative products). This plays down musical creativity as an overtly collective or collaborative activity, and presupposes a relatively stable and unified human subject. Furthermore, it does not allow for activity between domains, or for the radically creative challenge of interdisciplinary or cross-cultural music exchanges which result in hybrid genres. If it is merely the individual who makes the creativity manifest we would not recognize the myriad social forms that constitute the field of music: the musical associations and ensembles and the varied social relations that arise when people play music together. The point I am making here is that music occurs in a multiplicity of social spaces of the dominant culture, and counter- or sub-cultural genres, and is invested with a multiplicity of meanings underpinned by a multiplicity of practices and market forces, that, most importantly, constitute a multiplicity of musical creativities. Willis et al. (1990) support this view:

> In general the arts establishment connives to keep alive the myth of the special, creative, individual artist holding out against passive mass consumerism, so helping to maintain a self-interested view of

elite creativity. Against this we insist that there is a vibrant symbolic life and symbolic creativity in everyday life, everyday activity and expression—even if it is sometimes looked down upon and spurned. We don't want to invent it or propose it. We want to recognize it—literally re-cognize it. (pp. 21–6)

The singularity of the term 'musical creativity' does not recognize the sociality and the technological dimensions that underwrite how diverse forms of music are created, performed, and listened to; and neither does it recognize the multifarious categories of music manifest in diverse practices, of which a given singular category of musical creativity is but one member.

Aesthetic judgements are also situation-specific. If the 'work' or 'event' is part of the 'work' or 'event'[15] then it is not surprising that composers and songwriters may not agree as to whose intentions—composers, interpreters, or audiences—take priority. This depends on the cultural context or situation which is the context itself. For instance, for academically trained musicians as members of a symphony orchestra preparing to give a concert, instruments must have been invented, manufactured, and maintained, a notation must have been devised and music composed using that notation, people must have learned to play the notated notes on the instruments, times and places for rehearsal must have been provided, advertisements for the concert must have been placed, publicity must have been arranged and tickets sold, and an audience capable of listening to and in some way understanding and responding to the performance must have been recruited. This musical creativity is situated differently from the oral traditions played out in a Javanese *gamelan* where the centrality of mutual dependence and collective re-creation is underlined by ensemble interaction.[16]

But a theory of musical creativity, which is to say, an idea of what musical creativity is and what it is not, and of the role it plays in our lives, must be able to explain not just why members of one social and cultural group differ in their ways of '*musicking*' from members of another group, but how it is that members of one culture can come to understand and enjoy, and perhaps creatively appropriate the creativity of others. It must also explain when some forms of music creativity become dominant, sometimes across the whole world, while others remain confined to the social group within which they originated. One of my aims in this book is to make readers more aware of the nature of their theories of music creativity, and thus be in a better position to take control of and recognize their own creativity at play in their musical lives. A theory of musical creativity, like the act of creating itself, is not just something for 'musical' or 'creative' people but an important component of our understanding of ourselves and of our relationships to others. The act of musical creativity establishes in the place where it is happening a set of relationships between people, between the individual and the social group, between the individual and society, and between the society and the ever-expanding creative spectrum of web space.

For new-generation commercial music, web space and the peculiar properties of the ever-expanding web world—the medium through which musical culture increasingly organizes itself—provide a dynamic and complex context wherein all kinds of creativity nestle in the nooks and crannies.

In all of this is the recognition that values are germane to an understanding of musical creativity. The argument has been made that the context of musical creativity is not a single, static quality that can be described with any individualistic sense of universality. This context closely resembles a tangled web of shifting, contradictory realities that coexist, collide, and interface. Similarly, past

---

[15] Expressed by Dalhaus (1983) as oppositional and further debunked by Small's (1998) notion of 'musicking' (p. 11).

[16] See Brinner (1995) for a detailed account of Javanese *gamelan* where the context is created and invoked, and can be observed and analysed.

and present histories combine and overlap, forming both macro and micro histories that impact on the hierarchy of values in which musical creativity gets situated in time and space.

Constructions of dominant discourse

There can be no doubt that a certain concept of musical creativity is inscribed in the musical acts, tastes, and stylistic preferences of those who influence the market. Inasmuch as popular musicians create music destined for a market, and composers respond to a patron, commission, or brief, the musical scene that absorbs them cannot fail to heed the exigencies of this market. We know that Stravinsky was eternally aware of the society around him, the preferences of musical audiences, the lack of popular acclaim and the wages of social isolation. His return to eighteenth-century roots (known as neoclassicism) was not only an attempt at the restoration of authenticity to music from its sojourn into the privatized spheres of the incomprehensible, but also an effort to make music acceptable to a society not prepared to work at listening.

The categories of creativities involved in listening to music from churches to opera houses, temples to concert halls, and palaces to stadiums, illustrate the difference between writing for a congregation and writing for an audience. For Bach, writing for a formidable patron such as the Duke of Saxony-Weissenfels in 1717, or musical establishments such as the municipalities, the courts or church, which he himself had built up and trained for the music his choirs and orchestras were asked to sing and play, musical creativity was an amalgam of complexity and diversity. For Handel, writing for singers and players recruited locally in Dublin enabled him to write 'The Messiah'. The music requires one choir, four solo singers, and three instrumental soloists. For all its wonderful quality it is within the range of an amateur choral society. Given the centrality of performance creativity to these issues the point needs to be made that 'The Messiah' resists objec-tification as a 'work' in the sense of an autonomous score but rather it exists as a series of events for which sometimes substantial changes are made. Thus you have a 'Dublin' version, a 'founding hospital' version, as well as the 'versions' devised post-mortem by for example, Prout, Beecham/ Goosens, and Lam and Watkins Shaw. It was Handel who purportedly said 'and I think that I did see all heaven before me' when speaking of composing the 'Hallelujah Chorus' is a bit of Romantic self-promotion. Handel was a commercial composer, and his religious music is first and foremost commercial.

For Mozart, in the case of *opera seria*, it was for the prince; for Handel, in the case of religious music, it was for God, the Church, or for the patron. Similarly static canons exist in a number of musics across Asia, such as the *gagaku* repertoire of Japan wherein court music has been officially regulated by a government bureau since the early eighth century (Schippers, 2010). For Stravinsky (1947), however, the demands he made on the performer required a rigidly objective approach, called by him 'execution', which he characterized as 'the strict putting into effect of an explicit will that contains nothing beyond what it specifically commands' (p. 68). He was known to rail against the 'liberties' taken by performers who dared to interpose too much of their creativity into performances of his works. Thus, the concept of 'creativity' does not represent a peculiarly singu-lar quality situated in and through all musics. Stravinsky differentiated composing and performing in relation to creativity by the degree of enacted creativity inscribed in originating a piece compared with that of realizing it in performance.

The point I am making is that the way we think about musical creativity can lead us to assign a 'hierarchy of value' (Cook, 1990, p. 26), assigning a subordinate status to the production compared to the creation of music (as in the fetishization of composition), particularly if creativity is not a peculiar quality of the act. This status is totally at odds with the adulation of stardom (the view of individual charismatic performers who make creativity manifest in music) in the marketplace. All of this shows the intricate relationships of various musics with their environment, and the relationships between composer and performer, artist and audience for whom composers/songwriters/sound artists write and artists perform.

So, we have plenty of evidence for challenging the singular and individualist discourses on musical creativity. For young people involved in the dance music scene, the forms of collective association which are built around musical tastes and stylistic preference, exhibited at counter- or sub-cultural[17] music scenes, offer clear examples of the very acts of consumer autonomy and creativity that open up and reconfigure the potential multiplicity of creativities in music. According to Deliège and Wiggins (2006):

> There is no hope of understanding creative behaviour by looking at it from one discipline, using a single methodological approach even within a given scientific field . . . By its very nature, creativity requires confrontation, debate, questioning, integration. (p. 5)

Modern technology has allowed for the mass reproducibility of all musics. This makes it possible to speak of the ways in which society, with its download culture, has responded to the growth of the mass media by adding new forms of musical production and consumption. Moreover, collaborative and collective forms of creativity are inscribed in the music of youth cultures, for example, as portrayed by the mods and rockers in *Quadrophenia*, the well-known 1979 film based on the album of the same name by the iconic rock band The Who (Dillabough and Kennelly, 2010). Here we see a kind of 'symbolic creativity', which constitutes musical taste that is exercised by consumers and the 'creative' multimedia resources that they use to do so.

We are engaged in the process of creating music every time we realize our own version of a song. There is something more and something different that we do when, as users, we try to make our own meanings of music. The creativity of consuming is something that everybody does and claims by right as the buyer. So, it is not just giving expression to our own and each other's music creativity that defines us as human beings, but how the patterns of meaning are projected into music. These patterns of meaning are routinely stabilized and repeatedly observed, more generally but not only, in music history as powerful discourses or metaphors which come to condition how we think about things. A fundamental theoretical question arising from this is how to move beyond the tendency to think in terms of the nineteenth-century notion of a singular socio-musical reality, and rather recognize the multiplicity of musical creativities and their related practices of production and consumption in the emergence of sub-genres and hybrid genres.

The production and reception (and consumption) of music is integrative and collaborative. For example, although films tend to be known as their director's product, clearly there is crucial work involved by a film composer, musicians, producers, camera crews, actors, scriptwriters, and many others, just at the production stage. The same applies to the social production of television programmes and music written as signature tunes to soaps. The performing arts in general result in 'collective' products, in the sense that whether they have been composed by Mozart, choreographed by Martha Graham, or written by Brecht, they depend for their realization on other people: musicians, conductors, dancers, actors, and a variety of 'support personnel' (Becker, 1984). Thus, even if one accepts the potential multiplicity of musical creativities in today's highly

---

17 A. Bennett (1999) argues that those groupings, which have traditionally been theorized as coherent sub-cultures (for example, the now defunct British pop group Oasis and some of its fans promoted an image consisting of training shoes, football shirts, and duffel coats, which was designed to illustrate their collective sense of working-classness) are better understood as a series of temporal gatherings characterized by fluid boundaries and floating memberships. The nature of creativity, as with music itself, is both multi-faceted and a distinctly fluid form of expression.

technologized and mediated society, there is no single meaning and value accorded to the concept of 'music creativity'. For Sawyer (1997), writing on jazz improvisation, musical creativity 'depends on a shared system of creative conventions and no one can create music without first internalizing the rules and conventions of the domain' (p. 239). Then there are the electronic music experts, who are also representative of the collective as they constitute a realization of socio-cultural influences and involve practices situated at the intersection of electronic music, interaction, and social computing (Tanaka et al., 2005). Wiggins (2008) on the other hand, thinks that mainly Western 'art' music is 'a precious personal thing, almost like a religious construct, which is not open to question or even scrutiny . . . relative to both temporal and social context' (p. 109). Consider how musicians from different cultures situate creativity in their practice compared with the cultural idiosyncrasies of digital musicians who improvise with algorithms.

All this requires a recognition that the hegemony of Western classical music implies hierarchies of genre. For example, Wagner infamously transformed musical thought through his idea of *Gesamtkunstwerk* ('total artwork'), the synthesis of all the poetic, visual, musical, and dramatic arts, epitomized by his monumental four-opera cycle *Der Ring des Nibelungen* (1876). To try to stage these 'artworks' as he imagined them, Wagner built his own opera house, (the Bayreuth Festspielhaus). As another example, in London, at the O2 Arena, Take That offers up a visceral spectacle with an army of professionals supporting its production, the success of which depends on the judgement of observers who construct, contain, and constrain what is possible, what is supported, what is accessible, what is valued, and what is not. What is consistent between them is that they both reflect social groups in contexts wherein the form and content of the creative event is entirely dependent upon the conditions in which the creator(s) and creative endeavour is positioned; musical creativity is not value-free (Blanning, 2002). The audience, who also participates and engages creatively, makes connections in search of meaning from within their musical lives and social worlds. Behind the scenes at these different venues an army of professionals engages and explores the creative possibilities in the production of an event which can have the transformative effect of stimulating change by means of lighting, sound, marketing, etc. What they do musically can be construed—in some ways—as expanding frontiers between the new and the familiar. They do this as members of multiple musical cultures, each with their own musical affiliations. From this perspective, what differentiates these contexts and the musical creativities arising from them can be understood in terms of its relation to both cultural and social constructions of musical creativity. A value system remains firmly in place within the select world of the composer and the 'art' work repertory, on the one hand, and songwriters and popular culture, on the other, which positions musical creativity differently. A hierarchy of value reinforces the value-laden way musical creativity is talked about, and how it maps onto different individuals or social groups: composers, performers, and audiences.

Any attempt to explain or understand the value claims underpinning the concept of musical creativity as evidenced in the production and consumption of music entails a further conceptual dilemma in the idea of the 'artist-as-creator' working with divine inspiration, or as the lone genius involved in the creating the music. Must the generative force originate from a really high individual artistic order? Does it take music composed by a Great Composer to break free of one's time, without firmly and actively renouncing it? Wolff (1993) argues that the named artist plays much less of a part in the production of the work than our commonsense view of the artist as genius leads us to believe. Wolff addresses the key questions of the role of the audience and the concept of authorial dominance, and exposes the myth of the fixed, uniform and unconstituted creative source. She makes a powerful case for the demystification of 'artistic creativity' generally (Wolff, 1993).

In addressing the question of how musical creativity comes to be known and valued in particularized genres, we have seen that art and cultural forms appear in many guises, depending upon particular contexts, from the popular to the refined. But why haven't academics studied electronica artists, who do not use instruments as part of their musical output, alongside tribute bands and DJs, whose music is re-created or reinvented out of bits and pieces that were originally composed and performed by someone else? In terms of popular cultural forms, such as jazz, rock 'n' roll, and rock video,[18] the question of what constitutes musical creativity in terms which value all forms and practices (not only in terms of dominant, legitimate cultural forms of Western art composers) has not been addressed. Unlike the traditional Western orthodoxies of musical creativity, which have characterized our understanding of Western art composers, it is not clear how the consumption and construction of musical creativity comes to be known and characterized in our understanding of contemporary music and the construction of 'bourgeois subjectivity' (Cook, 1998).[19]

In sum, the Western canonization of musical creativity is a historically linked and limited definition of high art orthodoxies. By considering the example of Beethoven, we learn about the orthodoxies that privilege musical creativity as a uniquely autonomous, private (rather than public), personal (rather than social) realm that valorizes the individual. The generating force for musical creativity is not primarily of an individual nature but comes from 'the social within us' (phrase first coined by Vygotsky, 1971, p. 249), acting as a member of a human group. It is 'situation' specific, and is a construction that involves composer (generative), performer (productive and interpretive), and listener (exercising adaptive behaviours which involve them in production and interpretation).

From the habitus or social world of jazz clubs we know that stylistic change in the practices that generate genres such as jazz and rhythm and blues led to the production and consumption of bebop, moving away from the more formalized conventions of traditional jazz. Musicians use and engage with the raw materials of sound and repertoires for action, and produce or reproduce songs or use a framework, like the blues. Improvisation is the very context in which the construct of creativity takes shape. The effects of the habitus can be seen in the practices and beliefs to which it gives rise. For example, both sets of performers (whether players of bebop or any other subgenre of jazz) use their knowledge of contexts to generate appropriate action, and the appropriateness of that action—specific types of movement (tempos, energy levels, styles of movement) and the extent of interaction—then serves to define the context in which they interact. Neither the performers nor the listeners to jazz may believe that the composers of jazz standards merit any special deference with respect to how their songs should be played. Through their knowledge of and/or conformity to past practices, the performance we eventually see and hear comes to be and continues to be embodied in, and reflective of, its historical and social context (DeNora, 1995).

Alternatively, we can try to define creativity in terms of its situatedness, its 'context' such as (a) high art contexts: the insulation of individual artists whose identities are constructed as a social category of genius or divinely legitimated; or (b) contemporary contexts: musical creativity championed through contemporary practices; or (c) scientific and technological contexts: privileging invention and working innovatively, doing something that is done *to* as well as *by* the creator.

In the places and social worlds of religious ceremonies, space, time, sight, sound, and movement are employed, often with ritual behaviour in the form of repetitive motor actions, believed

---

[18] Aronowitz (1994) who argues 'that virtually all art is a commodified product of the culture industry' (p. 26).
[19] According to Cook (1998) the construction of bourgeois subjectivity within Romanticism (as the new mood across the arts was known) was the most important development (in terms of personal expression and how music came to occupy a privileged position) of the nineteenth century.

to be universal, applied across disparate cultures, times and places (see Levitin, 2008, pp. 194–5). In these settings, forms of musical creativity are infused with special meaning, as for example pitch-intoned changing which typically involve practices with order, regularity, and uniformity.

Web space offers mainstream rock groups and solo artists a dynamic medium to signal creativity and the ability to engage in, and with, all different kinds of music that employ situation-specific practices. This, for instance, might include the 'standard practice' of those who 'cover' (for example, Leona Lewis's version of Snow Patrol's 'Light up'); or 'remix' (Puff Daddy's remix of The Police's 'Every breath you take'); or do 'mash-ups' (on play stations, such as the Xbox® and Wii™ Guitar Hero®).[20] As with concert halls, arenas and opera houses, which distinguish themselves as sites of spectacles and speculation,[21] the centrality of place (whether in Greece, Vienna, London at the O2, the Bologna Opera House, or in Berlin or Paris) is a powerful site-driven signal for musical creativity of all different kinds. Such places allow humans to signal creativity through their capacity to engage and employ space, time, sight, sound, and movement for metaphorical communication between our personal and social worlds.

Moore (2010) provides a counter argument and brings the canon under fire when he argues against the basic principle of a canon being something that enshrines those things (works of art, masterworks) that are of autonomous, superior worth. He argues that 'canons are seen as arbitrary constructions reflecting no more than the tastes and fashions of dominant social groups or, at worse, as ideological forces that legitimate and reproduce the position and power of dominant groups' (p. 196). Others say: 'You can't think without a canon'. 'The canon determines how we judge the value of a musical work.' It is a judgement which is the product of procedures of a particular collective kind. Values are reflected and conveyed through the canon.

When music is examined under a critical gaze, it is subjected to discipline, order and correction, with the canon functioning as a basic tool in defining the scope of musical criticism. On one hand, the canon determines what music is worthy of study. On the other hand, it operates as a measure of the competence of scholars. The canonization of classical music (Kurkela and Väkevä, 2009) and popular music deliver alternative conceptions of music over to become secondary and marginal. In this case, the issue is the manner in which musical creativity is presented from the hegemonic perspective of the dominant form.

What is the relevance of the notion of 'de-canonization' to this discussion? In the domain of music and the phenomenon of musical creativity, the term 'canon' carries a variety of connotations, mostly pertaining to the authority and centrality bestowed upon 'great' musical genres, works, individuals, institutions, and texts in the worldview that academics impart to readers. In the specific field of music and music education, the concept of the canon may apply to our collective assumptions and beliefs regarding: standard pieces to be performed in a concert (or school setting); notable music educators whose methods are to be learned (Kodaly, Orff, Suzuki); educational organizations and institutions with which students are expected to engage, such as the Associated Board of the Royal Schools of Music (ABRSM) and Royal College of Music (RCM); and sources of music-related knowledge that are to be recognized as authoritative and complete (*Grove Dictionary* and Grout's *A History of Western Music*). Although the foundations of musical creativity and its role in teaching and learning may only be meaningfully understood in the context of social

---

[20] The idea of taking other people's songs to embody new meanings emerges from past practices constructed in different time periods and physical spaces, in communities from diverse cultural contexts.

[21] Concert halls are hypothetical sites of speculation and positioning in terms of musical creativity and the interplay between sound and form, convention and innovation, boundary pushing and traditional practice.

structures, explicit interrogation of systems of power and ideologies associated with institutions is rarely encountered in historical accounts of music or music education.

Conclusion

A vexed issue concerning a singular view of musical creativity in the early twenty-first century is why the dominance of the Great Masters of Western classical music continues to be postulated as the pre-eminent discourse running through political, social, cultural, and educational fields. The assumptions which serve to underpin existing models of musical creativity are put forward by, and inscribed in, studies of musical creativity arising from conventional tonal music. However, whether viewed through a psychological or socio-cultural lens, musical creativity occurs in a multiplicity of social spaces in which the contexts give and incorporate a multiplicity of meanings. These are underpinned by codified practices, which is to say acts based on generative principles, grounded in different discourses, the most dominant being Western classical music.

Musical creativity becomes apparent in different kinds of contexts in which the output of creativity and creative action occurs through practices involving thinking and action. The creative outputs are generally open to the participatory and discursive meaning-making processes of viewers, readers, listeners, and audiences, in which individuals interact with codified practices arising within the social space of traditions, conventions, communities, and networks. As with the field of music, musical creativity can be understood, to an extent, by an analysis of its specific historical and local, national, international, and relational contexts; but a proper understanding also requires an interrogation of the ways in which previous knowledge about musical creativity has been generated, by whom, and whose interests were served. This book responds to Bourdieu's call to counter taken-for-granted assumptions and challenge the familiar and accepted canon that privileges Western classical music, and argues for a new perspective on musical creativity.

The myth of viewing musical creativity as a singular phenomenon requires that musicians have similar understandings of what it is and how it is practised in particular genres. All music inscribes creativity, but the term 'musical creativity' is, as I will argue throughout this book, is an empty outmoded category unless we situate the production and reception of music more broadly in practices differentiated by distinctive creativities. As with practices of performance creativity, group compositional and collective improvisational creativities are temporally mediated, so the practices of audience and fan creativities are socially mediated. But creativities also define themselves through technological mediation which may reveal something about practices infused with a collective quality.

The myth of musical creativity as more generally realized by the isolated genius is perpetuated by the high art orthodoxies of Western art music which valorize composers' work as isolated and solitary. We are aware that many composers may work from home, but that, historically and culturally, composers practise creativity in interaction between people and communities networked within social and cultural contexts. Foucault (1977) has looked at artistic practice as self-technology, meaning the self-construction of images of self as an assemblage and construction. While we are encouraged to think of ourselves as individual creators and consumers, the reality is that we are working and living with social technologies. Social institutions have vested interests in keeping people as concert consumers rather than as concert creators.

The myth of compositions as fixed and finalized products separated in time from performance is part of a product-centric philosophy whose assumption is flawed. Works are not fixed. They are always being changed through interpretation or by the composers themselves. For game composers, for instance, the music is not a separate part of the product. Sounds cannot be fixed or finalized or finished. Sounds are not objects. The world of sound is primarily the world of activity rather than artefact.[22] The practice of privileging certain creativities is a practice of privileging only one aspect of the process of creativity.

Musical creativity, as with the field of music, has no boundaries. Yet we are constantly sold the idea that music is a simple three-step event involving composer, performer, and listener: an idea which privileges composers over performers and both composers and performers over listeners. This view does little to open the way to describing and interpreting the complexity of production, circulation, reception, and generation among consumers, producers, and creators of music, and the way in which individuals, within their social worlds and communities, interact. Musical creativity occurs in social spaces, in 'situation-specific' ways. Bourdieu's (1996) account of the 'field' and the 'social agents' who use differing strategies to maintain or improve their positions as composers (generative), performers (productive/interpretive), and listeners (exercising adaptive behaviours which involve them in productive and interpretive activities), constitutes a call for a more critical awareness of musical creativity in an expanded field where music has won a firmer place and meaning with the greater global public. The field of production involves consumers and producers in the production, circulation, and reception of changing forms of music creativities. This has an effect on what players can do, and thus how ideas and concepts enter into the field or marketplace of an interpretive community. Through this mediating process, ideas and concepts take on additional meanings as new practices are fashioned and old practices fractured. Musical creativities are revealed as the exemplary locus of diverse practices and discourse about practices, in this way offering unparalleled grounds for rethinking creativity itself.

Final thoughts

In journeying through the following chapters you will see that this book draws on a loosely framed approach in analysing the narratives of practice using the French sociologist Pierre Bourdieu's tools for thinking. One way of understanding the shift in perspective to the pluralism of musical creativities explained in this book is to replace 'this/or' thinking with a refined and developed 'both/and'. This recognizes the pluralist character of musical creativities and does not take this to inevitably entail relativism. So, what are the principal ideas associated with the theoretical premises that play a key role in bringing into the light and exploring multiple manifestations of musical creativity in the practices of real world musicians? The ideas of Bourdieu that I embrace are as follows.

- Habitus is a way of looking at data which renders the 'taken-for-granted' problematic. It suggests a whole range of questions not necessarily addressed in empirical research: How well adapted is the individual to the context they find themselves in? How does personal history shape their responses to the contemporary setting? What subjective vocations do they bring to the present and how are they manifested? (Reay, 1995, p. 369).

- The notion of cultural capital initially presented itself to me, in the course of research, as a theoretical hypothesis which made it possible to explain the unequal scholastic achievement of children originating from different social classes by relating academic success, which is to say the specific profits which children from different classes and class fractions can obtain in the academic market, to the distribution of cultural capital between classes and class fractions (Bourdieu, 1986, p. 243).

- As a space of potential and active forces, the field is also a field of struggles aimed at presenting or transforming the configuration of these forces (Bourdieu and Wacquant, 1992, p. 101).

---

[22] This view is strongly advocated in the work and writing of Murray Schafer. See Kahn (2001).

- The main thing is that they are not to be conceptualized so much as ideas, on that level, but as a method. The core of my work lies in the method and a way of thinking. To be more precise, my method is a manner of asking questions rather than just ideas. This I think is a critical point (Bourdieu, 1985).

- 'Ideas like those of habitus and practice, and so on, were intended, among other things, to point out that there is a practical knowledge that has its own logic, which cannot be reduced to that of theoretical knowledge; that in a sense, agents know the social world better than the theoreticians. And at the same time, I was also saying that, of course, they do not really know it and the scientist's work consist in making explicit this practical knowledge, in accordance with its own articulations' (Bourdieu, 1990b, p. 52).

- (Habitus × Capital) + Field = Practice (Bourdieu, 1984a, p. 101).

Part 2

Narratives of practice

Chapter 3

Originals bands

Musicians who dedicate themselves to a particular originals band, and the distinctive style of original music characteristic of that band, make choices in conformity with their tastes and dispositions relating to the way that the band—as a collective—predisposes members to play, perform, compose, and record in a particular way. Examples of this particularity include, for example, sound, identity, ethos, clothes, artwork, branding, signing or not signing to a label, interdependence of relationships, and top-down/bottom-up management models in the field of popular music.[1] For originals bands, the conveyance of 'originality' (i.e. the newness and unique-ness of a sound and the production of a distinctive album) exemplify co-constructed **production creativity**. Originals bands musicians engage in social forms which include the interplay of **entre-preneurial** and **collective creativities** and the establishment of a fan base and **fan-generated participatory creativity**, the latter supporting audience input and having an impact on what kinds of music are produced. In this chapter the descriptions of concrete exemplars of practice[2] are illustrative of the Bourdieuian principle of 'field positioning' (building reputations, gaining recognition, becoming known, accumulating fans), and prioritization of the practices of album producing, which opens up a multitude of possibilities in recording and mixing music. Some of the creativities realized relate to how bands struggle for dominant positions within the field[3] and mobilize their accumulated 'capital', the possession of power and prestige, to capture continuity and shape change as expressed through durable and adaptive practices.

[1] See T. Bennett et al. (1993), Cloonan (2005), Cloonan and B. Johnson (2006), and Green (2001) for inter-esting discussions of differences in originals musician and session musician attitudes and practices that underlie popular and local music-making.

[2] Steve MacKay (b. 1981) and Australian band Twelve Foot Ninja (TFN); Adam Scott (b. 1978) and Scottish band Zoey Van Goey (ZVG); Leah Kardos (b. 1979) and UK bands Helzuki and My Lithium and Me.

[3] In Bourdieu's work, a 'field' is a system of social positions (for example, a profession such as the law) structured internally in terms of power relationships (such as the power differential between record com-panies and bands). More specifically, a field is a social arena of struggle over the appropriation of certain species of capital—capital being whatever is taken as significant for social agents (the most obvious example being monetary capital and terms of record contracts). See Grenfell and Hardy, 2007, p. 11.

Introduction

Being a popular musician is an arduous occupation, and being a member of an originals band is even more so, not only because it is 'a long way to the top', but because hardly anyone trying to get there ever does so. It used to be the case that less than 15% of the artists signed to major record labels ever broke even, and only a minute proportion ever got signed.[1] These days, the opportunities

[1] For an interdisciplinary discussion of popular music's mythical status and the process by which it has been mythologized by its audiences, its chroniclers and its analysts, see K. Kelly and McDonnell (1999).

are fewer and narrower for bands signing to a major label and this is not always considered an aspiration or desirable. The economic rather than artistic impetus for change in the way originals bands work arises from the tension between preserving or transforming established practices and their hegemony. The struggle to introduce new forms of creativities can be considered as a struggle for cultural capital and the subsequent accrual of symbolic capital.

In writing their own material, members of originals bands accord creativity a central role. Creativity presents itself in different guises. There is the creativity sparked by dialogue and determination, and that arising from conflict and collaboration in attempts to create a unique sound, a smash hit, or a breakthrough album (all of which authorize discourses and activities in the field). In establishing a distinctive 'sound' and making a musical breakthrough, the quality of the communicated experience and the forms that it takes are key to understanding what is culturally valued. Creativity, however, is also constituted by, arises out of, and is inscribed in the dispositions and values, orientations and working practices of the bands and their individual members. However, which of these different aspects of creativity takes precedence may not be distinguished explicitly.

Creativity remains key to the success of originals bands. The members of a typical four-piece rock group—guitar, bass, drums, and vocals—are uniquely positioned to express themselves, whether in writing new songs, creating a new sound, style, studio resource, or other technological changes, and cultural values. The collective creativity of originals bands is focused on the production of ideas, images, and acts that may or may not 'fit' into an existing musical style, and may be realized in ways that are adaptive, unfamiliar, unexpected, surprising, or new. The production techniques of rock—idiosyncratic, progressive, electroacoustic, electronica dance music, hip hop and other contemporary styles—are frequently merged. This is exemplified by Trent Reznor, leader of industrial pioneers Nine Inch Nails (NIN), and by earlier fusion bands such as Frank Zappa[2] and The Mothers of Invention, whose 1966 debut album *Freak Out!* combined songs in conventional rock and roll format with collective improvisations and studio-generated sound collages. The musicians described in this chapter through their narratives of practice, aspire, whether at home, on the stage or in the studio, to transcend singular genre classifications, in order to produce new modes of discourse and new means of presentation. Audience and fan-generated creativity is encouraged through the creation of collaborative opportunities for remixing recorded material, for which digital technology has enabled new practices of participatory creativity.[3]

It is important to remember that what we might understand by the term 'musical creativity', namely, the familiar world of compositional creativity, tends to be taken for granted. This conception is not set in stone or universally accepted, either within or across, studio and performance contexts, or in the wide variety of genres associated with originals bands in the field of popular music. For instance, the social and technological circumstances that constitute the compositional environment and the practices of creativity of an originals band might show itself in genre hybridity, in global cultural crossover, or in not getting signed to a label, so as to be able to control the aesthetic paradigms specific to the balance of artistic freedom and the resources of a band as an

---

[2] Frank Zappa was also equally at home in concert halls, where he performed his own experimental contemporary art music. He was regarded as one of the most original guitarists and composers of his time, and remains a major influence on musicians and composers. He had some commercial success, particularly in Europe, and worked as an independent artist and was signed to major labels.

[3] See the NIN remix site on http://remix.nin.com for an example of how Reznor models creative processes by providing fans with tools and building blocks to play with their music and develop their own songs and remixes. See Väkevä (2010, p. 61) for a discussion of how 'what was originally "a mix" becomes material for new creative ways of projecting oneself in artistic-technological space. This discussion shifts the aesthetic focus from products to processes, from individual expression to communication.

aspiring trendsetter.[4] There are multiple creativities involved in coming up with new, surprising, and valuable musical ideas, in producing a new sound, or a new album, or in establishing a very large and loyal following.[5]

The popular music industry involves a hierarchy of intersecting 'fields'. A field, as Bourdieu puts it, is a 'space of positions' and a system of power relations governed by rules (1993c, p. 72). We can think of the field of music as a complex, consisting of particular spaces of action or social settings (e.g. a recording studio, or record label, which operate as insider social agents). None of these fields exhaust the issues posed by the question of what constitutes 'being creative', or can explain the creativity required to produce, or even propose, newness. The point here is that, in order to make an original band's particular sound stand out and be attractive, by associating it with supposedly familiar and other 'agreeable' values, it may well need to be located outside a common currency or particular style of music (as, for instance, with the birth of 'punk' or 'hip hop', both of which involved particular social groups taking a particular new musical direction). Bourdieu's work on the notions of field is helpful for understanding how creative practices are formed in particular forms of social production. In *The Field of Cultural Production* Bourdieu (1993b) describes the idea of 'field' as consisting of a 'separate social universe having its own laws of functioning' (p. 162), and as 'highly charged matrices involving a dynamic philosophy of human praxis' (Bourdieu and Wacquant, 1992, p. 127). In other words, a field of production can comprise specific forms of practice. In connection with the concept of music creativity and the concept of field are what originals bands see as pervasive influences on choices defined by entrepreneurial characteristics such as having innovative powers, dynamism, creativity, and drive as well as persuasiveness. These pervasive influences, according to Bourdieu (1990a), are 'durably inculcated by the possibilities and impossibilities, freedoms and necessities, opportunities and prohibitions inscribed in the objective conditions' (p. 54). So, within any one field, these influences involve power relations between those who occupy dominant positions and those who are dominated.

At the heart of the creative capacity of an originals band lies the concept of 'habitus', which can be understood as a compilation of collective and individual trajectories (relating to aims and orientations, tastes, and desires). A band can be defined by its habitus insofar as it involves the personal and collective history of its members. This is what makes it possible to produce an infinite number of practices, limited only by the structure of the field (Bourdieu, 1990b). The band's habitus is, of necessity, internalized and converted into a disposition that generates meaningful practices and meaning-giving perceptions (Bourdieu, 1984a, pp. 169–70). If a band's habitus demands that the band be in a position in which creativity enables groups or agents to designate how the value of specific forms of creativity is determined, then the band's habitus determines the forms of dispositions and attitudes towards practice and positions in relation to the field (see Appendix B for more on Bourdieu's conceptual toolbox of habitus and field). The band produces cultural and symbolic capital which relates to the prestige and recognition gained through success. The field of music is a complex consisting of many spaces of action. It is the interaction of habitus, capital, and field that generates the logic of practice. In particular, the concept of a field

---

[4] For a scholarly review of how the music industry works in the new millennium, its future prospects in the world of global entertainment, and the dynamics at work in the production of musical culture between the transnational media conglomerates, the independent music companies, and the public sphere, see Wikström (2009). For a helpful discussion of rock and pop music see, for example, Negus and Pickering (2004). For an outline of Bourdieu's habitus and the musical field, the exemplary agency of musicians, and the idea of socially heard (musical) voices, see Toynbee (2000).

[5] An example of this is how Trent Reznor and NIN model creative processes (See remix.nin.com).

adds to the possibilities of Bourdieu's conceptual framework and gives habitus a dynamic quality in relation to band culture.[6]

Why is the term 'creativity' invariably used in the singular when songs can be composed by individual songwriters or from creativity within and across band members? It is not enough to simply accept the act of song 'writing' as something self-begotten, unconscious, or deliberately learned and practised, as a 'written' craft shared by all songwriters. Once again, it is a question of broadening the concept of 'musical creativity' to denote more than the work of an individual artist, but rather involving social forms and behavioural modalities that favour associations and assemblages between musicians and instruments, composers and songs, listeners and sound systems.

Certain types of musical creativity are recognized and rewarded differently, the production context varies, and originals band musicians tend to play down, dismiss, or overlook, the act of 'writing', an act that is, itself, always informed by the available technologies, expertise, economics, and by the expectations of audiences. This is because, despite a band's individualism, its members together maintain a strong sense of collective identity. The collective nature of song writing also extends to the dispositions and orientations associated with being in an originals band, which give a sense of what is appropriate in particular circumstances and what is not. While the likelihood of individual musicians becoming highly successful professionals in originals bands is not self-evident, the practice of group composition inspires the popular musician with a sense of higher purpose and a position in a social space.[7]

This chapter will consider the contextual perspectives and personal histories of three professional freelance (independent) band members who have developed performing careers, and worked in a number of roles in the music business (coined 'protean careerists').[8] In addition, each musician has 'a sense of one's place' in the band as well as a 'sense of the place of others' in the social space of their respective bands, and a role in the shaping of the band's practices and habitus. Each musician is a passionate exponent of their respective instrument, and a virtuoso player with a huge repertoire of genre specific techniques at their fingertips. Each musician is beyond the entry level of careers in the music business, and is highly motivated about playing regularly in 'originals bands'[9] with fixed memberships who play regular live gigs. Each musician uses multi-track recording technology as a form of individual compositional creativity.

Steve MacKay is an Australian guitarist in Twelve Foot Ninja (TFN, see Fig. 3.1) a band based in Melbourne (Australia). Leah Kardos (Fig. 3.2) is an Australian pianist and vocalist in Helzuki and My Lithium and Me (MLM). Adam Scott is a Scottish bass player and the newest member of Zoey

---

[6] In Bourdieu and Wacquant (1992): 'The relation between habitus and field operates in two ways. On one side, it is a relation of conditioning: the field structures the habitus, which is the product of the embodiment of the immanent necessity of the field (or of a hierarchy of intersecting fields). On the other side, it is a relation of knowledge or cognitive construction. Habitus contributes to constituting the field as a meaningful world, a world endowed with sense or with value, in which it is worth investing one's energy' (p. 44). We see this investment of energy in both bands featured in this chapter, as characterized in, and through, the practices of the music industry. For interesting discussions see A. Bennett (1980) and Cohen (1991). See also Negus (1999) for a discussion of how corporate commercial concerns impact on band culture.

[7] See Green (2001) for a discussion of group popular music composition and individual popular music composition, the latter being associated with composition in the classical field.

[8] See S. Bennett (2010), Cottrell (2004) and Frith et al. (2001) for interesting discussions of the popular music and classical music profession.

[9] These are band musicians dedicated to a particular band and a style of music that is deeply felt to be characteristic of that band (see Green, 2001).

Van Goey[10] (ZVG, see Fig. 3.3), an indie pop band founded in 2006 in Glasgow (Scotland). Each of the bands, with the exception of MLM, plays a regular circuit of pubs, clubs, and student venues in local, regional, and national 'scenes'. Each of the bands uses multi-track recording technology to facilitate forms of collective composition. Each positions themselves differently in terms of the principles of building reputations, accumulating fans, and distinguishing the roles of artist-producer and audience-consumer. All the bands have released an album that is sold online, but each positions itself differently within the organization of the recording industry. ZVG, for example, has an agreement with the label Chemikal Underground,[11] which distributes hard copies and legal downloads for whomever they work with. For example, Chemikal has a business relationship with Linn Records. The relationship is established, very hand in hand, and ZVG acknowledges the symbolic capital and position of Chemikal Underground in the field. The bands that perform regular gigs sell CDs, vinyl, and other merchandise at those events.Steve's band, TFN, is primarily focused on autonomous fields of production, such as self-managing the distribution of albums, which goes hand in hand with, and situates, the principles of building reputations, becoming known, accumulating fans, and mixing up the roles of the artist-producer and the audience-consumer. This is illustrated by their first EP, and the **participatory creativity** of their growing fan base and related networks of reproduction, distribution, and consumption. Leah's band, *Helzuki,* which was originally a piano-rock trio formed in London in 2005, now positions itself as an 'art-rock' collective with a core membership of three main players: Leah Kardos, Kristian Purcell, and Matthew Roles. The band has recorded and released the self-titled debut album *Helzuki* (2007) and *The Little Bits of Nothing EP* (2010). Both releases are available for purchase from iTunes. Helzuki is also based on a similar model of independent self-management, a deliberate choice that allows the band to have complete creative control and freedom to evolve and experiment stylistically. By contrast, Leah's other band, MLM, is focused on semi-autonomous fields of production, whereby aspects associated with post-production, distribution, and consumption are the responsibility of others—managers, collaborators, and other stakeholders. Adam's band, ZVG, is also focused on semi-autonomous fields of production, thereby leaving the reproduction and consumption aspects of the industry sector to band managers. Each of these musicians has started up several bands, and played in guitar and piano-based popular and rock bands in their adolescence.

Within this coupling, we focus on the nature and significance of how a plurality of creativities is inscribed in originals band musicians' practices.

Positioning Steve in TFN

Steve describes himself as 'a guitarist'. He wears several hats, and plays the various roles of a guitarist, songwriter, lyricist, performer, bandleader, promoter, entrepreneur, costume designer,[12] event merchandiser, producer, teacher, and small business manager. Steve (as with Adam and

---

[10] ZVG was originally a trio. Adam Scott joined the band in April 2010 after working as a touring bass player from late 2009. The quartet recorded their second album, *Propeller Versus Wings* in May/June 2010 and released it in 2011. See http://zoeyvangoey.bandcamp.com/. You can listen to the first album on Spotify. They have played in venues with capacities of 300 to 2000 in Liverpool, Leeds, Dublin, The Hague, and Glasgow.

[11] Chemikal Underground is an independent record label set up in 1994 by the Glasgow rock band The Delgados. It was set up to release their first single, 'Monica Webster'/'Brand New Car' and went on to break many new Scottish bands in the 1990s.

[12] Steve was involved in the design of T-shirts, and worked with a fashion designer to create and custom the Ninja getup.

several other of the originals band musicians interviewed) is one of the 'net generation'—those born between 1976 and 1998, growing up on digital media technologies—and is an active and skilled user of video games, smartphones, the web, online networking, and digital technology. He has played on *Top of the Pops* (2003) with Delta Goodrem, works as a freelance DIY popular music producer at his home recording studio, as a national clinician specializing in Line 6[13] for AMG (Australian Music Group—www.line6.com) and as a contracted guitar tuition book series author for Hinkler Books. These jobs offer him access to a powerful business network (as, also, does his retail work at a local guitar outlet). Steve has successfully cultivated a career in music, and positions himself as a musician who fishes in a huge pond of business connections that are nurtured in virtual and real-life tradeshows and marketplaces. In this way, he locates himself firmly within a wider band scene. Steve has his own home recording studio facilities, and like many who work in the music industries, he is an extraordinarily talented individual whose role as a creative artist is respected and admired in the band.

Steve is part of the digital music revolution coined 'the new music industries',[14] wherein immense changes are currently working against record companies. Steve feels as if has been previously burnt by record companies and producers (Artists and Repertoire (A&R)).[15] His band, TFN, is preparing to release its first album inscribed with the 'collective identity' (i.e. the band's image) of its name. Unlike some signed bands, who can have a marketing department that assigns a savvy image consultant to transform the way they look, TFN has been left to its own creative devices in building its identity and depicting the image and storyboard of the multi-media project that is linked to the band. Image-moulding is important as it gives an opportunity to operationalize capital and exercise power over the field. The band shuns definitive social categorization, yet seeks to identify with their target audience and promote collective identity.

The practice of dressing up the act is nothing new. For Steve, the designer of TFNs image, the collective identity of the group is produced by individual members of the band wearing their own ninja-inspired costumes during performances, along with stage makeup, ninja-style contact lenses, and other symbolic gestures, which complement their stage act/performance[16] (see Fig. 3.1). The visual imagery of the band and its logo, and the images that characterize their stage act match the packaging of merchandise and online artwork, and define the band according to its

---

13 Line 6 is a retail company that specializes in guitars, guitar amplifiers, effects pedals, wireless microphones, and recording software.

14 Wikström (2009) provides a lucid and astute overview of what has happened to popular music since mp3 met the Internet at the birth of Napster, and how the music industries have changed and continue to do so in the grips of the wide-ranging, digitally driven shifts taking place inside the popular music industries.

15 Often seen as the gatekeepers and pressure makers of the recording industry, the A&R (Artists and Repertoire) agent acts on behalf of the record companies and labels promoters to search for and sign new artists. Many originals bands describe their encounters with A&R agents as people who are cautious and often contradictory. They don't like surprises but look for unexpected ideas only if they 'fit' into a style or sound. The pressure comes from the record executives who want to know where the hit is. They do not want to hear that the A&R wants the band to go on the road for two years and see where it ends up. They want to hear a radio song that has already gained an audience and what the band's plans are for the first album. The originals band's position in the field underlies the structuring of all subsequent experiences (e.g. the reception and assimilation of the message of the music and recording industries.

16 TFN is a multi-media band based around a spiritual-fantasy mythology story of the 'twelve foot ninja' (written by Steve and his girlfriend, Fiona Permezel, currently a medical student at the University of Melbourne). The story is essentially a creative play on two important concepts in spirituality: (1) the possible perils that may result from believing in the good–evil dichotomy; and (2) the potential for ruling over people, poisoning interactions, or 'energy stealing' by four quadrants of power-mongering behaviour: aggression, invalidation, manipulation and secrecy.

Fig. 3.1 Twelve Foot Ninja. *Left to right*: Shane Russell (drums), Steve MacKay (guitars), Nik Barker (vocals), and Damon McKinnon (bass).
Photo by: Amped Photography. © Dave MacGregor, 2011.

collective identity. These are customary practices of newly formed bands, which are actively appropriated as a source of identity and inspiration by their fans.

Steve comes from a rural region some 100 miles east of Melbourne, Victoria, in Australia. He attended a small primary school, a large comprehensive rural secondary college, and spent three months at a specialist arts high school in Melbourne before dropping out of year 12, despondent and disillusioned with school. He explains that he 'just wanted to play music, study from working professionals in the field, and play guitar full time'. What followed was a period of several years of family-supported and promoted home-centred music-making and one-on-one guitar lessons across different genres (classical, jazz, and contemporary).[17]

---

[17] Bourdieu (1996, p. 115) offers theoretical support for why we value what is 'popular' and what is 'classical', why the process of creating these super-styles is so very different, and how this difference is manifest in their varied, though overlapping, associated discourses concerning creativity. Cohen (1991) is notable here. She was concerned principally with music making, but notes the varied and overlapping range of

Steve: When I was six I heard my cousin playing blues guitar in my grandfather's lounge room one Christmas . . . I obsessed about guitars, playing guitar and listening to great guitar players. I went on to have many one-to-one lessons from reputable specialist teachers that I approached for lessons to help hone my technique. I remember Tommy Emmanuel playing (world renowned acoustic guitarist). As soon as I heard him play I thought it was just the best thing ever. I jumped right in and got all of his CDs went to all his concerts . . . There were many other lightning-bolt-type-artists that had made a name for themselves that blew my mind as a kid.

Guitarists, guitar practice and guitar playing occupy a distinct position in Steve's life. He positions himself firmly in the social space of specialist guitarists, and in the wider world of bands, engaging in a particular form of practice that will produce a particular form of cultural and symbolic capital. His initiative and creativity can be traced back to a dramatic decision to leave high school early and study at a specialist performing arts school, at which he hoped to assert his identity, get known and be recognized, and break with the perceived irrelevancies of a school that 'simply didn't cater for someone like me who could technically play but had no idea what they were doing.' We can understand this struggle as a disjuncture between habitus and field.[18] It is clear that he was aware of how important a performer's skills are, that acquiring skills requires countless hours of practice, and that becoming a technically brilliant musician requires prolonged exposure to experts in the field. This is an assumption that applies to many traditions in the classical art, jazz, and popular music worlds.

As Steve explains, his confidence and desire to produce the 'breakthrough album' seems to sit well with his taking responsibility for bringing the band members of TFN together. This is his latest project. The band members are a similar age, share similar educations, backgrounds, and interests, and have many friends in common. The vocalist lives off shares, the bassist is a full-time electrician, the drummer works in a printing factory and Steve works in a guitar shop three days a week. Collectively, it is the desire to 'make it' that unites and forms solidarity within the band members at the same time as it strains their relationships. It draws them together by providing a common goal and by being seen as a serious joint enterprise. They realize that 'the band' has a chance of 'getting somewhere'—but that the journey is neither easy nor straightforward.

Steve: I've learned a lot about what works and what fails from mistakes within other bands and after awhile you start hearing the same disputes reappearing in stories of band fallouts. I've been on the receiving end of disputes over publishing splits getting edged out of cuts for political reasons. It can get very ugly. You can get hung by your own rope . . . now, when I write a song with someone I get that important—yet creatively unimportant stuff—the financial stuff—out of the way straightaway. An even split is agreed upon and disagreements are worked out. If there are three of us, then the contractual relationship is written up/emailed, stating the writing split is at 33.3%. I've come to learn as a

---

discourses concerning local music-making culture in post-industrial Liverpool. Finnegan's study (1989) is useful in that, through its accounts of musical practices, it illustrates the wider dimensions of music making as an occasion for 'sociality'. Playing in a group or band, is, according to Fornäs et al. (1995) study of three young rock groups in Sweden, an important form of escapism from the more mundane aspects of everyday life, such as parental and school cultures (see relevant discussions in A. Bennett, 2000).

[18] See Reay (1998), 'Institutional and familial habituses and higher education choice' (pp. 519–29), who makes clear (as do Bourdieu and Wacquant, 1992) when habitus and field do not accord there are inevitable conflicts and disjunctures. For the white middle-class families in our sample such misfits between field and habitus were frequently manifested in a complex array of difficult emotions. For Steve, the disjunctures between habitus and the field of production can cause the disturbances and the impetus for striving, resistance, and/or new awareness of the need for change.

music producer and writer in the new music economy that retrospect really is the wisdom of fools and people conveniently get hazy about who actually did what—especially when there is money involved.

Working in the role of guitarist-producer, Steve is something other than an industry neophyte. He is neither a novice nor new to working in bands. Steve has learned a lot about group negotiation from earlier band conflicts. This band has 'a shared understanding about what constitutes' compared with 'what is just improvising or drawing from the "written" melody or harmony'. Besides mastery of the guitar and knowing many of the 'tricks of the trade', he wants both his band and its fans to recognize TFN's sound, songs, lyrics, and their originality.

TFN habits and practices

Importantly, the digitalization and digital distribution of music, and the mixing of artist and producer, and audience and consumer, are defining a form of participatory fan-based[19] creativity between the band and its fans through social media. Steve is an individual who adopts a collective approach to legitimate a particular band.

> *Steve*: We realize that you cannot succeed in the music industry without some level of business savvy. I'm not saying you need to be some sort of shark to survive; you just can't get on being some sort of ethereal bloody *mung* bean . . . It's like that art versus commerce argument; my view is a balance of both is necessary or you need a hell of a lot of luck. In terms of internal band dynamics, there always needs to be a leader, democracies don't work because the outnumbered will feel disenfranchised. We reach unanimity around creative choices and refer to a band agreement we wrote that is unemotionally attached to any individual circumstances to deal with disputes that seem difficult to resolve.

Online social networking through channels such as Twitter and Facebook connect and communicate with fans. This isn't new. During the production of their first two EPs, TFN continued to build a close relationship with their fans by regular publishing of a video-blog in which they discussed the development of their musical ideas. The tracks were listed on Facebook (and several are published on YouTube) during the album's production. Feedback is sought from the fan base. Conversations on Twitter and Facebook influence the creative process whilst promoting their upcoming album and gigs. These activities are all part of the immersive, multi-platform, multi-layered and important dimension of *connectivity*. As Wikström (2009) explains, 'Connectivity is a measure of how well the members of a network are connected. A network is considered to have a high level of connectivity if most of its members are connected to each other, and vice versa. In the new music economy, the importance of physical music distribution and the mass media has been radically reduced while the importance of the internet media has exploded' (p. 5). We know that originals bands use and develop different forms of creativity and employ different techniques in the making of new material. We also know there are different kinds of *capital* embodied in the way they work, whether individually, such as Steve, in pairs of band members (Steve and vocalist, Nik Barker), the whole band, or in a combination of these (as is the case with Adam's bands, which are discussed later in the chapter).

---

[19] What is crucial for the individualist and collectivist dimensions of decision-making in the process of actual playing and connectivity with the audience is that these two things frequently occur together as driving forces. This depends in part on audience's 'participatory creativity', which is very different from listeners' habits at a concert of classical music. At popular music gigs, the audience drinks, moves around and talks, as well as listens, which raises particular questions of how listeners construct their listening and its meaning.

We know that popular musicians are very disdainful of being labelled as purveyors of particular kinds of music. Some popular musicians like to think of themselves as playing music that is completely original.[20] But of course popular music is popular for the very reason that it conforms to particular stylistic norms. And of course, tribute bands are a vital part of the live music economy.[21] Here we see a real paradox of a habitus which tries to push the envelope, and place value on both originality (newness) and creativity: digital artistry, authenticity, authority, having and sharing ideas, and being disposed proactively to seek out new musical possibilities of mixing and meshing, and blending and binding ideas as a group. TFN knows it needs to do more than acquire notoriety in the independent music scene. 'How' and 'who' helps the band locate itself (and belong) in social space (with networks that ascribe certain capital), and develop its own material and identifiable sound and stage image (another form of capital) can be contentious issues.

TFN places the greatest value on connectivity with its fans, who are endowed with great power to influence decision making. The emergence of 'new media' is granting unprecedented connectability, along with direct-to-fan marketing and distribution techniques, which means they are working with their fans, not for the labels. Steve and his band also recognize other ways of building artist–fan relationships. Using Facebook and other social media as a go-between, TFN maintains a degree of intimacy and involvement, staying in direct dialogue with its audiences, as a default, yet creative ingredient in the mix. Traditional thinking about artist–fan relationships is being eclipsed by this trend, which has become so all-encompassing that, in the music business, we are seeing new models which embrace a more liquid view of creativity, along with increasing consumer empowerment and marketing tie-ins.

Steve has managed to convince his group not to sign to a label. They initially decided against it because, as Steve claims, 'We're an unproven band so labels don't benefit from this kind of investment. Contract terms are fairly weighted in the labels favour as the risk is substantially more'. He speaks with great confidence of the positioning of bands that prefer less commercial popular music (i.e. cultural) success: 'The closer we get to developing Twelve Foot Ninja's online popularity and the more we work efficiently with our available resources, and build our local networks, the more we can distance ourselves from the traditional forms of infrastructure of a major label'. TFN members invest all money back into the band, have a book keeper, accountant, management, and operate as a small business, slugging it out with an average gig rate of one a week. Without label involvement, TFN distributes discs via its website, and via digital download through iTunes. TFN is involved with a third party company that administers all of their iTunes downloads for a fairly small cut of sales. They are now starting to look at physical distribution because there is an emerging demand.

> Steve: You've got to know a lot about your fan base. I think a lot of bands and artists try and appeal to mass markets as soon as they start making some sort of measurable progress. This is often a fatal mistake. The early adopters of your music who spread the word about your band, incrementally recruiting your following for you, are the people you focus on and listen to.

Steve speaks with authority about TFN's album, its writing, the authenticity granted the group by the audience's perceptions,[22] and in reference to being thought of as 'the underdogs'. The

---

20 See Green (2001) for a detailed discussion of how popular musicians learn and develop self-conceptions as musicians.
21 See Homan (2006) for a detailed account of the tribute and cover band phenomenon and its place within the global popular music industry.
22 According to several TFN fans interviewed for this book, TFN engages with the fans as a creative act in itself. The fans judge the band on the basis of the website, which seems to be a multi-media experience

band's recently released EP entitled *Smoke Bomb* is intended for mass consumption. Steve is keenly aware of the social positioning of bands and their musical releases, and recognizes the politics of classification and creativity:

> *Steve*: The thinking behind the title is that it positions us in readiness for the release of our first album; the idea is that a smoke bomb confuses the victim before the blow is dealt to them unsuspectingly (the album). It is a bit tongue in cheek but my goal with TFN is to create something people can get absorbed in. Our songwriting methodology, song structures and arrangements have undergone a quantum shift in quality in the making of our debut album. I speculate that the actual procedure of writing has evolved and precedents have emerged which work. Our manager has a slightly cheesy but apt description of this process: 'forming', 'storming', 'norming' then 'transforming'. I think we are now operating in the latter of the four processes.

The songs are developed from ideas taken from the ninja story (these might be short sequences of notes) or from lyrics written by the lead singer, or from a lengthier and more structured composition. Generally, only one or two members of the band write the lyrics, one of whom is usually the vocalist Nik Barker, then the lyrics get discussed with Steve and altered collectively, as with all other aspects relating to the composition of new material.

> *Steve*: Generally the song writing process happens in one of four ways. The first is that I write all of the music (bass, drums, guitars, production) and give it to the vocalist to write lyrics and melodies. The vocalist brings what he has done to the studio and we workshop phrasing, melodic choice, and sometimes tweak the lyrics. The second way is when the bass player brings riffs to the table with some idea of sectional placement (verse, chorus, etc.). I work it up into a song bed then give it to the vocalist to write too. The theory is, if we get at least a strong verse and chorus with vocals, we can turn the ideas into a decent song. I (sometimes with the band present contributing ideas) arrange and write new sections to complete the structure in more detail. We do these things in that order to minimize time wasted working up songs with less than moving vocals. The third way is when the vocalist writes a song with basic guitar and vocals. I rework the music and re-record the vocals with the vocalist and harmonies and additional musical sections are usually added. The fourth way is when the band jams and comes up with musical ideas. Entire songs rarely come out of this process, but good ideas evolve.
>
> Whatever style it is, a reoccurring element of a widely recognized 'good song' is a strong melody. I think that when I write the music first, I sometimes have a tendency to venture to the dark side of the force, going mad with power creating some kind of musical mutant. At that point it is easy to lose sight of the actual song that I am trying to create. That is when it is good to be working with the vocalist. Melody and lyrics really frame the intention of the track and even though all of our music has a lot of stylistic juxtaposition, the intention is clearer when writing with lyrics and melody because they almost reign in the overall process. Our drummer often writes the drums, or I'll write the drums and he'll adapt them. I've played with him so long that a lot of the time what I write is what he'd play anyway.
>
> Our bass player has a lot of input; there's a lot of collaboration on the arrangement. The parts are usually there it is just a matter of which sections work best and what new parts need to be created.

rather being about music alone. For example, Joshua says, 'Emailing Steve from TFN means you feel part of something bigger than yourself. TFN is just incredible, and being an independent band they appreciate their fans in a big way'. A shared identity and shared territory, a projection of self and form of patronage—even ownership—is identified. The fans love the high impact, autonomy, and masculine identity of the group. Jack says 'They just draw you in closer and closer than any of the other bands I know. Their songs are awesome. Their style of playing is different. How it feels when you're being blasted over some speakers when they go into the chorus is the kind of style that just grabs me. I like that it's in your face and that you get to know the band really well.

Thus the representation of group creativity varies with the players' position within the band, the practices of which are developed not only by individuals but also collectively. There is no script or blueprint for realising and acting on the ideas of another, and neither is there any pattern to how multiple interests and ideas may lead to commercial success.

The key point is the way in which the band members integrate the individualist and collectivist dimensions of creativity. The particular forms of practice and the ways in which music creativities arise in TFN emphasize that the primary text of popular music is the recorded artefact. Particularly important is how Steve claims responsibility for collaborative writing, as classical and jazz composers claim the act of 'composition' itself, as being essential to music creativity. First, it tends to suggest that the work ends in an artefact or product; second, it implies the creation of a piece of music, the formal properties of which remain largely fixed (i.e. notated or recorded). Importantly, the computer plays a central role as a kind of 'creative partner' (term coined by Andrew Blake in *Popular Music: The Age of Multimedia* (2007, p. 74). The mixing desk, sound effects processing, and software programs offer high-tech facilities, employing layers of instrumental and vocal dub-influenced dance music, to include in acoustic-electronic mixes in live performance. The idea of recording technology as a new expressive 'instrument' is embodied in some music-making practices more than others, being differentiated by both category and context.

Positioning Leah in Helzuki, MLM, and Spider & I

Leah is actively involved with three projects. She was the founding member of Helzuki, filling the roles of songwriter, vocalist, and pianist, the other half of a production-based duo, My Lithium and Me (MLM), an electronic studio-based band in which she is a singer, multi-instrumentalist, co-writer, and co-producer, and Spider & I, a project that presents her contemporary classical album, Feather Hammer, released by record label Bigo & Twigetti in 2011, as a live performance work that has a second life outside of its creation and production. Helzuki is a band that has made a conscious decision to remain independent, prioritizing creative control and freedom to experiment. By contrast, MLM's output (electronica/trip hop) has been traditionally promoted and distributed through a network of channels that independent bands often have limited access to (radio/club play, synchronization opportunities, etc.). Finally, the Spider & I project is a multimedia endeavour, where Leah works with video artist Matthew Greasley on adapting and transforming Feather Hammer into a live performance collaboration.

Helzuki creates through improvisation; from jamming in rehearsal to free experimentation in the studio. The band's group compositions and studio productions aim to celebrate the individual style of each member, and to create something new and interesting out of these diverse influences. While Helzuki's approach to music-making highlights the difference and unique contributions of creative individuals from diverse musical backgrounds, MLM has a more deliberate stylistic aim, paying close attention to current sound and style trends, cutting-edge production techniques, and new technology. Whereas with Spider & I, Leah and Matthew take studio work and transform it within a live context, using Feather Hammer[23] as a starting point that allows for the creation of a unique and entirely new performance piece. The small stylistic details aren't as important for Helzuki as the overarching philosophy of inclusion and experimentation, whilst MLM is wholly concerned with details and Spider & I intends to create new works from existing ones.

Helzuki was formed in London in 2005 as a piano-rock band featuring Leah on vocals and piano, her partner Matt Roles on bass (both originally from Australia) and drummer Lex Lake, whom they met in London.

---

[23] For further information on the album see http://bigoandtwigetti.bandcamp.com/album/feather-hammer.

Fig. 3.2 Leah Kardos in her home studio (Glorybox Studios) in Bedfordshire.
Photo by Matt Roles, 2011. © Matthew Roles, 2011.

> *Leah*: The idea of forming the band came from the desire to combine eclectic influences (I from a clas-
> sical piano background, Matt from heavy metal). We were very interested to see what we could come
> up with. There was also a strong desire to do something completely different from the guitar-based,
> male-fronted bands that populate the unsigned London scene.

Since relocating the band to Bedford in 2008, they have lost Lex, but gained a male vocalist/
guitarist, songwriter and visual artist, Kristian Purcell. In addition to this core trio, other instrumentalists and small ensembles have been invited to collaborate in performances and recordings.
All core members of the band write and contribute to arrangements, and each member is encouraged to bring their unique set of influences to the table, and experiment with combinations.
Studio experimentation is also inclusive, with all members being actively involved in the processes of production. In 2008 the band gained unrestricted access to a DIY recording space, and
transferred all their creative activity to that environment. The stylistic impact of this, and of Lex's
departure and Kristian's joining, can be clearly heard in the stark sonic differences between the
two Helzuki releases.

> *Leah*: Having a guitarist join us was revolutionary—we had never had a timbral element in the band
> that could create atmospheric layers like that, our piano/bass/drums combo by nature always sounded
> rather tight and 'dry'. Kristian's guitar playing also freed me up to play the piano in a different way. Up
> until then I had been the sole harmonic rhythm instrument in the band, the only one pounding out the
> chordal accompaniment. When Kristian took that role I was free to experiment myself, play with
> sound effects, or even other instruments. He also sang, which again allowed me to step back from the
> spotlight and concentrate on the sounds we were producing.

The move to the studio was another big change for us, stylistically speaking. In the rehearsal room you are limited to the trio, in the studio you can play as many instruments as you like and multi-track yourself to sound like there's twenty of you. It felt like there was no crazy idea that was off the cards—with the technology anything was possible. When I look back at our two very different sounding releases, I can see in the first one our tight little trio trying to make a big sound with what we had—the second by comparison is so ambient, loose and atmospheric, it almost seems like a reaction to the first, a deliberate exploration of all the things we previously couldn't achieve on our own.

The studio space we use is built in the spare rooms of my house, so there was no limit on our use of the resources—which in the end I think was both a good and bad thing. Good in the sense that we could truly experiment, record absolutely everything and really examine it closely; bad in the sense that the unlimited access lead to a lot of 'tinkering' and changing things that at the time felt right and spontaneous but in the cold light of morning we might have had disagreements about. We were all involved in the production process. If one of us was performing in the live room, the others would be in the control room giving directions/creating stimuli for the experiment. We mixed and mastered the recordings together. It was really important to us that everyone's ideas and desires were accommodated. We sought input and feedback from our manager in London, whom we'd often email mix demos to. Her input was crucial—sometimes you feel like you're going crazy worrying about some minor production detail, with all of us so wrapped up in that process we really needed that objectivity from someone on the outside.

Creativity abounds in this recollection of her band's process and creativeness. This is a band, like many originals bands, whose members share not only material creation, which is to say the production of ideas, but bring into being collaboratively what *counts* as creative. This is conveyed in terms of terms of *how* creativity happens in the dialectic between individual and collective dimensions of studio creativity.

Leah: It usually starts with a recorded improvisation or a chord progression with a short melodic/lyrical idea. The members would then respond musically to this idea, and we'd just try anything. If it worked, then we'd go with that. The decision making was always by consensus. It was a similar situation when we developed new music in the rehearsal room back in London—one of us would show a new idea, it could be a fragment, a riff or hook, or just lyrics—and we'd jam it out and see if the idea had legs.

The DIY recording space allows for a bit of indulgence, especially in the road testing of new ideas. In the rehearsal room the potential of a creative idea is at the mercy of a snap group decision, whereas in the studio all of these ideas are kept. Sometimes going back to these rough embryonic fragments with fresh ears is really inspirational. Also, it has to be said, hanging out in the studio is a lot of fun. For us it's social—we drink wine, we laugh, we linger over the process. We know that we're not going to sell a million records, we're in this for the love of making music together.

Leah's other band, MLM, started as a David Bowie covers project in May 2010, the band forming after Leah asked her work colleague and fellow songwriter/producer Paul Ross to help her finish the project. Both Leah and Paul work as music technology lecturers at Bedford College. In the 1990s Paul was a member of electronic dance act Shiva, and was signed to Polydor Records and then London Records (FFRR). For Shiva, he wrote two singles—'Freedom' and 'Work it out'—that went to numbers 18 and 34 in the UK top 40 chart, both peaking at no. 1 in the UK club charts. From the start MLM set out to be a down-tempo electronica band, in the style of Massive Attack, Portishead, Lamb and The Knife. Live gigs aided by technology are possible, but the focus is on the production of recordings. Leah sings, and they both write, play various instruments, arrange, and produce.

Leah has invested large amounts of time and effort into becoming a musician, and described her musical background and upbringing.

Leah: I'm an only child of musical parents—my dad is a blues guitarist, my mother sings. As a child I was given piano lessons and, encouraged every step of the way, worked my way through the Australian

Music Examination Board (AMEB) grade system. Parallel to this, I grew up in a religious environment and from a young age I was regularly playing in my church band and learning how to improvise, vamp, and embellish my piano playing in a pop/gospel style. I believe both sides of my music education as a child—the classical training and the 'making-it-up-from-a-chord-sheet' aspect of the church band experience—have strongly influenced my creative practice. To this day my favourite way to write songs and compose is by improvising at a keyboard, and further than that, my music is almost always composed [by working the] chords first.

Doing music has always been integral to Leah's life. She grew up in a musically rich environment. There were values embedded in the religious group that her family belonged to. But hymns were not enough. Leah's insight, or moment of truth, came not as an answer but as a question, and an implicitly expressed question at that. What were the relative values of her different experiences of making music? Her 'classical training' and 'the church band experience' can be understood as aspects of the ubiquitous fostering of creativity, showing how musical creativity is possible even within the confines of distinct musical contexts and cultures. Clearly, Leah recognizes creativity and the process of being really creative in music. For reasons she discusses below, her creativity works as a rich repository of cultural capital, which relates to those forms of knowledge and practice which she values, as well as to educational qualifications, and then again, as symbolic capital which relates to the creative recognition gained through her bands' success.

When Leah reflected on the place that training and playing occupied in the construction of her identity in her teenage years, she detailed her creative experiences and explained how, at the outset, music functioned as a powerful agent for developing her creative identity, along with influences ascribed to technology.

Leah: After finishing high school I enrolled on the Bachelor of Music course at the University of Queensland, and felt compelled to abandon piano studies in favour of composition. At the same time I was becoming aware of more 'underground' popular music styles and artists/bands that engaged in sonic experimentation. This was the late '90s and I remember getting into jungle, drum and bass, trip hop and experimental electronica. Artists such as Goldie, Tricky, Massive Attack, Björk and Aphex Twin were hugely influential. I took courses in music technology and studio production and became a permanent fixture in the campus recording studio. I would book it all night long as often as I could, and often skip my daytime lectures to catch up on sleep. I'd just stay in there writing, improvising and recording for as long as they'd let me. I became obsessed with the creative potential of working with technology, with creating new sound worlds, with being able to create my own arrangements through multi-tracking. I researched Brian Eno's Oblique Strategies[24] and tried them out on my own material. I collaborated with any willing performers, setting up experimental performance conditions just to see what would happen. I was never thinking about making music in any particular style or creating an 'album' of works to sell, it was all about exploring possibilities. I actually missed my own graduation ceremony because I was in that studio producing something, so completely oblivious that I didn't even realize my course was over.

The creativities with which Leah seems to be primarily concerned during her undergraduate training, a time of socially navigating and constructing her own creative path, originate in music

---

[24] Brian Eno and Peter Schmidt's Oblique Strategies are a deck of cards, issued in five editions since 1975, which suggest methods of enriching the creative process via lateral thinking. They are designed to enhance working procedures and prompt ideas within a studio setting. Eno and Schmidt have stated that: 'These cards evolved from our separate observations on the principles underlying what we were doing. Sometimes they were recognized in retrospect (intellect catching up with intuition), sometimes they were identified as they were happening, sometimes they were formulated . . . they are not final, as new ideas will present themselves, and others will become self-evident' (http://www.rtqe.net/ObliqueStrategies/OSintro.html).

technology and studio production. Her motivation derives from technology and defines the nature of her creativity. Leah reflects deeply on, and is keenly sensitive to, her interactions with technology and the agency of groups of musicians that inspire creativity. Leah's relationship with music is primarily creative, and she refers to many forms or modalities of creativity including improvisation. Leah draws a firm line between 'piano studies' (and by implication 'performance') and the activity of 'composing'. What is also clear in Leah's outline of her improvisational model of musical creativity is her depiction of the composition/performance duality as respected partners in a creative dialogue.

There are at least two further issues that Leah brings to the fore in her description of her musical background, and which underlie much of the discussion that follows. First is the relational nature of the creativities at work in performance, and second, how recordings are indexes of creativity in performance. Since the success of bands, especially 'originals' bands, is attributed to the agency of creativity (for example, being able to create or originate 'new sound worlds'), it seems necessary to consider the creativities of both of Leah's bands, how she makes choices to actively realize her creative identity in female-fronted bands, and the different creative practices they exhibit.

Leah's bands' habits and practices

When Leah and her partner Matt decided to form Helzuki, it was out of a desire to 'combine our very different influences', and simply 'to see what would happen'. Matt has a background in heavy metal and grunge music, and Leah has a background in classical piano, gospel, and church music, with an urge to experiment with technology. Their first drummer, Lex, had very eclectic and different tastes, but also came from a background in hard rock and metal. They were all united by a general desire to do something 'a little out of the ordinary'. It is important to note that there are not too many female-fronted piano-rock bands going around (compared, say, to male-fronted guitar bands). The very idea of there being a gendered aspect to their work created a curiosity as to what they would come up with.[25] Matt and Lex would create riffs and grooves and Leah would piece them together into song structures. If anyone had a lyrical or melodic idea, they would try it out in the rehearsal room. While Leah wrote most of the lyrics and melodies, it wasn't ever explicitly her responsibility.

> *Leah*: It just seemed to happen that way since we wrote through improvisation and I was the one with the microphone in front of my face. Sometimes another member would write the entire lyric—an example of this is 'V8 Ego' from the first album. Matt had written this magnificent rant about a particular person who was annoying us at the time, it seemed to fit with an aggressive riff he'd written, so we decided to use it.
>
> When Kristian joined us, we'd share the lyric writing between us a bit more. We'd experiment with different methods, I'd compose music and he'd write lyrics for the song and vice versa. In some instances he'd write the chorus while I wrote the verses. We never saw our own lyrics as needing to be sung by us. I think we are both really keen on the idea of writing songs for each other to sing. Telling stories and communicating with a voice other than our own. The composer in me loves that sort of thing.

Helzuki never had a set 'mission', and while Leah, Matt, and Lex all had their own set of influences, they are not audible in the collective sound. For example, Leah's singing and piano style is,

---

25 See Dylan Smith (2010), who shows how in a highly masculine world explicit attribution is given to and incorporates the constructs of identity realization, learning realization, meta-identities and contextual identities (PhD The Institute of Education, University of London, 2011).

particularly at the start, influenced by artists such as Ben Folds, Tori Amos, and Amanda Palmer. Matt's bass playing is influenced by Kyuss and Skunk Anansie, and Lex's drumming was influenced by Faith No More and Calexico. Together they 'just sounded like us'. For Leah, what also compelled them to form a band and do what she describes as 'writing pop songs', was their collective influences and being philosophically drawn to The Flaming Lips' approach to creativity, in the sense that they employed diverse styles and clearly enjoyed and prioritized sonic experimentation over fastidious attention to detail.

> *Leah*: We were so focused on doing our thing. We were never about presenting a 'brand' or a definable 'new sound' to audiences. Our band was all about combining our diverse influences and having fun with it. When Kristian joined us as a new member, he brought with him a strong European art-rock influence, along with the new timbres of male vocals and ambient layered electric guitars, which completely altered the sound of our music. If Helzuki was all about a certain style of piano-rock, we could have merely hired a new drummer who played like Lex. Because all members of Helzuki have day jobs and their own individual artistic interests, and because we are an independent band with creative freedom to do whatever we please, the only priority is creating collaboratively and, now, using our studio to explore the limits of the sound we make together.

Apart from their demands on Leah's time, Helzuki and MLM appear to co-exist peacefully. MLM is a much younger project, but Leah and Paul approach it with what appears to be more business-like attention to detail, in the sense that they are aware of the music becoming a sellable commercial product in a competitive field, and understand the style and quality standards associated with the genre.

> *Leah*: Helzuki music is almost like a 'happening'. We start with the germ of an idea, it could be a chord progression and a few lines of lyrics, or maybe a pattern played on a looping pedal. From there we often experiment by adding elements, trying things out using our individual creative intuition. Sometimes it might be an improvised performance using one of Eno's Oblique Strategies (we have a set of cards on the mixing desk at all times!), and we'll record whatever happens and use it. MLM music is much more measured and thought out. With MLM, there is a lot more discussion and passing the project back and forth, each person fixing, working, and adding to it. There's no power struggle in the band, no ego tripping. We both just want the music to be as good as it can be, so the collaborative creativity happens as a result of constant reflection and evaluation. Certainly as a songwriter and singer, the music I sing for Helzuki feels more 'spontaneously me', even if the overall group composition/production is not what I would have chosen to do if I was working on my own. I've always got a head full of ideas when it comes to music, but I've learned that working creatively in a group is all about compromise and sometimes about surrender. The music I sing for MLM feels much more tempered and secondary to the style and overall 'vibe' of the production—and I think that is how it should be.

There aren't really any game rules for Helzuki, other than the need for any strange thing they come up with to be playable in one form or another. There has been a development of style and practice since the band located itself in the studio, and Kristian took some of the lead vocal duties, and also when Leah's role in the band switched towards string arrangement and a more traditional compositional approach using a score. An example of this is in the track 'Seen through glass' from their last release.[26]

> *Leah*: Initially the original chord progression came about from a piano improvisation, which I recorded and showed Kristian. He came up with the lyric and melody idea and recorded that on top. Then Matt wrote the bass line and we performed the percussion parts together. Finally I took away that first

---

[26] 'Seen through glass' can be found on iTunes.

element that held it all together and replaced it with an arrangement for string quartet. The resulting piece sounds like I'm not involved much at all. For some reason I get a kick out of that!

For Leah, the very idea of there being a gendered aspect to her work can come as a surprising creative realization of her popular/rock musician and composer/producer identity, which she actively realizes through the group creativity involved in both bands.

The key point is the way in which both bands realize a dialectical balance between individual and collective creativities. Like TFN, the particular forms of practice are multi-dimensional and multi-modal, and emphasize that the primary text of popular music is the recorded artefact. Again, the agency attributed to technology through particular forms of practice that produce cultural and symbolic capital plays a central role as a kind of creative partner.

Positioning Adam in ZVG

Adam's band ZVG is an 'indie' band (i.e. a band signed to an independent record company rather than a 'major').[27] The term 'indie' also refers to the sense of genre or style classification as exemplified by bands such as The Smiths and The Libertines. Most writers use the term 'indie' to describe any rock music produced by artists working within the network of independent record labels. Others see indie rock as a distinct genre of rock music with a specific artistic aesthetic, and care less about the context in which it is made. Many embrace both meanings of the word, believing that the aesthetics of the genre and its means of production are deeply intertwined. The band's debut single, 'Foxtrot vandals', was produced by the Belle and Sebastian frontman Stuart Murdoch, and released on seven-inch vinyl in October 2007. They released another single on seven-inch vinyl in 2008, which was produced by Paul Savage of The Delgados. Their debut album, *The Cage was Unlocked All Along*, also produced by Savage, was first self-released in 2009 and then re-released by Chemikal Underground Records.

Each of the band members engage in a range of freelance music-related professional activities.[28] Adam is also at the centre of a strong business network as a bass player. He knows what it is to be a musician in the music business and record industry in situations where casual and multiple engagements run parallel with membership and performance in multiple bands. Adam's standing, artistic reputation, and cache as a session player means that he works regularly as a bass player, and knows the orientation of specific networks in the music business.

Adam's band membership in ZVG entails popular live performances in Glasgow, Scotland, and the northern regions of England. The band is played on BBC radio, and has toured successfully across the UK. Its songs are recorded on a limited number of EP, CDs, and vinyl singles, and are available for download from the iTunes music store. Adam's membership in an originals band with a record contract involves him in a proactive and equal role in the creation of band material and the sustained application of a repertoire of creative skills in sound production. The record contract is a legal licensing deal rather than a traditional record contract. Chemikal Underground has exclusive rights to release and manage the music for a limited time period only, and ZVG retains publishing rights and ownership of the recordings. In a 'traditional' recording contract the band would have had to relinquish these to the label. ZVG is 'signed' but its label has no marketing department and sub-contracts this work. This is a common practice for indie labels.

....

[27] See discussion on 'indie' bands by Hesmondhalgh and Negus (2002).

[28] Steve crosses between author of guitar tutors, retail work, and guitarist for Line 6, a manufacturer of digital modelling guitars, amplifiers and related electronic equipment, and retail work. Adam crosses between originals band musician, session player, covers bands, and a part-time PhD.

Fig. 3.3 Zoey Van Goey. *Left to right*: Adam Scott (from Scotland), Matt Brennan (from Canada), Kim Moore (from England), and Michael John McCarthy (from Ireland). Photo by Campbell Mitchell. © Campbell Mitchell.

Adam is, as with Steve and Leah, a music omnivore who has invested large amounts of time and effort in order to become exceptionally skilled. His heavy dependence upon training and preparation is one of the many aspects of popular musicians' experiences. Training is also a source of creativity that is of great value in creative practice. It requires no undue intellectual application, formulae or method, and has the added advantage that it nurtures a reciprocity and interflow between members of the band—another underlying form of social capital.

Adam started taking piano lessons at around ten years of age, but, because of his love for AC/DC, Kiss, and later thrash bands such as Anthrax, he decided to move to guitar when he was 12. From about 12 to 20 years of age, he taught himself from records, and by using books, one of which was called *Lead Guitar* by Harvey Vinson, 'which contained many pictures of '60s and '70s moody-looking white male guitar hero types and rock language'. Adam read many articles in back copies of *Guitar Player* magazine. He did not take music at school and so could not read music, but nonetheless went on to study at Leeds College of Music from ages 20 to 24. An initial year-long foundation course gave him the opportunity to move on to a degree in jazz, the closest thing in the early 1990s to popular instead of classical music training. Adam was a first study guitarist who had the idea of becoming 'like John Scofield, a guitarist whose playing I really liked'. He had some excellent guitar teachers. In the second year of the degree he met a tutor called Graeme Hearn who was the college's 'contemporary classical guy', through whom he gained access to the college's electro-acoustic music studio, where he became familiar with composers such as Penderecki, Cage, and Feldman. At this time he was also a skateboarder listening to a lot of hiphop and US hardcore punk. John Scofield had been left behind in favour of free jazz. His final-year dissertation was, as he describes, 'a not very critical account of the music of John Zorn, a musician who I still follow. But despite having a degree in jazz, to this day I'm not a great jazzer'.

Adam went on to start a Master's in composition at the University of Huddersfield but did not complete it. He began to play with more bands, did some recording and playing work, and started 'being a bass player who could both read music and "rock out", and who could use samplers, synths, drum machines and sequencers. I also got into doing some web design at this time and learned how to programme Java which I did as a day job for a while'. In 2007, Adam did the Master in Popular Music Studies at the University of Glasgow. It was here that he learnt Max MSP[29] with Nick Fells which enabled him to take his Java programming ideas and apply them to his own music-making. He has recently started a second PhD, again at the University of Glasgow, examining creativity in popular music. Adam still spends a lot of time, as he says, 'learning new stuff by copying off records . . . I think this has been the best learning method for me as a player. A well-chosen record will quickly take you outside your comfort zones and give a wee taste of what it might be like to play with Black Sabbath, Ornette Coleman or Pete Brotzmann.'

Adam is a full time, freelance, professional mid-career electric and acoustic bass player who works in several bands. He plays in the Dave Peron Band, which is a four-piece jazz group. He also plays in a duo, BOZiLLA, which plays some 'covers' for which he makes detailed arrangements.[30] This is a highly skilled task that involves reducing music originally made by a number of musicians and instruments to a copy played by only two. His main creative activity, however, is ZVG (in addition to commencing a PhD on popular music and musicians).

> *Adam*: I describe myself as a bass player. I'm also someone who makes music using a laptop, which can be a compositional thing, or it can be a performance thing; so, a 'computer-y' type musician as well. I work chiefly with popular music genres. So, for instance, I play with a band called ZVG which is very much a fairly straight sort of indie-music-type-band, with a bit of spacey electronics in there as well, but it's sort of acoustic-y folk indie type music. Then I do a sort of a hip hop, dubstep thing with a friend of mine, which used to be called BOZiLLA, which has as a sort of hip hop, very electronic sort of sound. I also play in a jazz band on upright bass as well, which is with a friend of mine called Dave Peron, who is an alter-ego of the front man, Innes Smith. So I cover a number of genres on the bass. I know the tricks of the trade as a player very familiar with the field. I also pick up other casual gigs with bands doing musical theatre gigs. The ZVG thing, the BOZiLLA thing and the Dave Peron thing are very much projects in which I have a stake of ownership in. With ZVG it's all original music. With BOZiLLA, it's a mix of originals and covers.

----

[29] Max MSP is a visual programming language for music and multi-media widely used by composers, performers, software designers, researchers, and artists for creating innovative recordings, performances, and installations.

[30] 'Covers bands' primarily 'cover', or copy, well-known recordings or hits in a variety of popular styles. Their gigs take place mainly in pubs and other similar venues. Often, as well as copying previous hits, they produce their own original music, and are able to insert some of it into their sets, which involve about 70% covers and 30% originals. 'Function bands' can be thought of in the same way as cover bands except that they will be hired for functions such as weddings, parties, dances etc. (Green, 2001).

Adam confers a certain quality and classification and character on each of the bands he plays in. Being a musical omnivore, the particular forms of practice and creativities he has acquired are due to the relation between his habitus and his positioning within the field. Music figures largely in Adam's working life, and it structures his leisure pursuits. He is part of several music scenes in Glasgow and is confident talking about his established practices and positions in contemporary and jazz cultures, being equally proficient on electric and acoustic basses. He also writes songs as part of a collective but he doesn't describe himself as songwriter.

> *Adam*: I don't talk about myself as a songwriter, because I'm no lyric writer . . . I guess it depends on how you define 'song', but to say I write songs I think suggests I am in a lineage with people like Gary Barlow, Jack White, Joni Mitchell, Gene Simmons and Kurt Weill, which is not how I perceive myself. If I place myself anywhere, its more alongside producers-players-composers like John Zorn, Justin Meldal Johnsen, Squarepusher, and Brian Eno . . . The music that I've written myself, that I would say is music by Adam Scott, is instrumental music. The word composer has so many associations; it has many classical music associations, which I know it's a kind of silly attitude for me to worry about. It doesn't really make sense, but it makes the irrational part of me ask 'am I a composer?' The circles in which I move, people don't really talk about themselves as being composers, it's a crude word really and not one I would say gets used in the circles I move in. Possibly some of the musical directors with whom I work in theatre refer to themselves as composers. But I think when you're asking how I would describe myself, the bass player thing was easy . . . I think I generally avoid the use of the word 'composer'.

Being called a 'composer' clearly positions Adam differently from what he likes or relates to in his own professional field. Being a 'composer' relates him to a different world.[31] The ducking and diving of labels relates to Adam's view of himself as a musician both within and outside the field of music. Adam expresses concern about the 'crude' classification of 'composer', and is critical of the use of the word to describe his musical interests and activities. His tastes are wide, including jazz, rock, and heavy metal. He explains how he distances himself from 'commercial and elitist classical music behaviours that venerate composers, conductors and virtuosi, and where musicians are dot-readers beholden to the score'. However, he does like classical music and its sound world, and he works happily with classical musicians. The traditional role of an artistic avant-garde (whether as performer, musician, composer, or participator) is to challenge established hierarchies and the bourgeois values of the status quo. What he objects to are hegemonic attitudes and behaviours.

---

[31] To be a performance artist in the classical *world*—a great opera singer or chorister—involves a whole host of ideological forces that legitimate and reproduce the position and power of dominant groups. In learning a specific performance style, a specific repertoire, you learn the tastes and fashions enshrined in that genre—its art-objects, ideas, etc. Adam's ideas about the status of popular and classical contemporary genres are articulated here. Mikko, a Finnish keyboardist bears this out when he says: 'In high school, I led two musical lives. There was the life which centres on the kind of school music, you know, what you do at school together with others, particularly those who have or are having formal music tuition. Then, at home, I had my band that played covers and originals. A friend had a drum kit. Another friend had a guitar and an amp. On weekends we just went at it playing around with ideas, making up pieces together, some spontaneously, some recorded and worked on. It was really easy to do new things with my computer and to use computer sequencing for recording things. We weren't thinking about or targeting an audience or playing gigs or anything like that. We weren't thinking so much of traditions or bothering with any narrowly defined set of "classic" recordings taken from school or ripping off albums. We were friends who were self-taught, and loved making up our own music which pulled away from everything that was going on in school.'

Adam: I think musicians are a funny lot, they all deny the whole question and importance of genre.[32] You hear people say, 'Oh, we don't believe in genre, you know we're not a heavy metal band, we're, just ourselves', and all this sort of thing. And I'll be quite honest with you, I think that's a load of bull. I thought that even before I read some of the research people have done with musicians and their relationships with genre. In my own mind I would go into a session and I would think, 'Okay, this is this type of artist, they like these types of bands, they write these types of song and that might not be "classics" from the past that I particularly like and recognize and know as a genre, and I kind of know what the conventions of that genre are.' As the session progresses, I can contribute ideas about how someone might play something very differently in a reggae setting, or jazz setting, or in a dubstep setting. I think Frank Zappa, as a composer, band leader, employer, and cultural icon, provides and points to traditions in which the musicians must be literate to negotiate the anticipated and unanticipated during the improvised sections of, say, *Baby Snakes* (a DVD which features some great concert footage with keyboard player Tommy Mars and drummer Terry Bozzio playing together). In turn, the players themselves would then further Zappa's own understanding of music and improvisation, for example, Terry Bozzio or Aynsley Dunbar are different drummers to Jimmy Carl Black ... The idea being that Tommy Mars and Terry Bozzio come to understand Frank Zappa as a genre due to his standing in the musical and more broadly cultural fields. This understanding shapes their playing, much like my knowing about jazz or reggae shapes my own playing when I think it's appropriate.

Adam's focus on artists rather than albums, his awareness of mechanisms for establishing public recognition, his confidence in advancing an argument about genre labels, his ability to handle diverse genres and forms of cultural activity, and his evaluation of players and contributions to the creativity of trend-setting, show his concern with the kinds of cultural capital that might be at play here in the music field. He also displays a sense of his own place and a sense of the place of others, and an interest in the social positioning of certain genres. Because these field structures are constituted through symbolic capital, he recognizes the politics of positioning, and the canonical values of classical and popular music, whilst nonetheless contesting classification. Adam distances himself from setting borderlines between art and popular music, and indeed between classical music and popular music. Several examples of Adam delineating what kinds of cultural capital might be at play in certain popular music fields, and his conferring of status to certain styles over others, are featured in the following citation, which is, again, a recognition of the politics of classification and creativity, coincidental with the struggle for position within the field.

Adam: When I learnt to play bass I learnt to play by listening to records. I also learned about Motown by checking out some of their records, and then I found there was this book written about Motown bass player James Jamerson, and I went out and bought that book. These books and albums gave [direction to] people like me who blundered onto the field of bass playing going, 'Right! I've got this thing with four strings, what do I do with it now?' You know, I have this instrument, and the reality is I want to know how it works? What do I do? How do I realistically learn the ropes on how to play music and learn to develop musical skills on this thing? How do I get good enough, as quick as I can, to play

---

[32] A lot has been written by authors within each genre, and authors within each genre have written accounts of opposition between genres (Bourdieu, 1996). This phenomenon, which is sometimes referred to as 'genre-wars', is widely reported, especially the 'wars' between classical and popular genres as illustrated by Becker's (1963) famous study of 1950s dance band musicians and Berliner's (1994) reports on musicians who want to play jazz, but need to play dance music in order to earn a living, and thereby find themselves caught between musical worlds. Similarly, Cottrell (2004) comments on the different forms of capital and the status hierarchy accorded various categories of musician, and how different kinds of creativities are invested in different musical genres.

in or even start up a band? These so-called great 'lone innovators' gave me direction, they taught me what I wanted to get into, about celebrating natural talent and about learning band techniques to navigate the totality of bass playing in ways that are meaningful for me.

Forms of knowledge which are valued, and which lead to the acquisition of capital are associated with consecrated institutions of music. There is a sense here that these books and albums—cultural forms—are designed for 'people like me', by which he means musicians having no formal musical training but who gain musical competence and confidence through casual and formal encounters between band members. He is fascinated by the 'reality' of ripping off songs or licks by ear, coming up with new chord progressions, rearranging old songs, reproducing 'covers', recomposing and improvising, all of which leads to a very novel way of playing along with (or against) others, as 'natural' players with a very individual style can often do. He first learned about Motown by listening to records and then worked his way back to originals. Likewise, these forms of creativity gave rise to informal learning practices, which, as Adam suggests, are common to those 'musos' who have joined or started up bands with peers within a few months, or, at most, a couple of years of beginning to play their instrument. He emphasizes the importance of 'learning the ropes' as an aspiring musician who wanted to play guitar-based popular and rock genres. He positions himself on the side of having both practical and theoretical knowledge, that, in a sense, provides the potential for a new awareness of what Bourdieu (1993a) terms as 'having a good feel for the game'. We see in Adam, as with Steve and Leah, how habitus directly impacts on creative choices, and operates in relation to the field of music. There are fields within fields, and bands (and band habitus) within these fields within fields. Removal from the field or entry into a new game will generate a different set of responses dependent upon one's feel for the game (Sweetman, 2003, p. 534).

ZVG's habits and practices

Being in an originals band involves players as individuals, but, crucially, as members of a long-standing collective of finely tuned musicians, who are able to improvise, embellish, jam, and 'pick each other's brains' during group interactions in band rehearsals and performances.

> *Adam*: With Zoey van Goey, we come together to make a unique collective. I don't think we are an original collective, there are lots of other collectives that are a bit like us, maybe they are very like us—in certain circles there is a cultural object, understood as 'the four piece indie band with acoustic guitars and little Casio keyboards', but nevertheless we are Adam, Michael John, Matt, and Kim, who have unique individual experiences which, when put together, we use to pick each other's brains, navigate the process of making stuff as a band. Our collective pool of knowledge also, to some degree, dictates how we interpret situations as they arise and how we learn from the subsequent outcomes. We bring those things to the unique collective that is Zoey van Goey.

Adam's band seems not to follow a particular practice so much as act as a collective enterprise that works with shared ideas. On this level the core of the band's work lies in a way of thinking and talking. To be more precise, as a group the, members tend to ask questions rather than focus on new ideas. Adam considers this to be one of the most important forms of creativity: exploratory creativity. This is something all professional artists (and scientists) do. As discussed by Boden (2005), even the most mundane street artists in Leicester Square produce new portraits, or new caricatures every day. They are exploring their space, though not necessarily in an adventurous way. For Adam, this involves not just adding a new trick to their repertoire, but also about finding something that 'fits' within their established style, yet suggests or represents the development of a new sound, and is creative in an exploratory sense.

Adam: When you're working in bands you're trying to make uniqueness, you're trying to make some unique thing, be it a recording or a performance. And I think there's also commonality in that, as part of making your uniqueness, you're navigating decisions and choices as they arise, which are not known to you at the start of the process. At the end of it we're gonna make a record, or we're gonna make a gig, and I know that along the way we're gonna talk about it, or we're gonna play together. So I know that that's gonna happen. The specific decisions? What's going to happen along the way? I think that's the stuff you don't know. I think the creative process is in the making. It's navigating the unknown, and producing a unique object. Not an original object, like I would distinguish between 'original' and 'unique'. What I think about a unique object or piece of music is that if it's 'unique' it allows me to say that my piece is unique within a given genre. Or it might push that genre in a unique way. So, originality is to me about singularity. It's about the root, if you like, and I think it's very difficult to make roots in music. I'm not sure if you can make roots in music really. I think what you can do is produce uniqueness.

Adam explains how ZVG's 'uniqueness' is very differently constituted in practice.[33] While the band members share an equal split of both musical ideas and money, Adam is well placed to collaborate and contribute to the song writing, as can be heard on their new album, *Propeller Versus Wings*.

Adam: One of the first songs I played with the band was 'Escape maps' which at that time (late 2009) was a nice jazz waltz which I thought was OK, but I think the band as a whole felt it hadn't quite found it's place yet. Between then and when we recorded it in May 2010, the song was one we talked about more than played. Maybe around May 2010, Kim came in with a little recording of the song she had done at home on the piano. I remember she sang the lines quite freely, not really in the usual 4 or 8 bar phrases of pop music, and so she had shifted the placement of the changes and they were quite hard to follow. I remember MJ [Michael John] and I called this playing in 'Kim bendy time'. I think in the end for my own confidence I sat down at the piano and charted the chords out in standard Western notation, and this became the chart Kim used to play the song from when we recorded it. The final element in Kim's demo was this drum machine in 3/4 time, so there's this sort of polymetric feel; a shared pulse between 'Kim bendy time' and the drum machine. Towards the end of the song, bendy time also becomes 3/4 and the two lock together.

I played upright bass on the tune and to be honest I didn't have much of an idea about what I was going to play on it. I did a 'take' of just playing the roots of the chords following the chart. Then Paul (the producer) came in and said 'Try playing some fills like this' and he hummed some stuff to me. He hit record and I played a bit more—just jamming along really—whilst trying to remember what he had hummed to me, then the song ended and that was it done. I remember Paul's and Kim's voices coming in the headphones saying 'That was great', meanwhile I was a bit uncertain actually what I had just done. I think I was a bit surprised, kinda like 'Oh, is that it?' I went in to listen and was really pleased. We haven't played the song live since then so I'm going to have to learn the bass part at some point before we tour.

---

[33] For other originals band members, such as Norwegian Mikko, the experience of uniqueness is expressed this way: 'When I was 20, I ran an acid jazz band. It worked within a hybrid site of electronic rock, jazz, soul, and funk styles. The forms of creativity took many shapes. We'd start with a simple melody line (this usually comes from our female vocalist). We record this first with a click track. Rhythms, harmonies, and individual instrumental arrangements are built on top of that. We rehearse the songs at the same time with computer-based demo crafting. Feedback from the rehearsals was transferred to the computer demos. This is a kind of dance between composition and improvisational creativity, performance and listening creativity, voice and instrumental creativity, production and generative creativity. This can only bring clarity to our understanding despite the differing antecedents, which are aspects of a complex approach to a productive network that runs through and directs the nature of the collaboration that occurs within his band's recording session'.

Matt recorded the drums later and like my part, it seemed fairly jammed and improvised in the studio. Paul—a great drummer himself—would offer ideas and Matt would interpret those in his own way. I must say throughout making the album I really enjoyed watching Paul and Matt work together like this. Paul would slip Matt these little suggestions and Matt would fire them right back at him. It was two drummers who really respected each other, working on making great drum parts and sounds. If the album has a creative concept, I think it's one of being playful and open to just trying things out. Almost like sticking bits and bobs of stuff together and seeing how it sits. I think I've said it elsewhere but the ZVG test seems to be 'Does it make you smile?' You shouldn't take that to mean we were always having a riot in the studio though. Sometimes one or another of us would get annoyed about something and tempers would fray a little.

As you might expect with an 'indie' band, 'young hipster kids' and students provide a strong fan base. However, there are a lot of families at gigs, parents with young children in the audience.

> *Adam*: I think fans do contribute significantly to what is essential to the creativity of a band. I think that's one of the crucial things about popular music, that people can bring their own experiences, their own imagination. They find things in songs, create different meanings and memories that are unique to them, or unique to their group of friends, their town, and their group.

There seems to be a great deal communicated between bands and their fans; they work in close collaboration. Like musicians, fans operate within traditions and shared behaviours and understandings. Originals bands assign great importance to their fan base, especially when building a stylistic vision and working on stylistic developments. How the band experiments stylistically, whether the guitar eruptions work, or how an originals band, particularly on its debut album, defines its own sound says a lot about its fan base. The band members decide whether they'll feature macho posturing, include highly inventive and original takes on the concept of a rock song, whether they will consolidate or innovate, or go with an experimental, abrasive, new, beat-driven, title track. All these artistic and stylistic decisions will find some common ground with the band's fan base.

For Adam, the creative process is about making and navigating the unknown. He talks about the importance of producing 'a unique version of an object, not an original object'. He distinguishes between original and unique.[34] On the one hand, a variant can be unique in that it extends or pushes boundaries. Achieving 'originality' is about creating something completely new: a singularity that is difficult to achieve. In relation to his band, the uniqueness of their sound and expression– their music's own creative habitus—is more valued than its originality.

> *Adam*: Michael John is the guitar player in the band, and he would come in with some lyrics, and some vague sketch on the guitar, some chords, and he would sing that song to us. Matt, the drummer, who also sings, does something similar. Matt and Michael John (MJ) are the chief lyric writers. But then in terms of how the music pans out, the songs have ended up quite different from the original sketches

---

[34] Frith (1987) suggests that 'it is possible to identify with a song whether we understand the words or not, whether we already know the singer or not, because it is the voice—not the lyrics—to which we immediately respond' (p. 145). For another example, hear Thom Yorke's (Radiohead's singer) assertive vocal timbre on 'Creep', the song responsible for their early success. Yorke's singing on this track suggests a strong emotional investment and unmistakable honesty. His voice is dripping with meaning and originality. Mikko makes clear the value placed on originality when he says: 'With one band I was in we created an entirely new style of music which hadn't been played or heard in Finland. We spent a couple of years building it up from different genres. It was the combo of electronic instruments, electronic percussion, and we created a particular way of singing rock music. We had a female singer in this band and we created a unique way for her to sing and sound as well. We were together for five years.'

that they brought in on the guitar. And I think the reason for that is it has just been a case of all four of us chipping in some ideas, verbally or something played, and changing things around, making suggestions. Everyone comes in with some sort of idea. And it'll often end up being . . . there'll be one or two elements that we sort of hone in on, and the song comes to galvanize around those. But as I say, those things can come from a completely different source than the instigator of the song, if you like, which I would say is normally Matt or MJ . . . We have a written partnership agreement, though, which is split four ways.

Creativities of this collective kind are varied and overlap. Whereas interacting carries with it an implication of two or more different sets of ideas being compatible with another (taken-as-shared but never truly shared), co-acting is a process through which musical ideas and actions, initially stemming from an individual musician, become taken up, built on, developed, reworked, and elaborated by others. Thus they emerge as shared understandings for and across the group, rather than being any one individual's. Taken-as-shared dimensions are important in collective creativities, and could be used as a synonym for 'distributed'. Just as rhythms, melodies and harmonies might be shared or distributed, the sharing of ideas only makes sense if the player allows musical knowing and knowledge to be collective. Such a view is compatible with what Wenger (1998) termed a 'negotiated enterprise', wherein 'mutual engagement does not require homogeneity' and 'a joint enterprise does not mean agreement in any simple sense' (p. 78). Instead, he suggests that:

> Individual situations and responses vary, from one person to the next and from one day to the next. But their responses to their conditions—similar or dissimilar—are interconnected because they are *engaged together in the joint enterprise* . . . Their understanding of their enterprise and its effects in their lives need not be uniform for it to be a collective product.

> (Wenger, 1998, p. 79, emphasis added)

This is a complex system. Within the collaboration of joint enterprise the band members must be aware of each other's abilities or capitals in order to work together. Only then can they spontaneously cohere into functional collectives, or come together into integral unities with artistic potential that individual members may not have.

Group composition is fundamental to originals bands. Improvisational creativity also provides the means by which the collective is realized. The most common mode is certainly for a piece to be performed by those who have jointly contributed to its composition, but this is not always the case.

For Steve and TFN, Leah and Helzuki, and now MLM and Spider & I, and Adam's ZVG, collaboration means performing numbers they have learned from listening to recordings, from song sheets (involving chord charts), from the memory of one of the players, or, in a few cases, from notated music. The different backgrounds of the players are not necessarily distinguishable in performance (though they often mention someone else's composition when they are playing). Their performance depends on joint practice and development, with scope for innovation and stylistic freedom that is not bound by record company contracts.

Clearly, a plurality of musical creativities interacts neither as a single phenomenon or as limited to any one particular category. Each band, in its own way, integrates the individualist and collectivist dimensions of creativity as fundamental aspects of the practices of originals bands.

Concluding remarks

In this chapter, three originals band musicians shared detailed accounts of how they create their music. Each case illustrates manifestations of exploratory, participatory, individualistic, and collective creativities. The musicians speak about the differing roles and status of those involved in 'the game', of those 'in the know', and of the distinctions frequently used by musicians themselves regarding the hierarchy of values at work, both between and within various categories, and in the sociological potency at play in popular music.

Having a 'feel for the game', that is a 'practice sense' (or as in Bourdieu, 1993a, *sens practique*), as musician, as producer and as sound engineer, is a practice which has become a 'second sense' or second nature for the musicians featured in this chapter. This process is non-linear, multifactorial and relational. It involves multiple manifestations of creativities. Because there are many kinds of instruments, many kinds of microphones, many kinds of acoustic environments, many kinds of singers, and countless combinations which can be tested and tried, accepted or rejected, a complex, rich, and precise account of creativity can all too easily be reduced to a focus on just one social mechanism to explain all aspects of the complex mechanisms involved in original band creativities. In so doing, and as Bourdieu sees it, the consequences of these forms of field capital, when matched with a distinct band habitus, can lead to reconfigurations in the field, and thereby create particular markets in order to realize particular artistic ambitions (Bourdieu, 1984b). The agents, be they producers, musicians, engineers or record company executives, are always dependent on structures; and structures furnish the possibilities that they are predisposed to choose from. Those who think in simple alternatives need to be reminded that creativities in music are exalted by the complexities of creative spontaneity.

These musicians have learned many of the tricks of the trade and rules of the game. Their creative practices are informed by a sense of agency (the ability to understand and control their own actions). These possibilities of agency are understood in terms of the social structures that lie outside of the studio, and how creativity is vested in their working knowledge of the studio and their roles as record producers and sound engineers. They hold a lot of sway in their respective bands. They have accumulated a lot of cultural capital. They have the ability to wield power within the field, influence group decision making and get things done in the studio largely by existing outside the system.

For originals bands, the music is essentially defined by the recording rather than by the written script, and even small variations in performance can be crucial in the final product. This also extends to the visual components of the performance—costume, lighting, dancing, the physical movements of the performers—and the reactions and participation of the audience/fans.

For these musicians, creativities arise as a result of group activities in which every member has a major creative role. This group-based compositional activity is embedded in improvisatory practices leading to final products which, in some cases, are memorized improvisations, in some cases notated forms, and, in other cases are spontaneously co-created. In each case, the realities of creative practice (that is, how a song is actually composed, even if only in a limited form (partial lyrics only, or a riff to build on or sample) are that it becomes 'worked up' for live performance and recording. Popular music has many individual songwriters (see Cloonan, 2007; Green, 2001) and collaborative songwriting duos (e.g. Elton John who writes the music and Bernie Taupin, who writes the lyrics, and similarly with Carole King and Gerry Goffin (known as Goffin and King) (see McIntyre, 2010). The same was true of Rodgers and Hammerstein, Rodgers and Hart, and George and Ira Gershwin, who all had years of experience writing for Broadway. In contrast, it is usually thought that Lennon and McCartney worked competitively, and that each created the whole song themselves before George Martin came in. For all songwriters, however, the end-products are nearly always the result of combining contributions from a number of people.

The actions of musicians as social individuals, and the ways they create music, are influenced by issues and orientations relating to education, to environment, family, and to individual career aspirations and trajectories. Bourdieu's notion of habitus concerns these particular dispositions and attitudes towards practice. Among the associations that are considered key are exposure, recognition, recommendations, one-shot alliances, some medium-term collaborators and long-term running partnerships of the band. This is seen as social capital, since knowing and being known by certain hit-making names in the industry helps to validate bands. Word-of-mouth promotion by individuals and very loyal fans is more valued (as social capital) more than top-down media saturation. Social networks are rapidly becoming a widely accepted practice for music promotion in the digital age, along with the use of YouTube videos.[35]

For originals band musicians, their creativity, regarded as vital for challenging rules and conventions, along with innovation, which occurs when various forms of newness are taken up to establish a new practice, remains key to bands' durable and adaptive practices. This can be seen with Trent Reznor, who dropped out of college then formed NIN and went on to become an industrial rock[36] megastar after the breakthrough point of releasing The Downward Spiral in 1994. His seventh studio project early in March 2008, *Ghosts I-IV* made him a star. Collective musical creativities enable a different structure of artist-audience (producer-consumer) mapping, marking the complex nature of the relationships between youth, popular music and creativity, and their social reproduction in originals bands.

There seems little doubt that the strategies originals band musicians use to develop and improve their efforts to articulate their experience of the creative process broadens what counts as creativity. The narrative of a performance as constructed by an audience, itself a site for individual and collective symbolic work and creativity (Willis et al., 1990) is well documented. Both product and process are therefore dependent on the band habitus, the generative aspects of which serve to reaffirm the band. For Christopher Small this means valuing what people 'do' when they take part in a musical act. These actions—defined by Small (1998) as 'musicking'—involve a range of responses including taking part 'in any capacity'.

The creativity of originals bands ultimately rests on the inputs of individuals working together to mine the wellsprings of their own musical histories and favoured traditions. What is valued is not made to conform to the mainstream conventions in which their songs are situated. On the contrary, as more creativities are generated, the more categorizations are made possible.

---

[35] Wikström (2009) posits one of the more extreme examples: a Swedish baby boy William who was videotaped by his father while laughing quite adorably. The father posted the video on YouTube for his own mother to see. One year on, the 1 minute 40 seconds long video had been viewed more than 50 million times and is one of the most viewed videos on YouTube, ever.

[36] Industrial rock is a musical genre that fuses industrial music and specific rock subgenres. Industrial rock spawned industrial metal, with which it is often confused. Its artists generally employ the basic rock instrumentation of electric guitars, drums, and bass, and pair it with white noise blasts and electronic sounds from synthesizers, sequencers, samplers and drum machines. Guitars are commonly heavily distorted or otherwise affected. Bass guitars and drums may be played live, or be replaced by electronic musical instruments or computers. Industrial rock frequently incorporates the sounds of machinery and industry. This sound palette was pioneered by early 1980s artists (SPK, Einstürzende Neubauten, Die Krupps, and Test Dept), who relied heavily on metal percussion, generally made from pipes, tubes, and other industrial waste.

Key points

1. Exploratory and participatory, entrepreneurial, and collective creativities are integrated in the complex of originals band.

2. The underlying and defining principles of originals band culture and habitus include: (1) the creativities central to generating, prizing and prioritizing 'the new'. So for instance, reviewers will praise innovation, and competing agencies will use 'newness' or originality to establish style authority; (2) the creativities underpin uniqueness; and (3) the condition for the emergence of the individualism (or individuality) of the band is, for instance, to 'trail blaze' or rebel against already established norms). These bands are the quintessential expressions of the complexity of creativities in modern society, as also, is their desire to interact with fans' creative wishes for newness, originality and innovation. They realize these goals through entrepreneurial creativity which concentrates on what they do as bands that create new styles of performance, new identities, innovative use of instruments and sound producing technologies, and by encouraging fans to interact with, and own, their music. An originals band's career may be fast or slow according to the degree of recognized 'legitimacy' bestowed on them.

3. The collectivist dimensions of creativity can be explained in terms of abiding and shared values, and how they are constituted by balancing convention, expression and newness in sound, material, and meaning. There is no inherent conflict between the collective and the individual in these originals bands, and the concept of band habitus is a recurring motif even when not named in that manner. The individual musicians featured in this chapter illustrate a high degree of symbolic capital as professional musicians, reinforced by the accrual of multiple roles whereby the individuals manage or participate to consolidate the complex of band creativities.

Discussion questions

1. Some writers argue that there is no conflict between art and commerce, at least not in the music industry. Frith (e.g. 1978, 1983, 1987, 1988, 1996) claims that rock music, which sometimes is considered as a musical genre with relatively high levels of authenticity, is not created outside but rather inside the system of commercial music. Thus, combining creativity and commerce. How is the commercial aspect integral to the field? Does 'selling out' have to be a moral choice? How has the digital revolution changed the commercial music landscape? How does this impact on bands emerging today? In what situations/places with original bands would art yield to commerce (or vice versa)?

2. Part of the Mothers of Invention, regarded as one of the most creative and innovative originals group, Frank Zappa 'developed a musical style that was wildly eclectic, and thematically weighted to political debate and satire' (Shuker, 1994, p. 123) What do you consider is the criteria of the genuinely creative artist? How is the uniqueness of sound of originals bands socially constructed? In what ways do original bands reinforce and break with dominant popular, rock, jazz and classical conventions?

3. What do originals bands build reputations as creative collectives? What key choices are seen to be rooted in fine discriminations and judgements that position them positively in the field?

Chapter 4

Singer-songwriters

This chapter focuses on the plurality of creativities arising in songwriting, whether using notation or not, and on the performance practices of singer-songwriters.[1] These creativities include the **individual, collaborative, and intercultural** practices that uniquely define the songwriting process and the performance of songs, whether live, broadcast, or recorded. Individual and collaborative creativities include the overlapping practices and methods of creating songs, when **compositional and improvisational** modalities of creativity mediate singer-songwriters practices in ways that are different from the performance of songs, and when, again, the performance element is inherently different in recording and live contexts. This distinction is key to understanding songwriting as a plural, rather than as a singular creativity.

This chapter concerns the appropriation of other cultures, and the significance of the exchange relations that are central to intercultural creativity. Amongst other issues, it concerns how regulated improvisations can produce originality, and, with that, myriad preferences and songwriting practices. These cluster in the social space of small group interactions and activities that are interculturally meaningful, and relevant to creating a cultural identity within which the creative process unfolds. Singer/songwriters' creative activities or practices are endowed with cultural capital to varying extents, depending on: (i) particular ways of working with material; (ii) the reworking of this material in ways which interpenetrate and emerge from one another; and (iii) the partly unconscious 'taking in' of new forms of diversity, no longer defined by geographical borders, but following cultural interchange processes in ways which highlight the singer-songwriter's own distinctive and original creations.

Collaborative and intercultural creativities frequently occur together, yet play out differently, in the detailed accounts of the two young singer-songwriters featured in this chapter. This suggests that success does not depend on conformity to a definition of cultural practice imposed by the

---

[1] The term 'practice' refers to 'forms and ways of doing that are not simply the outcome of individual actions but also of wider structural factors' as put forward in Bourdieu's theory of practice. While it is important to view how individual singer/songwriters actively engage in creating and positioning themselves in their social worlds, using 'habitus' as the conceptual tool that Bourdieu intended, and as persuasively argued and illustrated by Reay (2004). It is the interactions between 'habitus', 'capital', and 'field' that generate a singer-songwriter's practices. See also de Certeau (1984), Hass et al. (2010), and McIntyre (2011, 2012).

music industries or by the field of cultural consumption (i.e. the audience),[2] but, rather, on a singer-songwriter's disposition as a cultural omnivore[3] who is able to emerge from numerous social sites wherein different cultures cohere and converge, providing space for intercultural creativity, and leading to the creation of something new.

2   This finding stands in contradiction to Bourdieu's view of visual arts practices, as discussed by Grenfell and Hardy (2007), who say that 'artistic success depended on conformity to a definition of artistic practice imposed by this field of cultural consumption. What was constituted was an artistic nomos, or organising "laws" of experience, which ruled production' (p. 111). In Bourdieu's work, a 'field' is a system of social positions, for example, a profession such as the law, structured internally in terms of power relationships, such as the power differential between record companies and bands. More specifically, a field is a social arena of struggle over the appropriation of certain species of capital—'capital' being whatever is taken as significant for social agents (the most obvious example being monetary capital and the terms of record contracts (Grenfell and Hardy, 2007).

3   The figure of the 'cultural omnivore' is a particular self-formation to show how cultural boundaries are being redrawn as the middle class draws culture into itself (see Skeggs, 2004).

Introduction

To work alone as a songwriter is rare. Whilst Irving Berlin, Cole Porter, Jerry Herman, and Frank Loesser worked alone, George Gershwin, Jerome Kern, Leonard Bernstein, and most of the songwriters of the popular music worlds did not. In fact, sharing authorship is increasingly the norm nowadays, as the structure of songs has changed from music *and* lyrics to backing track, lyrics, melody, *and* spoken rap.[1] Producers, sound engineers and chart arrangers all bring different talents to the mix, and may create tracks for songs they never imagined would be written over them. Co-writers and collaborators can be band members (as is the case with the artist featured in this chapter). Often bands work within a collaborative process giving bands credit for each song (like R.E.M.). Some bands have a principal writer or two, as is the case with The Who, for whom guitarist Pete Townshend writes the songs, or as was also the case in the first decade of Take That, before the main writer Gary Barlow agreed to involve all the band members in songwriting.

In addressing the question of how songwriters write songs in the worlds of popular music, including hip hop, wherein the lyrics mean so much, a central role is accorded to the types of creativity that are sparked by: dialogue and collaboration; the particular manifestations of creativity inherent in certain cultural traditions; generic conventions; the media and institutional conditions that shape distinctive song forms and styles, such as hip hop, rap, reggae, blues, and ballads; and the specific social, historical and political circumstances of the production context. The extensive use of the term 'creativity' in the singular in discussions of songwriting is because songs are generally assumed to be realized by an individual songwriter, rather than in any openly manifest form of *collaborative* production.

It is wrong to regard song-'writing' as something that is unconsciously or deliberately learned as a 'written' craft. Rather, it is necessary to broaden the term 'musical creativity' beyond descriptions in which the verb 'create' is used to describe a process of individual execution and distinguished by 'writing'. The notion of 'musical creativity' is not only singular and individual, as is so often assumed. Rather, there are different types of music creativity that are recognized and

1   The term 'track' refers to the use of backing tracks for writing lyrics. The terms 'melody' and 'spoken rap' are often mutually exclusive.

rewarded differently, insofar as the production context varies, and as musicians/lyricists tend to play down, dismiss or overlook, the act of 'writing', circumscribed, as it is, by available technologies and expertise, by economics, and by the expectations of their audiences.

There are numerous personal accounts of the process of songwriting from various songwriters. For instance, John Lennon differentiated between the process of songwriting to meet deadlines for a new album, and the act of writing 'real music . . . the music of the spheres, the music that surpasses understanding' for which 'I'm just a channel . . . I transcribe it like a medium' (Shuker, 1994, p. 102). Then again, from Paul McCartney's recollections of his creative collaboration with John Lennon,[2] and the distinctive collaboration between Neil and Tim Finn (members of Split Enz and later Crowded House), as well as collaborative projects between artists and musicians such as David Bowie and Brian Eno, and Bernie Taupin and Elton John, we learn that institutionalized expectations and the actual configurations of professional trajectories involve different types or manifestations of creativity.

Songs and songwriters, singers, and record producers display diverse manifestations of creativity, as shown, for instance, by the ways in which singer/songwriters, band members, and record producers come up with ideas. Quite aside from who thought of the idea first, or how that person managed to come up with it, songwriting arises through various approaches to group popular music composition, as seen in the previous chapter.[3] Then, there is the singer who writes, plays and sings. For Billy Joel, 'singing is the least of it. It's the changing-the-light-bulb part' (DeCurtis, 2005, pp. 137–8). Singing songs exclusively written by other people, as for instance Dame Shirley Bassey does, is considered much less successful and creative as song interpreters than singing and songwriting. For example Sir Elton John said, 'I started off as a piano player who wrote my own songs, and now, 32 years after the *Elton John* album, I consider myself as good a singer as I am a piano player. It's taken me a while to catch up. But I'm glad I write my own songs and don't have to rely on other people' (K. Kelly and McDonnell, 1999, p. 34). But of course he does rely on other people, as with Bernie Taupin, who writes the lyrics to his songs. Then there is the type of songwriting creativity illustrated by Michael Jackson's appropriation of stolen ideas in *Moonwalk*, which is based on making and appreciating novel combinations of ideas ripped off from, in this case, nature. Jackson made stylish, high-energy dance moves a part of his creative identity. Interestingly, it is possibly apocryphal that Toni Basil invented the moonwalk for Bowie's Diamond Dogs tour and Michael Jackson saw that tour and stole it! His 'moonwalk dance',[4] which he became famous for, was done for the first time while performing 'Billie Jean'. Jackson said: 'A musician knows

---

[2] See discussion of songwriting and songwriters in Shuker (1994, p. 102) and McIntyre (2010). For an interesting discussion of McCartney's view of 'divine intervention', and how others write by 'fooling around' see DeCurtis, (in K. Kelly and McDonnell, 1999, p. 34).

[3] The term 'group popular music composition' was first coined by Green (2001, p. 45).

[4] The *moonwalk* or *backslide* is a dance technique that presents the illusion of the dancer being pulled backwards while attempting to walk forward. A popping move, it became popular around the world after Michael Jackson executed the dance move during a performance of 'Billie Jean' on 25 March 1983 when performing at the Motown 25 TV broadcast. It subsequently became his signature move, and is now one of the best-known dance techniques in the world. There are many recorded instances of the moonwalk, similar steps are reported as far back as 1932, used by Cab Calloway. In 1985, Calloway said that the move was called 'The Buzz' when he and others performed it in the 1930s. In 1955, it was recorded in a performance by tap dancer Bill Bailey. He performs a tap routine, and at the end, backslides into the wings. The French mime artist Marcel Marceau used it throughout his career (from the 1940s through the 1980s), as part of the drama of his mime routines. In Marceau's famous 'Walking Against the Wind' routine Marceau pretends to be pushed backwards by a gust of wind. (For more information see http://en.wikipedia.org/wiki/Moonwalk_(dance))

hit material. It has to feel right. Everything has to feel in place. It fulfills you and it makes you feel good. You know it when you hear it. That's how I felt about "Billie Jean". I knew it was going to be big while I was writing it. I was really absorbed in that song. One day during a break in a recording session I was riding down the Ventura Freeway with Nelson Hayes, who was working with me at the time. "Billie Jean" was going around in my head and that's all I was thinking about.' According to *Rolling Stone* magazine's top 500 songs list, Jackson came up with the song's rhythm track on his home drum machine and nailed the vocals in one take.[5] Madonna, on the other hand, set trends by sourcing ideas from a rich store of moves from dance clubs, then coming up with creative associations that found surprising, valuable, and new combinations.

Collectively, record companies look to songwriters and their blockbusting songs as the single-driven symbolic repository for sources of huge profit. The current market was defined by the single-driven blockbusters of the 1980s—Michael Jackson, Bruce Springsteen, Prince, U2, Madonna. Even the seemingly 'anti-commercial gods of grunge' (DeCurtis, 1999, p. 34), who emerged in the early 1990s, conformed, however unconsciously or unwillingly, to that model. For record companies, a generation of creative singer-songwriters has been responsible for a large number of chart successes endowed with creative significance. The iconic creativity of Michael Jackson and Madonna, whose trend-setting multiple identities, music videos, and creative ability to reinvent themselves transformed the ways music is produced, and packaged, for MTV™ for instance. The vitality of the music industry lies in its potential to not only apply itself in different ways but in being able to adapt to change. The idea of tradition as a mechanism for handing down music, its culture, or its set of rules, is well documented. Schippers (2010) has argued that the 'traditions of Iraqi, Iranian and Indian classical music are perhaps best understood as a set of rules governing musical practice' (p. 44). These traditions can be handed down with little change. However, traditions that keep changing with, and responding to the demands of the time, can be creatively enriched. Here it is worth noting the speed of popular music's evolution, which has dramatically increased with the parallel evolution and proliferation of mass media, wherein development or change is no longer generational, and styles become 'old' in a few years.

This chapter introduces two singer-songwriters, a term given to artists who both write and perform their material, and who are able to perform solo, usually on acoustic guitar or piano. The first account is given by Pippa Andrew, an early-career musician who has a range of different songwriting (and arranging) practices, spanning classical, contemporary and popular musical genres, and bridging old and new cultural forms and practices.

The second account of songwriting is given by Roshi Nasehi, who performs with a 'backing' band, Pars Radio, which she regards as an integral part of her work as a 'song producer'. Here this term refers to the creation of a song, even if only in a limited form of scraps of lyrics or a riff, which is arranged or 'worked up' for live performance and recording. Roshi provides detailed accounts of the process of songwriting, from being perched on a chair, to fooling around with melodies and lyrical ideas on the keyboard, to the creativity imbued within creative practices ('indulgences') that are associated with freely improvised live performances and recordings with band collaborators from Pars Radio. She describes how she produces her songs using technology, and by drawing heavily upon her 'backing' band, and how she engages in the process of song performance, whether solo with piano, or with a band. Together, Roshi and Pars Radio, her three-piece band, create intensely original music that involves both modifications and adaptations of traditional Iranian songs.

Both singer-songwriters are in an early career phase as practising musicians and perform professionally across several styles of music: popular, jazz, and contemporary classical genres.

---

[5] See www.songfacts.com/detail.php?id=277.

Fig. 4.1 Singer-songwriter Pippa Andrew before a sound check in 2011 at a gig in Nottingham. Photo by Ben McKee. © Ben McKee, 2011.

Both musicians are, like Grammy-nominated and established divas Janelle Monae[6] and Imogen Heap,[7] fiery and energetic performers who sing, write songs, arrange, and perform, and have learned to mix orchestral arrangements with funk, soul, pop and rock. Both Pippa and Roshi work as freelance and session musicians. Awareness of, and knowledge about, the complexities of the music industry and the versatility required of them as they work require reflexive consideration, innovative use of technology, and innovation across distinct musical worlds.

Introducing Pippa

Pippa Andrew (Fig. 4.1) was born in South Wales and lived in and around Manchester when she was growing up. She is the oldest child of three, with one brother and one sister. She went to primary

[6] Listen to Janelle Monae perform live in the WXPN studios, and chat with World Café host David Dye about her imaginative creation of the ArchAndroid on her EP Metropolis: Suite 1, her collaborations with the legendary Big Boi of OutKast, poet Saul Williams, the dance-punk troupe Of Montreal, and punk prophets Deep Cotton, at http://www.npr.org/2011/04/01/132203681/janelle-monae-on-world-cafe.

[7] For more on Imogen Heap see http://en.wikipedia.org/wiki/Imogen_Heap.

school in Manchester and attended Cheetham's School of Music between the ages of 10 and 13 years. She was also a chorister at Manchester Cathedral. At the age of 14, she moved to a high school in Warrington and attended the Junior Royal Northern College of Music. She graduated with a BA in Music from the University of Salford, and is now studying to complete an MA in Composition at Leeds College of Music; a degree she completed in February 2011. Her first classical performance was as a violinist at the age of five. Throughout her childhood and teenage years she performed regularly on various different instruments, including violin, viola, voice, and, in her late teenage years, piano.

Pippa is a freelance singer who writes, plays, and sings. She plays keyboard, electronics, violin/viola, and guitar. She has written, arranged[8] and performed string parts for an album by Frameworks, a trip hop and hip hop writer and producer in Manchester, which is due to be released at the beginning of 2012 by Organik Records (California). As of January 2012 details of all Pippa's projects will be available at www.pippaandrew.com.

Pippa first got involved in popular music at the age of 19, and started learning about production at the age of 20. Her first band was formed for her undergraduate performance modules and was called Kaleidoscope Blue. Since then she has sung with and written songs for The Mobile Jazz Cafe, a Zimbabwean Jazz group, The Voice Collective, an acapella band featuring original arrangements of songs by, for instance, Stevie Wonder, David Bowie and Sufjan Stevens, and Malaika's Project, which features both her original songs and covers and is due to be launched in March 2012.[9] These groups can be described as 'mainstream' and 'marginal' bands.

Pippa's development of popular music skills, and songwriting in particular, came late (at tertiary level). She emphasizes that parental and teacher encouragement was a crucial factor in her early music training as a classical musician. (This is a common occurrence, as evidenced in findings reported and literature summarized by Green (2001, p. 24).) Her musical career, initially as a classically trained vocalist, pianist/keyboardist, violinist/violist, and harpist, and then, more recently, as a guitarist and electronics musician, has widened the parameters she originally set for her own creative practice. Pippa recalls learning practices among her earliest memories of formal music education, and mentions her parents early in her narrative. Their involvement was portrayed as particularly useful, supportive and central to her choice of a music education, and her choice of music for her higher education. Creativity is central to her earliest memories of music-making. She speaks at length about her creative energies and about being inspired by teachers, players, and new forms of creativity shaped by technologies and space, and about being creative as central rather than peripheral, essential rather than negotiable, to her music-making.

> *Pippa*: I've always really enjoyed making and creating music. My abiding memory is of always being in the school choir. I loved singing. We had a specialist lady come in who took the choir. Being in the choir was very much just a fun activity whilst at my first primary school. It was only when I was 10 and joined Cheetham's and Manchester Cathedral Choir that music became more serious. There was an

---

8   Record companies and some performing outfits make use of arrangers who are appointed as external personnel (rather than drawn from within the band) to make detailed arrangements, or reduce music originally made for a number of musicians and instruments to a copy by only two.

9   The Mobile Jazz Café is a collective of Manchester musicians playing original Zimbabwean Jazz compositions written by different members within the group, primarily sung in a mixture of Shona and English. The main songwriter is Pascal Makonese (see www.myspace.com/mobilejazzcafe). The Voice Collective is a Manchester based, 13-piece acapella band performing original arrangements of popular songs (styles incorporating pop, soul, jazz, rock and singer-songwriter) and original compositions, all arranged/written by members of the group (www.thevoicecollective.co.uk/). Malaika's Project is a Manchester-based collective of musicians performing songs written by Pippa Andrew. The songwriting stylistically incorporates pop, soul, jazz, world/folk, and electronic/production-based composition (see www.malaikasproject.com).

intense musical atmosphere at these schools. I mean we did five services a week, and practised up to five hours a day.

This assigns Pippa to a specific habitus, the significance of which Bourdieu (1996) explains as 'the one they put to work in their own production and in the appreciation of the production of other agents' (p. 271). Pippa articulates the significance of an institutional influence over and above the direct impact of family background, although it is clear that some families choose schools for their children so as to ensure access to a particular institutional habitus.

When Pippa reflected on her traditional music education, she referred to several compelling features of the musical creativities of her childhood. She emphasized how her talents were often championed and influenced by her parents. She speaks of creating her own music alone and with others, of the emphasis on traditional views of formal music learning practices, of being creatively engaged and inspired by classical music teachers, of the processes of music's creation through a free-form type of narrative, of developing 'good ears', of the prominent role of institutions and instrumental programmes from early years to university, of embodied modes of experimental and improvisatory character in music-making, of 'real' performances, and the notion that worth-while creative ideas arise in comparable ways with classically trained musicians.

Pippa was encouraged by her family, and by key 'turning points' when scholarships were won, opportunities invoked, influential people met, recognition received, and motivation to become a professional musician developed. These are all expressions that 'define the social conditions of possibility—and, by the same token, the limits—of the production and circulation of cultural works' (Bourdieu, 1996, p. 270). It was no accident that Pippa was propelled towards a career in the field of music. Associated with this, is the intra-musical nature of the field of work, and the ways of thinking about creativity in popular and classical music, in which fields the struggles posed are enormous.

> *Pippa*: All of my formal training had been in classical music. I was always desperate to formally learn jazz and pop forms . . . I loved writing my own original material, experimenting with vocal lines and stuff . . . and couldn't work out how to get involved in bands and stuff. So I applied to do a popular undergraduate course which specialised in popular and jazz music and recording. When I arrived, I'd never sung down a microphone, I'd never turned on a PA. I'd never been in a studio. The teachers seemed pretty negative about me being accepted onto the course; I felt a lot of opposition.

As Reay et al. (2005) succinctly assert, when habitus encounters a field with which it is not familiar (as with Pippa's experience of singing technique and amplification tools), the resulting disjunctures can generate not only change and transformation but also disquiet, ambivalence, insecurity, and uncertainty. For Pippa, the transition from a solo acoustic singer to being hooked up to an amplifier where all the senses have their roots in the lead, rhythm, and bass guitars plus drums four-piece rock group, knowing nothing about amplifiers, mixing desks, and micro-phones, was highly charged and caught between two musical worlds. Such phenomena are linked to perceptions based on specific hierarchized categories and the criteria of peer judgements that dominate inside the field, which in this case were Pippa's classical background and her encounter with popular and jazz music. The major oppositions among genres and the subtle, or not so subtle, differences observed inside the same genre and cultural practice can be clearly seen here. Pippa had plenty of ability but, as Bayton (1993) observes: 'Women have been largely excluded from popular music making and relegated to the role of the fan. Women performers have been more prominent in commercial "pop" than in "rock", but their place in all these worlds has been that of vocalist rather than instrumentalist' (p. 177). It is important to note that hardly any women work in production and music technology, even to this day.

Moreover, even in the presence of tutors and students (rather than paying audiences), many woman performers, particularly in all-male courses, find the idea of making the shift across genres risky and problematic. The music industry also plays a substantial role in legitimizing gendered meanings and interpretations of popular music's social significance that are essentially class-based (see A. Bennett, 2000; Willis, 1978). How well a musician learns the rules of how to enter the, mostly male, territory as a female instrumentalist and singer is an incredibly tricky and risky business. Pippa had a similar experience of learning to differentiate and appreciate the clash of practices that can inhere between classical and popular music genres:

> *Pippa*: I felt a lot of opposition to my classical instrumental training. It made me question myself so much, and I felt like I constantly had to justify myself as a musician. People just didn't know how to categorize me. And it's like they'd categorized themselves and they were trying to work out where I fit, in relation to them. And they just couldn't really work it out. And initially they all very much categorized me and put me in this 'classical box', which has a certain image that goes with it, and it has a lot of connotations, and people assume a lot about the type of musician you are, and also the type of personality you have, and by your appearance. You can feel a bit like a fish out of water when you find yourself in unfamiliar territory or boxed into one corner of the music world.

For Pippa, from the standpoint of performance traditions and performance styles in classical art music and the related classical canon, music creativity is not an elusive thing—pursuing it is not like catching butterflies or grabbing soap. When pursuing the object of her desires (to do music) she exemplifies the attitude of 'going for it' or, as Bourdieu and Wacquant (1992) say, becoming 'like a "fish in water": it does not feel the weight of the water and it take the world about itself for granted' (p. 127).

Pippa's songwriting habitus and practice

Pippa has a set of internalized dispositions that contribute to her status as a highly skilled musician. As one who locates herself confidently and strategically in the freelance labour market she is well placed as a new artist to gain commissions, be successful, and develop an enviable reputation 'as a musician who does a lot of performance, composition and production . . . (of) newer types of music, especially those that are more improvisation-based'. Finding your own internal motivation, a quality which social psychologist Teresa Amabile (1996), who has done extensive research on creativity within organizations, says is 'conductive to creativity' (p. 15) is important, as is being able to stay independent of demands and reactions from the environment, which is one of the characteristics of creative artists. Learning to cope with the ideological forces of people who are well versed in one or the other art forms happened early in Pippa's tertiary education. Whilst it is true that people are generally disinclined to admit any differences in the value of creativities that underpin distinct worlds of music, they privilege certain genres over others. So Pippa considered whether she should dismiss the entire domain of popular cultural forms, such as jazz or rock 'n' roll in favour of classical genres. Should she position herself, literally and symbolically, as a musician who is in touch with, and composing for, singers and instrumentalists of one single genre and not another?

> *Pippa*: I don't like how musicians get categorized by genre, and how this assigns who they are. It can be really hard to move back and forth between the worlds of classical and pop creativity, between performance and digital composition—or, more specifically, in people's unwillingness, to move between classical and pop aesthetics; there is a lot of exaggeration and misconceptions which don't always line up to the reality of people in real contexts.

Pippa's words imply a great deal about the significance of judgements of talent and taste, of a woman self-motivated to place herself in the spotlight of singing lead, and aware of the external power relations which act to polarize and produce hierarchies of creativity, particularly within institutions. What, how, and why choices are made when music is created, and the relationship between those choices and the kinds of creativities vested in particular musical genres, are played out in this narrative. It shows how prominent people influence music traditions, the working of musical canons, and the differing relations between students and classical musicians. At times, the personality of the student and tutor are complex, demands are equivocal, and the project sets up associations that students and teachers are not comfortable with. At other times, teacher and student, as with producers and composers, talk the same language, the demands are unambiguous, and both know and like what the other is doing.

> *Pippa*: I was always seen and identified as 'a classical musician' who had got lost. I was seen as looking in the wrong place. People thought that really I'd made a big mistake taking jazz and pop courses. I encountered a lot of resistance and opposition, you know, a particular kind of excluding attitude from teachers and students. I remember my first ever ensemble class: my tutor marched me down to the senior tutor and said, 'What is this classical singer doing on this course. She shouldn't be here'. OK, we all know there's a lot of differences between classical singing and pop singing, and one is the way you produce your sound, where you place your voice. But popular music has many individual songwriters who come from a classical background. While jamming is a bread and butter activity for popular and can be first and foremost an aspect of vocal performance, something very familiar to classical musicians, it's seen as so different from classical singing in the use of microphone technique, and the sound that you create for yourself on the PA. We were always expected to create or find our own sound in these ensemble classes, and I had no idea about that either. In classical music you do a lot of memorizing and copying but you also do a lot of composing and arranging as a classical musician. These kinds of activities are standard aspects of professional musicianship—being able to call on all manner of types of creativity—a certain punctuation of the flux of creativity, a punctuation that, not insignificantly, underscores the continued role of creativity in the 'event' of musical sound. This is the bread and butter of a performing artist isn't it? But these sessions were really about the technical side of music creativity; the creativity that underpins the production side of playing in a band which has massive impact you know. At that time, I didn't understand how to get your own sound, how to manipulate and position the microphone, how you avoid blasting people's heads off, how a cheap PA gives feedback and can blow your eardrums. After a while I got familiar with this equipment, and you quickly learn how to take control of the equipment, it becomes automatic. But without that experience, barring the miraculous—originality simply cannot occur and is least of all tolerated in these kinds of settings. It doesn't matter how much talent for music you have or ideas you have and want to share. Even how you structure a band rehearsal involves, itself, a different form of creativity. Having loud sounds blasted at you is physically very tiring and people get fatigued and upset quickly. This was my first experience of working and writing in a band. I'd written many songs before, but they were always just for me at a piano, something very private.

Genre is an important concept in relation to creativity. Pippa's words point to how discourses of creativity reflect and contribute to the formation of particular genres, how conventions shape creative practices, and how creativity invests in particular musical genres. Clearly, Pippa has signified that she communicated the genre to which belongs through musical patterns, timbres, texture, vocal sound, and style. These were associated by her tutors and fellow students with specific genre categories. How they went about distinguishing what were creative ideas from uncreative ones would have depended on how confidently she navigated between classical genres (such as lieder, ballads, arias, operas), and popular genres and the forms of textual codification that go with certain models of songwriting. When she reflects back on the process by which creative ideas arise, she reflects on what counts as a creative idea as well as *how it happens*. Whether she places a premium on song interpretation or melodic re-creation, the acceptance of conventions, however implicit, seems to be a compelling force.

Musicians position themselves according to a specific genre and, in so doing, position themselves in relation to one another. Positions adopted by classical musicians are often based on rules of production, on the accumulation of myths and false certainties, and the way in which musicians move from one type of music and audience to another. Becoming either a popular and/or a classical musician, together with the motives and consequences of pursuing one type of music and audience rather than another, as well as the related artistic conventions of the one compared with the other, are issues related to, rather than independent of, family, schooling and social networks, and the rise of female musicians to become composers. Pippa helps us understand how institutional habitus has a guiding influence on what counts as a good idea, and she differentiates between distinct types of musical creativities. She makes it clear who plays important roles, what the struggles are, what is possible and what is not.

From the point of view of the properties of the different genres considered as economic and cultural enterprises, such as the size of the audience and the value of the recognition implied in the act of consumption, the value of creativity varies. The opposition between genres is manifest in: the relations of power between performances that are live and those that are pre-recorded for the media; in the contrast between the aesthetics of pop performance and classical music performance; and in the ways in which contemporary artists challenge fine art practices with their hybridization of traditional forms. It also shows in their foregrounding of commodification and popular culture, in references to 'high art' and 'low art', the elevation of 'the work' or 'the album', and in the creativities which inhere in scored songs compared to their performance, and the ways in which this is realized on record and in a broadcast, as compared to a live performance. These distinctions represent artistic capitals gained by association with consecrated institutions of music, and exemplify the habitus which is located in the social, and, so too, in the creative act. This is a key point for the present argument. For not only are there a wide variety of factors relevant to the positioning of songwriting and singer-songwriters within the field of music, but music's creativities are also linked to the social and cultural connections of key artists in terms of institutional and educational cultural capital.

Pippa's positioning of projects within the field

Pippa demonstrates a strong pattern of educational capital, which derives from her association with a classical music education. She recognizes she is located within a complex matrix of influences, which are best represented as overlapping circles of family, friends, and institutions. The relative weights of these spheres of influence shift and change over time and there is an inevitable degree of overlap and blurring of the boundaries between peer groups, family, and institutions. Her own successful experience as a singer, composer, songwriter and professional musician bestows artistic capital on her, and assists in her struggle for field position. She thinks that the different disciplines she has worked within should be more interdependent, and that the movement between them freer. Some of the challenges and obstacles of established cultural practice, such as styles of singing, are described as follows.

> *Pippa*: There were always problems with the compositions I was supposed to be writing. For one module, we had to write and perform more of our own music together, and it had to be band music that we'd all written together in the ensemble. And that added to the difficulty, because we were put together in these ensembles. This meant you don't pick the musicians you were with, and we had, like, a drummer who was second study, so he wasn't fantastic on drums, he was into ska and reggae music, he wanted to play drum beats like that. Then there were the keyboard players who wanted to play ska and funk. The guitar player wanted to play soul and R&B, and the other guitar player wanted to play metal.

Any new artist entering the field must negotiate the conventions. That is clear. However, the consequences—in the form of inhibitions to be overcome—this has had for Pippa's creative practice, and the reception of that practice is unclear. There may be hidden discrimination at a grassroots level, and instances of opposition. The latter caused Pippa to reflect on her learning in ways that can help us to recognize the power struggles between the conventions of specific genres, and how any deviations become meaningful only when seen against the conventions of a genre. One can add to this the very distinct conventions operating between the physicality and coded genre of classical singing, and the abstraction of amplification and the virtual space of loudspeakers. She talked about connections between dress code and musical taste.

> *Pippa*: These were all 18-year-old lads who seemed to be quite set in their ways. They looked like what they liked in music. They all came in with different dress styling, saying, 'this is the sound of me': both in the guise of associating clothes as badges of authenticity and identity; but obviously, for them, their sound wasn't me. I recognized in that session that all I wanted to do was to prove to them that I could sing and play my instrument and that I would stick up for myself, but in a nice way, without destroying their egos. Once I established my singing abilities, it got easier. I was no longer a classical sounding female oddity. I was a musician.

As Negus and Pickering (2004) argue, 'The limitations of conventions are not that they are accepted, but that they are accepted as natural and never questioned as such' (p. 90). Certain conventions are valued as defining characteristics of the creative process. This bears on the values underpinning performance-oriented, codified practices of pop and classical music, in both of which new creativities build on and emerge from existing cultural traditions. Female guitarists are seldom seen in a setup that is skewed in men's favour, and in terms of a whole range of material and cultural resources. In other words, female guitarists are more often seen in female-only bands. For Pippa, her projected identity is a dynamic and mutually assigned construction. It arises from interactions between people.

> *Pippa*: How you define yourself is relative to why and to whom you are defining yourself. I define myself differently to different people and for different purposes. To some people I am a singer. To some people I am a composer. For my current purposes in performance practice, I describe myself now as a songwriter not a composer. However, I describe myself as a composer within my current academic work. It's interesting because when you're singing, you are in your own skin, you look outwards, and you don't see yourself as a 'woman'. You see yourself as a musician, a person who can do anything.

There is an important principle of gender corresponding to song habitus that has been described as 'mutual enactment',[10] and which, like creativity, positions the artist and provides the relations in which capital is organized and valued. Gender, like class and race, is not a capital as such, but rather it provides the relations in which capital comes to be organized and valued (Skeggs, 2004).[11] Gender is a performative act that can be produced *in* performance by both performer and audience. So, when asked about her willingness to break with genre codes, and what she learned about prejudices against tradition, Pippa replies with a crucial point concerning how the social trajectories

---

[10] Frith (1996) coined the term 'mutual enactment' as identity produced in performance (p. 115). In contrast, G.D. Smith (2010) argues that an 'individual's identity may not be mutually enacted or shared with members of an audience'. 'While it is possible to perceive that another person may possess a certain identity, this does not, however, mean that one inhabits or embodies any part of that identity—one merely observes it' (pp. 59–60). Musicians, in their different performance contexts, are able to reconcile the conflict between their different dispositions to, and organization of, practice, their performance identities, and their ways of perceiving and perpetuating creative practices, which coexist with valued traditions.

[11] Skeggs' (2004)interesting article introduces different models of the self-proposed in contemporary theory. She makes a cogent case for how practice and relationships to objects and people are central as central in how value can be realized. She draws heavily on Bourdieu's theory of habitus.

and hierarchies internal to each of the genres differentiate them from one another according to the degree to which artists conform to the specific demands of the genre through institutions (or academies), which sanctions the ethical and aesthetic (and political) taste of the dominant genre. She defines herself and her position by the balance of capital values accumulated within that holding. She positions herself as the industry 'neophyte'[12] quickly learning how creativity is perceived and practised differently in different genres:

> *Pippa*: To be honest I struggle with the traditional Beethoven at the desk composing thing. I think it's not something that I've ever spent a lot of time doing. I'm naturally quite a sociable person. I really enjoy that. I find it very difficult to be in a room by myself for long periods of time. I've never really considered it an important thing to be autonomous, and it's not something that ever occurred to me until the last two years. It's been made clear to me that if I am to do well I have to do this for my academic work. And since working on the trip hop album . . . and various other projects, such as The Voice Collective and Mobile Jazz Cafe and Kaleidoscope Blue, it's become more apparent to me that it is important from a commercial point of view, and it's important from an academic point of view, mainly because it appears to be very difficult to give credit otherwise. This is the system playing out. I recognize that. I mean you're not meant to submit anything that isn't entirely your work for academic marking. And for me that has posed quite a problem. In the real world, we know that composers do work together; they do get help, they create short-term opportunities for those they turn to, they give opportunities not only for opening up opportunities for themselves but also for making connections. I've put a lot of effort into putting time aside, and really trying to work hard, having a better relationship with just working by myself, but to be honest it's not something that I would ever want to entirely base my career on. Because for me music is a sociable thing, it's something that should be a sociable thing; it's something that has always been a social thing. A composer on a project always faces the ins and outs of studio politics, the technical demands of scoring for an orchestra and other important and serious elements of the game to be played here. There's a lot of politics in getting known as a composer, developing a reputation, securing ties with others, and moving ahead are all crucial and related.

Most highly successful singers are also celebrities who construct subjectivities, not simply through their music but through the construction of a particularized sound identity. The strength of audience interaction and feedback depends very much on the performers: applause; exchanges of physical gestures between performers and listeners; the song itself; and the particular qualities of the singing. Beyond the assumed individuality of the voice, however, methods of expression necessarily tend to be codified in order to be understood by others: emotional power is portrayed not only through the melody but also through the voice.

> *Pippa*: The more classical, traditional compositions that I've been working on, like the one I'm writing for the New Music Ensemble, have a big element of wanting to engage the audience in the creation of the piece. It involves a lot of audience involvement and participation in it, and it involves the players interacting with the audience, and with everybody in the room making decisions that affect the overall outcome of the piece. The idea is that everybody makes the music together. The piece is never played the same twice, meaning not that the fundamental structure of the piece has changed but that there could be differences in timbre, in decoration, dynamics, techniques, intensity—points which might seem superficial and yet greatly affect the final performance as actually constructed by both musicians and audiences. Jamming, being experimental, being exploratory, inviting surprises are all important to me, something that I took to the classical musicians, and had to introduce carefully, and has having something more in common with central components of the style of popular musicians.

So what distinguishes her songwriting practice in Kaleidoscope Blue, a soul-pop band, The Mobile Jazz Café, a Zimbabwean jazz group, The Voice Collective, a covers band which features

---

12 A neophyte is a new convert, newly ordained, novice, or beginner.

her own arrangements of songs, and Malaika's Project, which features both her original songs and covers? What manifestations of music's creativity are at play and characterize these groups? How is musical creativity practised and expressed . . . in different or similar ways? What are the non-obvious and even surprising features about genres of music that adhere (or not) to traditional notions of compositional, improvisational, and performance creativities? Are there coherent categories of creativity in Pippa's creative work in a range of venues—pub, club, and special function bands?

> *Pippa*: I started songwriting collaboratively with Pascal, a very experienced Zimbabwean musician, who emigrated from Harare, for The Mobile Jazz Café . . . Pascal is in his forties and he's got a great deal of experience in pop and jazz and, but also in Zimbabwean traditional music. Pascal comes from a very oral tradition involving a vast number of different types of music. In Harare they have a lot of Western kind of jazz and pop influences, but that's all fused with folk music. Well, not always fused by any means, but there is that element. Since I was about 11 I have been listening to African folk/jazz fusion from a young age. I've learnt and am still learning about Shona music traditions from Pascal. We incorporate the aspects of the culture into our collaborative process. We jam along and improvise vocal lines, which are framed by written instrumental parts that other people play as an arrangement we've written. The ideas for this music come out of just sitting together and talking and playing music, it's a social kind of jamming process. I feel so much freedom and so much confidence, because you have the freedom to make music and experiment, and improvise. There is a kind of ranking system as to right and wrong within Shona traditional music. You've got a set pattern that you're playing within a piece, and you play or sing variants. You go where your voice takes you. It's not in the kind of way that, if you were playing classical music, you'd be expected to stick to the score and produce the perfect performance. It's very, very different in Shona traditional music. The cultural and historical traditions of this music are very important elements in my songs. Pascal might bring to the table a first riff, or part of the lyrics and we'll jam together for a while, then I'll write the rest.

Pippa is presently in the grip of writing and recording her first album. This is, she says, her true calling. She is writing 10 songs, all centred around 'Malaika', which means angel in Swahili.

> *Pippa*: Malaika's a bit of an alter ego. So it's a project about a spirit of inspiration, a kind of guardian angel of the soul. And it's based on a lot of my friends really, who I feel have had to give up homes and relationships in order to pursue their music. And I've got a friend—he just left and went all around Spain and around Mexico for nine months—and he's just got back. And so it was kind of based on him and all the other characters that I know that have done this. There are 10 songs, 10 lessons, and each of the songs is based on different types of artwork, so it's really important to me that this communication of a story derived from the inspiration of different types of artwork also communicates creativity in what the songs convey; the co-creation of message is important to me . . . I'm quite methodical about my writing . . . My lyric writing process is specific and involves what has been called 'destination writing', which is I write a narrative. Then I highlight external and internal information, make a toggling system, make a rhyme scheme and then I fit the information from the destination writing into those patterns. I have a diary, which I write ideas for songs in, and so these songs also draw from my experiences. But it is really as much about the meaning that is conveyed through both the words and the music as how the messages are then re-created by the listener. So, I write my lyrics and then I write chord ideas and then I work up the melody and the lyrics to those ideas, and then I start working on an arrangement. I know some songwriters write the melody first, and then write the lyrics. But for me, it's about getting the lyrics right in the first place. Chord sequences offer up their own melodies over the top, so do the words. It's all interdependent, the flow of the song, the writing process and being the architect of new combinations of imagery, of music and of song material which may then be accepted, rejected, fused into a new cultural shape by whoever listens and relates their experiences to them. If I'm as successful as Imogen Heap, I'll be happy.

This is a young songwriter wanting to define a new aesthetic through the songwriter's capital, which for her involved a fluid range of musical practices representing remarkably different values and approaches (Bowman, 2004).[13] On the one hand, there is recognition and competing principles of legitimacy corresponding to individual and their political overtones. On the other hand, there is the principle of legitimacy, which requires that she gain recognition in the broader social space, hence accruing symbolic cultural capital, which can then be deployed through songwriting creativities within the field of music. Pippa places importance on creativity and communication along with certain forms of collaborative and cultural creativities. She writes as part of a tradition that draws on the practice of inter-textual referencing through the integration of previous texts into new texts, by way of which meanings operate at several levels. This lends itself to an original synthesis of different musical practices.

Introducing Roshi

Roshi has had many years of formal music education and training, including the successful completion of an undergraduate music performance degree. She is a protean careerist, that is, she self-manages her career and practises as a singer, songwriter, and music workshop leader. She is a classically trained musician who was immersed in classical instrumental tuition as part of her formal music education during her primary and secondary schooling. She is, however, enthusiastic about jazz, folk, traditional Iranian music, and popular cultural forms and genres. Roshi is a musician with an interest in popular and traditional musics and cultures with ideas about creativity wrapped up in manifest forms of collective and cultural production.

Born in Wales to Iranian parents, Roshi Nasehi is a singer-songwriter who presents her own evocative songs alongside interpretations of Iranian songs. Her songs reflect her origins. Her band, Pars Radio, features the electronic soundscapes/beats of Graham (Dids) Dowdall (Gagarin, Nico, Pere Ubu etc.) together with classical cellist Rachel Threlfall and experimental cellist Richard Thomas (Now, The Hola). It's an unusual sound world created through songwriting as a craft (as, for instance, the Tin Pan Alley manufacture of popular songs for all occasions) and songwriting as self-expression—in other words art (expressive of Roshi's life course). Roshi provides us with a distinct approach to creating with tradition. She takes the musical heritage and tradition of Iranian music, particularly folk, with its ancient beginnings, and applies a new performance style, which is not defined by a pre-existing repertoire of rigid rules, and seeks to introduce different values and create new sound worlds. Roshi creates distinctive variations on traditional Iranian music culture, retaining aspects of musical and stylistic relevance whilst evolving into a new culture using new recording techniques that enable considerable manipulation of sound sources. This has been a decisive and conscious move by Roshi to create something that is fresh, new, and different.

Many traditions attribute aural traditions to a song repertoire that survives in living musicians. Schippers (2010) has described the living national treasures that countries such as Korea and Japan recognize as crucial players in the survival of music traditions as examples of this. Fascinating, in this context, is the phenomenon of traditions being preserved and handed down in ways that combine traditional values with 'nuances of contemporary musical realities' using new technologies (p. 46). The music of singer-songwriter Roshi, with her Iranian-influenced song production and performance techniques, illustrates a kind of *cultural creativity* which comes with the learning

---

[13] Bowman (2004) characterizes popular music by its '(a) breadth of intended appeal, (b) mass mediation and commodity character, (c) amateur engagement, (d) continuity with everyday concerns, (e) informality, (f) here-and-now pragmatic use and utility, (g) appeal to embodied experience, and (h) emphasis upon process' (pp. 34–5).

of certain skills, with reflexive thinking about its traditional modes of practice, its set parameters, and its unconsidered possibilities. Roshi's type of songwriting and production is realized by exploring how a changing present affects a tradition and how a tradition affects a changing present, as will be illustrated later in this chapter.

Like Roshi, popular music songwriters can work alone, writing songs for themselves to sing, or for a band, or within a partnership or band membership. For an example of the latter, take Radiohead's Thom Yorke, who is the band's vocalist, lyricist, and is one of a collective of songwriters. The band writes collectively and is credited collectively. Even if in interviews he talks about his part of the process he is only talking about his contribution. He can't really be called the main songwriter. Of his songwriting style during the sessions for *OK Computer*, he has said: 'Writing as a witness. That was my ideal. A series of pictures, not even colouring them in really'.[14] The songwriters can be individualists (Jerome Kern, Irving Berlin, Cole Porter, George Gershwin, Annie Lennox) or collaborators (Lennon and McCartney, Elton John and Bernie Taupin, Morrissey and Marr). There are songwriters, as mentioned earlier in this chapter, who collaborate with lyricists and arrangers, and others who do not even play an instrument, but use computers to become writers and arrangers and share ideas with lyricists with whom they collaborate online. Roshi is a musician and recording artist whose creativity functions at several levels. She is involved in: (1) the creation of new songs, either within the Iranian musical tradition or as an innovation fed by technological elements; (2) improvisation, which is an important feature of many genres of music; and (3) the interpretation of existing music. It is not uncommon, and is found in many traditions, for the role of creator and performer to be unified within a single person; it is also not uncommon to separate these functions, with specialized musicians composing the songs without necessarily being part of the performance. Roshi's creative energy and artistic creativity shows in how she performs the re-creation of tradition, finding ways through which past cultural texts, forms and practices are negotiated and appropriated.

Roshi's music has been variously labelled as 'folk-experimental', 'genre-crossing exotic folktronica', and 'stunningly beautiful Welsh-Iranian torch song electronica' by reviewers. Roshi and her band Pars Radio create an unusual sound world, rich with individual interpretation and stylistic experimentation, which strives to be both a manifesto on creativity and a critical reflection and response to the juxtaposition of the old and the new.[15] Pars Radio, her band, is co-opted as part of a single chain of meaning and values, where voice is woven into a soundworld of cellos and electronica, applied in different ways, in a complex interaction that links the past and present in the interpretation and refiguring of Iranian songs and Roshi's original songs.

Roshi's debut EP *And Stars* was first released in July 2008 by GEO Records on 10" and CD, and then re-released in January 2009 following widespread acclaim across Europe (see www.roshi.biz/about.html). Her follow-up album *The Sky and the Caspian Sea* was released in October 2009 to similar acclaim. She has also contributed to many compilations and, in March 2011, released another EP of traditional Iranian songs called *Mehregan* by invitation of the Rifmountain independent folk label, who are based in Essex. This EP was the experimental EP of the month in the February 2011 edition of *Mixmag* (Fig. 4.2). As I will presently demonstrate, a type of intercultural creativity underpins Roshi's work as singer-songwriter.

---

[14] This quote is taken from an interview with Phil Sutcliffe, originally from *Q* magazine, p. 133 (October 1997) in Tate (2005, p. 153).

[15] Source of quotes is a review of the Mehregan EP in the February 2011 edition of *Mixmag* (http://www.mixmag.net/). The review was written by journalist Joe Muggs.

Roshi Nasehi:
Welsh wonder

TUNE OF THE MONTH

ROSHI FEAT PARS RADIO
Mehregan EP RIF MOUNTAIN
Electronic Iranian dreamscapes
Born to Iranian parents in Wales,
Roshi Nasehi is one of the most
singular voices working at the
moment. Here she interprets
some of the Iranian songs she
heard growing up, with subtle
backing from regular collaborator
and veteran experimentalist
Graham Dowdall, aka Gagarin.
Roshi's voice, although powerful,
remains contemplatively-paced
and generally subdued, and the
atmosphere it creates is like being
swept up in someone else's dream
of other times and places. If you
like music you can escape into,
this is a must. ♫♫♫♫♫

Fig. 4.2 Singer-songwriter Roshi Nasehi and Graham Dowdall, aka Pars Radio, with a review of the Mehregan EP, written by journalist Joe Muggs (February 2011 edition of *Mixmag* magazine, www.mixmag.net).
Photo by Brian David Stevens. © Brian David Stevens, 2011.

Roshi's songwriting habitus and practice

Roshi's individual interpretations of Iranian folk songs, as with her own songs, are sites of *co-opted cultural creativity* inscribed in both song production and song performance. 'Co-opted' creativity because she inspires and stimulates uniqueness in those who play with her, and 'cultural creativity' because her songs invoke a mode of cultural production: they use unfamiliar and novel combinations of traditional (familiar) Iranian music in creative association with new sound worlds coming from, as described by one reviewer, 'somewhere between Kate Bush and subdued avant-garde pop'.[16]

Roshi trained as a classical musician. Familial, educational, and ethnic *habitus* plays a significant role in her decision-making and these three aspects of habitus are key influences that operate synergistically with her musical background. As we saw in earlier chapters, *habitus* is a dynamic concept, a rich interlacing of past and present, individual and collective. Bourdieu describes *habitus* as 'a power of adaptation. It constantly performs an adaptation to the outside world which only occasionally takes the form of radical conversion' (Bourdieu, 1993c, p. 88). Bourdieu (1973) argues that one's habitus develops in relation to how much cultural capital one has within the given field. Roshi conveys a rich past of cultural texts, forms, and social actions, which are negotiated and appropriated in relationships played out at the school level.

> *Roshi:* I started playing the piano when I was nine years old. I had this very nice, but quite eccentric local provincial piano teacher who had lots of pets . . . She was encouraging, and I enjoyed it. There was

[16] See footnote 24.

a big singing culture in Wales; I sang a lot in school, and my dad played traditional Iranian violin music. My dad started re-exploring his violin when I started playing the piano. It was something instinctive. He plays traditional Iranian music on the violin, which is something that he learnt as a child. Hearing music in the family home encouraged me and encouraged him to buy a violin and to once again play the music of his origin, and mine. Being a first-generation Iranian he brought with him the musical heritage of his home country. But this musical culture appeared to be tightly conceived. Both parents played tapes of Iranian songs all the time. Mum would sometimes play classical music as well but at home the main music played was Iranian music in the most traditional sense. There were times when Dad would play an Iranian tune . . . he'd play it over and over to enable me to get the feel of it . . . he'd talk about some of the traditional aspects . . . we'd then try out some ideas together . . . I'd begin to play out another part on the piano . . . which I'd mix and fuse with classical bits.

Bourdieu argues that, next to taste in food, taste in music is the most ingrained. Roshi is passionate (and people do *love* their music) about the Iranian songs she grew up hearing. She experiences them as second nature. It is *felt*. The significance of music in the construction of identities and ethnicities is paramount in Roshi's deep-seated gravitation towards Iranian music. The centrality of this music, the way it was transmitted as a single cultural model directly from her parents, without explicit reference to other musics, is further indicated by the fact that, amongst all the realities of learning classical music, the inclination and talent required to learn it, and acquire a classical repertoire, were incremental and participatory. There was no formalized learning. Perceptions and expectations are significant because of the way in which they connect what constitutes creativity to the views, advice, and learning experiences of school friends, teachers and families. For Roshi, valuing the heritage music of first generation Iranian parents gets played out at a creativity level: it has a key role in transmitting cultural capital and uniquely defining her. While recognizing how enmeshed familial and institutional habitus are, Roshi articulates the significance of an institutional influence over and above the direct impact of family background (although it is clear that some families choose schools for their children to ensure access to particular institutional habitus).

Roshi: It was when I went to music college that creativity started playing a role in my playing and interpretations of pieces. I started having lessons from a world-class pianist. It was here that I learned the most directly musical of things is probably expression and musicianship. But then I was forced to have another rethink about myself when my teacher rightly told me that 'You're not bad. Look, you're even musical, and you got into in the college, OK because you're musically creative, but you don't really have much technique, and if you really want to make it as a pianist you need to practise for six hours a day, and you need to do your scales, and you need to do this, and you need to do that.' OK, so I wasn't a child prodigy who'd played a piece I'd composed myself at six years old with hands like Liszt! I had a go at it for about a year, but this routine and regime of becoming a technically brilliant musician takes so much practice and this wasn't for me really. It was very solitary. I didn't feel it was creative. While I felt there was potential for creativity, in the end, what I had to do in that moment wasn't creative at all, it was very much purely technique-based stuff . . . I spent a whole year working up a Chopin piece and others like that, I can't even contemplate or picture that now. I've come to understand I'd missed getting the kind of rigorous training which people need to have if they're going to become classical players and go on to be a world-class concert pianist. So I changed to composition in my second year, because I thought that would be more creative. But in a way that too had its own dogma.

So many music traditions, including Western and Eastern classical musics (as with jazz), insist on a long apprenticeship with a master. Becoming a 'technically brilliant musician' (i.e. acquiring mastery of an instrument and related performer's skills) requires countless hours of practice. The view that mastery requires rigid and prolonged exposure and absorption through an intense regime of regular lessons with an expert has become mythologized and romanticized in

Western music worlds[17] and has been well documented. But this is not necessarily common with singer-songwriters.

In a similar vein, the claim that creating new work in Western art music is associated with an inspired individual—usually a genius composer—sitting at the piano in his study painstakingly moulding or divinely pouring musical ideas into a masterwork; or that the instrumentalist/singer requires instrumental/vocal virtuosity to make it as a performer, are specific manifestations of myths in music, myths about music, and myths of music's production. Key to these beliefs is the role played by institutional habitus, which impacts directly on students' secondary and higher education destinations through the quality and quantity of subject and career advice provided in music.

Although Roshi doesn't question how she came to self-select herself out of the concert pianist career trajectory on the basis of her views of what is possible and what is not, she does question how people form impressions and identities around musical canons and recognizes how familial exposure to Iranian music increased her musicality and fundamentally changed the direction of her musical life and her songwriter creativity. She refers to the increasingly pervasive impact of creativity and creative strategies to engage with traditional and improvised musics. As Roshi indicates in her discussion of jazz (along with familial exposure to Iranian music), whilst improvisation plays only a modest role in contemporary approaches to the Western classical traditions, the concept does arise in her practice and persona as a songwriter. This provides additional support for the idea that the role of creativity is differently positioned at greatly differing levels of cultural capital in relation to the institutional habitus.

> *Roshi*: I came away from music college having invested a lot of time studying things that didn't seem all that significant to me. There is one exception though and that (one of the most significant and transforming experiences in terms of my musical life at the institution and my professional future) was getting involved in Keith Tippett's work at the jazz department. He ran free improvisation sessions and the college Big Band, and I was invited to sing in the Big Band.

One of the hallmarks of Roshi's development and deployment of 'creative practices' is the intergenerational transmission (i.e. handing down) of cultural capital (of the Iranian songs she was brought up listening to). Foucault's (1977, 1980) work on the construction and regulation of subject discipline and identity is helpful here, in that Roshi's identity as a musician, a singer-songwriter, is not simply imposed from above but is also actively determined by other individuals through a mix of family upbringing, and familiarity with culture and self-stylization. With Roshi, this shows in the complex movement back and forth between a variety of contexts in which she begins to integrate fully the insights from her earlier acquisitions of cultural capital (passed down by the family, particularly her father) and access to Iranian music with the social capital and currency of improvised practices powerfully underpinned by institutional and ethnic habitus.

> *Roshi*: Iranian musicians coming from the classical music tradition learn a huge amount of repertoire that's based on a complex modal structure and Iranian musicians learn to extemporize or improvise on these modes. So it's not dissimilar to jazz musicians, who may also learn all these kinds of things and in this way in order to play and extemporize on jazz standards, something which was taken further by Miles Davis in *Kind of Blue*, where he effectively developed modal jazz . . . My relationship with Iranian music is very much about performing individual songs. I mean sometimes I may know which mode a song happens to be in, but it doesn't really inform how I then present it in a very different sound world, with non-Iranian musicians playing non-Iranian designed and crafted musical instruments, working in

---

[17] See discussions on myths in Chapter 1. For more discussions on myths see Blanning (2008), Cook (1998), Small (1998) and the seminal text on myths by Weisberg (1986).

contemporary performance styles involving unusual arrangements of piano, experimental electronic, and string layers, etc.

It's not hard to spot how Roshi both expresses cultural values and creates musical practices through them. Using a dynamic approach to the Iranian music tradition, deriving its existence from a continuous process of change and innovation, the old music is continually exposed to new influences. Schippers (2010) describes approaches to tradition as a continuum from a 'static tradition' (which is characterized by a large corpus of songs aurally transmitted with specific meanings and tightly conceived uses, built on a closed system where musicians perform on specified instruments significantly without musical variety) to music traditions that are in 'constant flux' (from different interpretations by contemporary performers).

Roshi clearly recognizes her Iranian musical heritage and has the ability to make use of the legacy of cultural capital—her repertoire of artistic knowledge, values, beliefs, and information; she also has command over its application, which is necessary for her as a singer-songwriter to gain entry into the social circles and settings required for artistic recognition. She makes an explicit connection between culture and creativity when explaining the tangible structural forces used to create her music and its original soundworld:

> *Roshi*: In terms of arranging the Iranian songs, I make creative decisions that are born out of improvising as the essence in the moment of creating . . . something changes but many of the cultural ingredients are still present. I provide a kind of pre-planned framework, which we follow but, together with the other musicians in the band, we move between the purely exploratory to the more intentionally expressive musical possibilities, which opens up a lot of different kinds of sonic possibilities.

This means Roshi values highly, and draws heavily from, her understanding of the Iranian songs she chooses to explore and that being creative lies in taking the opportunities for extending and varying, transforming and elaborating, using acoustic and electrically or digitally generated forms. Roshi's view of the world, and her place in it, is an important consideration in trying to understand how songwriters navigate and assert cultural creativity in developing modern cultural products.

Studies of the effects of cultural capital on the educational success of male and female students have reached contradictory conclusions, and few studies have considered the role that habitus plays in ascribing creativity dimensions to educational outcomes (Dumais, 2002). However, in terms of Roshi's dispositional view of the world and her place in it, the stereotypes of the genius composer and child prodigy seem to have played a significant role in determining the model of creative practice she comes to develop later in her life.

> *Roshi*: And whereas other more traditional colleges would maybe have been doing Glenn Miller, and stuff like that, I really valued Keith Tippett, who is such a global figure, bringing us his own music, and music from South African jazz musicians like Dudu Pukwana and Mongezi Feza (who came to London in the 60s after realizing that the only way they could play freely was by escaping the oppressive social and political climate of their home country). Most importantly Keith led us to find our own music . . . I also got very interested in contemporary classical music and this contributes a lot to the ways I think about conventions across particular cultural forms and processes of change. An example of this is with George Crumb, an American composer. One of his pieces in particular, Vox Balaenae (The Voice of the Whale), made a really big impression on me. It's a trio for amplified flute, cello, and piano. I played and performed the piano part at college and Rachel (who I've gone on to work with in Pars Radio) played the cello part. It exemplifies processes of change and the use of extended instrumental techniques (for example he uses the inside of a piano) for genuine expressive purposes . . . It was around this time that I also got interested in the cultural elements of Iranian traditional music, in addition to jazz and I think these things will definitely stay with me.

Roshi shares a passion for creative engagement with musics that allow her to learn from them. She brings this passion to her band, whose members also learn from each other and share an interest and passion in this domain. Creativity in practice involves certain skills, experiences and tools, which they actively use in their practice. They continuously construct norms and structures through a creative process in which individual players explore a type of cultural creativity that is collaboratively developed. As such, Roshi utilizes the creative fertility of a directed ensemble.

Roshi's positioning of projects within the field

One of the principles inscribed in Roshi's world, a world endowed with cultural meanings and with valued practices, is to immerse herself in a performance which is indeterminate and contingent, with no *one* person in control—in a space of artistic possibility. Everything happens in the moment, and what is particularly salient is how the performance emerges from the actions of all those in her band. She is not purposefully breaking with conventions but rather helping to write into the music at each moment, an invention of musical space:

> *Roshi*: With Roshi featuring Pars Radio I think the nucleus of what it represents is about creating space in relation to each other; what I'm singing and what we're playing unites us. The creative decisions are about pure manifestations of sound and sound combinations. I'm inspired by the distinction of sound. I may sometimes use my keyboard in particular ways when the cellists are playing drones. But my intention here and my creative ethos are to work with the pure manifestations of space and simplicity. It feels much like a search where I'll begin playing a few notes at a time, then I'll be singing a kind of backing vocal part, which again will be purposively simple . . . I think much of this project is born out of improvising, actually. It has come out of listening to the music, of just coming up with ideas; a kind of new reading each time we play using a simple framework, founded on periodic turns and internal correspondences of narrative elements, situations, characters, locations, repeated several times with modifications. It's much more ethereal . . . an atmosphere created through the combinations of sounds and rhythms, it leads much more towards the kind of something where people should listen, and we're trying to kind of . . . You know, with the films as well, that we're showing (which were specially made for our songs by artist James English).

Roshi talks about a 'creative ethos'—a durable and generative disposition that guides and perpetuates one dimension, which aesthetically unites the other players in her group and from which 'the nucleus' is another dimension. This is how she communicates how the music is itself designed to function by 'what it represents'—by giving off a certain 'atmosphere'. This unifying principle is none other than dispositions, which create a sense of specialness, of immediacy, of qualities that make her music different and distinctive. This is an established group. It co-opts creativity gently oriented to 'what it represents'. In fact, her songs seem to have their own laws, they seem to exist in the form of a *song habitus,* born of a collective functioning as a sort of historical transcendental, whose norm is impressed, at each moment, on all the players.

> *Roshi*: We each respond according to the atmosphere. So, for instance, I write the lyrics of the song in such a way that there's a sense in which we can end the song flexibly. Flexibility of endings is important. It's very rare for us to say it's going to absolutely end at this point like this, and there's definitely been times when we've let things go on longer, or we've moved from one thing more quickly to the next thing, because we've felt, together, in the moment, that's been the right thing to do. And I mean I think that's happened, you know innumerable times I've had that experience. These kinds of flexible structures help us to develop a kind of collective modus operandi, and is the source of space . . . sometimes in gigs people have suddenly started dancing, and obviously it would be crazy to stop the music then. Although with this music it is more likely that it will be people sitting and listening, particularly when it's in a smaller more intimate venue, rather than a kind of outdoor stage venue. But you still pick up the

reactions of the audience I think, and respond creatively to it, and perhaps change what we're doing in response to that.

Roshi's narrative leads us to the principles of the performance creativity at play in her music. This creativity is orchestrated with other creativities, as with that of a habitus orchestrated with other habitus. The creative norm is shared, impressed and exchanged, at each moment, between players and between players and audience; such a creative relationship engenders the same assumptions and anticipations, which, ordinarily being confirmed through the performance, gives meaning to the act of music creativity in which they are immersed. This basis of the experience of creativity is the song habitus, the propensity of them all to orient themselves towards Roshi's project, recognizing her *position* as the leader and their capacity to realize her aspirations, which are recognized as legitimate. The subjective relationship that one musician maintains with another, at each moment, within the space of possibilities, depends very strongly on the possibilities which are granted. In this regard Roshi has the *recognition* and *respect* of her musical peers and this is *reciprocal*. Roshi has won recognition, making her mark and initiating a new sound, differentiating herself from other songwriters. Musicians' habitus can come together to establish a new legitimate configuration, thus establishing new forms of collaborative creativity. This is illustrated by the mutually constituting effect of key musicians' habitus and their positions in the music field; habitus influencing position and vice versa. For these musicians, *trust* and *respect* are crucial elements of their professional identity, and their creative selves, a world into which Roshi fits easily.

> *Roshi*: I respect these musicians very much, and I think if they wanted to write something for this project I'd be really happy to engage with it. Rachel doesn't really see herself as a writing musician, She sees herself as a classical cellist, and I think this is probably her most sort of contemporary project. The rest of her playing involves orchestral playing and things like that. Richard is involved in several projects and is really active as an improviser. Graham is also in many projects. He's writing and recording solo electronica under the name of Gagarin and working with really incredible bands like Pere Ubu. He's very prolific. Working together started really organically where, you know, I was playing by myself and people were inviting me to perform in various places, and I kind of thought oh it'd be really nice to have Graham for this particular concert. I thought it would be really nice to have Rachel, because we're good friends. And then it just felt really good. It kind of continued. Richard came in because we had this gig in a gallery space and Rachel couldn't do it but we still wanted cello. It became very clear that he was more than just a 'dep' and could bring something of his own so we decided to work with both him and Rachel. Although it's my project, meaning I'm bringing the material that we work with—it's interesting what comes out of all these different musicians with all their different experiences, and the way they may interpret certain things, and the things that they might add to the song. The combination of sounds is something that I find really interesting. I do still play other songs in which nothing else is needed, and it can be quite self-contained, just me on the piano, or it might be piano, or my voice and a loop pedal or it might be piano and just electronics, and then I'll need the string lines on a particular song so there's flexibility within all of this. We don't all play together all the time.

Although it is easy to lump songwriters in with musicians or artists, songwriters do hold a unique place in that, as Bourdieu (1996) aptly describes in relation to the notion of 'original project' they 'make a free and conscious act of *autocreation* by which the creator assigns himself his life's project' (p. 188; original emphasis). The songwriter draws on a specific domain of knowledge (or symbol system): a language of music, a knowledge of song structure, of lyric construction and associated conventions. The song habitus is a complex domain, which is 'the result of a long process of inculcation . . . which becomes a "second sense" or a "second nature"' (R. Johnson, 1993, p. 5). Once a songwriter has access to this stored information, that is, the accumulated field of works (a concept developed by Bourdieu in his book *Rules of Art* (1996)) of songwriting, they can manipulate this system to add to the wealth of the extensive popular song tradition. But the creative qualities that we would characterize as being the outcome of the individual creator, stand, according to Foucault (1977) in relation to the social function or multi-voiced discourse of authoring a song. He points out that the role of 'authorship' becomes one not of identifying who is designated author but rather the conditions of authorship. For Foucault, 'the function of an author is to characterize the existence, circulation, and operation of certain discourses within society' (1977, p. 124). In other words, the songwriter becomes a function of connecting individuals and discourses and makes their meanings mean something as part of a multi-voiced discourse.

Research suggests that the way songwriters learn to write is by imitating and emulating that which inspires them until their own styles gradually emerge (Green, 2001)—getting a 'feel for the game'. The charismatic representation of the songwriter is, according to McIntyre (2011) (who draws heavily on Bourdieu's 1993 concept of *habitus* in his analysis of songwriting and studio bands),[18] found to be inscribed in the position of the songwriter (in this case Roshi) at the heart of the field of production and the totally specific social space (her family) in which her (Roshi's) 'own project' is formed.

> *Roshi*: I practise a mix of things. I may score things before we meet for Rachel, who is used to reading as a classical player. Sometimes I do that, sometimes I write things out and . . . Richard as well can read, does read . . . and so that's sometimes a kind of quick and easy way. But then there's the other times where I haven't done that, and I've said oh you know, I can hear strings, but I'm not sure in which way. I might play something or might ask Richard to improvise something. I never write things down or notate things for Graham, because he doesn't read, so with him it's more kind of descriptive words I suppose, or just . . . all of us just, you know . . . I may just play, and then you know, ask . . . and they may just join in if they have an idea. So yeah, there's a lot of kind of different ways I think, even with Rachel, who's used to reading, and I can write, I can notate to an extent, . . . there are times when I won't do that because I may not have the faintest idea, and it may be nice to kind of hear . . . because, you know obviously they know their instruments much better than I do, what they think would really work, . . . Yeah, so it's kind of different ways. And then we've kind of no need to write anything down. But then there are other songs that are played very rhythmically and in that instance I may notate something. There's another song that I've written (called 'She Paces/And Stars') that the beginning is very rhythmic and it changes time marked by Graham's beats and with specific melodic patterns. Rachel plays a kind of plucked line that underpins what I'm playing on the keyboard. And Richard recently has been playing typewriter in that song. [laughs]

The point here, importantly, is that Roshi's creativity of practice can be characterized by how the borderline between the composing and improvising—like that between folk and experimental—is a fluid, constantly morphing one. Roshi's songwriting involves a significant degree of moment-by-moment, or improvised, creativity of the most obvious kind. But not every utterance will be novel. In the course of the song there may be hundreds if not thousands of musical events that seem to come from nowhere, and yet this is simply not the case. The collective consciousness, or 'cultural memory', of Roshi and her band's musicians means that the song's basic material is distributed within the community, rather than being either the property or the song of an individual.

> *Roshi*: I am extremely proud of the records that we've made, while I initially found the process challenging, you know, standing back and listening to the record, . . . To some extent I deferred to Graham as the producer to help me relax about the mix of elements on the record. I think we were able to

---

18 Bourdieu (1993a) 'a feel for the game', a 'practical sense' (*sense pratique*) that includes agents to act and react in specific situations in a manner that is not always calculated and that is not simply a question of conscious obedience to rules. Rather it is a set of dispositions that generate practices and perceptions (p. 5).

achieve this in terms of arranging the songs, and in terms of different ideas for production that's often gone in different directions in the moment, because you know, you're kind of listening back to things, and you think, well actually I could add a harmony here, or assert a different cultural interpretation there. I've begun to do this also in soloist mode using a loop pedal, and by layering up my voice, and multi-tracking of voices, you can achieve a lot of different kinds of sonic possibilities. I feel very excited about putting technology to work like this and putting new ideas out there.

My point here is that musical improvisation is a creativity of songwriting practice that shares its history with classical music, jazz and popular musics. For example, the jazz idiom in which skilled and deliberate jazz improvisers may perform a jazz standard, such as 'Summertime' by George Gershwin, pays witness to the borderline between composing and improvising. If we take a popular music example, then the two versions of 'Morning Bell' (on the album *Amnesiac*) will serve to symbolize the creativity of Radiohead in demonstrating how the borderline between music and noise—like that between rock and techno—is a fluid, constantly morphing one. In contrast, on the band's *Kid A* album, 'Morning Bell' is a tour de force in vocalic doubling and complex fusion of fragmented voice with machinic instrumentals. The difference lies in how the voice is used in song performance to either underscore, as subordinated to the instrumentals, in one version or pitched to resonate with the instrumentals in the other. This shows how the creativities of song performance can produce an expanded range of expressions that require an expanded account of the experience of creativity itself in the phenomenon of songwriting and song performance (and its contemporary Iranian legacy, as extended by Roshi).

Roshi's account of the creativity of songwriting practice, as multiple modalities, in effect, by collaborative/co-opted practice in a composed and improvised continuum, constitutes a temporal synthesis that affords an insight into a particular kind of cultural creation in which song performance is embodied.

> *Roshi:* It's a shared musical outcome. It can be something which is repeatable, or part fixed, so it changes with each performance Sometimes we fix on certain ideas, sometimes you think yeah, that's the line, that's the cello's lines, and this is what I'm going to play. But there may be some flexibility in the way that I sing or Graham may have a pattern or particular cool sound that he's using, and again there may be some flexibility in the order.

Roshi comes to the music profession from a culturally situated standpoint. Her cultural heritage exists because of those disposed, and able, to assure its continued reactivation. Roshi's song performance is also underpinned by a generative principle that draws on her Iranian heritage. This is particularly well illustrated in the song called 'Rachid Khan' (Rachid Khan is the name of the historical figure whose lover fears he has died in battle). In the recorded version there are cello drones and Roshi plays the strings on the inside of the piano. The song is performed[19] much slower than is traditionally the case to reflect the sadness in the words. A rough translation: Today is 2 days 'laloo'/Tomorrow will be 3/Rachid has not come/My heart burns/Rachid Khan the great/General of the town of 'Ghoochan' ('laloo' is similar to a female confidante). This is an Iranian folk song which is very sad and of historical character. It is sung from the perspective of his lover, who's saying to her confidante that she fears that he's died in battle. Traditionally, it is performed quite fast.

One only has to listen to one track of Roshi's album to recognize the conscious undertaking of intercultural creativity and of the force of social origin on which it is based. Roshi's father, Vahid Nassehi, provides the opening melancholic violin accompaniment in 'Zeeba Kenar' ('Beautiful

---

[19] Examples of Roshi's song performance are featured on the album *The Sky and the Caspian Sea*, which can be found at http://itunes.apple.com/us/album/and-stars-feat-pars-radio-ep/id283445469.

Corner'), one of the eight original compositions on the album. The songs and arrangements are subtle and low-key throughout, with Roshi's voice and jazz-tinged keyboard (usually piano) framed in a lattice of textural blips, scrapes, and interference from collaborator Graham Dids; cellists Rachel Threlfall and Richard Thomas add further colour and intercultural exchanges to the songs. Harmonically and lyrically, Roshi draws on her Iranian heritage, painting pictures of family visits to Iran in 'Night Swimming' and 'No Camels', celebrating illegal female swimming trips under cover of darkness, and meditating on conflicting feelings during a flight home. 'I'll take you back to my home in Wales/You'll be welcomed, you won't feel strange' she promises on 'We'll Go Down' with its ominous dissonant strings, and in the wonderfully titled 'Pills and Sheep' she laments that 'Pills and sheep seem unable to soften the fear' over starkly minimal piano chords, before breaking down into extended repetitions of 'I'm crumbling' as the song fades. In one of the traditional songs, 'Lor Batche' ('Lor Children'), Iranian folk and urban beats come together and feature layered vocal loops, which bring to mind Laurie Anderson.

Her album *The Sky and the Caspian Sea* has been applauded in reviews for 'refusing to be categorised' and for having 'an entrancing otherworldliness and admirable disregard of conventional song form'.[20] This, along with her previous album (see Fig. 4.2) illustrates a recognition of the value of the work in the discourses of direct or disguised celebration, which are among the social and cultural conditions of the music's manifestations of creativities.

This is Roshi making her mark, winning recognition; it means that she has created a new position, ahead of the positions already occupied, in the vanguard of popular songwriting. It illustrates the importance, in this creative struggle for survival (in accordance with the logic which characterizes the field of music and the recording industries), of all the marks and signs that establish a distinct identity.

This account of cultural creativity provides the background against which Roshi's life course, cultural experiences and skill set (habitus) is inscribed in her biography and the social world. Two conclusions follow: firstly, Roshi's identification with the cultural styles of song performance; and, secondly, the close correspondence that is found between positions and dispositions. The cultural values guiding her in her project produce creative possibilities which are a product of the relationship between, as Toynbee (2000) argues, 'the "push" of subjective disposition and the "pull" of objective positions' (p. 38). Crucially, possibilities emerge that are representations of her creative and reflexive self.

The song-performance schema and cultural practice attached to the use of drones, atmospheres, sonic textures, and her dad's solo, demonstrate Bourdieuan style 'strategies of distinction made possible by criticism [by reviewers in this case] [that] owe their particular effectiveness to the fact that they rely on a "total" oeuvre, which gives its author the right to import into each domain the totality of the technical and symbolic capital acquired in others' (Bourdieu, 1996, p. 210). In other words, Roshi's practice is shaped by multiple, interacting forces, including the cultural preferences and tastes that are formed in her family of origin. Bourdieu maintains that the cultural experiences in the home facilitate children and young people's adjustment to school and academic achievement, thereby transforming cultural resources into what he calls cultural capital (Bourdieu, 1977a,b; Lareau, 1987). As in other social relationships, family-school interactions carry the imprint of the larger social context, and individuals' experiences of musical culture and cultural forms can be a crucial mechanism through which music provides materials for creativity.

---

[20] Review in the online Freq magazine (http://www.freq.org.uk/reviews/roshi-featuring-pars-radio-sky-caspian-sea/).

The sense of creative or reflexive self and the 'meaningful particles that "reflect" and register self-identity, that provide a template of self' can be found in music (DeNora, 1999, pp. 31–56).

Third, in an understanding of Roshi's song habitus, building on Bourdieu's concept of habitus, which functions as a sort of 'historical transcendental' (1996, p. 271), we see Roshi's production of the songs reflects having the dispositions to act in a certain way, to grasp experience in a certain way, to think in a certain way, from which Roshi's positioning of cultural production, in terms of Iranian music's norms, as well as the transformative action of co-opted creativity is actualized, at each moment, as a type of *intercultural creativity*.

In principle, Roshi, in collaboration with her band, Pars Radio, creates a new technique, leading to new possibilities (in 'real life', as in her mind) for a given song, a songwriting style, and a song performance. The difference, as remarked above, is that the tradition can be changed, as can the musical styles. The deepest cases of musical creativity involve someone's thinking something, with respect to the music and its performance, which they couldn't have thought without the processes implemented in performance. A new style of music can come about if the creator/s change the pre-existing style in some way. It must be tweaked, interpreted, or even radically transformed, so that thoughts are now possible which previously (within the untransformed space) were literally inconceivable. This happens mainly in the song performance.

Whilst methods for navigating, interpreting, and changing traditional musics are well documented (see Schippers, 2010), Roshi illustrates how *intercultural creativity* uniquely defines her song production and performance style (i.e. the production of culture), and this is critical to thinking about the implicit developments in musical culture as expressed in the form of collaborative and cultural forms of creative practice. This is the key dimension of creativity, which leads to *innovation* because it is the source of challenge to rules and conventions.

Concluding remarks

Both Pippa's and Roshi's projects illustrate how *intercultural creativity* operate as a discourse between continuity and change. Bringing existing cultural elements together in a different arrangement is endowed with creative significance. In the process cultural and symbolic capitals are apprehended and accumulated in terms of interaction and self-fashioning in the face of differences (as in the process of choosing material artefacts and emblematic activities, and refashioning their relationships). All of this contributes to creative cultural production—to the sense of what is new and what the practice of 'cultural creativity' involves.

Both Roshi and Pippa are songwriters, working with new and traditional sources and performance elements, re-creating and re-interpreting ideas as cultural producers occupying a legitimate position. Roshi makes the most of the influence afforded by the accumulation of cultural capital—the repertoire of Iranian and artistic knowledge, values, beliefs, and information—and command over its application, which has gained her considerable artistic recognition. The generation of creativity ranges from cultural variation and counterstatement to abrupt breaks and fresh starts. A quality of newness accompanies her music. But, of course, there is new—and then there is new to the tradition. Pippa employs cultural practices and values cultural forms of expression and meanings which give her freedom from constraint of others and which facilitate the interests of capital. Of course, songwriters can and frequently do come up with ideas that are new to them, even though they may have been picked up from their culture or peer group, or borrowed from other cultures. In either case, they are already there: they are not originated by one individual mind. They include ways of writing songs, of playing and combining sounds—in short, any disciplined musical way of thinking that is familiar to (and valued by) a certain social group. Someone who comes up with a bright idea is not necessarily less creative just because someone else also had that idea before they did. However, if the novel combination is to be valued by us, it has to have some point.

The type of *collaborative creativity* maintained and embedded in the singer-songwriters' practices featured in this chapter are interestingly different from the forms of music's creativity demonstrated in earlier and later chapters. Both singer-songwriters accrue value in collaborative projects in which musical associations and ensembles produce their own social relations in performance. Not all songwriters do this sort of thing. For Roshi and Pippa, positioning their songwriting and song performance at the interface of cultural forms of expression (such as to articulate alternative notions of ethnic identity) and the market values of cultural heritages (and the locally situated nature of such experimentations with ethnic identity)[21] makes self-making and self-extension by experimentation possible. Here the self becomes a project to be worked on and extended; a self that reflects upon itself while simultaneously externalizing itself from social relations so that it can reflect and plan its future actions. Both singer-songwriters are defined by their individuality and reflexive self.[22] The emphasis is on the individual singer-songwriter's unique but shared access to particular knowledge. Their collaboration with other musicians is a source of value and is also their route to diverse creativities, including the expression of individual, collaborative, and intercultural creativities. Musicians, as Toynbee (2000)[23] argues, identify and select musical possibilities from what he describes as 'inside the radius of creativity' (p. 57): choices made within the field of works that intersect with the musician's habitus and the rules of the field (or canons) that they operate in.

Both Roshi and Pippa, although unable to escape structural forces in general, can decide on which forces to act on and which to ignore. Both live out, biographically, the complexity and diversity of the dominant symbolic value system or dominant theories of popular music songwriting in the music industry that surrounds them (see McIntyre, 2010). As Pippa's and Roshi's songwriting practices have distinctively shown, cultural differences, the requisite reflexivity, and access to particular cultural knowledge and techniques can play a significant role in making distinctions between, and the development of, intercultural and collaborative creativities. It is this model of the singer-songwriter habitus accruing value in the conversion of its different forms of cultural capital, be it consciously or unconsciously, that, I maintain, expands the notion of music's creativities. We should be alert to such shifts in the dominant forms of music's creativities, especially in the recognition of the nature of the value that is attributed to collaborative and intercultural creativities.

---

[21] Back (1996) offers a useful model for understanding the locally situated nature of such experimentations with ethnic identity with the notion of 'cultural intermezzo', which refers to a space in which different cultural sensibilities merge and new identifications are formed.

[22] The *reflexive self* is one of several different concepts of self discussed by Skeggs (2004), who argues that the cultural resources for self-making and the techniques for making the self can be made from cultural practices, which can then be stored in the self. This is then related to Bourdieu's notion of habitus, which is premised upon the self-accrual process, which in turn conceives of culture as an exchangeable value in which some activities, practices and dispositions can enhance the overall value of personhood.

[23] Toynbee (2000) draws primarily on Bourdieu's work on cultural production, whereby it is suggested that 'the musician-creator (individual or collective) stands at the centre of a radius of creativity. The creator identifies and selects musical possible within this radius according to her habitus, but also the rules of the field of musical production—conventions, techniques and so on. Crucially, options here are tightly constrained in that the radius of creativity traverses a limited set of possibles' (p. 21).

Key points

1. **Intercultural creativity** emerges out of, and builds on, existing cultural traditions—that is, it requires a tradition to build on and access to the cultural resources for self-making as singer-songwriters develop the semblance and interplay of **individual** and **collaborative** creativities.

2. The defining practice of **intercultural creativity** is the desire for a degree of continuity—through socially reconstructed selections of tradition—and for change, realized in creative activities that accrue value in cultural conversion and exchange. Value inheres in the creativities that these singer-songwriters practise as variations on styles of performance, while building new types of musical relationships and using new technologies.

3. Intercultural creativity can be explained in terms of what is culturally inherited and what is reconstituted by creativity's requirement for renewal by extension and transformation. As illustrated in this chapter, songs are often constructed in a sequence of multiple takes, overdubs, and editing, which constitute separate creativities that can become manifest at the level of **intercultural** practices. These practices are not only open to negotiation but are often renegotiated with the singer-songwriter's collaborators (to realize creative possibilities) in live performances and performances for the media. We may hear identical versions of a song of central significance in the recording work or we may hear different renditions of a song in performance. Either way, a strong performative element inheres in the many manifestations of a song performance across different kinds of creativities, which are articulated in different ways at different times and in different combinations, whether in the scored or non-scored work of singer-songwriters, including: (a) song performances for studio recordings; (b) song performances in live concerts (and in live concert recordings, where there may be a set of rules of artistic production applied but where song performance and an editorial song work element converge); (c) scored song work (which can involve compositional and improvisational modes of creativity) of specially recorded studio sessions (for an album, single versions or remixes); and (d) unscored song work involving collaborative creativity in specially recorded sessions.

4. The sheer diversity of creativities that emerge in relation to singer-songwriters illustrate that songwriting has a performative dimension right from the start. This is also illustrated in the importance of cultural meetings and regionalism, which provide opportunities for **intercultural** creativity, involving cultural practices, through the formation of a *dominant set of cultural repertoires*. These inspire the **individualism** of the singer-songwriter in ways that bring existing cultural elements together in different (and novel) arrangements. As Vygotsky (1971) puts it, creativity is 'any human act that gives rise to something new' (p. 7). The significance of cultural resources for self-making, of cultural experiences that inform cultural styles of performance, and of cultural knowledge and relationships with objects and people, are central to the realization of creativity.

Discussion questions

1. How has your own creative practice been influenced by meetings with another culture, a social group, a sound, or genre? How have you managed to show your understanding of what shapes and defines your creative practice to others in interaction? What are the communicative and interactive processes that challenge intercultural creativity? What are the fields of tension you have identified in your creative practices?

2. If creativity is a constant characteristic of human intentional activities, what are the cultural aspects living within the songwriters you admire that are revealed as part of their creative act?

3. What are the taken for granted assumptions and qualities that form and distinguish collaborative and cultural constructions?

4. Have you ever considered whether you should dismiss the entire domain of popular cultural forms, such as jazz or rock 'n' roll in favour of classical genres? How do you position yourself, literally and symbolically, as an artist and audience member who is in touch with, and perhaps even composing for, singers and instrumentalists of one single genre and not another?

Chapter 5

DJ Cultures

This chapter focuses on the plurality of individual and collective creativities that arise in the practice of DJing.[1] DJs talk about and display sociospatial performance creativities that require of them the *mystique*, *power* and *ability* to read or interpret crowds at every moment.

A DJ's resourcefulness is displayed in their knowledge of how to play to a crowd, in their understanding of dance 'moves', in their having a feel for and mastering and, in a practical way, the execution, content and appearance of DJing. DJs know how to deploy and create music to 'move' a crowd; the collective experience of space is as important as the mutual tuning-in and of the construction of the 'we' of collective creativity. They know what the 'game' requires. They know how to move a crowd, and to how guide the collective experience of club cultures. These transformative sociospatial performance creativities are characteristic of, and form part of, the cultural capital that constitutes the field of DJing (associated with a particular DJ's production style and acts, in a particular local club and music scene, at a particular point in time and place). Although the emphasis is often on style, technique and trendsetting (i.e. innovative remixing of records or mashups of digital data), the creativity of individual DJs tends to favour specific knowledge of musical styles or identifiable genres, as well as knowledge of the complexities of subgenres (there are nearly one hundred distinct subgenres within dance music). Techniques in mixing can be highly innovative and offer a sense of exclusivity, a different way of experiencing sound (breaking with established methods), in order to situate each dance scene.

DJs are keen to develop transformative performance creativities as forms of capital in the collective act of creating club cultures and the socially functional reality behind 'getting gigs'. In sum, the 'whole package' comprises a reputation, an extensive record and sample collection, having a style and identity of their own, and building a fanbase that can lead to celebrity status.

---

[1] Dance club music has been described as 'disc culture', a term, coined by Thornton (1995), which refers to a musical activity wherein recording and performance have swapped statuses: records are the originals, whereas live music has become an exercise in reproduction. Club cultures celebrate technologies that have rendered some traditional kinds of musicianship obsolete and have led to the formation of new aesthetic principles and judgements of value. This is not about songwriting, guitarists, or classical-popular genres of difference, but rather about the work of producers, sound engineers, remixers and DJs.

Introduction

In addressing the question of how DJs—the heroes and creators of dance scenes—continually display transformative performance creativities in the production of the 'atmosphere' or 'vibe' of disc and club cultures, it is necessary to depart from the Romantic conception of musical creativity and the idea that music is the work of a lone creator, and begin, instead, to address some of the issues that arise from the emergence of a new kind of entrepreneurial market-oriented artist. This requires that, rather than adhering to a fixed or single notion of musical creativity, consideration be given to a number of different constructions.

DJs position themselves as 'turntable musicians' who perform elaborate mixes that require much rehearsal (with names like 'the running mix', 'the chop mix', 'transforming', etc) and create new music in the process of mixing. For DJs, records are the raw material of their performance just as, with sampling, they have become the raw material of composition. House records are *not* recordings of performances but are actively *performed* by the DJ. Ironically, while DJs may be musicians, they are rarely performers in the pop sense of the word. As cultural figures, DJs are known by name rather than face. Although in the mid-1990s, in a minority of London clubs, the 'cult of the DJ' led to the practice of facing the DJ booth whilst dancing, this has not become widespread. Any effort to articulate the creativity of the DJ's performance invokes a language or discourse of sound, use of vinyl, and production of digital sets re-composed at home and improvised 'live' at the club. The creativity inherent in DJing is integrally wrapped up with and manifest in the forms of subcultural production of 'club cultures'.

The global phenomenon of 'club cultures'[1] is markedly different from that of live music cultures. Records are the musical instrument of club cultures. The scene is all about the buzz and energy that results from the interaction of records, DJ and crowd. 'Liveness' is displaced from the stage to the dance floor, and from the worship of the performer to the veneration of 'atmosphere' or 'vibe'. The crowd becomes a self-conscious cultural phenomenon—one that generates shared moods that are immune to reproduction. As such, subcultural authenticities are often inflected by issues of nation, race and ethnicity.

This chapter introduces highly successful and creative DJs who are able to create 'buzz', 'vibe', 'mood' or 'atmosphere' in the spatial interaction between DJ and crowd. DJs create music associated with certain sounds and crowds. In Thornton's words (1995), they 'assert their cultural worth', claim their subcultural capitals' and 'offer alternatives' to 'subverting dominant cultural patterns in the manner attributed to classic subcultures' (p. 115). The DJs featured in this chapter are: the legendary Jazzie B, founder of Soul II Soul (Fig. 5.1), a black British *disc culture*,[2] who emphasizes the strength of community ties outside the dance club, seeing the 'vibe' as an affirmation of a politicized black identity (Thornton, 1995); Rob Paterson (Fig. 5.3; see also www. examiner.com/djs-in-new-york/interview-with-rob-paterson), a trans-Atlantic DJ based in New York City who 'spins' urban dance forms such as hardcore house and techno, and whose 'sound' is characterized by particular samplings in subcultural sites of new creativities; XUAN Liu (Fig. 5.2; see also www.facebook.com/i.am.XUAN.liu or www.djXUAN.com), who interacts with crowds in Taiwan (where DJs' creative agency is most important to music culture, see for example, Born,

---

[1] Club culture is the colloquial expressive given to youth cultures for which dance clubs, and their 1980s offshoot, raves, are the symbolic axis and the working social hub. The sense of place afforded by these events is such that regular attendees take on the name of the spaces they frequent, becoming 'clubbers' and 'ravers'. See Thornton (1995).

[2] 'Disc culture' is a term coined by Sarah Thornton in her book *Club Cultures: Music, Media and Subcultural Capital* in which she argues historically 'in the 1990s, records have been enculturated within the night life of British dance clubs to the extent that it makes sense to talk about *disc cultures* whose values are markedly different from those of live music cultures. What authenticates contemporary dance cultures is the buzz or energy which results from the interaction of records, DJ and crowd. "Liveness" is displaced from the stage to the dance floor, from the worship of the performer to a veneration of "atmosphere" or "vibe". The DJ and dancers share the spotlight as *de facto* performers; the crowd becomes a self-conscious cultural phenomenon—one which generates moods immune to production, for which you have to be there' (1995, pp. 29–30).

(2005) and is responsible for an 'underground'[3] house scene based on soulful, funky and deep house music; and top-flight Australian Simon Lewicki,[4] also known as 'Groove Terminator' (Fig. 5.4; see also http://en.wikipedia.org/wiki/Groove_Terminator), whose distinct practices reflect variations on the experience of creativities according to the norms that prevail for DJs (as, for example, with the introduction of MCing over his sets, setting trends for 'rave' or 'warehouse party' practices). Simon also works as a recording artist, multi-platinum producer, remixer and as a creator of music for major corporate brands, campaigns, television shows and motion pictures.

For every music scene, the DJ, or 'turntable musician', has his own dance club culture and distinct set of media relations. DJs are most important to 'disc culture'. They respond to the crowd through their choice and sequence of records; seeking to direct the crowds energies and build up the tension until the event 'climaxes'; they are expected to have their finger on the pulse of the event in order to give the dancing crowd what they need and want. DJs are artists who are present in the construction of musical experience.

How do DJs create with records? DJs improvise with records or electronic gadgets, usually backed up by immense sound systems. They produce variations on hit records by taking them apart, adding new drum tracks, superimposing tunes or bass-lines, and generally paying strict attention to the quality of the sound and efficacy of the rhythm. Improvisation is central to the process. The idea is to not only keep people dancing but to respond to the dancers and to develop a kind of 'disc culture'. Thornton (1995, p. 66) describes 'disc cultures' as being all about position, place, sound and timing. The scenes have their own fashion systems, their own clothing codes and their own subcultural capitals, which all act as signs of the young and the 'hip'. The media plays a crucial role here, being the main disseminator of these capitals. (The media is a series of institutional networks essential to the creation, classification and distribution of cultural knowledge.)

This chapter illustrates how the concept of musical creativity is not based on any rarefied or fixed object, process, attribute or quality. As with the flow of cultural and social expressive power, and as is inherent in everyday life, DJing is both a practice and an event, situated in the flow of time and occurring in a broader context of culture and history. Any effort to articulate the acts of musical creativity is linked with the sociality of dance culture and club cultures, in which multiple meanings are generated. In this chapter I will provide capsule biographies of four DJs with four geographical understandings (UK, USA, Australia and Taiwan) of what DJing is about.

Also important are turntable technology and the expanding resources of recording, which are, in themselves, new expressive instruments that reposition DJs in the field. What matters in the

---

[3] 'Underground' is the expression by which clubbers refer to things subcultural. More than fashionable or trendy, 'underground' sounds and styles are 'authentic' and are pitted against the mass-produced and mass consumed. Undergrounds are exclusive worlds whose main point may not be elitism but whose parameters often relate to particular crowds.

[4] Simon Lewicki, also known as Groove Terminator, is an Australian electronic music artist. Originally a hip hop DJ, he eventually began spinning house music. He was featured in the 2000 Australian edition of the Ministry of Sound's Club Nation series, as well as several other Ministry of Sound compilations. His song 'Here Comes Another One' was the theme of the popular Australian (and worldwide) reality TV show *The Block*. Starting in late 2004, Lewicki's song 'How Life Should Be' has been featured in a series of television commercials for Progressive Insurance and the Sci-Fi Channel's Stargate series. He is also in several other bands, one being Tonite Only with Sam La More, which was launched in 2006 and is signed to Hussle Black, a sub-label of Ministry of Sound. In 2009, Lewicki started the Electronic Rock San Francisco duo Jump Jump Dance Dance with singer/guitarist Chris Carter, also known as DJ Snakepanther. Their eponymous debut album appeared in August 2010. Associated acts: Chili Hi Fly (2000-2002), Tonite Only (2005–2006), Jump Jump Dance Dance (2007-present), solo career (1997-present).

accounts of DJs featured in this chapter, is not how, with hindsight, we make objective judgements to establish relative values for musical creativities, but what functional value each configuration or manifestation of creativity has, contemporaneously, within the practical logic of the field. In this chapter, I will present examples of DJing practices in which creativities include the assemblage of various bits of songs to the remixing of entire songs to mashups made in DIY studios. The practice of remixing, or 'turntablism', is increasingly part of the realities of 'digital musicians' (i.e. musicians who make music by utilizing mainly or only digital technologies) and musicians whose practices are enabled by both conventional music-making and digital technologies. My intention is twofold. Firstly, I aim to provide an overview of each DJ's personage and practice (i.e. habitus or set of dispositions), offering some indication of how they each inhabit different yet similar musical networks and worlds, and what characterizes the practical sense (or logic of practice) that DJs comprehend and negotiate as forms of capitals ascribed to explain the particular club culture in which they perform. Secondly, I will explore DJ practices as creativities of place, sound, and scene.

I begin with the auteur[5] and iconic DJ (and entrepreneur) Jazzie B, who details the ways that DJing inscribes and enunciates individual and collective creativities, and describes the capitals upon which DJing origins were shaped in the mid to late 1970s.

Introducing Jazzie B

One of the biggest urban acts responsible for revolutionizing the modern R&B movement in Britain, Jazzie B (born Beresford Romeo in London, England), has played a seminal role in British dance music history. He was the founding member of the musical collective Soul II Soul, created in London at the end of the 1980s. Soul II Soul comprised: Jazzie B (singer and vocal dialogue/keyboards/programmer), Nellee Hooper (producer/mixer/arranger), and Philip 'Daddae' Harvey (percussion), along with a changing roster of other musicians. Soul II Soul was one of the most successful musical exports from the UK during the late 1980s and early 1990s. Their name became an umbrella for several of the operations of founder Jazzie B. These various parts of the Soul II Soul jigsaw included sound systems, gigs and the group itself. It was as much about a lifestyle statement as a musical movement, and a sound system; it was all about position, context and timing.[6] Its subcultural capitals are not only about being 'hip', but also about the dissemination of a philosophy, and the institutional networks essential to the creation, classification and distribution of cultural knowledge. The subcultural ideologies of Soul II Soul drew attention to a particular black style of innovation, involving a particular music scene, sound, place and time. Jazzie B was the ninth of a family of 10, several of whom began running sound systems in the 1960s and 1970s.

> *Jazzie B*: I didn't have any real professional sort of teaching or anything. I wasn't deemed to be a professional musician by anyone around me at that time I was growing up. We were just hacking at it. I was never into classical music but a guy once who was heavily involved in it described it to me. It sounded like a rush. Learning an instrument held no real relevance to what I really wanted to do. Principally, all of my ideas stem from being a DJ. I started as a DJ. This means taking loops and beats and using various different bits of outboard equipment to enhance the sound we were using. Technology was really majorly important for us. I was making music for myself and for my following. I think that's the best

---

5   The auteur is broadly defined as an author or creator who stands at the pinnacle of a pantheon of performers, and who works and enjoys high respect status amongst performers and fans. Although auteur status is not always dependent on chart success, significant market volume is a corollary of cult status and recognition.

6   See the interesting detailed biographical account of the early stages of Jazzie B's emergence within the DJ culture in the UK at http://en.wikipedia.org/wiki/Jazzie_B.

Fig. 5.1 DJ Jazzie B in a Beijing club in 2006.
Photo by Anders, China.

strategy that any musician could take out really; you do it for yourself first and if everybody/anybody else is interested, then fair enough.

Working under the name Jah Rico, Jazzie B's first gig was in 1977 at the Queen's Silver Jubilee around the time that the 'Northern Soul' scene of the 1970s was all kicking off in Wigan in the north of England. Populated by the white working-class youth who danced to obscure Afro-American soul records from the 1960s, the scene was considered by many to be the strangest and most unlikely manifestation of the entire black music experience.

> *Jazzie B*: My whole thing comes from a reggae background. I focus on listening to the groove. I'm very interested in the groove. I love melodies and the top line streams and chords and so on and/but I'm very interested in the groove. But now, that would be deemed to be an old-fashioned aesthetic. Now, a lot of the music is quite industrial, quite hard and reflects the times that we're living in. Nowadays, the bedroom DJ can have iconic status in terms of the music industry.

Jazzie B changed his group's working name to Soul II Soul in 1982 when he founded a 'black' music collective interested in sampling and other computer technologies.

> *Jazzie B*: Our sound was principally based on a mish-mash, or like now we call it like a mashup of electro, which was like hip hop with an R&B/reggae idea with elements of disco. And, like I said, the ideas of the melody and choruses were catchy.

Jazzie B's DJ performances are known for their 'soulful' musical style. Exploring new computer sound possibilities, using vocals, and starting a new line in clothing—dubbed 'Funki Dred'—Soul II Soul consolidated the British trajectory of the 'dance' genre. Their debut album *Club Classics Vol. One* reached number 1 in the UK Albums Chart, and was certified triple platinum by the British Phonographic Industry. Jazzie B illuminates a particular relationship contextually linked to particular places, sounds and people.

> *Jazzie B*: Nellee and me were arch rivals originally. He was from Bristol and an organization called 'The Wild Bunch'. I used to infiltrate that territory quite a lot with our sound system, and we had quite a lot of following from Bristol as well. We used to play at blues parties in Bristol. I had quite a lot of family

members there and quite a big following. I think the initial meeting was with Milo, who was Nellee's partner at the time, and he was the person everyone was after, technically. He was just an incredible DJ and the guys would sometimes travel down to London, and after a while we built a relationship. Nellee brought the idea of really refining the ideas of what we were trying to do as a sound system to the commercial market. Before working together, Nellee was involved in production and was heavily into percussion. So when we were doing the clashes and stuff like that, we used to have an SP1200 that we would programme. And we were doing some pretty outrageous stuff during those early days. And Nellee used to 'cut up' really well; he's a very good turntablist. So after putting the beats together sometimes he would scratch and cut things up. He refined the idea of making a more polished sound. We saw ourselves as being most like Parliament, P Funk. When Nellee came along, he polished and popularized the sound while my bit was built on being a bit of an entrepreneur coming up with and building the ideas and things of nature.

Soul II Soul also had great success in the United States, where 'Back To Life' reached the top 10, and was certified platinum, and the album (renamed as *Keep On Moving* for the US market) reached the top 20 and sold over two million copies. The group also won two Grammy Awards: 'Best R&B Performance By A Duo Or Group With Vocals' for 'Back To Life', and 'Best R&B Instrumental for 'African Dance'. Jazzie B was awarded an Order of the British Empire (OBE) in the 2008 New Year's Honours List, and in May 2008 he was awarded the first Inspiration award at the Ivor Novello Awards for being a pioneer and the man who gave black British music a soul of its own. The ways that Jazzie B continually displays innovative performance creativities can be found in his specific references to the exploration of new practices and new forms of identity and distinctive trend-setting sounds in DJ production. His style was novel, his technique broke with normal rules, and his creativities led to highly innovative methods that are now seen as the precursor of 'a soul sound' (see Fig. 5.1).

Jazzie B: The industry was really a lot different during the eighties, very different, black or crossover or main stream. We managed to have such a presence in the whole 'dance culture', which was a very new terminology used in 1988. Because we were a black band, or a black organization, we had to break the black circuit first in America. And when Soul II Soul first came out in America we had to actually change the title of our first album. Compartmentalizing and marketing is so important in America. The original album was called *Club Classics Vol. 1* in the UK, but in America this title would pigeonhole us with being just 'club music'. So we had to change the title. Well, the record company ended up changing the title of the album to *Keep On Moving*. The other thing that helped break Soul II Soul in America during that period of time was the fact that, to be honest with you, the mid-west of America didn't really recognize black British music. So, at a cultural level, we were able to really break barriers. Although, we didn't really even necessarily see ourselves as a band, it was more of a collective; this was all very new for America 21, 22 years ago. Black radio was emerging during that period too and we were heard as something new, something different, and something that they could relate to but couldn't quite put their finger on. So our timing was really, really good. We were recognized by black America first, and then we broke the college circuit, which was very important in terms of you actually having a real meaty, hearty following. That would have been anywhere from outside of the major six or seven cities into the mid-west of America. A few years later we ended up with Grammies and keys to seven cities with a sort of amazing status in America.

We cannot say whether Jazzie B's schoolteachers ever berated the young Funki Dred as he fell asleep at the back of the class with the words, 'You'll never get anywhere mucking around with that sound system instead of doing your homework'. But if they did they could not have been more wrong. It was revising his knowledge of the essential elements of roots, dub and reggae that made Jazzie B who he is today, the founder of Soul II Soul, whose staple anthems changed the practice of soul sounds, and who uniquely positioned Soul II Soul in the music business, coordinating the exploitation of both song, sound and merchandising.

One does not merchandise people or things but intangible rights. In the case of the performing and recording sound system and artists involved in Soul II Soul, the merchandising consisted of the artists' individual names, trade names, clothing, logos and artwork. These were used in two (and more recently three) principal ways to exploit their merchandising rights: touring, retailing and web merchandising, which has come into its own in the past few years. In the end, it is really an issue of the significance of acts of creativity (carrying with them conventions, rules, codes and procedures) in which thinking the impossible becomes the catalyst to an 'impossibilitist creativity'[7], which demands the disposition (habitus) that allowed Jazzie B to challenge the conventional practices of the day and to break with the field as it existed at that time; and in this way reactivate the field and bring about an innovation in the way DJing and sound production was perceived. The logic of practice can be seen in the execution, content and characterization of the values that underlie it.

> *Jazzie B*: You've gotta kind of die for your art. You've gotta be willing to be ripped off once or twice in your career. You've got to learn to levitate on another level. You've got to take risks, and think the impossible . . . What still sounds absurd to me now, is the idea of me giving away music—making music free on MySpace or the Internet or anything like that—which sounds impossible to me, I mean even as a collector of vinyl, I go trawling through stores around town, you know, trying to look for the perfect beats on a weekly basis. And that's something that I still do, it's a little bit of a hobby of mine to go out and buy music. I haven't come to terms with the idea of giving away music, yet! But there are a few guys on the label that are having to do that now.

As he shows in his account below, the elements of a particular, black style, and an innovative strategy that radically transforms the sites where these musical cultures cohere and converge, results in a complex amalgam of creativities. This includes a particular music scene, the development of a particular sound, and an understanding of the role of locality and fandom, and how it all took place.

> *Jazzie B*: The person who produces music or sound has become much more involved, in fact, in the production of, you know, what is in fact a multimedia artefact, or a piece of multimedia. The notion of a performance artist is now in fact what used to be a musician. And I think there is real consideration, in the sense that, whatever the sound is, that it looks right when it goes with what's happening, seems to be the way in which, for example, You Tube breaks many people who are what you were describing as bedroom DJs.
>
> In actual fact, Soul II Soul with my idea of the Funki Dred, which was principally based on an idea of being a black person with various religious beliefs, and growing up in London with all of its multiculture, we searched for an identity. My philosophy is a happy face, 'a thumping bass for a loving race'. [It] had a huge impact, particularly when we went to America, and what made us stand out from everybody else was the fact that we had this flamboyant hairstyle and the way we dressed. And I can even remember those early hip hop guys and the way they dressed. It wasn't until Run DMC and people like that came along and made it something identifiable within our own neighbourhoods; something that we could identify sound with vision.
>
> But the game has changed dramatically. The artist or the acts now empower themselves. Artists become the label, become the producer, become the distributor, become the promoter. With the idea of Twitter, Facebook etc. the followers can get really close up to the artist.

The distinct practices of Jazzie B introduced new forms of creativity that were contextually linked to a 'whole way of life' that celebrated star producer DJs who marketed a clothing range as part of the development of a club culture featuring the Soul II Soul sound system. The whole corpus of Soul II Soul music became closely associated with a particular social setting, a philosophy

---

[7]   A term coined by Boden (2005, p. 44).

and a particular sound and lifestyle. This led to it attaining cult status in the US market. Jazzie B contributed to the key factors distinguishing DJs, the values that underlie them, and a certain DJ habitus.

Introducing Shiuan Liu (artist name XUAN)[8]

XUAN is not a 'typical' Taiwanese. He was born in Taiwan and migrated to the USA when he was eight years old. Like many children of Asian middle-class parents, he was expected to learn a musical instrument, and he played classical piano from the age of five until well into his twenties. He began to take an interest in popular music after moving to the USA. His first few years of involvement with popular music included playing in the school band, playing for a theatre group as a rehearsal pianist, and playing 'pop songs to woo girls'. In the meantime, he was identified as having 'gifted' classical piano skills, and was accepted onto the Juilliard School's very selective pre-college division. He was very aware of the way musicians operate and function. He would 'hang out' at record stores, and shop for records like any other teenager who likes music. In college, he started 'shopping for beats', 'buying albums' and 'collecting records'. (This is part of the DJs habitus or 'way of life', and is anchored in the symbolic capital of 'buying albums' as expressive 'instruments'.)

XUAN DJs at club and corporate events, at which latter he understands his role as a 'music director' or 'show producer' (XUAN's DJ work spans from corporate gigs to nightclub gigs. Figure 5.2 is an example of a semi-corporate gig. In this case, XUAN was invited by a university's design department to play at their booth at the design fair.) The role of DJ in the context of club events, corporate events and fashion parties is differentiated according to the context, as explained later in this chapter, and manifests itself through changing forms of social creativities, and the building of a brand of identifiable sounds whilst working within the often tight limitations of a specific dance music or a specific corporate scene (see Fig. 5.2).

For XUAN, the creativity of a DJ involves a specific social and cultural engagement with music, space and production, as well as the consumption of music by a special community. DJing involves his stage persona and style, which he changes in accordance with different contexts. What this means for XUAN is as follows:

> XUAN: My name is associated with house music. My name is also associated with corporate events like fashionable, high-end club parties.

The club and corporate scenes are as diverse as the different tastes in crowds. XUAN plays to all kinds of crowds and music scenes, and has built a name for himself as someone with a style of his own: a DJ who is open to the exploration and reinvention of popularized forms that appeal to people's different tastes.

> XUAN: People's tastes are different. Some clubbers like a much harder, aggressive beat, something like 'hard house' but even faster . . . I also work in club environments where the audience gives you instant feedback; but it's not like they tell you what to play, it's a visceral engagement; I respond and interact with them . . . you have to know the scene . . . There are a few dedicated crews putting on events that feature 'techno' and 'new-school' who give a nod to house DJs like me in their line-up . . . it's important to stick to a sound that identifies me.

Being a DJ, then, may demand a certain disposition (habitus) to allow the creativity required to be successful to flow, or, perhaps, to not be locked into a certain habitus; to be willing to experiment,

---

[8] XUAN is an artist name that is spelled out in capitals.

Fig. 5.2 DJ XUAN performing at a semi-corporate gig in Taiwan.
Photo courtesy of Shiuan Liu.

to challenge and define new practices. The techniques of DJ production include the ability to alter the uses of technologies and space, to be able to adapt mixing (or reconstructive) practices, and to have a status and effect that is dependent on the music and technologies associated with the club culture of a particular place. Expectations of DJs vary considerably, as illustrated in XUAN's view of the creative process:

> *XUAN*: In the old days, the ones who had the rarest records were the best. A lot of time was spent hunting down records. In the process of collecting the music, you start to build a map in your head of how the songs will sequence together in a club, how that sequence will move the crowd etc. But today, everyone with a broadband connection has access to unlimited amounts of rare tracks, so now the skill is much more about careful selection and finding a sound and style of weaving those sounds together that represents YOU. Some DJs (myself included) with some studio background will seek to differentiate themselves by making special edits of tracks they like, in essence making remixes that only they will own. I have had formal music training, so I also differentiate myself from other DJs by playing the piano while I spin, thus adding another sonic and visual layer to my performance (and it's also something other DJs can't do). Another way is to work with new technology and equipment that opens up possibilities for live performance that weren't otherwise available. Software like Native Instruments' Traktor Pro, Ableton Live and controllers like the APC40 now allows DJs to mix four decks at a time, or do live resampling and re-looping—essentially creating new music on the fly. It's a wild time to be

a DJ because there are so many tools now and ways of performing but, to me, I still think the most important aspect of performance is to take the audience on a journey and move them, mind, body and soul. Doesn't matter how you do it, but the old timers did so much with two decks and a simple mixer, I don't think you need much more than that.

The social and symbolic value of music is encapsulated in the relationships between musical production and consumption. Attali (1985) reminds us of the psychological potency of music, as well as its power as an economic commodity. The production of music, the creation of place, and the deployment of music in the exercise of power and mystique, led Attali to a consider the practices by which something as local and particular as Western classical music can be mobilized as a universal discourse. Attali recognized the simultaneously material and imagined qualities of musical production, through processes that both localize and give form, and that are forged through musical practices that are intimately bound up with production in space and place.

> XUAN: Of course I'm gonna be shaped by the local culture. But I still see my strength in being able to bring elements from a different culture into [the] work I do in this culture, such as 'Western pop sensibility' and 'underground dance music vibe'.

It is not easy to balance the demands of commerce and creativity, few are able to overthrow or challenge the 'game'. They do not believe in the game, but they continue to define their interests within its parameters, narratives, and values by making a 'virtue out of necessity' (Bourdieu, 1990b, p. 54).

Music at once defines and reinforces the disposition of power within the musical spaces of dance clubs and corporate events. DJs appear to practise a particular form of sociospatial creativity that has the power to create an atmosphere and influence moods and emotions.

> XUAN: I think Taiwan has a lot of influences, and people here are very adaptable and practical, and it allows for interesting fusion and incubation of all sorts of musical styles . . . I think clubbers recognize artistry with DJs who create new soundscapes from old just like anyone else.

What is implicit in this is the way XUAN understands and constructs the Taiwanese club habitus, and how he responds creatively when a set of dispositions meets with a particular problem, choice or context. In other words, XUAN's DJing can be understood as a 'feel for the game' that operates at a level that is at once particular and unconscious. XUAN is clearly influenced by the cultural rules, systems, laws, structures, agendas and values that function effectively as habitus, and then serve as the specific sociocultural conditions or contexts for creativity in Taiwanese club culture. XUAN is not blind to, but, rather, conditioned by a shared cultural identity. It is this shared cultural trajectory that produce the habitus, or what is happening around him, and the imperatives of the field as he sees it in Taiwan. This is seen in the way he draws a clear distinction between furthering and improving his own standing and capital within the cultural field. This ability to analyse and respond to particular club contexts by means of diverse performance practices is, of course, a large part of his identity and image as a celebrity DJ.

The place and mediation by the DJ of dance music is everything. Much the same creative process can be seen in the field of sport. The need for sports people to have strongly exercised and finely honed bodies is equivalent to a DJ's finely grained knowledge of recordings. Being a sports person requires that one fits as closely as possible to the demands of one's chosen discipline: a rugby body, for instance, is very different from that of a distance runner. Of particular interest is what happens when sports people move into different fields, such as public relations or the media, where there is no 'coincidence' between their bodies and their new work. The overwhelming impression is of awkwardness, not just in what to say or when to say it, but also in the relationship between their bodies and their new surroundings. Their lack of a spontaneous understanding of where and how to move, how to use their facial muscles, when to laugh, and so forth, can make them seem like a fish out of water.

Hence, drawing from Bourdieu, we can recognize that a cultural producer occupying a legitimate position will require considerably more than simply raw talent for mixing records. Aspirations, ability, a knack for constructing soundscapes that create 'environments', the know-how to make use of cultural capital (a repertoire of musical knowledge, values, beliefs and information) and command over its application, are all necessary for the DJ to gain entry into the social circles and settings required for recognition. So, when XUAN is asked how he prepares for each event, and what he thinks is specific to his production process as a DJ working with dance genres in Taiwan, he says:

> XUAN: Of course, each event is different. I constantly get new tunes so I work that into the CD folder. The production process begins by listening to a lot of tracks. So we have to search for those tracks. It used to be paying a visit to our favourite record shops, but now most of the listening to and buying tracks I do online. The next part is to listen to the tracks. For me, I breeze through them quickly before I purchase, and I also put them in my iPhone so I can listen to the tracks while I travel, doubling up on my time. As I'm always work with a lot of new tracks, I also sort them by genre and variety, and burn my favourites to CD, make a CD cover with their names, and put them into my CD book. It used to be taking a vinyl record and putting it into the 'crate', which I liked better. Now, most tracks I play have no physical form and I'm doing all the cataloguing and setting up playlists on the computer. Then, before a show, I listen through the tracks again to map out a general game plan, a rough sequence and flow. This is more of a fallback option than anything, as, usually, once the party gets moving, it's much better to play tracks depending on the spirit of the moment, rather than some predetermined sequence . . . I play a lot of corporate events. Each has different methods of playing and preparation. With corporate events, you first must meet up with the clients who will brief you on the product and the vibe they are promoting, and you have to source music along those lines. For example, at a recent gig they asked for something very futuristic and slightly cold for the beginning of the night. And during the 'party time' (which is really like a cocktail party), they wanted slower, more 'chillout' music. So you prepare according to how similar and like-minded they want the social character of the crowd at the club to feel.

In creating a club scene in which the 'social character' accords with the nature of the event, the DJ seeks to create and enunciate a feeling of community and a sense of collective presence. This is a distinct creative practice, contextually linked to highly particularized social norms and cultural nuances. It is a feeling of belonging that the DJ is seeking to communicate. This is done by interlacing records, the DJ and the crowd.

> XUAN: The crowd for corporate events expect different things from the crowd at a dance club. Many corporate clients, who don't know the club scene as well, will expect a turntablist scratch show from every DJ (which I don't do). Instead, I have put on shows where I work with violinists or guitar players or other live musicians to give the performances a more visually appealing element. At a recent gig, a new luxury hotel opening, I worked with two beautiful female musicians playing traditional Chinese instruments, to give the clients the visual and audio vibe they wanted.

In dance clubs, people dance, of course, but for the most part, clubs that exist entirely for dancing and music are almost non-existent. People, alcohol, girls, and heat and noise is what clubbers want. This means that there is a close relationship between creativity, originality and social affinity at particular events. Nonetheless, the centrality of music in this social world is further indicated by the fact that music is the only cultural attribute that is almost always mentioned on flyers promoting clubs. Usually the music is specified by a short generic list: 'techno', 'hardcore', or 'alternative', for example. The musical aspect is also emphasized by naming the DJs who are associated with certain sounds and crowds. That XUAN plays mostly house music, which covers a lot of subgenres, such as 'funky' and 'soulful house', means he likes 'to get deep and minimal sometimes' but,

Fig. 5.3 DJ Rob Paterson performing at a New York club.
© Arnaud Stébé, 2011.

as he says, 'when things heat up I can also transition into more pounding, tougher sounding mate-rial, even breakbeats. He does not play what many people call 'trance'. Nor does he play hip hop, though, as he says, 'a lot of these musical boundaries are getting blurred these days'.

The creative process is determined by the moment, via the musicalized marking out of urban spaces, and a lot of things are unscripted. XUAN's own sound comprises samples of Asian instru-mental phrases, which are put over rhythms to make them into dance music. Dance musics coexist in Taiwan through the interplay of style, space, and commercial and cultural influences from overground venues and commercial clubs,[9] a pattern that we see again with Rob Paterson.

Introducing Rob Paterson

Rob was born in Manhasset, New York, and went to a suburban public school in Setauket, also in New York, and then to college in New York. His first big gig as a live performer was at the Metro

[9] For a fascinating discussion of different styles of clubs and practices in mainstream overground and subcultural underground scenes, see Toop (2004, pp. 233–46).

(Chicago) in July 2002. He has since worked in many dance settings.[10] Rob shuns definitive social categorization, preferring to describe himself as a creative artist whose life's ambition is summed up in the following extract (Fig. 5.3):

> *Rob*: As a musician, I make and perform music . . . I find that being labelled as 'a producer' is one thing but I could equally be called 'an engineer' or a DJ. But whatever I call myself it all boils down to music, audiences, crowds, production types and wanting to put something very special on and developing my own sound.

As with all of the DJs featured in this chapter, Rob was considered by those around him to be talented in music. He came from a family that was not established in the music industry and achieved high levels in grade music examinations for at least one of the several instruments he played, which included piano, trumpet and guitar. In his first year or two of college he performed as a solo singer-songwriter, playing guitar and singing original songs with a loop sampler. He describes himself as 'a musician whose musical practice is the product of free, individual expression'. He stresses his own individuality and uniqueness in terms of what it means to be a musician, and the positive effects of digital technologies, insofar as it can be used to disrupt the trajectory of the conventional musician. Being diverted this way is something that often happens to traditionally trained musicians.

Rob explains the competition for capital within fields with reference to the transition between one field and another, by which means he suddenly gained capital (public recognition, status, and the ability to take creative control) through access to digital technologies that inspired and facilitated his creativity. Creating music within a field, with new rules, discourses and creativities, corresponded to a logic that was clearly offering him new ways to earn a living from something he loved doing. This is what followed:

> *Rob*: In my junior year at college but I kind of had this revelation—an epiphany—with a little bit of help from my friends. I got some exposure to the right stuff by two friends who I pretty much owe everything to at this point. They showed me how to record with a computer, and it blew my mind. Until then, I'd felt imprisoned by my own creativity and yet really nervous about the riskiness of music-making which often felt like you were going out on a limb. The fact is that prior to that I was working with little tape decks and stuff. You know, like where I had no control over what I was doing, except for the 'live' take. So that really kind of set me off on a new path. It was a new start. It set me up with new networks and sources to new challenges and tasks . . . So, in my junior year I switched colleges, and I switched to music . . . What I could do exploded with newness. What I could trial and taste expanded into new territories. It was like learning an instrument all over again. It fascinated me . . . I'm the type of person where it's all about ideas. I'm always kind of on the edge of the next idea, I guess, and this was the biggest 'next set of ideas'.

The 'new path' was important, too, in terms of affordances, which is to say the tools and networks that entered his life due to his peer networks, as was also his openness to change. Rob's sets range from funky-breaks to 'nu soul' to 'electro'. His style deviates from the standard house, electro, trance mega-club genres because of his musical background and interests.

> *Rob*: I used to be a singer-songwriter, my favourite artist was Nirvana, I had never heard good electronic music. During my freshman year at college I was exposed to artists like Boards of Canada,

---

[10] Rob has his own home studio in Stony Brook, New York. Rob also produces music as a solo artist, ranging from downtempo to dance and grunge music. He is developing a career portfolio writing music for films, producing audio clips for various websites and working part time as a music producer with Philip Shearer at Communicate Media Studios for Manyc Records, located in the South Bronx. He also freelances as an audio engineer, producer and performer, and works regularly as a professional DJ.

Atari Teenage Riot and Massive Attack. I saw Radiohead during their Amnesiac tour in Toronto and it turned my world upside down. I had never heard or seen live sampling and it left me inspired. I bought turntables, a sampler and a Roland 909 drum machine to take my performances into a new direction.

Rob realized his new direction was catching on when he started winning competitions:

Rob: I won the 'Art for Progress Clash of the Artists' DJ competition in 2007. The main prize was a spot DJing at the Winter Music Conference, which was an amazing experience. I am very fortunate to have such a loyal fan base as a fairly new DJ, especially on the web. I remember entering the contest and letting as many people know as possible about the vote, but not necessarily to vote for me. The last thing I want to do is be some selfish, self-promoting performer. I managed to place in the top three during the online vote and went on to win the competition at the live event.

Success in competition is a cultural capital whereby artists are allowed entry into or repositioning in the field itself. For Rob, being recognized at the time for what he is doing as a DJ in this way has been pivotal evidence of support. What he is talking about here is not simply an abrupt challenge to the conventional art of the day, but a symbolically different way of DJing, analogous to a different way of seeing the crowd and *co-creating* new forms, sounds and social conditions, which together constitute the elements (or logic in Bourdieuian terms) of the domain of creativity, which is vested in his DJ practice at this point in time.

Rob: It's your job to get people to dance and to get people excited. And you really have to understand how to read people and read a crowd . . . there's no better feeling than getting a crowd to completely lose themselves in what you're doing. Everybody wants to have a good time and if you can be part of that in some way, and do your job which is, you know, playing the right music, or paying attention to what's being played and reacting . . . It's very community-driven . . . like my fans here are people that I met out at clubs or online boards. It all stems from this really amazing network that happens. And there's something about dance music and clubs. There's definitely a drug component that's always there with nightlife and all that. But that's not really what's driving the need to want to come together. It's a scene where you don't have to change who you are to fit in, let's say. It's not about fitting in at all, it's not cliquey, it's not like that at all. It's a really good feeling to be connecting to that same kick drum. It's not just about the shaping of the sound . . . You have the power to really shape the way that the night is going to go. It seems to me it starts off as a technical thing, being able to beat, match and play records together. But then it blossoms for me in terms of going way beyond that.

Indeed, as will be demonstrated shortly, for the most part, DJing is associated not only with musical fragments heard in urban dance mixes, but also with the whole issue of musical taste and what it signifies for young people. In this context acknowledging drug culture is important since it fits in with a philosophy of 'shaping the experience' and certain dance music styles. Being free to choose, not only between various musical styles and combinations of sounds, but also how such choices are lived out, and what they are made to stand for, is implicit in this type of DJ performance. It is not rigidly bound, but rather assumes a fluid character in terms of what is actually going on in subcultural dance music events. As with DJ performance, clubbing is not a singularly definable activity and consists of different crowds moving between different musics in different rooms (e.g. house music on one floor and hip hop on another), wherein DJs simultaneously compose, arrange, produce, and perform by remixing other artists' existing recordings. Significantly, the differentiating principle is never the 'thing' in itself, but it is rather the *performance creativity* that uncovers the extent to which various DJs hold similar capitals in the field.

Rob: What you know and knowing a lot about a lot of things is synonymous with being successful. It's not just about having ideas. The farther you get along the path the more you realize this. I work with music probably between 12 and 15 hours a day. I've really come to learn that it doesn't matter what you make, or what style or genre you make it in, there's always rules you must follow, rules you can push, and rules to break. Let's take 'techno'. It has always been a style of music that is technology-driven; I mean it gets its name, you know, really from the process of people who were building their own drum machines and synths. And, the farther that they pushed the technical side of it, the more they were respected. But when the creativity side is not tech-driven, it is something very different. People who are always pushing to get the new software, or the new synth, they'll actually appreciate in value . . . I think what I try to do is make the 'normal' conspicuous and the 'new' mundane.

Just as the concept of DJ performance creativity resides in the positioning, context and subcultural capitals built up between the DJ and the distinctive club culture, so, also, does the raw material for blurring the boundaries between production and consumption. Through their use of new types of technology, DJs have radically altered approaches to musical composition, challenging existing notions of musical style. There are examples where a DJ's mix/remix has eclipsed the popularity of a commercial single, sometimes even replacing it altogether! With increasing eclecticism they have created new mixes that fuse elements from contemporary music and the sampled soundtracks of urban dance; mixes that redefine conventional notions of musical taste and break with the field as it exists at that time. We see this pattern again with Simon Lewicki, also known as Groove Terminator, a top-flight Australian DJ/producer, and the first to firmly establish himself as a major international recording artist who has produced, recorded and remixed many of Australia's major recording artists.

Introducing Simon Lewicki (artist name DJ Groove Terminator)

Simon was born in Australia and was originally a hip hop DJ. He was featured in the 2000 Australian edition of the Ministry of Sound's Club Nation Series, as well as on several other Ministry of Sound compilations. While maintaining his career as an active recording artist, multi-platinum producer and DJ, he has also composed and produced TV and radio commercials for Coca Cola, Nike, Vodafone and many others. He currently lives in Los Angeles, where he DJs and produces, and makes frequent tours as a guest international DJ at clubs in Europe, Australia and across the USA. From an early age, within a particular cultural setting and urban youth practices, he has learnt the production and practical operational knowledge required of a DJ. Simon's DJing was characteristically produced within a system of close-knit local networks, crossing over between radio techniques and pioneering club disco work, which uses record mixtures and super-impositions of 'beats' or 'break beats',[11] samples of rock music and funk with some MCing over sets.[12] Exercising entrepreneurial skills has proven the viability of the venture, and generated cultural capital from a young age.

> *Simon*: I grew up in Adelaide in Australia. My step-dad was the station manager and he put together the first community radio station in Adelaide. My mum used to do a show on Saturday afternoons, and so I'd go in with her, and sort of mess around in the record library and sort of make myself tapes. And then someone offered to teach me to 'panel', which is to run the equipment in the studio . . . I'd also find ways to sneak into the studio during the graveyard shift and make these crazy mix tapes for myself

---

11 Toop (2004), explains 'drumbeats' eloquently as 'A conga or bongo solo, a timable break or simply the drummer hammering out the beat—these could be isolated by using two copies of the record on twin turntables and playing the one section over and over, flipping the needle back to the start of one while the other played through. The music made in this way came to be known as beats or break-beats' (p. 236).

12 Simon was one of the first to practise MCing over sets in ways foregrounding 'rave' and 'warehouse' 'arty' techniques.

(a)

(b)

Fig. 5.4 Groove Terminator (Simon Lewicki) DJing at: (a) a Los Angeles dance club; and
(b) an outdoor concert in Sydney, Australia.
Fig. 5.4a: Photo by Andy Amos. © Simon Lewicki, 2011; Fig. 5.4b: © Simon Lewicki, 2012.

all night, and then I started a high school radio programme, one day a week . . . Around the age of 17 or
so I was at an age of going out quite a lot, and in the last two years of high school, I really got the bug
for it, and I started DJing in nightclubs, even before I turned 17. I'd lie about my age to get in and stuff.
And I pretty much got the bug very early on. So we're talking the mid to late 80s. I was there doing that
for a while, and then at the first advent of the first wave of hip hop culture and then with 'house music'
coming in and everything, I kind of got swept up in that. There was three things basically you could do

within hip hop culture, and that was dance, or do graffiti, or DJ. I was a terrible dancer and I was a very, very average artist. It was the music that really excited me, so I basically kind of fell into it that way. I was always making tapes for my friends. And it was sort of about sharing great music.

For me it was always about sharing great music with people. As I got more into DJing for dance floors I sort of understood more about the whole theory of DJing, and the rules behind it. And the thing is that it's like the sort of technical ability of the whole thing, which you can pick up fairly quickly, like you can do elementary sort of things, you can pick up like in a day. The thing that took me ages and ages, like years to really get my head around was sort of the programming, being able to like read crowds, and the whole big DJ cliché of taking people on a journey and being able to move them throughout the night. I was very lucky when I started doing clubs, I'd do the DJing from beginning to end, so I was playing for eight hours. You'd get to work the room from beginning to end and that really helped me get my grasp of reading a crowd. Just knowing what to play next is, I think, probably 85% of DJing.

Simon sees DJing as a co-creative experience shared between the DJ and crowd. He was one of the first to pick up on break-beat music in Australia, synchronizing beats with a particular sound, personal mystique and identity, which orchestrates a powerful interaction with the crowd. His DJ name, 'Groove Terminator' is a 'brand' with celebrity status that infuses all aspects of his DJing. Simon has won awards, prizes, and received nominations (including the Best National DJ). His song 'Here Comes Another One' was the theme of the popular Australian (and worldwide) reality TV show *The Block*).[13] Simon is currently also engaged in continent hopping guest gigs (see Fig. 5.4).

Simon: I picked up very early on that there was a basic sort of rotating rule of three operating throughout the night. I learnt this by basically hanging around with other DJs, trying to pick up tips. The rule of three is play one they know, a new one, and something they love But not necessarily in that order, but it's like that's the rule of three that you'd always go to as a working DJ going out doing mobiles or weddings. It's a rule I apply doing really cool inner-city clubs as well. When you're reading the crowd you can tell if you've got tracks or songs that are playing with a lot of energy, so you're just going to wear the crowd out instantly. You want to keep them there for hours, but also, at the same time, if you're like the resident at the club, as opposed to the guest DJ, which is the culture of DJing now, sort of the resident, you need to be able to work the bar as well. So you need to get people worked up, and get them sweaty for a couple of songs, they need to go off and drink, and spend some money behind the bar, and then you need to get them to come back and dance on. When I first started out I really enjoyed that whole aspect of it, it was great. It was just really hard sustaining that energy for eight hours; it's a long graft.

Now, it's a very different club culture than when I started. Now DJing is more about the cult of celebrity. It's a guest DJ culture scene where it's about your name on the flyer, at the best dance venues in country, where you're billed by your brand. People come for you. People trust your brand, you're trusted as an artist, people trust your taste; you're afforded that position by the crowd, who trust you and go with you and they know what they are going to get when they get that person. My thing is, especially in the last 10 years, from club DJing to making my own records, and then doing the 15 minutes of being a pop star crossover, pop star DJ thing. In America I'm not known as GT or Groove Terminator, I'm Simon in Jump Jump Dance Dance writing and producing band stuff and genre-bending. In Australia, I'm known as GT and DJing the records or going out like the Chemical Brothers with a big light show. There's a DJ circuit . . . what I call 'the jobbing DJ', where you've got your equipment or you work on a guest DJing circuit and go into the club, get put up in really nice hotels and you swan in and play records. It's taken nearly 15 years to get a good market share there, to get my name known.

The emphasis is on branding and building specific knowledge. The importance accorded to having access to socially embodied history and the cultural capital required to 'read' the crowd

[13] See http://en.wikipedia.org/wiki/The_Block_(Australian_TV_series). *The Block* is an Australian reality television show broadcast on the Nine Network. The show sees four couples compete against each other to renovate a home in an apartment block and sell it at auction for the highest price.

resides in the values that underlie them. There is an emphasis on style, technique and the innovative remixing of records, recording techniques, styles and mashups of digital data. The logic of DJ practice is immanent in the building of an identity, a celebrity DJ status, and a certain DJ style for each scene, club and circuit. DJ success depends on independent control over technique and style, but, perhaps, most of all, on a whole lifestyle and individualism, which matches perfectly with the art of the club scene.

> *Simon*: Preparing for a gig sees me thinking about the music. You spend a lot of time, in the first 15 years, going into the record stores, several times a week to shop for imports. These days it's so easy to jump online and go trawling through online stores. I get sent most of the music I play these days though. But you have to spend a lot of time listening to a lot of music. Thinking about a specific gig, you do a lot more preparation, thinking about the type of club, the space, the place and that sort of thing. You think about if you want to keep it cooler, or keep it a bit more commercial, or what sort of vibe you want to produce. Then I think about the tracks and sets, the first song and option four or five other tracks. You think about potential goal posts or points in the set you'll move between; where you can transition from point to point, and where you can change in direction and can move around. The points are flexible. You need to be able to move those, because the crowd may react differently to what you expect. So you need to be able to change the mood up quite quickly without it becoming a train wreck.
>
> When I'm DJing I always tend to think of working out how I can blend a song into another song and what new music I can create out of blending these two seemingly disparate bits of music together. That's what I enjoy most, the mixing of tracks.

Technology is a huge catalyst for creative choices. It enables the DJ to alter, adapt, deconstruct, innovate, and use record mixing in different ways to move different crowds. Underpinning the practice of DJing is: (i) the music's embodiment of social connection; (ii) the dialogical performance practice between DJs and audience; and (iii) a unique kind of critical listening and choosing, which is essential to the DJ's creativity.

> *Simon*: One of my favourite DJs is Fatboy Slim. He has always been a big inspiration, a big idol of mine. His big crossover single 'Rockafeller Skank', I remember when he played it. We were together doing a 'Big Day Out' tour, in a big festival in Australia, and he had a version of the vocal of that. Underneath, he had put together the lick from the 'Rolling Stones', 'Satisfaction', and it was just incredible. The crowd just went absolutely ballistic, because they were hearing these two incredibly well-known pieces of music, and he'd mashed them together to make this completely new piece of music, and that was really exciting and new. That was a really big turning point for me. I was like aha! You know. I kind of run with that idea now. I'll deconstruct things, maybe not so obviously, but in a slightly cooler way. That's very much his style, and that's what he does, and he's brilliant at it.
>
> I make my own sound and create my own sort of vibe and that's what I look for and what keeps me excited. It's all also about using technology, showing your dextrous abilities and your technical prowess in deconstructing and reconstructing the songs. You've got to have the tools available and you've got to know your genres in order to repackage a genre that you may want to bring back. It's also about self-marketing. As a DJ, you see yourself as a creator, a creative individual. I don't think I've created a genre yet but I've made some massive discoveries with mixing genres that have really grabbed me and crowds I've played for. And being at the top of the game, and one of the biggest in the world, means you're seen as a celebrity and getting Grammy nominations as part of the mainstream community as a whole.

Simon finds himself in a dynamic and ever-changing process. He is a DJ who has been defined and recognized across diverse social and cultural contexts and time-specific and scene-making practices. Simon often speaks about DJing as a sort of 'game', which one may be either in or out of. The rules of the field of DJing, itself a product of the conditions of a particular place, venue and time, are defined in terms of its sociocultural conditions of production. As I have already noted, DJs occupy a specific time and space. They are good players, winners, who work to a set of rules that govern how the game is played, what is and is not allowed, and how deviancy is dealt with. However, DJing seems to depend on intuition and game-sense as much as on mastery of explicit procedures. DJs implicitly agree to be ruled by the conventions and immediately set up personal relations with the game, as well as with other DJs. The 'rules' of the game concern the creative sense of 'interaction with the crowd' and the commonly accepted practice of, as Simon describes, 'getting two different records which will blend in with each other, to create a magical third piece of music where you're deconstructing and putting things together again'. This practice is not present in some genres or styles but is a big part of GT's brand. The venue or club is understood as a field site, a structurally identifiable space that marks out the sphere of social activity.

For Simon, DJing is the exemplary *structured* field, which is also *structuring* in practice. In other words, creativities arise in real time performance in dance clubs from interactions between DJs and crowds, and they constantly seek appropriate music in which both find degrees of shared meaning—constructing and constructed according to the intents and the limits of the venue. DJs are regarded as highly collective and as highly individual.

Simon possesses ample skill and knowledge and is known for his ability to move and influence a crowd. He has an abundance of relevant capital; he has the social capital (that is, the necessary networks and personal charisma) that can build up a strong reputation. This gives him the luxury of creative choice in deciding which gigs he takes on, and how he acts and thinks in response to the crowd and the opportunities that present themselves. His knowledge of genres and musical styles, his tastes and his 'good taste' for the better-known aspects of the culture—rapping, scratching, beat-box mixing and MCing—are founding principles of the process that legitimizes the distinctiveness of DJs in terms of their hip hop style roots and their positioning of themselves as 'taste-makers'. Establishing DJ status and mystique binds the DJ and crowd. This process is part of the strategies that DJs adopt over time to position themselves with an eye to which clubs, gigs and crowds will be chosen and played to at the pinnacle of the DJ's career.

Concluding remarks

In contemporary society, the idea of musical creativity as the work of its (unique) creator leads to too exclusive an approach, one based on aesthetic *prescription* rather than on informed *description* (and construction) of the cultural practices through which people (as shown in the practices and discourses of the DJs in this chapter) endow music with meaning (in the course of clubbing). To understand this, should we apply a theory of music or a theory of creativity? In the end, the two prove inseparable, partly because of the way in which theory is implicated in the creative process of DJs, and partly because the practice of creating dance music is emergent, contingent, responsive (as in the interplay between bass player and drummer in a band), with DJs depending on their knowledge of and interaction with the crowd: its generation, style, taste and values. A jazz bassist may pick up a recurring rhythmic fragment from the drummer, just as a pianist may pick up a recurring fragment from the bass-line and harmonize it as a comping pattern. Similarly, the circles of interaction are made up of exchanges between the DJs and the crowds, and, as with experienced improvisers who often perform together, such adjustments and negotiations occur spontaneously, almost instantly.

The DJ's relationship with the dance crowd is crucially important. Ultimately both the DJ and the crowd need to grasp each other's intentions, the former through the DJ's performance, and the latter through dancing, both of which feature multiple dimensions of musical creativity in terms of originality and the value accorded to meanings experienced within the club scene. The work of the DJ includes: giving form and meaning to the creativity sparked by a kind of fictive, parallel universe within a club scene; setting up playlists on a computer; sequencing, beat-matching, mixing and remixing sounds and songs for a live audience; and generating the 'buzz' or energy which results from the interaction of tracks. The types of creativity a DJ depicts appear to be fluid and constantly change from one situation to the next. At the same time, they are embedded in clear-cut social and cultural contexts, with values ascribed to distinctive subgenres, usually specified by a short generic list (for example: 'techno-hardcore-alternative-trance'; or 'ragga-hip-hop-jungle'; or 'funky-soulful-house').

The music is always invoked by naming DJs who are associated with certain sounds and crowds, thus enabling new creativities and sites of authorship. The changing status of the DJ is implicit in the potent mix of youth, media and cultural conditions that shape distinctive musical forms and styles. The star producer-DJ's habitus, 'as with bands like the Rolling Stones are caught up in the logic of 'disc culture' even if the dominant strains of their myth are about Mick Jagger as dramatic performer, Keith Richards as virtuoso guitarist and a legacy of gigging and live stadium shows' (Thornton, 1995, p. 31). The DJ's performance creativity allows for and *demands* 'invention and improvisation'.[14] However, the DJ must simultaneously respect the 'rules of the game'. Moreover the creativities are performative and transformative; they embody a physical expression of a collective experience. Sounds are remixed live with other sounds. Break-beats are put with other elements of recorded sound and music. Both temporal and technological mediation is embedded in the practice of creating something new. There is a fusion of re- and de-composition.[15]

The invariable use of the term 'creativity' in the singular is because it is generally (and fallaciously) assumed to be realized in the individual rather than in any openly manifest form of collective production. It is, however, as we have seen, necessary to broaden the remit of the term 'music creativity' to denote more than a process realized by the autonomous individual. As in the case of songwriters, so in the case of DJs, we must acknowledge that there are different types of musical creativity that are recognized and rewarded differently. DJs are distinguished by the particular sounds of 'disc culture'. The DJ's relationship with the dance crowd is crucially important, and both the DJ and the crowd need to grasp each other's meanings, one communicated through dancing and the other through the DJ's performance. The DJ lives in the social space of dancing and dance culture—in the 'scene', which results from the interaction of CDs, DJ and crowd.

Whilst there is no shortage of superb social accounts of the record hops and disc sessions of the 1950s and 1960s, the discotheques of the 1970s, and the clubs and raves of the 1980s', the creativities of DJs and dance culture and the overarching distinctions of its practice have received much less attention. Particular club cultures are associated with particular places and tastes. Club crowds (they are not called audiences or fans) congregate on the basis of their shared taste in music, their consumption of common media and, most importantly, their preference for people with similar tastes to themselves. Particular club cultures manifest particular meanings and values, and, in turn, build affinities with the meanings and values of the culture as a whole. These cultures therefore house ad hoc communities with fluid boundaries, hierarchies of what is authentic and legitimate in popular culture and what can and cannot be called current.

A great deal of work has been done in this area, with particular attention paid to empirical studies of youth's social and cultural hierarchies.[16] Thornton's study (1995) was one of the first extended academic discussions of dance culture, and her use of Bourdieu's approach has been influential. More recent literature[17] has provided insights on common themes, such as an ethnographic focus on the social patterns of club culture at a local level, an emphasis on the positive aspects of dance

---

[14] 'Invention and improvisation' are terms coined by Bourdieu (1990b, p. 63).

[15] 'De-composition' is a term used by Berleant (1987) and refers to the process by which musical material is broken up, and ideas are recycled and remixed.

[16] For further discussion see Becker (1963), Frith (1978, 1983, 1988, 1996), Frith et al. (2001); Thornton (1995).

[17] See Longhurst (2007), for a comprehensive review of the literature.

culture, and the way in which the clubbing experience (dancing, music, dress, sex, drugs and the 'vibe') can lead to the production of new identities for the participants. There has also been research in the area of blues, folk and country music, and their locales, by cultural geographers and popular music scholars (see A. Bennett, 2000; Shuker, 1994). The emergence of 'localized alternative music', with processes that both localize and give form to new practices, has been well documented by Shuker, who argues that 'local sounds provide marketing possibilities by providing a "brand name" which consumers can identify with' (1994, pp. 210–211).

Locality and youth culture are intimately bound up with the production of club cultures wherein space and place are fruitfully brought together in urban dance music forms (such as the club cultures of *soul*, *house*, *techno* and *jungle*), as has been illustrated in this chapter by Jazzie B, XUAN Liu, Simon Lewicki and Rob Paterson. These DJs stand for very different geographical locations, and yet together form a set of cultural repertoires that illustrate how their distinctive 'scenes' and 'vibes' contribute to and illustrate transformative sociospatial performance creativities.

Key points

1. DJing is a distinct fusion of individual and collective creativities: an amalgamation of style and sound arising from sociospatial performance creativities that emerge as a co-created musicalized marking-out of urban spaces. DJing practices emphasize the identity of the community and the strength of community ties outside the dance club, seeing the 'vibe' as an affirmation of a living culture wherein DJs bridge the gap, insofar as they are professional collectors and players of 'originals' as well as mediators and orchestrators of the crowd. In this context, the production and reception of popular musics generate a wide repertoire of possible actions. DJing predisposes individuals towards certain ways of interacting with a crowd and behaving in ways that are expected of DJs. DJing involves sociospatial performance practices that celebrate the eclecticism of contemporary music in sampled soundtracks of urban dance mixes. This process produces its own social relations within performance, with sociospatial creative techniques of arranging, remixing, performing and combining real and sampled sounds, and when a DJ and a crowd interact through music to create a unique happening. Sociospatial creativities are illustrated in DJing practices, which are endlessly capable of altering, adapting, experimenting and innovatively using technologies and record mixing to move different crowds in real time and space.

2. DJs value stage persona and the creation of a unique sound. What DJs do with vinyl is also important. Some produce digital 'sets' at home, whilst others do it 'live'. Being different from the rest and having a style of your own is important, as is having a healthy fanbase. Throughout, key motifs or characterizing features of transformative performance creativities are originality, innovation and authenticity. Originality involves issues of 'originality' in sound. In this sense, turntable technology and an expanding resource of recordings are, in themselves, new expressive instruments developed by DJs. Authenticity is about being natural to the community or subculture. Both forms of creativity require an extensive knowledge of the social context, and the place and crowd in which the DJ exercises a strategic intention to navigate according to the rules and then play with the possibilities and options that produce the practices. But, at the same time, the DJ is driven by the values and expectations of transformative performance creativities. Innovation occurs when new kinds of genres and new kinds of assemblages in the creative process give rise to new trends and fashions in music's micro-social manifestations.

Discussion questions

1. All DJs are alike in important ways. All DJs are different in important ways. Is one of these statements more important to understanding DJing and DJ creativities than another? Why?

2. What is the importance of the link of spatiality and DJ sound systems, as featured in a number of practices, to constructing place-based identities and inscribing the individual and collective nature of music creativities at dance clubs?

3. What are the effects of the flux-form-of-existence of a DJ's digitalized music that gives it a special capacity in spinning social connectedness?

Chapter 6

Composed musics

This chapter presents the musical creativities of three contemporary composers who explore myriad ways of composing music for concert halls, opera houses, music theatres, and popular music venues.

Composing entails an amalgam of music creativities. The spectrum of practices featured in this chapter range from **individual** and **collaborative**, **cultural** and **inter-cultural**, and **audience—generated** types. The compositional spectrum of three composers from three diverse cultural settings share practices with a complex of technological and temporal mediations. Representations of participatory and exploratory creativities also feature in alliances and collaborations with specific contemporary ensembles (Topology, ELISION Ensemble, Crash Ensemble).

Composers' concepts of the development of performance creativity can include: (i) the defining of a musical work in performance; (ii) performance-composition creativity; and (iii) recordings representing performance-composition creativity. The differentiation here is often brought about by the composers' direct engagement and associations with contemporary ensembles.

In this chapter the following points are emphasized. (a) Musical creativities can emerge from the individual expression of an internal world—a practice driven by the individual composer—and, at the same time, can arise from the external social realm and the scripting of social action, as evidenced by the participatory and improvisational modalities utilized in innovatory performance practices in relation to the technology used by specialist contemporary music ensembles. (b) The same composed piece played in a different setting can generate considerable differences in practices. Multi-dimensional issues relating to **listening creativity** include unique combinations of context and inspiration, freedom and constraint, communicative musicality,[1] and originality. (c) Collaborations with contemporary ensembles or performance artists invite the development of new practices such as separately composed elements that are then brought together and combined into something new, or collectively created at the same time. (d) Musical creativities can be inherently sound-based or notation-based, cultural or intercultural, as manifestations of the temporal modalities of compositional, improvisational, and performance creativities, all of which create new kinds of relationships, and radically shift the balance of power between participants. The performance of composed musics involves considerable audience-generated creativity.

[1] A term coined by Malloch and Trevarthen (2009), who explore the intrinsic musical nature of musical interaction.

Introduction

Creativity is the locus of what composers do. The mythology built on an historically constructed conceptualization of musical creativity that understands composers' practices in terms of the Romantic view of four successive phases—preparation, incubation, illumination and elaboration—has long been dismissed.[1] The great majority of present-day composers are university-trained and are university teachers, which makes their lives very different from that of the composers of the nineteenth and most of the twentieth century in terms of their specific social, historical, and political circumstances. As argued in Part 1, the fact that musical creativity is a concept built around nineteenth-century myths and cults of 'genius' should not cause us to neglect questions concerning the notions of musical creativity that lie at the heart of much of what we most value in musical culture. The influence of these myths and cults should not be underestimated in any generalizations that we make about any aspect of the creative process.[2]

Emmerson (1989) provides one account of the compositional practices of composers, such as Stockhausen, Ligeti, Xenakis, and Berio. These practices involve verification as well as trial and error, using 'aural testing' and 'experimental analysis'. This technique replaces traditional notions of composition based on imagined sounds or carefully notated manuscripts, and refocuses on what is essentially a test procedure involving immediate sound feedback from a set of 'action repertoires' that form the basis for developing and discovering ideas. Computers and synthesizers, connected by digital technology, which is referred to as musical instrument digital interface (MIDI), enable the composer to continually record, store, revise, and hear evolving drafts of their work in musical data format.

Accounts of composition by Emmerson (1989), Berleant (1987), and Goehr (1992)[3] remind us of the dangers and inappropriateness of accepting any single theory of its nature. The trend amongst contemporary composers is to cast doubts on the compositional format of commissioning, promotion, and publication of musical works that has been with us since the late classical era. They claim that the 'masterwork syndrome' is archaic and discriminates against true experimentation (Goehr, 1992, p. 143). Emmerson (1989) was critical of Western musical practice because the composer was: (i) allowed the creation of just one version of each composed piece; (ii) denied revisions of works judged in final form on the basis of a 'once and for all'; and (iii) in the control of and responsive to power brokers in the arts as defined by the critics.

Many contemporary composers challenge traditional assumptions, preferring more collaborative aural and oral means, based not only on notation but also on collaboration and improvisation. It can be argued that the imbalance between literate and oral modes of musical expression is exemplified by the practice of improvisation in composition. By writing a composition within the context of an ensemble, the composition process becomes the result of collaboration between the players and the composer. Of particular interest is that a new trend has emerged called 'meta-composition' (Bahn, 1997). This refers to the composition of dynamic structures for musical performance, group coordination and improvisation. The general concept of musical organization reflects a non-linear compositional process involving hyper-media performances. This might include involvement in jazz performance and algorithmic-based and electronic music. It is not unreasonable to hypothesize that compositional technique, and indeed the final composition, is a reflection of the interplay between numbers of diverse approaches, in particular improvisation and notation. Questions remain concerning the differences between composition and improvisation. Some insights into these differences may be gained from investigating how we think about composing and the purpose of composing.

---

[1] See Burnard and Younker (2010) for a critique of this view.
[2] One of the cornerstones of contemporary beliefs about musical creativity is that whilst we are all born with a creative potential, few of us are touched by genius.
[3] See S. Bennett (1976), Berleant (1987), Emmerson (1989), and Goehr (1992) for related discussion.

Composition as object

Interestingly, Campbell and Teicher (1997) reported on the distinctive forms of aural traditions of music creation in a variety of musical cultures and described traditional Vietnamese music as 'compositions'. The festival-ritual music genre (*nhac le*), chamber music from the central (*nhac Hue*) and southern regions (*nhac tai tu*) are 'fixed' traditional melodies that are preserved in partially notated forms but learnt using an aural tradition. The adaptive process of performing a traditional melody with opportunity for the performer to elaborate their own versions adheres to the Vietnamese musician's motto of 'learning a dead song (but) performing a live melody' (Campbell and Teicher, 1997, p. 36). The nature of the compositional process was characterized as:

> No part of the process of musical creation and performance predominates over the other: conceiving a musical idea and shaping it into a melodic form by the composer is no less important than the re-shaping and personal interpretation of it by the performer.

> (Campbell and Teicher, 1997, p. 36)

These cultural interpretations of composition inform us about the composer's experience and the identification of a piece as an object which is not bound to its maker. Additionally, a composition can exist as a fixed product or as an evolving piece that is revitalized in and by each performance. This suggests that composition could be considered as a form of processual object, which is continually redefined through performance. Clifton (1983) described it this way:

> By and large, a composer moved from a general understanding of what has to be done to a specific feeling which is the result, not the cause, of the actual production of the composition . . . The composition as a complex object of 'feeling and knowledge' is understood by uncovering its sense . . . If we prefer not to simply confer significance onto a composition, the binding of feeling and understanding can help us remember the intuitive origins of implicit significations . . . [but just as] . . . the composition is *presented* by a performance . . . the composition is not reducible *to* the performance. (pp. 78–9)

Identifiable composed musics

Wolterstorff (1994) proposed that composition was guided by the 'rules of completeness that specify what constitutes' a composed work for 'a complete playing' (p. 118). This view was echoed in the writings of Margolis (1977) and Goehr (1992), both of whom considered that a necessary pre-condition for composition was a work-concept that affected the way compositions were judged, valued, and received. According to Goehr (1992), a function of the composition is to produce an enduring artefact which:

> . . . is *not* generally thought to be just any group of sounds, but a complex structure of sounds related in some important way to a composer, a score and a given class of performances. (p. 20, original emphasis)

Margolis (1977) emphasized that the explicit intention of a composer is to produce a musical manuscript or score as 'a record' of the creator's 'determination'. He maintained that the process of composition incorporates the selection and rejection of ideas on the basis of the goals of composing, 'since in the course of composing a work he [*sic*] normally considers a great many more [ideas] such than he actually settles on' (p. 247). Margolis developed this notion to suggest that the composer's intention is not just to ensure a particular 'kind of performance', for what is a performance without interpretation, but that the nature of composition requires the composer to create a certain 'kind of sound-sequence-occurrence' (p. 244). Subsequently, composition can be regarded not only as an adaptive process, revitalized in and by performance, but one based on an attentiveness to creating a piece that is 'properly formed'. Similarly, Wolterstorff (1994) claimed that composition results in the production of identifiable kinds of pieces. For example, he described a 'norm-kind', which contains certain 'properties'. Certainly, a composition has both an identity as an object of work and as an object in and of itself.

As the use of musical scores as permanent records was the standard practice in nineteenth century Western music, the composer's ownership through authorship of the music enabled his or her music to be preserved. Performances in earlier centuries were often less notated, and involved improvisatory practices in which performers embellished and elaborated on the score (Goehr, 1992). Goehr argued that composition is characterized by the fixed and repeatable score that identifies the piece as 'property'. Certainly there can be little doubt that composition is the dominant ideology of Western art music.

We cannot simply say that composition is a way of constructing an exactly specified work characterized by deliberate intention. The practice of composing is not simply determined by goals which direct judgments that the piece be worthy of being preserved as an artefact and replicated in future performances. Similarly, it is not sufficient to say that what it is to compose is defined by the goals of composition. When we expand the contexts within which composers create music, as demonstrated in non-Western cultures, composing can be applied to a piece that can be revitalized in and by each performance. Is it sufficient to say that composition involves an act of forming or constructing something that reflects changes through time? Is composed music bound up also with the broader institutional forces that provide the basis for its production and reproduction, whether elite or religious patronage, or whether subsidized by public or private funding? Are composers concerned with conscious control, clarifying intentions, refining, evaluating, and revising ideas? We know composition can involve an interplay of oral and notated traditions, or be exactly specified products or encompass purely oral forms that do not lead to a single version of a piece for replication, but how do we conceptualize the changing forms of musical creativity that arise in the practice of composed music?

What is central, then, is to understand how contemporary classical composers think about and practise their own forms of musical creativity. Hence, the purpose of this chapter is to explore the significant dimensions of musical creativities as played out in the practice of composers who are drawn from three socio-economic art worlds.[4] Ultimately, we are trying to understand musical creativity as it is defined in composers' practices and ways of thinking. We are not trying to eliminate differences between individuals: on the contrary, we are trying to find the creativities behind composers' practices. That being said, I am aware how difficult it is to present such analyses. In my early attempts of such an analysis I ended up with a mountain of text after trying to present a comprehensive picture of 20 composers, using small chunks of dialogue. The result was a misrecognition of their practices and creativities. I have therefore settled for illustrative discussions of selected composers who share a 'feel for the game', using these as examples of professional composers endowed with demonstrable mastery and achievements in three distinct contexts. The first of these is when academia supports music written in institutions of higher learning. The second is commercially supported music written for film, television, theatre, and popular media. The third is that of independent composers.

Of course, the habitus of these composers is fluid and permeable. Even if the context is an institution of higher learning, academic institutions are not the only influence on the composer's status and success. Academic composers can have performances of their music outside academia,

---

[4] Becker (1984) defines an art world as 'the network of people whose cooperative activity, organized via their joint knowledge of conventional means of doing things, produces the kind of art the art world is noted for' (p. 39).

their scores and recordings published, and their music reviewed in the press. They can have private patrons, and be awarded special honours and prizes outside academic institutions. Cultural capitals can be acquired in centres of musical production and consumption, such as recording labels, albums, grants, commissions, premiere performances, and private patrons, which can help them become established and provide the influence of social environment and material resources as a power base for musical choices.

Most of the 20 contemporary composers who were interviewed are university trained and working in academia, wherein contemporary music is discussed, analysed, and played. But there are also other networks supporting composers in the musical and alternative art worlds. These networks can function as composer collectives (e.g. the Camberwell Composers Collective; Aosdána, an Irish association of artists created in 1981 on the initiative of a group of writers and with support from the Arts Council of Ireland, some members of which receive a stipend to allow them to work full time at their art), or can belong to creative communities that give rise to codifying practices inscribed by the field of a particular group of experts, such as electronic music live-coding groups. In these networks, composers determine the direction in which the networks develop collectively.

The kinds of influence academic institutions have on composers (as with those featured in this chapter who originate from Ireland, Australia, and the UK) depend to a significant extent on the type of institution and its size, the composer's relationship with their colleagues, and the types of student that they teach. The attitude of the department to composers, their public, and the outside world, are all important elements that contribute to the diversity of environments from which this sample of composers is drawn. Some composers seek funding as composers-in-residence at schools, which gives them specific compositional and performance opportunities, and provides the schools with new music.[5]

Besides students and colleagues, academia may also provide opportunities for composers to build relationships with communities around the institution. Federal agencies and government councils also award grants for the creation, production, and performance of new works, as well as offering a performance outlet. There is also the possibility of commissions for new works, either through research grants or as research fellows. Many universities, especially the larger ones, can develop their own public, and function like regional cultural centres. Composers can also work consciously to build an audience from the local community by hosting concerts. Many are expected to sustain an international reputation, and so may travel extensively during the academic year. Indeed, the growth of the university as a performance environment has accelerated rapidly under the influence of composers. To varying degrees, teaching may also influence a composer's work, as with chamber music arising from academic situations. Whether teaching constitutes an appropriate complementary activity to composition has long been a subject of heated debate.[6] Either way, creativity is the locus of what composers do.

All of the composers who granted me interviews between May and September 2010 had received grants, hold undergraduate degrees in music or art, and had institutional affiliations or teaching positions at the time of the interviews. Several also seek their living outside universities, working as professional musicians, book writers, and researchers, or work as composers-in-residence in a range of educational and community settings. How musical creativity is rendered and retold by contemporary classical composers is crucial to understanding the dynamics and significance at the heart of much of what we most value in culture and society.

---

[5] See Burnard and Swann (2010), for an account of one such project.
[6] Pasler (2008) makes the case for the political economy of composition at the American University in 1965–85.

In this chapter we trace the way creativities are manifested in composers' habits and practices, through the accounts of a sample of contemporary classical composers. What is going on in their practices? Is it the heroic image of composers as creative individuals who work in a solitary, sustained effort on a commissioned and notation-based composition project for a long period of time?[7] Do contemporary composers operate in and/or seek out networks of people or groups as collaborators to help make choices about what they will play and how they will perform a piece, negotiating generative priorities and performance directions?

Creativity enters into virtually every aspect of a composer's work. What counts as evidence of musical creativity, and what difference this concept makes, both in practice and in possibilities, is the subject of the questions addressed in this chapter. As with all composers, musical creativity is played out at every step of the way, and yet can we assume that music and creativity, interesting partners as they are, inhabit the same conceptual space in composers' minds and practices? Given that we know there are myriad different ways in which contemporary classical art composers work, should the concept of musical creativity be used in the singular because it is the highest form of creative practice, which is realized by the individual, rather than in any openly manifest form of collective production?[8]

This chapter provides descriptions of concrete exemplars of the practices of three contemporary post-classical composers' work in Ireland, Australia, and the UK, as well as in mainland Europe. Their creativities are illustrated through their discussions of the nature of their compositional work, their work in performance, and through performances of their compositions.[9] As distinguished composers working in academia, engaging simultaneously in diverse (large and small) projects, receiving commissions from some of the world's most eminent cultural institutions, with works published and recorded by major and independent labels, they provide evidence of how multiple creativities are constituted socially and over time.

All position themselves in relation to a classical formal music training, and have accumulated plenty of cultural capital from consecrated sites (see Bourdieu, 1996), which lends them cultural capital (Bourdieu, 1996). Their profiles demonstrate a 'self-assured relationship to the world'

---

[7] Notation-based composers produce a written score. Given the centrality of musical notation in the discourse of classical music, a written score may, as is the case for the composers featured here, serve several purposes. Performers can be given wide-ranging degrees of leeway; but the unwritten rules of the game, unless otherwise stated, are such that this leeway may be relatively small or very large. The idea of being true or faithful to the score, and therefore to the composer, is something agreed between the composer and the performers, particularly, as in this chapter, where all three composers are affiliated with, or founding members of, performance ensembles, for which they work in close alliance. In the case of Liza, her group is described implicitly as a 'creative laboratory'.

[8] See discussions in Deliège and Wiggins (2006).

[9] The connectedness of modalities of creativity, such as compositional creativity, improvisational creativity, and performance creativity—rather than the notion of a piece as something autonomous—is a common practice, in which composers bring together a stock of possibilities and supplement these by *creating* further possibilities, working closely with, and composing for, a particular chamber ensemble. This conception of creativity refers to composition as a musical 'work in performance', and links to a ubiquitous kind of creativity illustrated in terms of 'performances representing works' (a term coined by Nicholas Cook). For Donnacha Dennehy it's the Crash Ensemble. Liza Lim works closely with Elision, which functions as a 'creative laboratory'. Robert Davidson works closely with and composes for a Brisbane post-classical quintet, Topology, known for managing to 'cater to audiences with no specific interest in modern chamber music. It isn't until one sees a boundary-blurring performance like tonight's that one understands how the group has managed to acquire such a unique following.' (See QUT Festival Theatre, Brisbane Powerhouse Review: 17 September 2010, http://www.topologymusic.com/).

(Bourdieu, 1984a, p. 56), with creative practices that are applied in different ways, adapted to new situations and grounded in the everyday experiences of both the individual and social realms. In the field of music, which has tended to polarize the study of creativity as either individual, or collaborative, or collective effort, they open up new ground. The composers illustrate a number of characteristics of collaborative creativity by acknowledging, borrowing and building, and integrating cultural and intercultural collaborations. Each is rooted in a particular context that is bounded by what the field and their own practice means for them.

In the narratives that follow, we see how musical creativity as part of the composer's habitus, is specifically named and described, how it is talked about, developed, extended, and applied rationally and consciously over time. We hear a collection of shared, alternative, and sometimes opposing themes intersecting with each other and coalescing around the dominant situational models of individualism and social spaces. This finds expression in varied and overlapping discourses of creativity.

Of the 20 interviews, the accounts of the three notation-based composers[10] featured in this chapter articulate important differences between various sorts of creativities (creativities that take different forms and which are particularly prominent) and dispositions, which are evident not just in attitudes, approaches and values, but also in their particular creative practices. As mentioned earlier, each of these composers also works as a recording artist with those who are more traditionally schooled in the classical arts, and/or are popular music artists with a classical bent. (See, for example, Sufjan Stevens, David Bowie, Radiohead, Brian Eno, Battles, The Knife, Frank Zappa, Jónsi, Owen Pallett, Björk, Dirty Projectors, Kayo Dot, Joanna Newsom, Katie Noonan, Kate Miller-Heidke, all of whom who have often engaged with contemporary art music.) This practice goes back to The Rolling Stones who put the first sitar on a Western pop record ('Paint it black') and the 1970s prog-rock and art-rock movements.

We begin with Donnacha Dennehy (Ireland), then move on to Liza Lim (UK), and end with Robert Davidson (Australia). In all three cases, what counts as 'musical creativity' differs not merely from practice to practice but also as the composer's habitus is constituted in moments of practice as a complex interplay between past and present (Reay, 2004). Thus, musical creativity is not defined simply or primarily in terms of the creation of musical works, but rather in terms of the modality of creativity (e.g. improvisational, compositional, performance, and listening creativities). Musical creativity becomes a means to the end of making music not as an end in itself but as something that composer, performer, and listener all have a hand in creating and co-creating. For example, Robert Davidson asks performers to read his scores as improvisers and composers, creating a co-authorship that comes into being through creative listening and music-making.

Introducing Donnacha Dennehy

Internationally renowned Irish composer Donnacha Dennehy (Fig. 6.1), of Trinity College, Dublin, has received commissions from the BBC, WNYC (Public Radio New York), RTÉ, Amsterdam Funds Voor der Kunst, the arts councils of both England and Ireland, and from many individual ensembles. Noted performers of his work include Dawn Upshaw, Bang On A Can All-Stars, Orkest de Volharding, London Sinfonietta, Percussion Group of the Hague, Ensemble Integrales, Electra, Prism Saxophone Quartet, Joanna MacGregor, and Jenny Lin. He has also collaborated with artists working in video and dance.

---

[10] Each composer works in higher education at universities as follows: Donnacha Dennehy at Trinity College, Dublin, Ireland, Robert Davidson at the University of Queensland, Australia, and Liza Lim at the University of Huddersfield, Yorkshire, UK.

Fig. 6.1 Composer Donnacha Dennehy.
© Sophie Elbrick Dennehy, 2011.

Donnacha studied composition at Trinity College, Dublin, and at the University of Illinois, Chicago, USA, where his main teachers were Salvatore Martirano and William Brooks. He pursued further studies in electronic music at The Hague, and at IRCAM, Paris.[11] Returning to Ireland, he founded the Crash Ensemble in 1997 to concentrate on the newest music, exploring multi-media. He now lectures in music technology and composition at Trinity College, Dublin. His work has been featured in festivals such as ISCM World Music Days, Bang On A Can in New York, Sonic Evolutions Festival at Lincoln Center, Wien Modern, EXPO 2000 in Germany, the Ultima Festival in Oslo, the Gaudeamus Festival in Amsterdam, and State of the Nation at the South Bank. Forthcoming commissions include pieces for the Kronos Quartet, and Dawn Upshaw with the St Paul Chamber Orchestra. His first full-length album, *Elastic Harmonic*, was released on NMC in June 2007, and Nonesuch Records is releasing *Grá Agus Bás,* a new album of his work which was released in May 2011 (see www.nonesuch.com/albums/gra-agus-bas). In 2005, Donnacha was elected to Aosdána, Ireland's state-sponsored academy of creative artists.

When Donnacha's father saw that he was interested in music, he purchased a piano and a record player for the house (neither was there before). As he says, 'my family are not particularly musical, but very encouraging, particularly of the creative aspects of my life'. Donnacha's father was also a playwright, although he earned his living primarily working for an insurance company. He has just retired from working in the Dublin libraries, and is now writing full-time. His grandmother was a fiddler, and his father's sister had a strong interest in classical music, both as a player and listener. Donnacha's mother works as a ward clerk in a convalescent home. As he explains:

> *Donnacha*: I remember my mum being very fond of Elvis, and my father of the Beatles, and some classical. Also both were interested in important Irish cultural figures such as Sean O'Riada, John B. Keane, Brian Friel, Tom Murphy etc. Both had a strong interest in going to the theatre. My father had wide

---

11 IRCAM (Institut de Recherche et Coordination Acoustique/Musique) is a European institute for science about music and sound and avant-garde electro-acoustical art music. It is situated next to, and is organizationally linked with, the Centre Pompidou in Paris. The extension of the building was designed by Renzo Piano and Richard Rogers (http://en.wikipedia.org/wiki/IRCAM).

radio listening habits. I remember his waking me up one Saturday to listen to Varese on the radio when I was around 11 or so as he found it fascinating.

He started flute lessons at the age of nine and piano lessons, as a second instrument, at ten. As a teenager growing up in Dublin, he had a strong passion for listening, and was influenced by the potentialities of American minimalist and post-minimalist music. He was not particularly encouraged by any teacher ('in fact, often actively discouraged') at this time. I was encouraged however by a very unconventional harmony teacher and composer from England called William York—he did have a big influence on me (he also set up an ensemble in Dublin devoted to new music, which unfortunately lasted a very short time). There were, however, lots of musical influences from Irish music and experimental rock, and approaches to sound use, not just in the use of electric guitars but also electronics and related working methods of electronica/experimental rock worlds.

His earliest memories of music-making invoke a complex response to the productive tensions and 'collisions' between forms of cultural inheritance and resistance, as well as the powerful potentialities of new music invention. Donnacha saw himself bound not so much to tradition as to the musical significance that is brought to it.

> *Donnacha*: The most important thing to me when I was growing up was playing and composing music, these were things I did together from a very young age. But a lot of my educational environment didn't encourage creativity though. There was no music taught at secondary school. I also had a lot of problems with authority towards the end of my time at secondary school, serving detention every week for the last two years! . . . I remember playing my own pieces into a tape recorder and then transcribing it. I'd make up pieces which were improvisations too. I used to give them names like 'symphonies' [he laughs]. And then there were all the punk pieces I wrote when I was 10. But at this time I was also hero-worshipping Stravinsky and Bach and Stockhausen of course, who was finding new ways of composing, and, of course, there was all the Irish music in there . . . I grew up knowing that music can be something of the past and it can be something made in the present . . . I have always been fascinated by the craft of composing and by the physicality of the sound. Many composers have quite a cerebral or at least distanced approach to the 'sound' of the piece, whereas I work directly with it. It actually inspires what I do on many levels, even structurally. I want to feel the impact of the sound, even when it's gentle—it has to make an almost bodily impression on me. In one of my pieces 'Grá Agus Bás',[12] there's an almost overwhelming aspect to the sound of it, particularly in the centre, and in the final ascent. Aside from that, most of the gentle parts are deeply informed by this overtone-spectral approach to the harmony which actually results in strange timbres that I feel directly.

Performed sound becomes the raw material for new dynamic structures of composition. The musical composition is constituted in its sonic production and reproduction, not in a score. Electronics form a big part even of Donnacha's acoustic pieces such as 'Grá Agus Bás'. For Donnacha, recordings embody performances: the work is not embodied in the score but, rather, it is the performance that represents the work. Even though, today, the majority of composers in the post-modern post-classical tradition still produce scores, for Donnacha the composition exists in the performance, with the recording being the key to individuating the work—a kind of documentation that is in step with the way rock musicians represent the work of album making or recording as a single stage in writing down the sound.

> *Donnacha*: Writing 'Grá Agus Bás' (2007) was actually a step in a new direction for me. I had never really done anything substantial with any of Ireland's indigenous folk traditions prior to this, except for when I was a child of 10! I actually felt it was a big risk for me, especially with the normal experimental/

---

12 'Grá Agus Bás' has just been recorded (along with 'That the Night Come', the piece Donnacha wrote for Dawn Upshaw and Crash Ensemble) for a forthcoming release by Nonesuch Records (www.nonesuch.com).

new classical audience. But I was drawn to the material in a very creative way, and really sensed a sort of potential for me with a very specific type of extant repertoire—the unaccompanied sean-nós tradition. I have since worked even more with this material, sometimes quite directly in making 'spectral' sean-nós settings, at other times using it to influence melodic and ornamental patterning in my music (my recent Yeats setting for Dawn Upshaw and Crash Ensemble, 'That the Night Come' (2010), and also very abstractly in a much more abstract instrumental piece such as 'As An-Nós' (2009) . . . Also, very importantly for me, is the fact that I've developed a lot of what I'd consider my landmark works for Crash Ensemble—many of those scores remain basically incomplete for years, with my revising them based on rehearsals, performances, etc. Also the musicians know my music so intimately that there are some details that I don't need to put in, and it's only when other groups want to do it that I finally produce as detailed a score as a I possibly can . . . But I do have a strong interest in 'controlling' the way the music may work—this is in strong contrast to an approach of a composer who wants to have the performers create the piece anew in an improvisational manner in each performance—for them the idea of a fixed score is not of interest at all.

From the age of 10, he has been an avid listener and practitioner within the contemporary classic avant-garde scene, attending, for instance, the Dublin Festival of 20th Century Music and contemporary concerts of music by Stockhausen and Cage, amongst others. Although he acknowledges the plurality of rule systems within contemporary music, from total serialism and its offspring in the neo-complex methods of the likes of contemporary composer Ferneyhough, to aleatoricism, to system-based compositions, and to what looks like an increasing orthodoxy in spectral techniques, his music is not based on any one of these systems.

Along with performed sound, another significant element in Donnacha's practice as a composer involves his innovative use of technology. This is at the root of what Donnacha does as a composer—looping material on the computer to hear what it yields, transforming it, and then figuring out the way forward.

Donnacha: For me, everything I hear I feel as energy of my composition; sound has a physical impact on me, that I think 'oh, that's really interesting', or you think 'oh God, that sound feels boring' . . . So I sort of listen to it all the time, and sometimes you'd hear a particular combination of sounds that would just lodge in there, in some sort of physical way. Or a way that a composer, when you least expect it, can surprise you. And of course there is a powerful connection created with something you're feeling and seeing at the same time.

He feels and sees the physicality of sound as he is playing it back—often at loud volumes—through loudspeakers, and then making generalized mockups of the whole thing (without the details filled in) to get a basic idea of the overall shape so that this overall shape then informs the way he treats the material within. What also matters is how Donnacha locates himself in 'cultural collisions' between elements from Irish traditional music, electronica, rock, and a kind of post-minimalist territory. This situates him as a composer in different conceptual spaces as illustrated in his approach to the composing of 'Grá Agus Bás':

Donnacha: To begin with, I had to immerse myself in as much of the sean nós tradition as I could. Vital to this was the helpful assistance of the sean nós singer Iarla O'Lionáird. Iarla would come to my house when he was in Dublin (usually for other business, as he is a busy successful singer), and I would record him singing much of his repertoire entirely unaccompanied. I also sought out transcriptions made by English musicologists (working under the auspices of the London Folk Music Society) who travelled around Ireland at the start of the twentieth century. I was especially interested in the transcriptions made by Martin Freeman because he covered a lot of the songs in the region that Iarla came from—Cork and Kerry. I then transcribed all the recordings both by hand and using a piece of software called Melodyne. I used the software in order to (a) really see clearly the deviations from normal tuning without my ear tidying them up intuitively, and (b) really put a microscope to some of the ornamentation patterns.

Some of these ornamentation patterns were then translated into straightforward, almost minimalist figurations for the instrumentalists. Importantly I was drawn to the sean nós tradition not only for its own very obvious merits but also for how it intersected with my already existing musical vocabulary and interests.

I have become increasingly interested in the relationship between pure overtone-based harmony and resulting timbres. You see, almost any sound can be analysed and reconstructed by breaking it down into its pure time varying overtone patterns. I wasn't so much interested in reconstruction however but in the new types of timbre possible out of using harmonies made up of these 'pure' frequencies. Anyway, much of the so-called 'microtonality' of sean nós singing, which might be viewed as wrong in a strictly equal-tempered harmonic environment, could actually fit very well with a much more 'spectrally' enhanced type of harmonic language that I was already using. Also the smaller rhythmic level of my music is based on repeating and varying patterns too, and I wanted to infuse these patterns with material taken from ornamentation patterns in sean nós singing. Importantly, I was not interested in paying homage to the tradition but rather using it as an imaginative springboard for my own creative voyages. However it's probably important that I actually come from Ireland and this material has such strong resonance for me. I would feel uncomfortable doing the same with indigenous African music for instance—it would feel like I was raiding that imperialistically or something. As much as I enjoy something like the Tropenmuseum in Amsterdam, I also feel uncomfortable about the colonialist relationship between it and the indigenous cultures of Indonesia, Surinam, etc. that are so beautifully represented there.

The visceral nature of Donnacha's creative practice, and the impact of its dynamic complexity, is manifest in the way his music appropriates and explodes musical conventions in an amalgam of diverse and sophisticated components, starting from 'feeling my way, often accidentally, and then generating a kind of rationale for it as I get more of a feel for it' and getting 'involved in "making" something'. He is 'literally often painting the sound of the piece right from the start using these kind of elaborate mock-ups, which actually help him to generate the material, as it were, viscerally. He describes his practice as 'instinctive'.

Donnacha: Each piece is compelled by some sort of problem or opening up to something new. Actually that's usually quite exciting for me. The fact that I'm writing an opera and setting texts in new ways but also doing something new for me . . . there's various discoveries that compel me . . . Because you have to spend hours and hours every day doing the details, you can't afford to lose sight of what you're really trying to do. I have these notebooks, these moleskin notebooks that I have all the time, that I sort of scribble down ideas, abstractly, and eventually I get a kind of image though, this is sort of when I'm preparing a piece, of what I actually want the piece to do. And I usually have a kind of image of what I want the whole thing to do, and actually I would say that one of my things is that I usually have a fairly good idea of a kind of bird's eye vision of the piece. But there are always shocks and surprises along the way.

Donnacha highlights the central significance of different kinds of creative process as a practice that varies considerably and is distributed across different kinds of media, involving multiple takes, overdubs, and editing. The process starts with 'messing around at the piano or I often do a lot of stuff with overtones'. Improvisation remains key.

Donnacha: Especially important, so as to avoid doing something similar, or where you're almost destined to just copy what's been done before. In a way you have to have some non-explainable element to it . . . and a lot of improvisation can fall into a kind of standard mode you know. There's also a thing where I stop listening to stuff related to what I'm composing too, in case it would too directly influence the composition as well . . . In a way you have to have some non-explainable element to it.

Technology figures prominently in Donnacha's creative practice. He records 'everything'. Then he plays it back and listens, 'tying this up, trying that out, sorting out problems'. Thus the compositional practice is multi-dimensional and multi-modal, and is manifest in iterations as he responds emotionally and viscerally to what he hears. This iteration is a main part of his compositional process.

> *Donnacha*: Sometimes I do stuff just writing straight onto the computer, and then figure out what the constraints are . . . figuring out how something is to work over it. So a lot of it is that I'm sort of generating material, or whatever, and figuring out how to do it by mixture of sort of playing it and thinking it . . . And then sometimes I just focus on setting a particular sound . . .

This is a composer who is drawn to the immediate raw sonic and visceral impact of sound, which is the reason that electronics and electronic mockups play such a role in his creative practice.

> *Donnacha*: I find that I become wise after the fact as I'm working with the material, that it then seems to have this inevitability as I'm developing it. But you would never predict that inevitability in advance about what you actually wanted to do with the piece.

The use of 'mockups' as piano reductions signifies that a strong performative element inheres in recording 'the performance of sound'.

> *Donnacha*: 'Mockups' are abstractions of the piece. I use them in a way so that I don't actually fall in love with my mockup as opposed to the piece that I'm trying to write. I use the computer at each stage in the process. Sometimes I switch between two platforms to get an idea of how it's going. Sometimes notation is limiting too for certain pieces. Some pieces I've written out by hand because I haven't been interested in the way that the computer will do it. Sometimes I work in a feedback loop with musicians [here he is referring to his group the Crash Ensemble during both performance and playback] . . . I have them play back something I've worked up partially scored or I set up experiments where I do certain things with the computers and do other things only by hand. If you do recordings and you record yourself, you're thinking it can change and you can think of it in a different way. Musicians playing drafts of your compositions engage in a kind of creative translation; they're translating between something you've written and something they are doing spontaneously in a process of discovering something new . . . it's like trying to get the details tied up to something but while seeing a kind of a big picture that's driving it . . . it shows varieties of looking at the same thing in different ways.

Donnacha practises a kind of composition-performance creativity as a process of discovering and actualizing new possibilities. Performers are adding these possibilities, and as a result, the work changes by way of performance creativity. The composition is somehow worked *into* the performance. The composition does not grow beyond the intent of the composer; however, because Donnacha has a firm conception of the work, and defines his own creativity in terms of the musical work in performance and its constructed meaning. But Donnacha is right, this process varies considerably as stages are compressed or articulated in different ways, even when it is identified with the recording, the composition grows beyond him. He has no real control over its reception. It becomes something else in the minds of listeners, and even then it changes according to cultural context. The result is that there tends to be many manifestations and recombinations of composition-performance creativity.

The 'mockup' brings about a creative fertility, which operates at different levels, involving specific types of creativities that function in different ways at different points in the creative process. The process drives a vision or imagined whole ('a kind of big picture'). The 'mockups' hold a complex set of intentions supplemented by actual performances. Compositional and performance creativities together create possibilities—possibilities that are actually inherent in the work but that do not exist without the musicians, for whom performances are discoveries of inherent possibilities. Donnacha locates how these 'mockups' function and the significance which is brought to them:

> *Donnacha*: With my more elaborate mockups, I can just shift around a sound to see what the impact of that sound is in combination with others feedback from performers. For example, in a piano trio that I wrote it

doesn't really sound like a piano and two normal string instruments. You'd think it's got electronic modifications when you first hear it. That's to do with the way the overtones connect with each other to produce
this kind of sonic effect. Not sonic effect, so much as a sonic mass. So I mean in some way I'm really precise,
like trying to get the details tied up to something, but holding firm on the big picture that's driving it.

In this view, Donnacha emphasizes the participatory role of his Crash Ensemble (his new music
ensemble) in giving feedback, and the social and individual significance of having a strong association with a contemporary ensemble—a community to which the composer implicitly has 'all these
[musician] friends that you can call on'. The relationship between the virtual space of the musical
score and the physical space of its performance is not one of detachment but, rather, one of complementarity. Donnacha acknowledges that the creative impulse is triggered through composition-
performance creativity, which forms a part of the intimate tie between players and composers. His
work and practice of 'workshopping' with the Crash Ensemble figure centrally, and as an essential
part of his composer's habitus, wherein highly consecrated cultural capital is a major constituent, and
through which he takes up a significant position within the wider social space and field of music.

> *Donnacha*: I think for me the creative impulse is definitely individual. However I would be stone not to
> be influenced by my environment, such as where I live, what I listen to etc. There's no doubt that my
> having set up Crash Ensemble has been vital to my development as a composer. In some pieces I very
> much do thrive on interaction with players in the group. And 'Grá Agus Bás' was one of those! For
> example, it was essential to work with our cellist Kate Ellis in working out all these gymnastic fast pat-
> terns made up of natural harmonics. I came to her with a number of ideas in advance written out, and
> then modified them based on what worked best/seemed the most natural/produces the most sonically
> interesting result, etc. This then influenced the entire writing for the strings. Also, because I know the
> players so well, it really affects how I write for them, as I kind of know inside out what they're really good
> at. I also often take much more risks for pieces for Crash as I know that they will be very tolerant of my
> making lots of changes during the rehearsal process. This kind of workshopping I find invaluable.

This successful contemporary chamber ensemble provides opportunities for performance play-
back and performer feedback. Here it is the Crash Ensemble that discerns and probes Donnacha's
music, not in the sense of performers working collaboratively but rather inspiring individuality in
terms that further his practice of composition-performance creativity. This has to do with editing,
selecting, assembling, arranging, and ways of individuating the work and evaluating different
versions, of writing down in sound multiple renditions of a piece in performance. In a discussion
of the aesthetics of rock music, Gracyk (1996) argues that in rock the work is in the recording. For
Donnacha writing a score is as important as the renditions of a piece in performance.

> *Donnacha*: The wonderful thing about a score is that you have something there in a document that
> allows it to be performed so many times, by different people. I do like that . . . of course it's amazing
> the difference at different performances. You can hear things in pieces that you never imaged, whether
> that is the outcome of certain players inputs or some conductors as well . . . Even if the piece isn't that
> original, there can be new emotion that one gets from conducting it, playing it or listening to it. That
> is where I liken myself to an architect that's built the building. What happens to it is up to those who
> live, work and play in it. I find that's exciting. But not all composers write on paper. Not all scores are
> fully notated. This is where the type of piece determines the amount of collaboration or inputs and
> influences from others and where the computer is central . . . it helps me to compose a piece written
> around what the players can do . . . There is an awful lot of solo effort involved and an awful lot of need
> for processing on your own. You need a quietness . . . you need space to create.

History shows that the 'solo effort' of creative accomplishment is common in the accounts of
composers' practices, as are the centrally positioned performers or chamber groups that they
work with, compose for, and seek feedback from. Individual and social creativities rely on the

interaction and judgment of others, and because of the process of appropriation and connection to social relations, networks, thought communities, and collectivities of which they are a part. Thus, the manifestation of composition-performance creativity is never solely an individual phenomenon (M.S. Barrett and Gromko, 2007). The Crash Ensemble is itself a form of cultural capital, in that it orients actions and inclinations without strictly determining them. The ensemble is a site of incorporated history, the source of practices and perceptions which reproduce that history, and which provide opportunities to experiment, negotiate, and make judgments within the social system in which specific works are created.

Introducing Liza Lim[13]

Australian composer Liza Lim is Professor of Composition and Director of CeReNeM (www. cerenem.org), the Centre for Research in New Music at the University of Huddersfield, Yorkshire, UK. She was appointed in 2008, having worked as a freelance composer for 20 years. Liza's research and composition work has been focused on the area of intercultural exchange, looking particularly at Chinese and Australian indigenous art, aesthetics, and ritual culture.[14] Liza's early work examines the role of ambivalence, particularly in diasporic cultural conditions, as a space for the transformation of cultural knowledge. This is allied with a strong interest in the politics of translation and other kinds of transactions in cultural meaning, which she has explored in three operatic works, The Oresteia (1993), Moon Spirit Feasting (1999) and The Navigator (2008). Her compositional work in the area of narrative multiplicity is informed by analyses of Chinese poetry, calligraphic structure, and the many traditions of folk stories that 'don't add up'.

Liza's collaborations with Chinese, Japanese, and Korean musicians inform her interest in kinaesthetic approaches to performance, whereby the physicality of gesture is interrogated as the basis for formulating new approaches to instrumental technique and listening. Key works in this area include 'Koto' (1993), 'The Alchemical Wedding' (1996) and three important commissions from the Festival d'Automne Paris, 'In the Shadow's Light' (2004), 'The Quickening' (2005) and 'Mother Tongue' (2005). More recently, her explorations of Australian Aboriginal culture, through research and collaborations with indigenous artist Judy Watson (Glass House Mountains installation project, 2005, Queensland), and with Yolngu women elders of the Gumatj clan from Yirrkala, in her role as curator of the music series 'As Night Softly Falls' for the 2006 Adelaide Festival, has led her to look at aspects of indigenous aesthetics and non-Western epistemologies of time and space in art, music, and story-telling.[15]

---

[13]   For more information on Liza's background and works, see http://www.ricordi.co.uk/composers/index-liza. php and http://www.ricordi.de/lim-liza.0.html?&L=1.

[14]   Liza has been recognized internationally through major commissions, regular performances at key venues in Paris, Berlin, Munich, Venice, and London, and a distinguished publication history with Ricordi (Milan, London and Munich). Awards include the Paul Lowin Prize, Fromm Foundation Award (Harvard), Australia Council and Ian Potter Cultural Trust Senior Fellowships. Her key works include 'Machine for Contacting the Dead' (2000), commissioned by the Ensemble InterContemporain, Paris, in association with the Cité de la Musique's exhibition of archaeological artefacts from the tomb of the Marquis Yi of Zheng, and performed in Paris and Basel in 2000. Related to this work is the opera Moon Spirit Feasting (1997–99), commissioned by the Adelaide and Melbourne Festivals, which investigates Chinese ritual culture and theatre as an evolving form under diasporic conditions in South-East Asia. Following seasons in Australia, the opera toured Berlin, Zurich, and Tokyo in 2002, before making a return season to the Brisbane Festival in 2006.

[15]   The relation of composer to audience is an important issue for Liza (who works for/composes to no specific audience).

Fig. 6.2 Composer Liza Lim working on the pencil score of 'Mother Tongue' (2005). This was a work jointly commissioned by the 2005 Festival d'Automne à Paris, Ensemble InterContemporain, and ELISION Ensemble.
Photo by Daryl Buckley, Brisbane. © Daryl Buckley, 2011.

Liza has brought her formative experiences with the ELISION Ensemble in crafting individual approaches to instrumental sound to her work with much larger forces written for the Sydney and West Australian Symphony Orchestras, Bavarian Radio, and South West German Radio Orchestras exemplified in works such as 'The Compass' (2006), 'The Guest' (2010) and 'Pearl, Ochre Hair String' (2010).

Liza's most recent project 'Tongue of the Invisible' (2011), commissioned by the Holland Festival and musikFabrik, points towards new directions with an interest in distributed creativity bringing improvisational sections into her music as a way of exploring the shifting states of the mystical poetry of the fourteenth-century Sufi poet Hafez. About the work, she says, 'One of things I wanted to explore in my work "Tongue of the Invisible" is this aspect of the untranslatable dimensions of the poetry, or the multiple translations that sit side by side. The layers of meaning point towards but ultimately can never fully express this idea of union adding to the almost painful sensation of longing in the poetry. The librettist of the work, writer Jonathan Holmes, made a wonderful version of lines from Hafez, placing them in a 7 × 7 grid. Every square of the grid has a line of poetry and one can trace one's own path through the poem—each line reflects on every other line and every pathway leads you through the poem—you get a sense of the work as a multiplying unity. The music also reflects the immersive structure of the poem by creating spaces that are sometimes composed, sometimes improvised so the creativity of all of the participants is drawn into the realization of the work as a world of multiple meanings.[16]

Liza has two younger sisters, neither of whom works in the arts or music industry. Both her father, an ENT surgeon, and her mother (an audiologist) are now retired. Liza, as with the other

---

[16] From an interview with Vrouwkje Tuinman in the monthly feminist *Opzij Magazine* (May, Issue 6, 2011), http://www.opzij.nl/.

composers interviewed in this sample, was self-directed towards composing, and from early adolescent years spent a good deal of time and energy exploring the experience of composing.

> *Liza*: I have been writing music since I was at high school. I have thought of myself as a composer since I was about 11 years of age. I'm now 43, so that's over 30 years of work. I would say that the kind of exposure I had at school, particularly to contemporary music and the notion of making your own music through improvisation and composition, was the formative thing which turned me into a composer.

As with Donnacha, a strong home influence with parental encouragement and a nurturing school environment were key elements in preparing Liza for a male-dominated musical world.[17] Liza is a composer who has developed a strong reputation based on the gains achieved from taking chances, tenacity, individuality, energy and vitality, skillfulness, innovation, and having a distinctive voice. Some of her earliest formative experiences came from being part of a community that encouraged this attitude and creative disposition in music. At the age of 11, Liza was encouraged by her teachers at an independent/private school in Melbourne to turn from piano and violin studies to composition.

> *Liza*: My first instrument was piano and then I started learning violin around that time. I wasn't particularly clued into music as a child at primary school. It was the impact of going to a particular high school that I think kind of really switched on something inside of me . . . I owe everything to them . . . Perhaps unusually I began composing with a graphic score phase and experimenting with sounds rather than traditional notation. But I would say it was a little bit later that I had more of a sense of trying to create my own language and developing my own voice.

In these early years, teachers and peer musicians have a major impact on young people developing their musical identities and identifications as composers. Such influences, as discussed by the other composers, form part of the social context in which they are situated, such as family, bands and school. Liza's teachers, peers, and the school community encouraged her ('everything I wrote got played') and made composing seem not a peculiar thing to do. Being recognized as a composer came without any direct pressure. Equally strong patterns of capital were formed, but this time derived from educational, social, and cultural capitals, gained by association with consecrated institutions of education and arts, along with social networks. Liza was accepted and widely acclaimed as a young and gifted composer during her formative school years, when she found her self-identity, reputation, and distinctive voice as a composer of new works.

> *Liza*: At the heart of my work has been much collaboration with many musicians. And they have certainly been, I would say, also, the formative kind of impulse for a lot of my work . . . fellow students, all the way along. In fact I still work with someone I went to school with, the singer Deborah Kayser who was in my last opera The Navigator (2008). So, very long-term collaborative relationships with key performers are what I would say has really characterized my work as a composer . . . I had the most fantastic sort of level of support from people around me. Everything I wrote got played . . . Some of the early works I wrote were for the school orchestra where there was a sense of 'give it a go'.

At the individual level, music reinforces social relations, in particular social and personal networks. The formation of a composer's identity, their generational processes, and the central role of the creative process can be seen as dependent on discursive frameworks within an 'emergent process that involves a social group of individuals engaged in complex, unpredictable interactions'

---

[17] See Reddington (2007), for a discussion of female musicians in the male domain of rock music; see also Green (2001), for a discussion of gendered approaches to students composers; see also Pasler (2008), for interesting discussions about the challenges for women in developing careers as composers.

(Sawyer, 2003, p. 19). This type of creativity has been described cogently by M.S. Barrett and Gromko (2007), who propose that individual creativity is situated 'within social communities where members practice problem finding, problem solving and productive evaluation. The creative product, therefore, is one that bears the stamp of the history, culture and social interactions within the community of which the artist is a member' (p. 227).

One of Liza's important communities is ELISION, a contemporary music ensemble that creates opportunities for experimentation.

> *Liza*: Working with ELISION[18] offers me all types of opportunities for just plunging in and trialing and testing ideas . . . that's why I said that the contact with performers was absolutely critical, because for me the creative laboratory is crucial for finding out what works and what doesn't work, in a very concrete sense . . . And it's not just the technical, but it's the interpersonal level as well that's really important here. In a sense, much of the work I do is a customization of sound that derives from these contacts with performers. These are the idiosyncratic aspects rather than anything else. I've always tried to characterize the work I do in terms of trying to move further and further away from any sort of generic sense of what is happening, towards an evermore specific and finely tuned sense of the particular: *this* moment, *this* sound in *this* way, *this* type of energy in relation to the performer.

The dualism of individual and inward and socially constituted and outward practices is shown in the discourse of individual creativity, which is defined by the intent of composing, but situated within the community of which the artist is a member.

> *Liza*: Another aspect of the way I'm in dialogue with a wider context is the way my compositional work often focuses on aspects of intercultural exchange looking particularly at Chinese and at Australian Indigenous art, aesthetics, and ritual culture. This hasn't been an abstract study but very much something arising from interactions with different kinds of performers and artists from various traditions . . . I did study with a number of different composers in Australia and abroad. I went through my undergraduate training as a classical performer. It was a bit later that I was part of a composition course. I was often left to my own devices as well. So I would say that the contact with composers was a different kind of input from the other kinds of experiences I was having with performers . . . While the contact with performers was absolutely critical, I did study with two teachers who emphasized musical craftsmanship. One was the Australian–Italian composer Riccardo Formosa, who took a very artisanal approach to composition with a sense of the hand-crafting of every sound and with things like orchestration . . . sound for me is also key . . . Looking for different solutions for how a sound can transform, listening for what happens when you push the sound in a certain way, being very specific in terms of its qualities and knowing certain things about the boundaries of where things start to morph, so that I can actually compose with these different degrees of transformation . . . This close connection to the morphology of sound has been honed by the experience of writing pieces which are for a specific situation with performers . . . There are particular performers that really inspire me and so a work is made in close collaboration with the performers and they form part of the interaction.

Central to Liza's experience of 'individual creativity' is the assumption that there is not merely an accidental, but an essential relationship between the work and its written and aural manifestations. The work is not static but essentially historical and social in nature. As she puts it, 'the performers form part of the interaction' of its generative origins. These meanings live on, and are renewed in, each new performance; and, as in creative collaborations (or collaborative creativity),

---

[18] The ELISION ensemble is a chamber ensemble specializing in contemporary classical music, concentrating on the creation and presentation of new works. The ensemble comprises a core of 20 virtuoso musicians from Australia as well as other parts of the world (www.elision.org.au).

this process is profoundly affected by the nature of the social and cultural relationship between artists.

> *Liza*: I have an ongoing concern or interest in Aboriginal aesthetics . . . since 2004, I've experimented with different ways of realizing these ideas. I've a collection of works where what I'm looking to create in these works are qualities of sound which are highly mobile, and quite three-dimensional. So if you imagine a point on a surface, you can move that in any direction, and then drop below the surface, that is, the sound can be understood in a spatial way, the sound can take on different qualities of density and opacity. The types of vocabularies I might use to describe what I'm doing with the sound or how it develops come from meteorology—weather patterns and dynamical systems. And so that connects with a particular aesthetic world, which prompts me to look for new techniques to realize these structures. An example, is the use of a 'guiro bow' in my piece 'Invisibility' (2009) which looks at the behaviour of strings tuned at different tensions and rough and smooth bowing surfaces to create sounds that have this three-dimensional mobile quality, the quality of 'shimmer' that is so central to Aboriginal aesthetics . . . It's about just looking for different solutions to making new sonic textures, asking, what happens when you create a situation where there are a number of interacting forces influencing the behaviour of sounds. It is not like I'm measuring it in . . . [a] strictly quantified empirical way with a sliding scale of effects. It's more about investigating categories of sonic behaviour and their interaction and I am able to internalize the qualities of the sounds and be attuned to their dynamic qualities so that I can compose with these different degrees of transformation in behaviour.

Liza's habitus is essentially distinct in the unusually potent configuration of social, cultural and symbolic capital as the constituents of a successful field strategy. Here we see creativity take myriad forms embodying an indigenous culture's aesthetics (or cultural creativity) as they become manifest in text, mimicry, and signifying, and as re-created in forms of contemporary musical mediation (or intercultural creativity). Creativity eschews any absolute state as it is continuously changes and transforms. These qualities reflect the principles that structure this composer's artistic practice, the capital configurations of her habitus, and her endowment of symbolic capital. To gain acceptance in these terms is indeed to gain legitimation of, and justification for, aesthetic transcendence, which gives a sense of uniqueness transmitted through the originality of artistic expression. New music by contemporary composers can struggle to displace a whole aesthetic scheme of perception, and, in so doing, can transform the structure of the field. To this extent, what takes place in new musical creativities should be seen as gaining legitimation for an aesthetic that must be understood, as Bourdieu (1996 wrote, to be 'historically necessitated' (p. 252).

Creativity is also bound up with the reopening and re-creation of cultural source material, in improvisatory inclusions, and in the physicality of performance, another type of creativity wherein language, gesture, and bodily significations are condensed in musical performance.

> *Liza*: There are some major effects of socialization[19] from which you get so many messages; you can lose contact with your own specific individual creativity . . . there's even more pressure now with new media and technologies which is about moving away from the highly individual, with an overriding message about conforming to a utilitarian, economically driven view of things . . . society is a very big teacher . . . but in a way, I think that individual expression in all areas of composition even if it only holds a very tiny place in the bigger picture has value by virtue of offering a different kind of message about what the nature of exchange might be . . .

---

[19] Here Liza alludes to the struggle, perseverance, and will necessary to pursue a serious career as a composer and the general ironies of gender and the stereotyping of female artists in society. In discussing women's music and female composers (never seen though is the equivalent 'male composers'), contemporary reviewers, as society generally does, continue to use gender stereotypes and critics' telling use of vocabulary. See Pasler (2008) for relevant discussion in the chapter 'The ironies of gender'.

I'm receiving impressions all the time, for instance from different parts of the world when I travel, my interactions with people and situations and then there are impressions from specifically musical situations as well. I have built up a very aural-tactile-formal sensorium of impressions and I think my work arises from this 'lived experience'—sometimes in quite concrete ways, at other times in very unforeseen and abstracted ways where it would be difficult to trace the sources.

Some of the work I've done with performers, particularly with Asian, for instance, Japanese, Korean and Chinese performers, has focused on particular modes of performance practice where this sense of the kinaesthetic touch is an intimate part of the musical meaning of the work. And so in those kinds of projects, I'm connecting very directly with that specifically musical-aesthetic kind of information.

These things are whirling around, and I know that they do have an impact on how I think musically. But in terms of actually producing anything, definitely it's the regular time I spend at the desk that makes it happen . . . I mean I'm a believer in working every day, and what happens is that after a certain point you build up a momentum and that actually carries you through. For me, that's the great pleasure with composition, the feeling of freedom within yourself when I'm in a really good place creatively.

Liza describes her creative practice as the work ('regular time I spend at the desk') of a composer as both the self and social being. Here, compositional creativity is a dialectic involving an act (writing 'at the desk') of individual expression (that 'can hold a tiny place') in relation to a complex set of musical-structural-cultural properties. Whilst it potentially involves a complex set of intentions, these are supplemented by actual performances and the development of performance traditions. Thus, we can say that seeing how music comes to offer particular things means seeing how it constitutes aspects of the social world. Yet, what counts as creativity differs, depending on the context, which creates different possibilities.

> *Liza*: There are certain things I might write for specialist contemporary music solo performers that I feel are not possible in the same way with an orchestra. Over time, I've shifted from thinking about these differences as constrictions in a negative way to becoming very interested in the creative possibilities offered by more bounded situations.
>
> I'm hardly ever concerned about what the audience will think, because if you start worrying about whether people are gonna like you, I think that's the end of you as an artist. To shoot for artistic originality is to feel complete fearlessness, you've just got to want it so much that you're going to do it no matter what anyone thinks or says or does . . . It's not really about the mastery of the materials. One is trying to go beyond the pre-existing forms of 'language'. And when I say 'a language', I include the most experimental work as well as the more traditional mainstream kind of approach to making music.

There are at least three ways of characterizing creativity. First, as 'artistic originality' (or artistic creativity), which can be described as when works have a stock of possibilities that originate as the unique artistic intent of the composer—unique in the form of site-specific practices that require 'fearlessness' (risk-taking, individual independence). Second, creating a work, the primordial value of which is 'compositional creativity', because it is the guiding principle of genre 'mastery', is constituted by and depends on that which has gone before in 'pre-existing forms of language', including experimental and traditional forms of music-making. Whilst classical performers are bent on fidelity to a score, they nonetheless acknowledge, perhaps, that a piece of music may exist without one as a developing structure that arises from the activity of music-making, whether improvised or aural. Third, recognizing the latter activity, there is music-making as 'improvisational creativity', when music is made and played differently in various social contexts.

> *Liza*: I begin from a place where I think I'm offering something that is very finely focused and individualized. For me, that's my job. An important aspect of the point of art seems to me that it can hold a multitude or perhaps infinite number of possible meanings and experiences for people. So for me,

I'm not saying I want people to feel a certain kind of way, but really what I would like is to offer something that opens out towards a sense of many possible meanings.

This plays into the social context of music, where there are certain kinds of occasions and situations
where people's expectations are for entertainment or for something which is going to positively reinforce their sense of importance and status . . . then there's the opening night, which is always the
invited audience of very important people with expectations of a certain kind of glamour. Unfortunately,
this aspect of social reception can often get confused in discussions about accessibility . . . I'm more
interested in an audience that's incredibly engaged, that has this language for engaging with a whole
range of works . . . Most people like what they already know, that's a kind of conservatism, rather
than necessarily going out and seeking experiences that are completely new.

Here Liza speaks of vocabularies of reception that will allow you to have more or less contextual
resonance. She speaks of the physicality of gesture as the basis for formulating new approaches to
instrumental technique and listening. The social space and how the venue plays out, as aspects of
the ideological rules of genre, illustrate how venues function as cultural institutions with consecrated artistic capital. Liza does this through a consideration of her beliefs that go with genres, and
how these are often articulated in assumptions about creative and cultural practices, aesthetic
identities, and the broader sets of social relationships and creative actions of production, mixed
with consecrated cultural capital derived from national and international cultural fields.

We conclude this discussion of the types of creativities, meanings ascribed, and appropriation
of capital connected to Liza's work as a composer, with the following points:

1. Creativity is defined by the interaction between developing inwardly directed practices that
   constitute the 'self', as ascribed by intention, individual vocabularies, musical languages,
   original voice,—individual creativity—and outwardly directed social creativities: practices
   such as the social modes of creativity that take shape in 'the creative laboratory' of working
   with ELISION (in developing new performance techniques, mixed media or cross-arts, and in
   forms of indigenous cultural and intercultural aesthetics as manifest in the compositional and
   improvisatory modalities found in performance, cultural, and intercultural creativities).

2. For Liza, the range of ways in which the self and social realms enable multiple creativities is always
   in motion.

Introducing Robert Davidson

Robert Davidson is an Australian composer. He studied composition with Terry Riley in 1995 in
California, following studies with Philip Bračanin at the University of Queensland, where he
undertook doctoral studies in composition and now lectures in that subject. Before taking up his
current academic role, he was first a bassist with the Australian Opera and Sydney and Queensland
symphony orchestras and then worked as a freelance computer programmer. Since 1996, Robert
has directed the multi-genre quintet Topology, with whom he plays double bass. He also features
on vocals, guitar, and electronics. The quintet has played at numerous festivals around the world.
Many of Robert's works focus on the relationships between speech and music, often including
video elements. Robert's compositions are regularly performed, recorded, and broadcast around
the world, and all of Australia's professional orchestras, and many leading soloists and ensembles,
have commissioned and performed them. His many works around themes include voice portraits
that use recordings of figures such as Gandhi, Churchill, Clinton, Whitlam, John F. Kennedy, and
Amelia Earhart.

Robert is the second of four children, his siblings all being engineers, and not active musicians.
He grew up in a typical middle-class home with music in the house—radio, records, some playing
and singing, plus a lot of music at the Uniting Church in Australia. His parents listened to light

music (Bacharach, Mantovani), popular music of their younger days (The Seekers, The Beatles, Cat Stevens) and some classical music, and encouraged his interest in music. He attended a government (state) primary and secondary school, and his first formal involvement in music-making was at around 11 years of age. He emphasizes the way some knowledge was constructed and some knowledge was excluded in these learning situations, letting us see how the opportunities offered by a particular teacher at a particular school at a particular time in his schooling, was significant. This teacher was enthusiastic, evidently engaged with the music she was taking her students through, and was interested in letting them talk about the music they were interested in, and in finding out what their own musical personalities were. She helped Robert find his own creativity, so much so that he 'felt validated'. That being said, he was not introduced to classical music until age 16, in the final years of secondary school. He describes himself as 'someone who owes a lot to my classroom music teacher'.

> *Robert*: I learned that creativity is messy. I learned the idea that someone owning a piece of music is problematic. I'm totally into the concept of 'musicking', as articulated by Christopher Small, that music's what you do. I don't think a piece of music is an object, it's an action, it's not a thing, it's something you do and so it's a temporary sort of illusion. The way Bach was played in the eighteenth century is different to how the music is played now. It's actually a different sort of music, and it means something totally different today . . . Every time there's a new cover version of a song it's going to be quite different . . . Other people are doing the whole authentic-performance-practice-thing and protecting it in its 'original' form, so there's no damage when alternative versions are created. For me, my music teacher taught me how you can emerge from music history needing to question why it takes particular forms . . . I'm not wanting to make any claims that I'm particularly unusual or special in these things. All that I have done is drawn from approaches taken by composers from Bach and Beethoven to Percy Grainger and Frank Zappa and to contemporary bands . . . I'm just a typical case of a composer who's interested in alternatives to what's been handed down as the correct sort of way of thinking about the hierarchy of composer-performer-listener and wanting to question that.

Robert's explanation of his musical background and experimental trail includes popular music production and style. He is a new kind of musician-composer who advocates that one should not promote one style over any other. For Robert, no division exists between 'popular' music and 'classical-art' music. This, for him, is a distinction that is being eroded in digital culture. As a 'composer-performer-listener' he sees the need to practise, to develop, to evolve as a musician who questions and to resist classification.

> *Robert*: I've played in bands since I can remember playing music. My current group decided to get together because of being friends; the instruments were a secondary consideration, so there's already a congeniality there. We had already played together in other groups and things so—it's nothing weird; it's just what contemporary bands would do, they just stick with their friends.

Robert names many people who have had a strong and guiding influence on him. He makes it clear how all kinds of musical activities, mentors, musicians, and music have played important roles, what the struggles have been, what is perceived possible, and the convergence and cross-fertilization of genres, audiences, musics, and types of creativities that have become blurred through the eclecticism of contemporary concert and theatre practices.

> *Robert*: Well I guess my main way of thinking of myself is as a composer. But I like to blur the boundaries of composing and performing, producing, presenting, arranging, you know, improvising, working with other musicians. And at the moment I'm making an arrangement for the Brodsky Quartet and my group, Topology, of an Elvis Costello piece that was originally a ballet score. And I treat that as much a part of my practice as composing a brand new piece or performing a piece or collaborating with very different musicians. So I see myself as a composer, performer, arranger, improviser. I do a lot of arranging

which, in my view, is a kind of re-creating defined a bit differently from how others understood it. I am not so interested in realizing another composer's ideas . . . I'm mainly interested in taking somebody else's idea and then making it my own (or making it our own in Topology) and seeing it in a new light; and that's something which is how we depart from, say, maybe a contemporary music ensemble within contemporary classical music is that we wouldn't normally be sticking to what the composer wrote, we'd have to change it in some way. Even if somebody wrote us a piece we'd normally change it in some details, so we would very rarely just be realizing a score . . . We did some fairly extensive market research and people don't really see us [referring to his group Topology] as 'classical music', as related to groups such as ELISION or Ensemble Offspring (both of whom we admire) . . . We do sit in the cracks, as do many people—I mean, it's quite common these days to be breaking across several categories and that makes it both exciting and confusing and difficult to market.

At one time it was commonplace to assume that 'classical/art' music blazed an experimental trail that popular music then exploited. In many instances that was true, but composers are now able to exploit their work commercially, writing for theatre, writing in institutions of higher education, and for arts organizations, as well as making ground-breaking musical discoveries by blurring distinctions between concert and theatre music, between the analogue and digital worlds, along with the use of electronically generated sounds. For Robert, creativity in his musical world is defined through his ensemble Topology, whose cooperative activity, organized via the members' joint skills, knowledge, and friendship, produces all kinds of creativities that are at the interface of both individual and social dimensions. He defines his creative practice as follows.

Robert: The music I make is influenced by where it resides—its 'primary text', which has an important influence on its priorities; with a Mahler Symphony the musical work probably resides primarily in a score. With a lot of popular music, the primary text is in the recording. I think for us the primary text is probably the live performance. Anything else is just serving what happens there. The score is dispensable; the recording—well, it's good to have, it's an artefact, but it's not the main location of the music, because it leaves out the central aspect of our bodies in a specific space. I think where the music happens for Topology is in the gig, and the audience role is crucial. And again, I find it quite inspiring to look back at musical history and see that, say, Bach would often borrow a bit from one piece and put it into another piece; repurpose things, rescore things, because the score was not a monolithic, fixed thing. I think that's great—it's just whatever's going to work for that particular situation. Perhaps the score was not so strongly the primary text for Bach as our current views of him would suggest. I do have 'works', but they're flexible, because they exist primarily as live performances.

The 'musical score' or 'masterwork' is really just a set of instructions to performers, to make certain sounds at certain times. The score, or any notated representation, is no substitute for performance creativity, or the interaction between musicians, or between musicians and audience, or any other aspects of being 'live'. That is to say, the extent of creativity will be the perceived success, or otherwise, of the interactions as they take place during a given performance of a piece of music. The fact that the musical score is more frequently the object of study, a 'readable' substitute for the act of performance, is a by-product of the evolution of various academic and commercial interests. Goehr (amongst other critics), in her seminal book *The Imaginary Museum of Musical Works* (1992), has critiqued the concept of the musical work. She argues that it was around the year 1800 that the romantic principle that musical invention depended on the self-expression of the individual composer-genius, who must refuse to follow established rules or submit to external controls, came into being; and, with it, the arrival of a 'work-based practice' which centred on the belief that musical works were perfectly formed and finished. Following on from this argument, Cook (in press), amongst others,[20] highlights the central significance of the

20 See related discussions in Chanan (1994); Frith (1988, 1983); Thornton, (1995), and Toynbee (2000).

recording, which manifests performance creativity ('work in performance' and 'performances representing works' and 'recordings representing performances'). Gracyk (1996) argues, similarly, that in rock music the 'work' now consists primarily of the recording, saying that it is 'the history of production rather than notational determination [that] is the key to individuating the work' (p. 32). The point here is that recordings are worthless these days because of downloading. Both record companies and artists have almost given up recording being worth anything. The question arises as to whether the artform is still there, or is it dying out to be replaced by live performance which is, these days, the way artists make money.

The consequences have been profound. Robert alludes to the myths that have been used in the cultivation of public opinion from the eighteenth century onwards, which have promoted the image of the solitary genius composer, such as Mozart or Beethoven, working in isolation. Robert, on the other hand, gives primacy to the individual and collaborative dimensions of composed musics; of the performance relationship, which he thinks are fundamental to composition, and central to his creative practice.

> *Robert*: I still definitely believe in creating work in isolation and you know, really, you please yourself first, there's no doubt about that, and that's the thing I suppose, I don't want to pander—I don't want to give people what they want to say, make it market-commercial. It's very much about being authentic about being one's self and trying to reach a true expression of what you really are . . .

These basic aesthetic assumptions guide Robert's intention to produce new music in which composers speak as themselves. Similarly, as discussed by Toynbee, writing about popular musicians and creativity (2000), what is premised by live, recorded, and broadcast music as much as in the composition of a written score, is a concern with the 'truth to the subject, a full issuing out of music from the inner being' (p. 61), a concern for the self, and the social realms of thought and action as a composer. For Robert, the key aspect of his composing habitus is the way it disposes him as musician-composer to play, write, record, or perform in a particular way. One of his characteristic practices is through performance possibilities that arise, and are realized by and through, an interplay of oral and notated traditions, or those that encompass purely oral forms which do not lead to a single version of a piece for replication. What defines composition for him is his intention.

Robert talks about what he thinks and does as a composer, and about the social context through which he negotiates his position within the field. As well as reconceptualizing traditionally held ideas about improvisational creativity in the light of particular social relationships, his practice is located at the junction between the individual appropriation of the 'self', as defined by his own compositional intentions and by larger social relations. Robert also reflects on the collective processes behind his creative fertility, and the experimentation and innovation that arise as a social practice that is played out in his participation in particular social groups.

> *Robert*: Improvisation was actually far more important than we sort of have come to think since the middle of the nineteenth century. I think it's a real shame that improvisation has so vanished from classical music. Because I think it was so vital and important, as it still is in jazz. And the way that there's been that real divide between composers and performers, the idea of the authority of the composer as an unassailable genius, I find pretty irritating . . . it is also about embracing their individual journey and the need to have individual ideas. But it's also about creating a scene around yourself, and that's connected to the scene around Topology. People are part of a scene because it's collective, and the reality is that the people we see as these lone geniuses never actually are, they always are part of a really vibrant scene which throws up the stuff and they're just the surface of it or part of it.

Robert works across genres with multi-media (moving image and projected text), which enables him to understand a complex amalgam of ever-expanding creativities, as opposed to the minimization of notions of musical creativity through constantly looking for creative homogeneity. He does not engage with musical creativity in an insular or singular mode of apprehension, nor does he engage with it in an abstract act of understanding. His experience of creativity is based on the degree to which he realizes and goes beyond the illusion of the separation of composition and performance. He sees himself as a composer who is consciously influenced by and reinforces particular social relations, and who forges alternative views of his creative role and social agency through live performances. He does not split creativity up between the composer, producer, musician, and audience, but rather sees himself as part and product of his 'scene', which comprises all of these elements and more. Robert's creative practice reveals a fusion or interaction between inwardly directed practices which constitute the 'self' within a compositional act defined by intention and self-expression, and through outwardly directed social practices, particularly those involving his group Topology, and others, through which he mobilizes an entire professional network ('creating a scene around yourself'). Within this social positioning, or 'scene', Topology forms a community to which Robert belongs, whose compositional or performing activities are a way of practising collaborative creativity through the social and individual significance associated with it. Robert goes through a process of self-reflection, emphasizing the social basis on which his music is constructed, and, in so doing, establishes a social position, complete with its own logic of practice that emerges along a continuum between collaborative and collective, and individual creativities.

> *Robert*: I exist as a composer who writes for other people, and also now I'm developing a solo act which is a different identity; and I work with different bands. But my prime identity is wrapped up in the group I play in, write for and manage . . . we sort of combine the ability of bouncing ideas off each other in improvisation, individual work with notation which you can use for planning and things, individual work on development, and put it all into the stew . . . We're using what we know, what chamber music offers—improvisation, recording—and all these things can offer in the creative process, trying to sort of embrace all of it, which is not far from what maybe Frank Zappa would have done or various prog-rock bands . . . This is why we often do a lot of collaborating. We often seek out people who are doing things which are quite different from us because we want to be stretched . . . this is probably started by being invited to play in a theatre show—the whole way of rehearsal and creative process . . . in what ideas you take from theatre, dance, performing arts, visual arts, or comedy . . . the creativity comes in how you negotiate the constraints.

Here, Robert characterizes a composer's habitus that is firmly entrenched in the persona of the individualist composer whilst also being embodied in the ever-changing score of live performance, which for him represents the 'primary text' of creativity. Creative action is characterized by how it blends the 'popular' (high volume capital within the local field) with an artistic appreciation of established contemporary compositions, the consecrated cultural capital of which is derived from a large audience involving national and international cultural fields. Robert's creative practice is articulated at the intersection between his own actions and ideas as an individual, with those others who take them up, in the space of collective decision-making. This is where the individualistic and inward, and the socially constituted and outward practices together represent the 'primary text' of creativity.[21] What this means is that Robert's composing habitus constitutes a series of individual and social practices that negotiate possibilities between the 'primary text' of the live performance and the social and individual significance that is brought to it at one and the

---

[21] For further discussion of the inward and outward practices of creativity, see Westerlund (2008).

Fig. 6.3 Composer Robert Davidson, members of Topology, and TaikOz musicians talking with a concert audience at the Brisbane Powerhouse (where Topology is in residence) in November 2009. TaikOz is a full-time contemporary music ensemble based in Sydney (specializing in percussion music and Japanese Taiko drumming).
Photo by Elleni Toumpas, Australia. © Elleni Toumpas, 2011.

same time.[22] In short, Robert sees the production of contemporary music as a site of both a struggle for individual position as an individual composer, and a drive to act on behalf of the community and for the collective good. (See Fig. 6.3: the relation of composer to audience is an important issue for Robert, as it is for composer Liza Lim.)

Concluding remarks

This chapter has explored the meanings of 'musical creativities', and what is distinctive about them, from a sample of composers' practices. For these composers, what is distinctive about musical creativity is a sense of social location and the occupation of composer in the social space. Accordingly, as we have noted, there is no singular form of musical creativity in these accounts of composing and, indeed, creativities have been shown to be plural.

We have chosen not to make explicit comparisons between the composers' practices. Instead, we invite the reader to compare the reflexive accounts in this chapter and the discussions in Part 1 and Part 3. This can then provide a backdrop to changing ideas about musical creativity, specifically, and creativity generally. We can then carry forward our discussion of the realization of musical creativities, finding common ground in Csikzentmihalyi's[23] (1999) words: '[what] we call creativity is a phenomenon that is constructed through an interaction between producers and audience. Creativity is not the product of single individuals, but of social systems making judgements about individuals' products' (p. 313). This characterization is fundamentally based on the assumption that creativity is a psychological phenomenon, and that the social context has an

---

22 For discussion of scripting social interaction in collective improvisational performance and Western 'art' music see Cook (forthcoming).

23 Csikszentmihalyi is pronounced 'chicks sent me high'.

impact on individuals' motivation to engage in creative activities. Yet, it remains a widely accepted view that composers compose in isolation, and that the acts of creativity in which they immerse themselves are the consummate expression of individual selfhood rather than any openly manifest form of collective production.

As this chapter shows, it is wrong to make the general assumption that compositions are realized through an individual's isolated compositional creativity. Some forms of transcreativity arise from crossing boundaries of genre (classical, jazz, popular, contemporary). Some are developed by changing the primary modality through which a process is articulated (improvisational, compositional, or performance creativity). How this happens may or may not involve working and playing with others, and may be intentional or unintentional. Some compositions are fully scored and others are not.

Writing about the socio-musicological perspectives of the nineteenth century, Emmerson (1989), Berleant (1987), and Goehr (1992) remind us of the dangers and inappropriateness of accepting any single theory of the nature of composition. The work of the contemporary classical art composer goes beyond that of the predominately score-based activities, for the primordial value of the score no longer exists. The controversies and debates we have examined in this chapter provide evidence that musical creativities are realized as individual practices in socially and culturally mediated spaces. There is little doubt that the sociopersonal perspective on creativity, as espoused by social psychologist Amabile (1996), provides insights into the ways in which a number of components converge. These include social environment, task motivation, intrinsic/ extrinsic rewards, domain-relevant skills (musical aptitude, experience, and training) and creativity-relevant skills (adaptability, openness, flexibility, originality, and innovation). Amabile directs our attention to the social dimensions of creativity and human beings' abilities, as social creatures, to act as independent agents who profoundly affect each other as they interact and coordinate actions around both individual and socially agreed goals. From this wellspring of ideas comes new ways to view the composer within the contemporary art world—a world in which composers work and play with, and with respect to, others. The synchronous positioning of family, early socialization and the social environment plays a crucial role in conferring and defining the composer's social, material, and musical cultures (or habitus).[24]

Categories of evaluation and judgement are contested. Different creativities are inherent in different contexts. Contemporary composers challenge the traditional assumptions of the lone genius. Many opt for a more collaborative aural and oral means of composing, based not only on notation but also on collaboration and improvisation (Burnard, 1999). By writing a composition within the context of, and in collaboration with, a performance ensemble, the process of composition places the focus on mediated social action at a collective and interactive level (Becker, 1984).

---

[24] Bourdieu (1993a) describes the idea of 'field' as consisting of a 'separate social universe having its own laws of functioning' (p. 162). A 'field of production' is made up of specific forms of practice, methods, and principles of evaluation. Bourdieu's notion of 'habitus' concerns those particular dispositions and attitudes towards practice that a person acquires, unaware of their constitution according to particular rules, in ways that such dispositions seem natural. These dispositions relate to modes of perception, thinking, and ways of evaluating one's own actions and those of others.

Westerlund (2008) describes the dualism of the individualistic and inward and the socially constituted and outward practices as the interface between the social and cultural lives of an individually experienced musical agency. Similarly, DeNora (2000) emphasizes how musicians actively draw on different music differently to 'regulate, elaborate, and substantiate themselves as social agents' (p. 47) while engaging in particular 'inward' practices. This implies that music is used as a medium through which composers negotiate their position, which is to say that being a composer means positioning the self within a field of production in terms of specific forms of practice, methods, and principles of evaluation of both practice and forms of knowledge that are valued, and which therefore constitute cultural capital in the field (Bourdieu, 1993c).

The common approach of sociocognitive perspectives is that individuals make novel variations, but from sociological perspectives, such as that of Becker (1982), where the focus is placed on mediated individual action. In other words, like any creative endeavour, constituting the self as a composer has many aspects, all of which involve the self and social realms of thought and action. From the accounts of these composers and the literature, the act of composing itself involves forming or constructing something that reflects changes through time.[25] Composing involves thinking about ideas and fixing retrievable elements. It is concerned with conscious control, clarifying intentions, refining, evaluating, and revising ideas. Composing can evolve in an organic way or be envisaged as a whole. The final form can be retrieved through notation or recalled in memory, but writing music down takes the place of memory. Compositions can involve an interplay of oral and notated traditions, be exactly specified products, or encompass purely oral forms that do not lead to a single version of a piece for replication. What defines the experience is the composer's intention (Burnard, 1999).

Yet because, as most studies show, professional composers, as with professional musicians, are socially distinct[26] and retain key links with notions of agency and autonomy as artists (A. Ford, 1993; McCutchan, 1999; Pasler, 2008), we should be cautious about making or accepting any grand generalizations about this or any other aspect of musical creativity as a singular conception. What constitutes musical creativity in the practices of contemporary composers, and what defines their expression of musical creativity, and the extent to which these views are shared, remains linked to institutional viewpoints and practices. This includes: the ways composing is learned and taught; the conditions for learning and the cultural background of the creation of new music; and sociological issues such as power, ideology, inspiration, agency, freedom, personal expression, audience–artist relations, and even the microprocesses of sound and notation. It is not surprising that such developments generate opposition as well as support, since they challenge some of the most basic assumptions of modern Western societies. Studying and teaching composition, as many of these composers said, is a transformative experience.

----

[25] The study of creativity, and the social system in which children and young people undertake composing and other related musical practices unique to children's musical cultures, is argued elsewhere (see for example, M.S. Barrett, 2005; Burnard, 2005, 2006a,b).

[26] That is, full-time performing musicians and composers rarely play with rank amateurs, although as social anthropologist Ruth Finnegan (1989) noted, a study of non-professional music-making in the English town of Milton Keynes found that many amateur ensembles actually include semi-professionals—people who earn their living in some area of the music business or teaching, though not primarily from performance.

Key points

1. Composers' accounts of their creative processes provide evidence of a multiplicity of musical creativities. The nature of the activity is characterized by the complementarity and interplay of multiple types of creativity (individual and collaborative, cultural and intercultural, reception-venue and audience-generated, participatory and innovatory). Composers also use technology as a mediating tool to support innovation.

2. The nature of creativities as manifestations of musical work in performance links to and is illustrated in terms of: (i) performances representing works; and (ii) recordings representing performances; and (iii) composed pieces in performance.

3. Individual (or self) and social (collaborative and audience-generated) creativities favour close relationships between musicians and instruments, composers and scores, and artists and audiences in ways that embody myriad music creativities.

Discussion questions

1. What are the differences between construing 'the self' and 'the social' as context, as adherent quality, or as constitutive of music creativities? Are they different in important ways? How do the self and social realms interact in the creative process? Are these distinctions important? Why? What do you conclude about the relative importance of attending to individual and social dimensions when learning what distinct musical creativities are implicated in the development of musical practices?

2. How might criteria appropriate to the evaluation of musical creativities differ from creativity to creativity? What instructional practices might such goals imply in teaching contemporary classical art composition?

3. Discuss how types, classifications, categories, and styles obscure particularity and individuality. Do you believe it reasonable to claim that some musical creativities are valued differently from others?

4. To what extent do current elementary, secondary, and post-secondary educational institutions currently address such questions?

Chapter 7

Improvised musics

Improvisational creativities that are embedded in real time, or 'live' performance practices, are particularly pertinent to my questioning the narrowness of the customary concept of musical creativity. In focusing on 'live' rather than 'recorded' performance practices, my concerns, first and foremost, are with the generic qualities of improvisational creativities, covering a range of settings, practices, and techniques, from collective aspects of concert (formal) to community (informal workshop) ensembles, from freely improvised to culturally specific, and from acoustic to digital forms, such as 'live coding'.

The five musicians featured in this chapter all improvise in real time; and represent a diversity of practices from admitting anything, to strictly defining everything in advance. I have purposively selected certain types of improvisational creativities (based on diverse assumptions underpinning self-social and traditional-digital premises) that differ sharply from the compositional practices featured in the previous chapter. These musicians' accounts shed light on the status accruing to improvisational creativities in the fields of electro-acoustic, community, folk/traditional, and computer music. With so much already written on jazz improvisation and jazz musicians,[1] I have not specifically featured the collective creativity of jazz, but rather, referred to those whose affiliations are aligned.

There are at least three themes in these narratives of improvising musicians' practices. First, improvisational creativities and their practices can be laden with, or lack, any particular musical idiom or style. Second, they involve creating and re-creating music. Third, improvisation sometimes involves creative community practices in which individual musicians follow, create, and break conventions collectively.

[1] For discussion on jazz improvisation see Alperson (1984, 1985), Berliner (1994, 2006), C. Ford (1995), Haddon (2006), Kenny and Gellrich (2002), and Sawyer (1997, 2003).

Improvisation and real time performance practices

Musical improvisation means either the creation of something new, or the changing and reworking of existing material in a novel way. It is characteristic of some Western art music (particularly of the Baroque), jazz, folk music, and of various musics from around in the world. Improvisation can involve specified and non-specified musical parameters.

Improvisation was considered pivotal to the training of instrumentalists because it enabled performance without the aid of notation. Even prior to the mid-1800s, the playing of an instrument involved the spontaneous invention of music. In the seventeenth century, composers' reputations rested on an amalgam of roles, amongst which improvising was a popular pastime. Documentation of the improvisational activities of Mozart, Beethoven, and Chopin indicates that improvisation was regarded as a viable alternative to the performance of notated compositions. Indeed, whole pieces were improvised containing lavish embellishments, ornamentation, and cadenzas (see Blanning, 2008; Goehr, 1992).

Contemporary musicians and their practices of improvisation take on a range of meanings depending on whether they value process or outcome. Berliner (1994) described this difference as follows:

> When players use *improvisation* as a noun, referring to improvisations as artistic products, they typically focus on the products' precise relationship to the original models that inspired them . . . When artists use *improvisation* as a verb, however, they focus not only on the degree to which old models are transformed and new ideas created, but on the dynamic conditions and precise processes underlying their transformation and creation. (p. 221, original emphasis)

Understanding improvisation requires us to examine how new possibilities are generated or authored. Pressing (1984) characterized improvisation as a 'learned' behaviour. He argued that musicians 'cultivate' the ability to draw on a personal repertoire of ideas and motives from a repertoire of known motor actions and musical conceptions based on the conventions of a genre. Pressing referred to these acquired skills as 'habit hierarchies'. Such creativity is always informed by the musician's habitus. At the same time, improvisational creativities appear to involve and express a sense of togetherness through interaction with all the players who are involved. This draws the listener into an engagement with the behaviours, intentions, and identities of performers. As Toynbee (2000) argues, it is the listener 'who authorizes possibilities' (p. 42) for the place and sound of *social authorship* and *voice*. Everybody, however, experiences the performance in a different way. This is crucial for the present argument, and has important implications for the expansion of the concept of creativities in music that I want to develop.

We often use metaphoric language to describe and envisage particular performance practices in popular, jazz, classical, or contemporary music production. Improvisation has been described as a 'journey', a 'dance', a 'groove' (Berliner, 1994), a 'conversation' (Sawyer, 1997), a 'personal voice' (McMillan, 1996), a 'space of possibles' (Toynbee, 2000), a 'performance art par excellence, requiring not only a lifetime of preparation across a broad range of musical and non-musical formative experiences, but also a sophisticated and eclectic skill base' (see Burnard, 1999; Kenny and Gellrich, 2002; Smilde, 2009). The descriptions used depend on the symbolic hierarchy of the genres and the social value attached to each of them, as well as on the meaning and value attached to the space of possibilities that improvisational creativities occupy within Eastern or Western performance traditions.

These metaphors serve as descriptive functions for improvisations, and help to illuminate some of the experiential qualities in the complex interrelationship between the field and the musician's habitus. Wolterstorff (1994) argues that 'a necessary condition of improvisation is that it *not* be the performance of a work' (p. 119). He emphasized that any attempt to understand the nature of improvisation must be embedded in an understanding of the particular *practice* from which the music emerges. Furthermore, Wolterstorff proposed that the nature of music is determined by the context in which the performance practice is 'sounded out'. In this chapter codified practices are inscribed within the contexts of traditional and community genres, and institutional and concert settings.

According to L. Solomon (1986), improvisation can be thought of as 'the discovery and invention of original music spontaneously while performing it, without preconceived formulation, scoring or context' (p. 224). Some improvisers practise without a preconceived notion of the kinds of music they will create, but rather tend to allow their music to dictate its own form, so that every performance uses a 'forward-looking imagination which, while mainly concerned with the moment, will prepare for later possibilities' (Bailey, 1992, p. 111). Similarly, Campbell (1991b) reported on the chance-embedded processes that are wedded to improvisatory practices, and described the mysteries of musical spontaneity as follows:

> Musically speaking, improvisation may be more than the sum of its component colloquial explanations: 'To wing it,' to 'make it up', to 'blow it out,' to let ideas tumble out on specific preparation or

pre-meditation. It is the musical response to an unpredictable impulse or feeling. It is the intricate balance of performance and composition, all at once. It is deserving of its air of mystery, its magic to empower both performers and listeners, and its status as a quality whose skills may be acquired by the performer through informal listening, observation and experimentation, and through formal training. (p. 21)

John Cage (1912–92), widely known for experimenting with unusual sounds, was a composer whose composition happened by means of the *I Ching*.[1] In 1951, he produced the *Music of Changes*, a four-volume work for solo piano, in which every sound was chosen and placed by chance operations. The result was what Cage called 'non-intentional music', meaning that though the music was produced by chance, what it created was fixed as a piece of music thereafter. The following year he wrote the infamous and paradoxical *4'33"*, four minutes and thirty-three seconds of silence, dating from 1952. My point here is that in trying to find new ways of putting sounds together (and, by implication, identifying new types of creativities), Cage developed entirely different types of performances, some of which used improvisation in order to re-establish the uniqueness of the act of music-making. Cage's promotion of 'live' art that explored sound and sonority and the world of noise, legitimated a certain kind *indeterminacy* and *immediacy* in real time performance practice. For Cage, improvisational creativity was embedded in the sounds made and played out in real time and, the bounds of the structures that branch out in multiple directions, based on the choices made during performance. For Cage—and this is true of freely improvised music—the piece only exists when it is being played: the full possibilities of a piece are in its life.

In contrast, jazz guitarist Derek Bailey (1992) described freely improvised music as follows: 'diversity is its most consistent characteristic. It has no stylistic or idiomatic commitment. It has no prescribed idiomatic sound. The characteristics of freely improvised music are established only by the sonic-musical identity of the person or persons playing it' (p. 83). For many musicians, free improvisation is a way of engaging creatively with music in a different way, where the music is exempt from 'the inevitability of genre' (Toynbee, 2000, p. 108) and the 'particular player's persona' is free of what is already known.

Nettl (1974) speaks of improvisation from an ethnomusicological perspective by locating it within a collective, cultural context. He claims that the culture influences the sounding-out of created music during the course of a performance in which the amount of improvisation varies. This notion of a continuum of improvisational variation can be described in terms of graduated points of independence from a given musical model, which reflect existing performative genres in various cultures. These ritualized genres are 'reproduced anew in each performance' involving 'component units—building blocks, stock phrases, and formulaic patterns—of a model piece' (Nettl, 1974, p. 13) that are recast, rearranged, and renewed. These performative genres can range from what Nettl (1974) described as 'ritualized' to 'improvisational' performances depending on the degree of independence from the musical model.

There is no word equivalent to 'improvise' for classically trained Indian players. The two terms they use are *upaj* and *vistar*, which mean 'to grow' and 'to spread out', respectively. Neither of these terms have 'spontaneous' connotations, because much of Eastern music is predetermined and fixed in nature. The Indian *raga*, Javanese *gamelan*, Arabic and Turkish *maqam*, Persian *dast-gah*, and group African drumming are examples of *ritualized* performance in which there is only limited opportunity for creative spontaneity. Nettl (1974) suggested that what we consider to be improvisation may in fact be culturally specified composition.

---

[1] The I Ching, also known as the *Classic of Changes, Book of Changes* is one of the oldest books in print.

In some West African drumming ensembles there is a structure already scripted and imprinted in the minds of the players, but not notated. There will be a master drummer in charge who uses stylistic idioms, techniques, and structuring principles, one of which is that they are free to improvise. Organization of time is one manifestation of improvisational creativity, which occurs as an official function reflected through improvised rhythmic patterns that the master drummer is free to play over the underlying pulse, interacting with multiple ostinatos in cooperation between multiple players to reinforce their status.

A different kind of performance creativity can be used in the performance of a folk tune, or a mariachi strophe, or in the solos of Japanese *syakuhati* (vertical bamboo flute) players. Improvisational creativity sometimes interacts with the idiomatic morphology of an instrument, or may consist of deliberately finding new ways to play an instrument, which is highly idiosyncratic to Derek Bailey's (1992) approach to improvisation (Baily, 1985).

In his study of jazz musicians, Becker (1963), described their performance as 'deviant'. He argued that the ethos of jazz fosters a disregard for the rules of society in general through a desire for freedom from outside interference. Berliner (1994) interviewed 50 jazz musicians over a period of 15 years in order to gain a better understanding of the 'improviser's world of consciousness'. He wrote that 'the sense of exhilaration that characterises the artist's experiences under such circumstances is heightened for jazz musicians as storytellers by the activity's physical, intellectual and emotional exertion, and by the intensity of struggling with creative processes under the pressure of a steady beat' (p. 216). Nardone (1996) identified similar themes in the experience of improvisation in a phenomenologically informed, psychological analysis of the life-worlds of three adult improvisers. These themes included: (1) ensuring spontaneity by yielding to the musical flow; (2) experiencing a consciousness divided between an awareness of rhythm and maintaining creativity; and (3) the immediacy required in moment-to-moment musical responses.

Live coding is the improvised algorithmic programming of a computer and the mapping from code to musical event in front of a live audience (Collins et al., 2008). Its distinctive real time programming (or live scripting) takes the form of various performance practices including: (1) a composer-programmer with a laptop computer on a concert platform, playing out high-risk coding in real time performance, often as an unaccompanied soloist, but also in ensembles, which reduces the stress of solo programming a computer in real time concert conditions; or (2) interactive explorations between two or more laptop-networked composer-performers, perhaps with electroacoustic and live analogue elements, creating a real time interaction between these performers and the laptop players; or (3) a laptop orchestra engaged in programming a live gig with any combination of acoustic sound devices, traditional, and general acoustic instruments. In a live coding performance audiences do not usually witness any of the expressive physical movements or gestural forms of performer musicianship. The music's distinctive quality is its temporal (improvised) character and its presentational immediacy through live scripting.

Clearly, there are numerous conceptions, social scripting, and distinctive practices of improvisation.[2] In freely improvised musics, structures, patterns, and variations are played out differently to improvisational creativities as in real time performance practices of the inherently collective improvisational performance of traditional folk musics or those of live coding. Thus, in collective improvisational performance, practices are categorized in the field and will differ according to

---

[2] For a comprehensive review of improvisation in music and music education see Azzara (2002, pp. 171–87).

distinctiveness of genre and style and, as Cook (forthcoming)[3] has argued, the scripting of social interaction.

Whether improvisers codify their practice within jazz, popular, folk, or ethnic and cultural communities, the extent to which they improvise new music or re-create music varies significantly. The key point for the present argument is that such diverse styles of live music performance provide a basis for exploring the collective and communal aspects of improvisation, positioning an array of different improvisation creativities of increasingly complex colouration and extended forms, which, together, have important implications for the broadening of the model of musical creativities I am developing here.

In this chapter, five musicians are featured from a range of social and cultural origins, who generate practices that derive from differences in habitus and the ways in which they inflect positions in the field. The following five narratives represent each musician's habitus and their particular notions of sound and sonority exploration, as well as illustrating how indeterminacy and immediacy are applied to real time performance practices.

The first featured musician is David Toop whose improvisational creativities involve electronic, electro-acoustic and digital sounds. Using established technologies, along with acoustic sounds and more conventional instruments, played by David or others, he aims for a complete and original musical experience. Whilst his music directly manifests his persona, it is also bound up with the broader institutional forces that provide the basis of its production: sounds are shaped, reshaped, transformed, and restructured using digital tools; or he uses a combination of acoustic sounds and digital recordings in real time performance.

David Toop: where a musician's habitus intersects with multiple fields

David Toop (Fig. 7.1) describes himself as a musician, composer, sound artist, writer, and curator. He sets the stage, at this point in the chapter, for a consideration of the eclecticism of improvisational creativities. Using his talent for navigating acoustic improvising, studio loops and samples, digital networks and interactive technologies, David brings together experiences of working in the context of experimental music, live electronics, acoustic ecology, and sound-based and soundscape genres, in both improbable groupings and as soloist.

David grew up in Waltham Cross, Hertfordshire, where he was educated at a state secondary school (Broxbourne Grammar School), which he left in 1967 to study at Hornsey College of Art. He grew up in a very conventional, lower middle-class house, with, as he says, 'very little what we would call "high culture", or none really'. There were very few books in the house. His parents, as he recalls, 'listened to a bit of easy listening music, and my dad liked military band music'. His father was very disapproving of a career in music and actively discouraged it. The realities of life as a musician, and the dilemmas faced as a musician in meeting those realities, has led David to explore practical, musical, and literary ways to fundamentally change the way we think about the meaning of performance and the nature of sound itself, whether electronic, acoustic or a mixture of both.

[3] In an article on improvisation, performance, and Western 'art' music, Cook (forthcoming) explores the historical and political and aesthetic reasons that are drawn between jazz improvisation, which is seen as embodying utopian values of social interaction, and the performance of Western 'art' music, seen either as embodying establishment hegemonies or so having no social content at all.

Fig. 7.1 David Toop in performance.
© Patricia Titsch, 2011.

David is one of Britain's most celebrated writers of books on music.[4] In a chapter entitled 'Silent music, secret noise' in his *Haunted Weather*, he asked, in conversation with Derek Bailey, 'how does an improvising player discover new material, or fresh approaches to old material, in the heat of the moment, from within routines that are hardwired into brain and reflex?'. David thinks, 'playing is a negotiation between fixity and fluidity. To play is to learn and unlearn, a state of refinement and state of becoming that have the power to undo each other's work.' (Toop, 2004a, p. 245). Derek said that 'even if you're groping around for more clichés, you have the feeling you don't know what's in front, and sometimes you don't. Sometimes you can find things, but then it comes out of the impetus of playing . . . I don't know how that works'. In this section, we address the question of what kind of thing improvisational creativity might be.

In the extract that follows, David meditates on the meaning of live performance, on the act of listening, on the nature of sound itself, on creating sounds acoustically, electronically, from computers, or from our environment, whether using recordings of wind or electrical hums in musical composition. A deconstruction of the concept of musical creativity threads its way through his undoing and redoing of the idea that there exists a singular core of creativity to which everything in musical experience relates.

> *David*: I tend to think of creativity as something that can happen to anybody, and is either an innovative response to a situation, or it comes seemingly out of nowhere, and finds some new way of thinking or acting. But we get it mixed up with art. And of course art comes from creativity, as does, you know gardening or cooking, getting a tractor out of a ditch. To an extent, it depends on the difficulty of the challenge, and how you approach it, I suppose. If you have an innovative response, you know then that kind of creativity can flourish in any aspect of life. Working with sound, working with music is

---

[4] David Toop is the author of *Rap Attack* (1984, 1991, 2000), *Ocean of Sound* (1995), *Exotica: Fabricated Soundscapes in a Real World* (1999); *Haunted Weather: Music, Silence and Memory* (2004a).

very collaborative. So you're constantly working with other people. It's actually very difficult to separate out what you do from what other people do. And there is no individual string which is separate to yours. And particularly working in improvisational settings, you know if you're working in an improvising trio then you can't say, 'This is mine', or 'This is yours', because that never exists. Even in the moment of conception, which is in improvisation extremely brief, or to the self possibly non-existent, it's a response, as much as anything. It's always a relational thing, yes. Even in the sense of isolation there is the feeling of a response, or the need for it. [And] even when I do a lot of solo music performances, which is something I don't particularly like, but for various reasons it happens a lot, and it's never just the self, it's always some . . . exchange with an acoustic space, a physical space and the audience, a set of circumstances. And that's one of the problems of it, you know you can work up this perfect act, then it's overwhelmed by these circumstantial effects. And that of course is one of the aspects that makes it interesting as well as very challenging, what you do and can be changed so powerful, by these apparently passive effects. It's a tricky world.

For David, then, the creativity of music, of particular things and experiences of music, sound, and noise, is not radically separated from 'response' or 'context' in creativity. Contingency and situatedness, constraints and freedom, are not contaminants but basic conditions of all human creativity; and the differences between various types of creativity are more a matter of degree than of kind. Computer creativity is marked by brilliance, affordances, freedoms, but the world of musical creativity is attenuated and mediated by constraints. As David implies, music creativity worlds are not cut off from the social, or inherently illusory.

David: I think there is, in anybody who improvises, a desire for some version of freedom, or their idea of freedom . . . The only difficulty with that is when that meets other people's idea of freedom, or the impossibility of freedom, or freedom with a big 'F', or you know, the notion of some sort of political freedom, or whatever . . . I mean it's always deeply problematic. But no, I don't [laughs]. . . I don't . . . No, I don't have any problem with those things so far . . . I mean that's very much a part of my teaching. When I work with students in improvisation classes one of the first things we talk about is the notion of freedom . . . we talk about improvisation, what it means to them. Very often it means to them some hazy idea of freedom, so we talk about the possibility or the impossibility, and begin to try to unpick what the rules might be, in a very general sense, and also a specific sense, you know given those particular people. What's clandestine? You know, what's under the surface? What's going? What's preventing us from certain actions? You know? What's holding us back in certain areas? Why aren't we doing this? Why can't we do this? Why do we make this sound, not that sound? Why don't we all just break out in a popular tune? You know, if there was absolute freedom then . . . well, it's unimaginable actually, because already we're limited even by thinking about it. It's like the moment when I heard AMM[5] for the first time, which was a revelation to me, I had a sense of it, a sniff of it, and of course that was why it was such an epiphany to me. I then went to hear them many times after that in the following few years, and it didn't have that same sense of freedom. I mean I loved it, you know and it was very influential on me, but it didn't have that. And of course partly what was happening that first time I heard them was that they couldn't do what they wanted to do. They were constrained by the circumstances into making something that was . . . in a way lacked . . . And it's funny to talk about AMM in terms of cohesion, because you play that to a lot of people even now and they say, 'Oh my God, it's just chaos, anarchy'. But I hear it, I'm very familiar with it, and I can hear the form. I can hear a lot of the time why events are taking place. So it has a shape to it, it has a very clear identity and shape to it. It's not by any means chaotic or undifferentiated, or indecipherable.

....

[5] AMM was a pioneering free-improvising group formed in 1965. Founding member and drummer, Eddie Prévost, including the early lineup of saxophonist Lou Gare, guitarist Keith Rowe, pianist Cornelius Cardew, and cellist Lawrence Sheaff—through to the current duo of Prévost and pianist John Tilbury, pursued a unique sonic course, unswayed either by academic orthodoxy or the conformist pressures of the market (Prévost, 1995).

The notion of 'freedom' in music is most often associated with 'free' improvisation. Such practices do not adopt 'stylized' techniques or conventions. Otherwise, as will be seen later, cultural creativity comes from the practice of a particular tradition and the learning of certain skills, rules and parameters (as related by folk fiddler Hazel Fairbairn). Freely improvised music, as described by guitarist Derek Bailey, 'has no prescribed idiomatic sound'. The characteristics are 'established only by the sonic-musical identity of the person or persons playing it' (Bailey, 1992, p. 83).

This is a very helpful way of thinking about improvisational creativity, although, even if the generic norm of freely improvised music is 'freedom', it can still be a practice produced within communities, underpinned by either a strong social framework (exemplified by Rod Paton, who calls it a 'click' (Paton, 2010)), or an aesthetic goal, when the improvisational nature of group collaboration (as illustrated in Rod Paton's workshops and AMM) generates possibilities that derive from differences in musicians' habitus, and the ways it inflects and deepens their connection with the music and each other.

In posing the question of how a player discovers new material, David brings up the issue of constraints. Bourdieu, in his book *The Rules of Art* (1996) rightly, points out that there can be no negotiation of creative possibility without constraint. To begin with, when we learn anything new, as children or adults, we start with certain basic rules and procedures. We recognize these, and follow them in order to acquire the basics of any skill. While the acquisition of skills is a necessary step in the development of a musical practice, the issue of who is competent and what is competent, as with who is creative and what is creative, inevitably entails some form of value judgement. So, the acquisition of forms of constraint is integrally connected to the creative opportunities available to people, and to structures and relations of power and authority within the community.

David says he is 'not a comfortable performer, or a virtuosic musician nor a risk-taker either'. He says he 'hates driving fast cars and flying'. What he likes, however, is 'constantly undermining any sense of excessive dependency on that feeling of knowing what you're doing . . . you have to unsettle your base with un-preparedness. So it becomes a dialogue, between the preparedness and un-preparedness'. This is a crucial concept that has important implications for improvisational creativities. As seen in the passage below, the teaching/learning relationship provides a conflicting choice between learning and preserving a meaningful identity, and what emerges is a mismatch or tension between learner and teacher.

> *David*: I've played guitar since I was 11 years old. I started off playing twangy guitar stuff, . . . like The Shadows and The Ventures, and then I played R and B, and played in a couple of bands when I was a teenager. And then I got into noise guitar. I mean after that a hybrid of everything I knew. I always played the electric guitar, solid body guitar, a Fender Telecaster. Because I'd been experimenting a little bit with the guitar, I'd been listening to African American music, and I used to go and see Jimi Hendrix, but it was Bo Diddley particularly, music from the '50s and early '60s, that was pretty experimental for its time . . . And so I'd been playing around a bit, and interested in the organization, and what seemed to be the un-organization, not disorganization, but un-organization of music . . . I took up the flute when I was [about] 17, and a certain point a few years later I decided I needed some education. And so I went to a . . . jazz player, and he gave me a couple of lessons, which I stumbled through, and then I think [in] the third lesson he said, 'Oh, I'm busy at the moment. Why don't you just sit down and listen to this record', and it was Paul Horn's *Inside the Taj Mahal*. It was Paul Horn just playing solo flute with the echoes of the Taj Mahal, and I thought well I know this stuff, I'm not going to pay for somebody to play me records that I already know about. And I didn't confront him about it, but I stopped going. And maybe he just felt that I'm wasting my time trying to teach you conventional flute technique, you know where you're going anyway. Or maybe he was being lazy, I'm not really sure. But whatever, I have never been able to succumb to the pedagogical discipline, either as a learner or a teacher . . . I think that to be open to learning all the time is a source of that thing we call energy. Being constantly open to new ideas is hugely important, for human beings.

Contemporary artists often reflect on formal music lessons as being a long way from artistic practice, of utter irrelevance compared to the informal learning of popular music. They wish to turn to, rather than away from, sound and sounds that inspire, enthuse, motivate, and attract deep commitment—to go back into the 'real world of music'. It is no surprise that David is drawn to the 'experimental', not as someone who is attracted to a particular canon or tradition, but as someone who loves working in many different areas, having many different audiences, being a free improviser, and resisting feeling constrained, or being 'locked' in.

> *David*: If I listened to Delta Blues players, I could tell, untutored as I was, that they were using a different tuning, and I was attracted by the sound of that tuning, and I wanted to follow that path. It wasn't about a trajectory of composition, you know, that had come from Wagner, and Debussy, and so on . . . And then going to a concert when I was 18, and hearing a group called AMM play, and it didn't seem like a musical performance, it was a way of organizing sound that was very unfamiliar, and hardly anyone appreciated that it was a musical performance, maybe except me. I found it so powerful . . . it was an epiphany through which a constellation collected around various events that interested me around 1966, when I was pretty young still, still at school which connected me with ideas of decomposition and destruction in art.

As an improvisational musician who does not read or write music, it is no surprise that David offers insights into improvisation: (1) as an original practice of both individual (or personal) and social creativities; (2) as giving opportunities for authorship and co-authorship, the possibilities and potential that arise from dispersed social networks; and (3) having links with those who have gone before and those who come after, and all those composers, performers, and listeners who have a hand in creating the music.

David's compulsion to both integrate and separate the creation of music from the practice of improvisation clearly has implications for him as an acoustic and as a digital musician insofar as digital technologies reconstitute sound and sound devices as numbers, modified so that their nature is changed. It is interesting that he positions himself firmly as a guitar player within a history of rock music, playing in bands which draw upon a tradition of distortion and the deliberate incorporation of noise from the 1960s. David is not a composer of fixed scores, like the traditional Western classical or jazz composers. He does not read or use notation. He does not hold any strict allegiance to the composer's score. He did, however, recently 'compose' an opera, not in the European tradition of opera, but by using his laptop, by developing ideas through workshops, and documenting a timeline template to communicate with an ensemble comprising five instrumentalists and three opera singers. The music has its own natural path of growth whilst at the same time represents the embodiment of a collective performance practice. To an extent they find what they are doing, and where they are going, along the road they travel. As with free jazz improvisation, David seeks for relationships within an evolving musical continuity. This is a practice that has a collective ideology and definition of that creativity and creative experience.

What interests and fascinates David about improvisation within the digital domain is 'the possibility of constantly challenging the stability of the musicians identity'[6]. David is a composer/performer, curator, author, sound artist, and digital musician (see Fig. 7.1 showing David in performance) who is interested in the performance practice of computer music. His interest in and approach to the digital domain of improvised performance practice can be seen in the activities of his group, Unknown Devices: the Laptop Orchestra, a large ensemble of free improvisers playing laptops, convened by the Sound Arts and Design Department of the London College of Communication, and the University of the Arts, London. The genesis of the 'laptop orchestra' is connected with his university work, which involves workshops grounded in musical performance

---

[6] From the Laptop Orchestra website: www.vimeo.com/4863417.

activity, and what it means to be part of the community of music improvisers. Within this community it is possible to develop new aural cultures and yet blend voices in a genuine dialogue, in which no voice is simply absorbed or drowned out by any of the others (some of this can be seen in action at www.vimeo.com/4863417).

> *David*: I called the group 'Unknown Devices' . . . In this group we think of sound itself as a material, to express it more carefully as an event. I have certain strategies which move towards a condition of listening rather than composing and judgment straight away. Being open, flexible, and adaptable, and with people who want to set up an environment like this, is the strategy of invention. We've done quite a lot of performances now . . . it's an incredible experience to play in a group of say 20 people improvising in a venue like Tate Britain or Tate Modern . . . we talk about the 'impossibility' of the situation, and how not to make a music which is a kind of 'mutualized mush', you know, which takes up all the qualities of these different tastes, these different skills, these abilities and reduces them down to [a] wishy-washy type of hybrid . . . moving beyond the dependency of jazz licks, or that entrapment within you, of a particular stylistic genre, in disrupting the expectations of people from differently constituted musical worlds.

This is a community of players who develop laptop-networked improvisational practices. The production of 'newness' is essential to improvisational creativity. Each of the players responds to 'disruption' positively knowing that it enables them to create something new together; that the creativities that bring them together unite them as a community.

Naturally, there are different ways in which improvised performance practices take place. In a small group (such as a string quartet or small jazz group), there is a good degree of room for a genuine dialogue among all of the players. Jazz pioneer Dave Brubeck has argued that 'jazz is about the only form of art existing today in which there is freedom of the individual without the loss of group contact' (1992; cited in Berendt, 1992, pp. 161–2). What follows is an account of a real world practice by a musician who develops improvisational creativities in community practice, and considers what it means to be a part of a community of music-makers.

Community musician[7] Rod Paton exemplifies a practice of improvisation that has emerged from a community-genre of music. His work embodies the concept of '*Lifemusic*'. *Lifemusic* refers to a community of practice in which members interact through collective engagement with improvised music. The musical receptiveness and communication required of such music demands trust at emotional, social, and cognitive levels, and thereby promotes empathy amongst the players, granting them authority and legitimacy as creative agents in a workshop community.

Rod Paton: improvisational creativity as a living process —a community art

Rod Paton (Fig 7.2) is a composer, horn player, writer, and community musician who teaches at the University of Chichester. He describes himself as a jazz and improvising horn player. He has performed with many of Europe's leading players, including broadcasts on BBC Radio 3 and has appeared in the Czech Republic, Germany, and Finland. His CD *Ascension Jazzmass* was described in *Jazz Journal International* as 'a memorable document of the human spirit at its open-hearted and affirmative best'. In his book about improvisation as a community art, *Living Music* (2010), Rod shows how his particular approach to musical practice forms the basis of what constitutes group improvisation 'at the core of community art'.

---

[7] Community musicians devise and lead creative workshops in health care, social care, in prisons, and the wider community. For discussion on the concept of lifelong learning in music see Smilde (2009).

Fig. 7.2 Rod Paton playing at a jazz club called the 'Smoking Rabbit', Brno, Czech Republic, December 2008 with drummer Radim Kolar and bassist Ruda Drozd.
Photo by Michal Sedláček. © Michal Sedláček, 2011.

> *Rod*: Improvisation is the primary creative function: nothing comes into being without it. Improvisation means, literally, to work with the 'unforeseen'. This means that each living moment requires an improvisatory decision to facilitate movement to the next living moment. For me, working directly with unforeseen events is a form of magic. Improvised music is directly in touch with living process—hence '*Lifemusic*'.

Lifemusic is a particular musical practice that Rod has developed over many years as a method of group improvisational music-making that facilitates creative music in workshop settings. For Rod, *Lifemusic* essentially reflects the lives that people lead. *Lifemusic* is based on the principle that 'everybody is musical', that 'everybody can be creative in music', that 'since we start from the understanding that nothing can be "right" or "wrong"', 'there are no wrong notes in music', that 'the music is the raw material', and the potential of that material is 'to draw forth, to create music'. Rod's theory of group improvisation is complex, and links directly to the actual musical practice and the responsibilities of those who take part in the dialogical character of his participatory workshops. For Rod, 'what fits as the music is carried along on the wave of its own logic is the free, creative decisions of the players'; his concern, as facilitator, is explicitly with what performers actually *do* and think they are really *doing*, regardless of whether or not this corresponds with any pre-existing norms.

> *Rod*: *Lifemusic* comes back to my concept of improvisation, my theory of improvisation and the idea that when people are improvising music certain things are happening which define creativity. To begin with, I think they're very much taken into the moment. A person, as it were, connects to time when making music, meaning that they're brought instantly into the here-and-now . . . and that the mind is completely concentrated in that moment. The next part of the definition concerns a mental or psychological trigger which suspends reality or literal thinking in favour of the imagination which is fired up, not just to be inventive, but to actually break down the distinction between what we regard as real and concrete, and what we think of as unreal and imaginative. There is a kind of barrier between what we

think of as sensible and rational and everyday and the things that we think of as happening to us when we're asleep and we're dreaming. Creative improvising dissolves this barrier, and the mind is therefore able to travel, not exactly into the unconscious, but into a kind of suspended state between conscious and unconscious. Here I use Victor Turner's term 'liminality' or 'the liminal state' to describe that[8]. And I think what happens when that point is reached is that the mind can become truly creative. And what happens then—and this is a very important part of my definition of *Lifemusic* as well—is that the ego self is kind of taken out of the picture and what is then firing the creative process in place of the conscious ego is a kind of archetypal energy, a living process which connects people not just in time, but in space.

As with Christopher Small's idea of 'musicking', which associates equality of human relationship and participation, the 'life process' that connects people in *Lifemusic* involves a stance, a particular mental state, a joint endeavour, the intention to find rapport through improvisation. Indeed, the ethnomusicologist John Blacking (1973,) remarked on observing the intricate interaction of two African drummers playing together, stating that through such interaction, two people might achieve an empathic experience unavailable in any other way.

> *Rod*: With improvisation in general and the *Lifemusic* method in particular, I encourage groups of people to enter a particular mental state anchored by what I call a holding form. The idea is that you start off with a conscious idea, a riff, a pattern or an interactive game of some kind, and you play with this for a while, quite consciously and openly. But then something new kicks in, and I notice this again and again with improvising groups, provided that they've been set-up and encouraged, and facilitated in a sensitive and empathic way so that they have permission to break the rules! A short while into the improvisation something shifts, something else takes over, the original (conscious) holding form is abandoned, you can feel it happening, I can almost smell it coming nowadays. I think 'Yes, we're just about to take off . . . we're just about there', and suddenly this thing kicks in and everybody knows exactly what to play. There is an overwhelming sense of shared purpose at this moment. You might have a group of 10, 12, 15 people, but suddenly when that thing kicks in—and it might take a couple of hours of work, or it might happen very, very quickly—they are then being truly creative, because they've suspended that adherence to the external rules, they've let go of the handrails and they are in direct or internal contact with the collective or group intention.

Rod describes here a way of thinking about collective music-making and improvisation. Improvisation is a profoundly social activity. From its earliest manifestations, in the caregiver–infant dyad, to its mature expression, group improvisation involves interaction with the acts and intentions of a collective—a mutually supportive gathering or group of people who come together to share a sense of togetherness, processes of social bonding, and to share in group musical practices (Cross and Woodruff, 2009). Yet, the distinctive practice of collective creativity as applies in jazz improvisation remains inherently communal in nature and much more than acting in the moment (see Fig. 7.2). The nature of improvisational performance, the themes and events of the play, the rules and relationships between the field and the individual are emphasized.

> *Rod:* I think it was Art Blakey who claimed that jazz improvisation was the highest and most demanding level of musical performance. Classical music mostly lays out clearly what is expected of the performer through detailed notated scores so that however technically difficult the music might be, the performer really only needs to interpret the wishes of the composer; free improvisation, on the other

---

[8] Liminality (from the Latin word limen, meaning 'a threshold;) is a psychological, neurological, or metaphysical subjective state, conscious or unconscious, of being on the 'threshold' of or between two different existential planes, as defined in neurological psychology (a 'liminal state') and in the anthropological theories of ritual by such writers as Arnold van Gennep and Victor Turner (http://en.wikipedia.org/wiki/Liminality).

hand, allows the player to be totally creative and this is only as demanding (or not) as the player chooses it to be. But jazz, at least in its most standard forms, both lays down fairly strict parameters of style plus the underlying structures of the music (chord changes or modal forms) but then requires the player to be highly inventive within this framework, often in close collaboration with others.

For me, as I guess for many, learning to play jazz within that remarkable tradition which developed historically through blues, ragtime, swing, bebop, and modal jazz was like a self-imposed need to 'win my spurs', to show that, although my preferred mode of expression was 'free' improvising, I could also improvise in a way which others would recognize as skilful within a specific idiom. This would hope-fully lend a kind of credibility to the free stuff I did at other times. But this was ultimately someone else's problem and I was fortunate enough to meet and occasionally play with others (such as Evan Parker, Paul Rutherford, Elton Dean, Gus Garside) who simply ploughed their individual furrows to come up with highly original and personal forms of creative expression.

Yet, I return again and again to jazz, as a composer and as a performer because, historically it seems to be the music which, more than any other, carries the deep ambiguities of modernity within its syn-thesis of African and European musics. This is not just through a combination of modal tunes and tonal harmony, fixed pulse and free rhythms (though in essence that is what it does) but more about an aesthetic which reconciles African and European perspectives. Mostly though it is about *soul*! Jazz is a music which was born of genocide, slavery, repression, and unimaginable collective pain, and it manages to draw from this darkness an extraordinary resilience which required the deepest form of creative artistry. Art Blakey had it about right.

This emphasizes a point made earlier about the importance of social systems and the scripting of social interaction. Musical improvisation depends very heavily on an implicit tradition, on tacit rules, and an internalized body of works (Berliner, 1994). Improvisation seems inherently com-municative insofar as it involves creating music together in cooperative contexts that provide the conditions for a profoundly social activity from which the self is nuanced and positioned to locate itself within a collective. It takes place within a wider social arena, as a process that requires musicians to be sensitive to the inner states of others. It shows itself as a manifestation of self-other sensitivity, with enhanced empathic processes and empathic relationships that rely at their core on a most intent *listening* to each other: a practice of empathic creativity between interacting players.

When asked how he responds when someone says: 'But, you know, you've got to learn to play an instrument before you can perform on it', he replies:

Rod: Actually, you don't have to learn formally to play an instrument if you choose the right instrument . . . It's true, you can go to a master balafon player and after years and years you become incredibly skilled in that instrument. And it's a very sophisticated instrument too, it's an amazing instrument. But you can also take somebody who's never played a balafon before, put a stick in their hand and say: 'Just make a sound and make it meaningful' . . . One of the mantras which define the *Lifemusic* method is that every sound has a meaning. If you play a sound and hear the meaning in it, you're making music. You don't have to practise for 10 years to do that. But if you do practise for 10 years you'll make a dif-ferent kind of sound and a different kind of music and, obviously, naturally this will be more skilful or at least technically complex . . . but that does not make it better, or more expressive or more socially useful—just different. But group improvisation can also move players from being completely bound up in their own musical worlds and playing chaotically to finding a connectedness with each other . . . The movement between the chaos which comes when each individual is wrapped up in their own stuff and the collective entrainment which comes from empathic listening is a dance between two extremes and this dance is always creative. For me, it's also important for music to connect to the ways that we aspire to live, not just functioning as an entertaining accompaniment to life but as an essential part of our personal and collective narrative of living . . . I've met so many young people who come to me and say I've got Grade 3 violin but I can't be creative, because I can't play unless I've got music in front of me, or I can't improvise unless I learn to play an instrument formally. And that seems to me to be incredibly sad. People with no musical training whatsoever can be incredibly musical and creative . . . When people engage in improvising music together, creating something fresh and new, they celebrate total engagement in the creative process in the here and now. When that 'something' clicks in everybody is on the same level and working to exactly the same end.

Rod believes that creativity between people through improvisation is a living process that can be central to, and a thriving aspect of, everyone's lives. He considers improvisation central to what happens not only in blues, jazz, rock, and world music but also in many other styles that enable musicians to engage in creative acts. He sees improvisation as a state of mind, an attitude, an approach, a particular kind of creativity between people through music, which in turn brings about an inner experience that fulfils some of our basic human needs. For Rod, being creative through group improvisation is a practice characterized by its 'escape from notation, from scores, from staves, from clefs, from barlines (prison bars), from fixed notions of "right" or "wrong", from conductors, from seated patrons, from equal temperament, from composers, from teachers, from grade exams, from analysis, from all the stuff that imprisons music and renders it comatose'. He sees group improvisation as involving shared intentions, the alignment of our own emotional states with those of our collaborators, constituted by mutuality of action in the collective processes that underpin creative musical group practice: this notion seems central to the practice of empathic creativity. We can define the experience as mutual affective alignment underlined by a creative process.[9]

The next featured musician is traditional fiddle player, Hazel Fairbairn, who uses conventions and traditions as integral elements of a cultural creativity that recognizes both the individual and the collective. Hazel uses the generic codes of traditional fiddle playing, shaped by sets of rules that are extendable, and which are associated with particular social formations across time and space. Her music is always imbued with personal, cultural, and collective memory.

Hazel Fairbairn: traditional performance practices

Folk fiddler[10] Hazel Fairbairn (Fig. 7.3) describes herself as a self-employed, professional fiddle player who plays Cajun, Eastern European, experimental electronic, Scottish, and Irish fiddle styles. She manages and plays fiddle in a professional Irish and Scottish Ceilidh Band called 'The Ceilidh Allstars',[11] which includes guitarist John Lawson, dance-caller Mary Panton, and bodhran player, Mark Russell. They play in barns, ballrooms, concert halls, and on stages. Hazel has played in many bands, including Mervyn Afrika's Kaap Finale, a Soweto-style township jazz band, and a non-mainstream and uncategorizable group called 'Horace X', which fused diverse world music fiddle styles with sequencing and sampling, and has travelled extensively, performing in folk festivals across North America, mainland Europe, Scandinavia, and the UK. In 1991, she

---

[9] Features of musical interaction that inspire empathic creativity are discussed further by Rabinowitch et al. (in press).

[10] Hazel changed her description of herself in email exchanges after her interviews from 'Irish fiddler' to 'Folk fiddler', because, as she explained, 'not being Irish, nor playing purely that style it seems more authentic, little though I love the word, to describe myself as a Folk fiddler'.

[11] See Fig. 7.3 and Hazel's bands playing at: www.facebook.com/video/video.php?v=10150566931410173#!/ pages/Horace-X/121387338633 and on YouTube: Performing Live on stage at the Ely Folk Festival, 12 July 2009 (www.youtube.com/watch?v=63GK53bt_Ww). For audio streaming of several music samples see www.acallstars.com/. See also an example of another Irish band playing in the context of a Cork Pub setting, uploaded by Eoin Bouzouki 1975 on 4 October 2010.

Fig. 7.3 Folk fiddler Hazel Fairbairn.
Photo by Steve Bond. © Stephen Bond, 2011.

busked her way across Europe, playing in a professional street music fiddle-guitar-accordion cajun and bluegrass trio.

With a portfolio of capitals (musical knowledge, education, life experience) including a PhD from the Ethnomusicology Department at the Faculty of Music, University of Cambridge and University College, Cork, in 'Group Playing in Traditional Irish Music' (1993), Hazel's particular understanding and interest in group performance practice is important in the context of this chapter (Fairbairn, 1994). Her PhD concerned group playing of traditional Irish dance tunes, with a focus on the balance of individual expression with communal playing. Hazel's work as a fiddle teacher and workshop leader has been affected by her insider and academic knowledge of the field of traditional live music performance. Her orientation is informed by the interplay of a musician's, and an academic habitus. Her undergraduate music lessons weigh on her when she teaches the fiddle or leads a workshop. She has taught traditional fiddle playing for 20 years, developing an alternative to the classical violin syllabus and strategies for traditional folk skills and instrumental styles.

Her particular interests are in aural learning, and its positive impact on rhythmic conception, the ability to improvise, and the creative process in playing music. Negative teacher/learner relationships, sadly accompanied by stress and demotivation, plagued her at an undergraduate level.[12]

---

[12] See Smilde (2009) for research findings that point directly at the challenges facing the education and training of musicians today, and the need to recognize the vastly changed world that musicians must now navigate as lifelong learners, and in order to continue their professional development.

Hazel: I've always felt quite stultified by classical music. I found it quite oppressive and I think that is reinforced by the teaching, or the way that I experienced the teaching. Particularly once I started lessons at the Guildhall School of Music . . . as part of my university degree, and that was when it got really quite . . . quite bad . . . [laughs] I found my teacher's perspective was problematic. She was used to people who were practising eight hours a day, very dedicated. Not really trying to do anything other than the one thing, achieve this very sort of precise goal. And then she had me, a part-time student whom she found difficult to understand at all. She couldn't understand me, my attitude or anything about it and I think she must have found it frustrating. And so she got cross . . . it wasn't a good relationship. It was very much based on, I suppose, scolding is the word that comes to mind. You know, scolded for not practising, scolded for playing it wrong, scolded for playing the wrong notes, scolded for tapping my foot . . . I always reacted badly to that learning culture. And I think on the other side of it, my experience of playing by ear was a much more kind of much scruffier, much more informal, and with fewer rules that I was aware of. And there were probably rules that I wasn't aware of, but less explicit rules about what you could and couldn't do. And it felt different . . . Like once I was at university I'd sort of played a little bit with different bands, and started playing the viola with a South African kind of Soweto jazz band. And it just felt different, it just felt like a different experience. I actually felt joy playing music, rather than feeling quite repressed and anxious about whether I was playing it correctly. And it was that feeling partly of social involvement, and just quite deep fulfilment that I hadn't experienced playing classical music, even though, you know, it was to a reasonable standard. I'd never experienced that fulfilment.

Within institutions concerned with the formal training of musicians there are those who break out of the traditional categories, and redefine the work, education and training of present day professional musicians. To fulfil a particular role, a professional musician may sing or play an instrument, or become a composer, songwriter, orchestrator or arranger, performer, leader, or teacher. But Hazel sees a need to reformulate the idea of what a musician could be, with freedom to choose, taking account of the musician's 'own' music, rebellion against certain musical learning processes, and the exploration of what the musician has beyond technical proficiency on an instrument. Musicians now need many strings to their bows. The nature and challenges of being a professional player, whose style of performance or musical genre belongs to more than one tradition of musical practice, has been a subject of much discussion in recent years (S. Bennett, 2010; Schippers, 2010; Smilde, 2009).

Lively debates still flourish around what constitutes 'authenticity' in the teaching of a musical tradition, and how certain individual or group creative processes shape the material's continuity, variation, and selection. Hazel explains some aspects of the 'folk processes of re-creation', and how these aspects address the importance of individuality, in relation to personal and collective identity, and what she considers to be authentic Irish performance practice.

Hazel: Well, if you went specifically to an Irish traditional session and someone started a tune and you didn't know it, you wouldn't play. You wouldn't just jam over it . . . the only time that you would deviate from that tune would probably be once you were fairly well entrenched in the tradition and fairly well known to the people you're playing with. It's not something you would do as a newcomer, and you would probably get quite a lot of bad feeling really if you did. So it's not like it's a big free for all . . . with Irish music the tune is the shared currency, the tunes are what everybody knows . . . You have to play a lot of the tune skeleton in order to identify the tune. So the room for personal freedom is really on the level of ornamentation and tiny little changes in the sequences of notes that you use. You know, in a sort of very traditional way there isn't a huge amount of room for individual interpretation. But then no two people play the tune the same way, and you would recognise a player instantly within a bar for their sound and how they treat the tune. So it's quite a subtle thing. I think creative practice defines how a particular person uses slides, ornamentation, exactly how they would execute a roll, being like a turn but more of a rhythmic effect, or a grace note. And then there's a lot of regional variation, so you could tell whether they come from Donegal, or whether they come from Kerry, because they have different styles. Obviously, this is slightly blurred now because people can listen to music from anywhere. But even within that there's regional style, so it's a very intimate thing within a group of musicians from one area.

In addressing how possibilities for re-creating music are generated through free associations in 'conversation' with constraints, Hazel explores the very nature of Irish music. As a field of cultural production, Irish fiddling does not operate and cannot be played or re-created without reference to existing conventions that enable it to be recognized and differentiated from other traditional musics. Hazel characterizes these conventions in terms of having a strong individualistic or personal aspect in harmony with the collective knowledge of certain musical patterns, motives, and associated sonorities. Hazel explains how learning Irish music-making is located at the interface of the individual and collective identity of the player, in its own domain and in larger social relations at one and the same time. Learning is accomplished by watching other players, by listening and copying, by observing how genre rules inform the postures and movements and the spacing and pacing of musical events, and by assimilating unwritten principles of collectivity and authenticity.

> *Hazel*: Well, the best metaphors that I have come up with for it are: one: when you're having a conversation or telling a story, you don't make up new words. You don't re-create the rules of the language in order to express yourself, so you're operating within the system. But you're gonna say things differently on different days, you're gonna say them in different tones of voice. You're gonna express yourself more or less formally, depending on the person that you're talking to. And I suppose improvisation I would think of in that kind of conversational way, is it's very context-dependent and it's very much expressed in terms of the language you're speaking. The second metaphor is doing martial arts. You're gonna go through a drill. You're gonna spend hours and hours and hours learning how to do a particular kick, a particular punch, a particular block. And then when you're actually doing sparring or free-fighting with somebody, you don't think about any of that. You don't think about your technique, because you're too busy trying to stop yourself getting hit, or trying to land a punch on the other guy. So all of that knowledge is there, but it's not something which is cluttering up your conscious mind. It's there and you can draw on it, but consciously I think if you're improvising well then you're not thinking about it. And in that sense I think, you know, it's not like you just make everything up from first principles, you're very much drawing on tricks, on riffs, on rhythms and tunes, on fragments, on core progressions that you've picked up over the years. But you're not putting thought . . . you're not thinking too hard about how those are gonna be put together. So you can be thinking about something completely different, like, I don't know, what you're gonna have for breakfast the next day. And it'll still . . . that means that you're gonna improvise more effectively then, than if you're actually engaged in conscious thought about what you're gonna play next.

Hazel identifies several creative and cultural practices that form part of a broader set of social relationships. These are integral elements of her practice of improvisational creativity. Listening to others and responding with 'something new' gives the impression of a mutual exchange. But this immediately raises the crucial question of how, if Irish group music can be thought of as a kind of dialogue, who is speaking? Do we hear the players themselves in conversation? Are these voices really their own?

> *Hazel*: There is a very strong hierarchy and there is a master or apprentice element in traditional Irish settings . . . that's where I've thought about it and studied it. But certainly there you will get a nucleus of people who are very much controlling the sessions and it radiates out. If somebody arrives, like a close friend or, someone you know is a very important musician, then they'll have a seat made for them near the middle of the session. But it radiates out, you know, so it's kind of totally acceptable to be just passing through and not knowing anybody in the session, it's absolutely acceptable to draw up a seat on the edge of the session and just play along with what you can. It takes a sort of a concentric circle

effect . . . I suppose, again, you can look at the sort of martial art analogy, and very often people that are very good musicians that go and play in sessions, are not necessarily getting loads out of it themselves musically. But, they're doing it because they learnt through going to sessions and they want to keep that tradition going. It's also a social thing, it's a way of keeping links with a group of people . . . But the two things that people experience as being barriers to joining in, are the speed that people play at and not knowing the tunes. So really it's a combination of repertoire and being able to play quickly. For Irish sessions the more tunes you can play and if you can keep up with the session, then, you know, that's gonna make you more and more adept as a player and that's what's valued.

Knowing the tune is one key aspect of habitus, in the sense of the way musicians are disposed to play and perform. Bourdieu calls such an orientation a strategy, meaning a semi-conscious but characteristic practice (1993b,c). How do we know to what extent a performance is original? Is the virtue of novelty that it somehow reproduces personal creativity? For Hazel, the key aspect of musicians' habitus is what players think and do—their creative 'practice' in a particular genre. This emphasis on the self-interests of the players and how they mobilize their accumulated 'capital'—their musical power and prestige as expert players—as they compete for dominance in the performance of traditional Irish tunes, is important to what kind of improvisational creativities arise in contexts of cultural production. Debates around the concept of authenticity by Karpeles[13] (1953, cited in Wade, 2004) and Negus and Pickering (2004, p. 112), amongst others, raise the following three defining factors: (i) continuity from the present to the past; (ii) variation which springs from the creative impulse of the individual or the group; and (iii) selection by the community, which determines the form or forms in which music survives.

> *Hazel*: Obviously, it depends, to some extent, on the musicians involved. But, you know, if people are listening to each other they will adapt their playing to each other so that, you know, they kind of . . . Maybe one of them will play slightly differently . . . but, they're probably both playing slightly differently from normal in order to find a place where they meet in the middle, where their styles can gel. And certainly you get musicians that play together more easily than others, because their styles are closer. I think there is that kind of . . . and it's quite a subtle thing, it's . . . As you say, it's quite nuanced. But then you do also get people that don't listen, so you have to fit in with them, 'cos, they're not gonna fit in with anyone else.
>
> If you've got like three or four people who are playing together, they can all hear each other. It's a very different situation from if you've got 30 people playing together in a really noisy pub where it gets a bit insular, everybody's just sitting there playing the tune and it's like lots of parallel lines. And there's very little interaction between people, so in a way the bigger the group of people, the less interaction there is. You know, whereas two or three people can really start to communicate. So . . . I suppose, in a way, it's almost like . . . the listening thing is almost . . . it's so central it almost doesn't . . . it almost goes without saying. I mean, obviously, some people don't listen, but I . . . to me, it's all about . . . if you're improvising you're listening and you're responding to the sound that you hear. Obviously, not if you're sitting playing on your own, but if you're playing with other people then you're listening . . . you're listening to them. And I would tend to listen to them more than I would listen to myself. And just that moving that focus to the other people, means that there's more chance of something new coming out of my own playing. Rather than repeating . . . going round and round and round in the same patterns.

But good new ideas do not automatically translate into accepted cultural practices within a specific cultural framework or field. Personal and cultural creativities arise when a traditional player realizes and creates a variation. The individual absorbs a practice from the culture and

---

[13] Karpeles defined authenticity in folk in the *Journal of the International Folk Music Council* (IFMC) (1953, p. 23). Authenticity and authentic performance practice in folk music is defined by Bonnie C. Wade (2004, p. 141).

changes it in a way that may be judged to be valuable by the field, thus providing a new cultural framework, constructed through interactions between tradition and innovation.

> *Hazel*: I don't write music. I think my identity to music is very much the performer or player. So, for me, the creative side of it is to do with improvising and playing, and what I can and what I can't do with a tune or a style that hasn't quite been done before. So I play a tune sort of slightly differently from how everyone else, or a lot differently from how everyone else has played it.

Thus, personal and cultural creativities have a participatory dimension in that they presuppose a community of people who share ways of thinking and acting, who learn from each other and imitate each other's actions. Personal and cultural creativities drive change within musical traditions. Musical cultures tend to become differentiated over time, and they develop increasingly independent and autonomous styles, but they can also become increasingly integrated when players seize the opportunity to develop a network of contacts that enables them to integrate personal and social creativities.

> *Hazel*: I think bands are forming their own sounds, their own identities, rather than everybody kind of going for the same sound or identity of an Irish group with at particular sound, there's now lots more different line-ups, different sounds. There is a particular sound which we think of as Irish music with a particular instrumental expected line-up. There's possibly been a little more experimentation with, you know, adding different instruments. Bands like Lau are actually experimenting a lot and blowing apart that 8-bar-phrase thing and actually going into much more extended exploratory sections. There's also bands fusing traditional instruments in traditional music with other styles of musics. You've got things coming together like an Afro-Cuban beat in an Irish jig, bringing a kind of fusion.

One type of improvisational creativity that arises in traditional music has been historically coined 'the folk process of re-creation'. Hazel asserts the primacy of a process of interweaving musical material which is given with material that is being newly created as one listens. In most folk music performance traditions, the process of improvising—individual players creating variations in melodic ornaments, articulation, phrasing, speed or dynamics—results in 'recognizable variants' (Wade, 2004, p. 110). This process may involve personal and cultural creativities when the dominant mode of engagement is in understanding co-construction as a new consciousness: understanding what it is to be creative together, as well as the role of self in a community of music-makers.

We have seen how a type of group improvisation creativity, developed by Rod and referred to as '*Lifemusic*', arises in community workshop settings. This process of group improvisation allows for the emergence of empathy through creative practices. What links traditional music and *Lifemusic* practices is the development of self-other sensitivity. Both are real world live performance practices that emerge in community. Both occur in off- and on-stage settings in which group members stay together attuned to the music as it comes into existence. The players pursue shared values and trust in participatory music-making—in situations wherein personal, collective, and empathic creativities are at the heart of live performance practices.

The featured musicians that follow, Andrew Brown and Nick Collins, are composer-laptop-musician-programmers working with 'live coding'. This is a radical practice of computer-mediated creativity within a particular community, and is facilitated by relatively small-scale modes of production. Live coding involves using laptops as instruments on which to improvise on-the-fly programming for live audiences, who watch their work on projections of their laptop screens, whilst hearing the music being generated in real time.

What follows in the next section is characteristic of a view of improvisation in the digital practice of 'live coding' and live coders. Andrew Brown is a musician who sometimes performs as an unaccompanied soloist but, more often engages in interactive coding in live coding duo performances with Andrew Sorensen, acquiring legitimate cultural capital in and beyond academia. The innovative dimension of live coding lies in a new approach to the process and context of improvisation. Bourdieu's (1996) assertion that creativity and capital are interrelated, and have an embodied aspect, allows us to consider the extent to which Andrew articulates a different kind of creativity to that of Nick, and what kinds of capitals are associated with live coding engagements in algorithmic composition for different individuals.

Andrew Brown: the generative rules of improvised live coding

Andrew Brown (Fig. 7.4) describes himself as an Australian composer, performer, and researcher in the field of computer music. He recalls being interested in music from a very young age, singing at church, and 'banging knives and forks on tables and doing percussion things' at home. He started learning piano formally around the age of 10 and continued through high school. He went on to take a music degree, majoring in classical piano. He was always interested in popular music, and played in rock bands when he was school. He did a stint as a professional musician, touring Australia, before completing university. His interest in technology and computer music began with playing keyboards and synthesisers. At senior high school, he was taken to a concert by jazz pianist Keith Jarrett, and 'was just blown away and did the whole buy-every-album-go-to-every-concert' thing.

Andrew is Professor of Digital Arts at The Queensland Conservatorium, Brisbane, Australia. His academic work, research and teaching is in technologies that support creativity and learning, computational music and art, and the philosophy of technology. He is also a musician, author, and previously the research manager for the Australasian CRC for Interaction Design. His creative activities focus on real time audiovisual works using generative processes and live coding performances. His first live coding concert was in 2005 with his colleague Andrew Sorensen: 'It really did need two of us at the time to make anything half decent, a solo concert was a long way off. It was terrifying. We were praying that the software we'd written wouldn't crash'.

Thinking about the type of creativities identified and expressed in Andrew's practice of live coding has to begin, I suggest, not with the indeterminacy that arises through improvisation, nor with on-the-fly programming, but with how he characterizes the nature and value of the 'computer creativity' underpinning the programming practices, and the interplay of human and computer creativities. Unlike Nick, Andrew focuses on the principles of the communicative form, and on aesthetic judgements about live coding performance. The creativity here is of a collective kind. The field membership requires a degree of technical skill, interdisciplinarity, and intellectual enthusiasm for virtuosic displays.

> *Andrew*: [Live coding] is a music performance practice, or sometimes a multimedia performance practice. It is where you type computer code to write software that generates the art form that you are working on . . . The audiences are usually the same kind of audiences you might get for other experimental music and art works. You know, usually a sort frequenting an underground kind of venue and things like that. Although it also has a fairly strong academic interest. So sometimes conferences and those kind of academic events are very interested in it as well. The academic interest comes from a couple of directions. One is people who are interested in media art generally and the other is those people from computer science and technical backgrounds. So the artistic people are kind of interested in 'How can you do some sort of interesting things there?' 'What is this crazy stuff you are doing?', and 'I don't understand anything you are doing?' And then there are the computer scientists going 'How can you possibly do that. That's crazy. You are typing code live and how can you not make any mistakes?' So they see it as a kind of technical *tour de force*. And the artist people just see it as it comes up, as a crazy thing. [both laugh] . . . Commonly live coders come out of either a classical music training where eight hours of practice a day for 10 years is necessary, or out of a pure science background where a similar discipline is required to apply the skills . . . And like all marginal practices, there's only potentially

Fig. 7.4 Andrew Brown performing at a live coded concert in Brisbane, Australia.
© Andrew Brown, 2011.

going to be a small audience. This is why I think it has found a home in the 'academy' because it is about new practices and new knowledge, and there is a new basis for enquiry, and a new kind of research which goes with that. Academics and artists are people who are interested in both. It is also how the culture keeps changing with the technology . . . I sense there has been a swing of the pendulum, backing away from the perceived need to be simply novel for its own sake and an embrace of the role novelty plays in creativity and how that defines society.

The forms of knowledge, conceptions of creativity, and skill required in the execution of live coding demand a lot of discipline and practice. So, Andrew observes that, to some degree, this strongly insulated field membership and position-taking denies the possibility of judgements in the aesthetic realm having an 'objectivity' independent of personal background. It is, for sure, an emergent mode of performance practice, and as Andrew sees it, not for the untutored and unsophisticated musician.

The generative principles cross fields within fields, including media, music, and maths, and can be understood in terms of making visible the coding as a procedure of a particular collective kind. Visual presentation presents the data flow directly, in a what-you-see-is-what-you-hear format, which audiences may consider important for formulating judgements about the performance, just as seeing a pianist or violinist perform virtuosic and inventive passages may suggest creativity of superior worth by virtue of some feature that is extrinsic to the music itself. Ideally, there is no difference in creative agency between graphic and text languages but a different in expressive flexibility and a different capacity expressed during performance. Value also lies in the differences between graphical programming environments[14] (Max/MSP and PD) and text-based languages

---

[14] There is an interface paradigm for computer programming where commands or functions are represented visually as blocks and a program is constructed by assembling blocks together into a flow chart diagram by connecting blocks with virtual wires. This style of coding is called visual programming.

and libraries, such as Impromptu, SuperCollider, Csound, and Chuck, and the preoccupation with the fantastic marvels of execution that are now in fashion. Andrew values creativity, invention and communicative values, and the complex interaction between artist and audience.

> *Andrew*: In relation to the audience's experience of a live coding performance, one of the reasons that live coders have displayed their code is because they are aware that if they weren't to do that, the practice would seem very opaque to the audience. From a technical perspective, most people don't understand what is going on. If you weren't to display a code you would expect most people would feel even more uncertain about what was going on . . . When you're an audience watching someone playing a piano or a violin you kind of understand through experience about what is hard and what is easy and what is possible and what's not possible, so you can judge virtuosity. There is a strong connection between those gestures and sound. Whereas in the live coding context, or even in many electronic music performances, most audiences members are not familiar enough with the techniques involved to be able to really make a good judgement about whether or not that person is performing virtuosically or otherwise. Because they just don't know what is possible and what the boundaries and possibilities are . . . the display of coding is one way of revealing or lifting a lid on what's going on.

Interestingly, and crucially, the code is only used once before being discarded at the end of the performance. Often it is not recorded, thus preventing a repertoire to be established, and, perhaps blocks a canon of works to be referenced. What happens, then, if there are no accumulated artefacts? How is the value of creativity, the act of creation itself, communicated from the self to others, from particular to general, in terms of what live coders do, and have done, and how does this impact on the critical assessments and judgements made about what is new?

> *Andrew*: It is such a small community. Everybody sort of knows everybody's stuff [laugh] so you can't necessarily just go to a concert and redo a performance because the next concert is going to have half of the people who were at the previous concert. So you need to keep moving forward. But I imagine if there were more performance venues and so forth I would certainly repeat a work and play again. But I don't really want to repeat a work again to the same audience. I would rather do something new and push myself forward rather than simply replay a work that I might have done at a previous concert. There is also the issue of variation from one performance to another, which can be much larger for a jazz performer than it is say for a pop music performer, or for a classical music performer. The live coding thing is up the end of the spectrum closer to jazz where every performance is or shows evidence of innovation and of creativity. What is interesting here is that, as with jazz, there is a strong tendency to want to value a particular performance by capturing it, recording it and moving on. From my own experience, there is or can be quite a wide variety between different performances of the same work; some of which I am quite happy with, and others which I am not.

Here we start to gain awareness of what live coders are grappling with, and how certain types of creativity are recognized and rewarded. An incredibly creative and communicative aspect of live coding performance and generative practice is that the coding makes visible the algorithmic composition of sound and music in real time, and makes possible changes to the program itself in real time. So the coding presentational display for the audience establishes a strong correspondence between time and sound as the improviser controls temporal flow and sound generation. This is the special character of the creative act of live coding, and what informs the self-understanding and strategies of live coders as much as it impacts upon the critical assessment of what artists do and have done.

> *Andrew*: While I don't think that economic circumstances are having an influence on live coding because of its limited commercial impact, I do think that technology has had an influence on live coding . . . I'm not sure that we have a shift in types of musical genres and styles that people like to listen to though . . . it's back to the sort of live coding aural culture which privileges the live performance.

> It is one of the reasons why some colleagues don't do audio or video recordings of their performances . . . You can't find a video recording of Nick Collins on the web. This is different from the practice I share with Andrew Sorenson. We are quite happy for those recordings to be public. It's not a uniform position. But nevertheless the act of sampling and taking materials and so forth is not so critical in comparison with what someone does in the moment with them during the performance . . . the creativity is in the improvisation and the communication and interaction with the audience . . . giving the audience a real experience in a space that has to live.

The question arises as to what kind of communicative creativity enables interactions between the artist and audience that are different, within an aural culture that values live performance and originality? Although the various creativities are used in different ways, as Andrew sees it, all of them are useful in some context or other. What he means by 'creativity', its unfolding and its applications in relation to live coding, is also constitutive of dispositions such as curiosity and openness, and the relative distinctions between novelty and newness; if, that is, what is novel for people refers to what is fresh, unusual, forward-looking, and new-fashioned, or if it refers to what is strange, different, unfamiliar, unique or original), particularly as these categories relate to how certain types of creativity are recognized and rewarded in academia compared with industry.

> *Andrew:* I think creativity is strongly tied to a curiosity, an enquiry. I think that people who are creative are interested in what might be, and what could be, and what the opportunities and alternatives are, and being not usually satisfied with the way things are in the status quo, and they're kind of excited by things which are a bit novel and new. I think there's a difficulty in characterizing creativity in relation to novelty alone, however, because things need to be appropriate, and so I think a big part of being creative is actually having quite a solid understanding of the context, and of the field so that you know what is appropriate.

Andrew highlights some of the quandaries about the context of creativity, and the connections between the simultaneous tasks and processes of composition and performance. There are complex issues in this context concerning: performance and performing acts; the conditions that foster creativity, such as curiosity and openness, novelty and newness; coding that makes visible the algorithmic composition of sound and music created in real time from a program specification, and the possibility of changing the program itself in real time; and the creative possibilities of how these relate to what is at stake, in terms of currency and conventions.

> *Andrew:* Live coders illustrate the dissolving of the difference between composition and performance. Given that the person who is doing those things is the same person, almost always, you don't play someone else's work, then I think that's definitely a difference from what you would conventionally see. However, I don't think it's unique to live coding, I think that a lot of the electronic dance music cultures, and stuff like that, are starting to get there. Although, having said that, DJs of course play music that's written by others, and so there's more of a division there, but in the experimental electronic community, and probably in the folk music community as well, interestingly, where there is less of a great divide.

Here, the type of improvisational creativity being recognized in musical practice has a special character, which Andrew identifies as being common to certain generic conventions. Live coders, as with composer-musicians working in dance clubs, folk clubs, and electronic music aural cultures, are described as improvisers, for their modes of composition involve a kind of improvisation. They make use of the most exhilarating aspects of real time improvisation in musical practices, whereby existing rules and limits apply in ways that result in both respecting those rules and altering them. On the one hand, how live coders play within, or seek to challenge, conventions is indicative of what is at stake, and what is considered high risk for live coders. For Andrew, live coding is certainly about the application of aesthetic judgement (rather than about the criteria) but it is more so about musical processes and this is the 'compositional' aspect of it.

> *Andrew*: [These are] things I would like to hold on to concern a sense of continuity and momentum so that a work doesn't seem to have spots in it where it gets dull and uninteresting. So just to maintain the level of interest, and therefore hopefully the audiences engagement, requires an appropriate momentum, a sense of moving forward and evolution in a work. But one other thing which of course is tricky in the computational world is that, given that most of the live coding practice involves generative music which has a high degree of indeterminacy in some of the processes, you can just be lucky [laughs] in some events that all the computational random choices work out nicely, and at other times they don't. You really do put yourself in the hands in the machine, and the reason you do that is because that is part of the excitement. Sometimes it turns out much better than you could have imagined. So you kind of take the risk that on occasions it is going to be just really exciting and come out amazingly, even better than we had planned. There are other occasions where parts of it are not going to work as well as you would like. You know that's just the risk profile you take on.

One of the central motifs expressed by Andrew is the idea that creativity involves the computer as a conduit through which computer-creativity may affect him as the locus of an 'autonomous' agency of its own. That is, the live coder is never sure what the laptop will throw back at him/her. The laptop does not just reflect the live coder's creativity; it has creativity of its own. If we think of creativity being attributed to computers, so that the computer is not merely a 'tool' made use of by a 'user' (live coder), but more of *a creative partner* having a particular type of agency, then we can more readily see why Andrew considers a computer can be seen as a creative partner.[15]

Live coding involves the performance practices of an original 'piece', which is a work that may or may not be planned in advance, but admits multiple performances. Live coding performance is an improvised music wherein creativity can be understood as the practical outcome of a specific combination of structural determinants and conditions and which is enabled through 'improvisation', in that playing within the bounds of the structure can go in multiple directions based on choices made during performance. It is rare that a performance is recorded but some pieces are (such as 'Full Slate' which was discussed earlier). Some composer-programmers, as with Andrew and his Australian duo (*aa-cell* with Andrew Sorensen), exhibit creativities that intersect as 'on-the-fly' interactive explorations and constructions using an interpretative programming language, such as the Impromptu system based on the Scheme language). They rarely repeat whole concert programmes but do post up their performances on YouTube.[16] These pieces are consumed by other live coder networks. In the contemporary world, the field of power is primarily, but not exclusively, shaped by these interactions, competitions,[17] collusions and tensions between the players, the field of cultural production, and their values.

---

[15] For further discussion of the notion of partnership and other of these points see Brown (2001) and more directly related to live coding in Brown and Sorensen (2009).

[16] www.flickr.com/photos/madpixelist/sets/72157623109139757/.

[17] See Nilson (2007) for a description of a 13-round 'Code Out; For the World Programming Federation Finger Weight Belt' competition for live coders.

Nick Collins: the discourse of real time scripting and a new genre

Nick Collins[18] (Fig. 7.5) describes himself as a UK-based composer, performer, and researcher in the field of computer music. He lectures at the University of Sussex, and has research interests in machine listening, algorithmic composition, and the history of electronic music. He is an experienced pianist and laptop musician, active in both instrumental and electronic music composition. Live coding is but one of many musical activities Nick takes part in, his other work embracing many possibilities opened up by new technologies, in particular the creative potential of the computer for exploring, manipulating, and transforming sound.

Nick has a first degree in mathematics, a Master's in music technology, and a PhD in computer music. He learned violin between the ages of 7 and 11, and hated it at the time, despite which he enjoyed the challenge of playing again in orchestras for a year at the age of 30! He then took up keyboard (age 12–15), 'essentially teaching myself' and engaging in 'obsessive self-study', taking Grade 8 and A-level music, and has continued in this way to the present[19]. Nick describes himself as something of a 'digital musician' particularly oriented towards live performance.

> *Nick*: Rather than the composer-pianists of the nineteenth century, I see myself as a twenty-first century composer-programmer. People are an implicit and untangleable blend of characters and change as the context suits; . . . I am certainly happy to be labelled a digital musician where this might simply mean someone working at the cross-disciplinary juncture of these types.

Here we glimpse an assumption involved in the production of digital and new audio cultures and practices. Technological innovations have certainly played a decisive role and revolutionized our thinking about the new breed of musicians. As noted by the early experimenters, such as Cage and Schaeffer, digital technology, as with the tape recorder after the Second World War,[20] has revolutionized music. Nick's choice for his first degree was mathematics although, in reality, as he explains, he 'probably practised piano and instrumental composition more than maths at university'. He 'didn't program a computer until my Master's', during which he made a detour through music technology to become a composer-programmer. For Nick, live coding is a performance practice that produces an improvised piece from real time algorithmic judgements:

> *Nick*: As a sort of live maths, it's like a rap battle but with programs. It's a very experimental thing and we are still figuring out the best ways of doing it.

The audience watches the coding on projections of the computer screens and hear the music being generated in real time. For example, a performance of one of Nick's pieces 'Full Slate' starts from a full page of code projected on a screen; from which point the live coder works backwards, deconstructing the text. It aims to foreground a new kind of musical composition, and privileges a particular live performance practice whereby a new audio culture is mobilized by the interplay of human creativity and whatever constitutes computer-controlled/machine creativity. (For an example, see Fig. 7.4. The live coding performance took place on 20 September 2009 in Plymouth. The concert had a seated audience. The visuals involve two projected laptop screens, plus some further live code, VJed visuals by Dave Griffiths, with all overlaid on the planetarium's curved

---

18 There are no videos or recordings of Nick Collins performing his piece 'Full Slate', because it is an improvised piece. It inverts 'traditional' blank slate live coding, meaning that, starting from a full page of code, the live coder works backwards. However, there are some general live coding resources which give some ideas of the style: www.toplap.org/index.php/TOPLAP_videos_and_screencasts.

19 Some recent works for piano and electronics are listed at www.cogs.susx.ac.uk/users/nc81/music.html.

20 The first US tape recorders were built around 1948, though German radio used AC-bias machines for war broadcasts in 1941. Schaeffer's first tape-recorded composition was written in 1951.

Fig. 7.5 Nick and Matthew Yee-King in a live coded concert performance on 20 September 2009 in a planetarium in Plymouth with multiple screen projections overlaid.
© David Griffiths, 2011.

screen just behind the performers, and hence spattering light across the performers as well.) But, as Nick suggests, 'People have some problems with these kinds of performances'.

> *Nick*: The main complaint usually is that it's not sufficiently gestural, too unlike ordinary musicianship. You must be prepared to accept some failures and ugly moments of sounds . . . it has often proved a controversial practice because it disengages from the traditional immediate gestural work of musicians, yet it offers a new form of improvisation, embracing the computer program and what that might mean to musicians . . . You can still perform with programming, with some sort of framework within which you expect to create a performance, where you may not know beforehand everything that will come out.

Accounts of live coding such as this provide material for understanding new types of musical creativity. Live coding involves the creation of a novel performance tool in the form of a programming language and improvised performance. Creating code live is inherently risky, not least because of its lack of visual excitement for audiences. Nick speaks of the principles of the communicative form and creative act, which are likened to, but transcend, the conventions of improvised jazz musics. Even that which seems individualist, is socially scripted and this is reflected in the nature of the act of creating sound with computer languages.

> *Nick*: A few years back I spent a month explicitly practising a set over and over, day after day, for an hour each day, as if I was about to go up on stage. There was a marked improvement in the level I could live code and it was rewarding to see real efforts translated into sound created with computer languages that are immensely rich infinite grammars. It's a great intellectual challenge and a new territory.

What are the principles underpinning the intellectualism and creativity of the field of live coding, of real time scripting during a laptop music performance, and what are the improvisatory skills and risks involved?

> *Nick*: Some have argued that the code is like a score. But the code is much more general than a score—when you are live coding you are not necessarily making a fixed rigid thing, you may be making an

interactive program, and as you rewrite this program that gives one level of interaction. You might also be interacting with the program in other ways: waving at a camera, talking into a microphone . . . It is like a musician practising improvisation in the traditional sense, where you don't know the exact order of notes that can come out in the concert. But you may practise certain gestures or certain ideas that might be useful to you in those situations. So if someone is live coding they may be constructing from scratch the algorithms that are running on the machine, the algorithms that eventually lead to the music. Now how would they practise that? What they may practise is improving the quick recall of certain effective coding instructions . . . That doesn't mean they know in advance exactly what final shape the algorithm will have, that's being negotiated in the performance. But you can improve the number of possible gestures you can have access to. In the same way a traditional musician practising improvising would try to increase the size of their repertoire and techniques that they can employ in a live situation.

The ideological rules and internal language of 'communicative musicality'[21] that inform jazz artists, DJs or punk rock bands, for example, what postures, clothes and movements are appropriate for frontline singers and instrumentalists, and what these signify and communicate to audiences, are uniquely specific to the originality, the peculiar quality of an act. For Nick, the ideological rules and internal language of live coding performance is not confined to a community of avant-garde composers, nor is it about the production of musical objects. What is unique to live coding and its ideology is the dominant knowledge structures and position[22] of the live act of algorithmic processing. That is, this form of creativity is about the possibility of coded crashes, of improvisational lucidity, of algorithmic engagement in fast coding, of live coders writing themselves into their world, developing their 'voice' through expert computer programming and scripting.

> *Nick*: Live coding itself doesn't say the music must be in such and such a style, or the visuals have to be in such and such a style . . . To be slightly more specific about types of performance, things that might actually be attempted, I have a performance called 'Full Slate': it opposes the idea that you start with a blank page and try to build something up. So I began with a pre-written part, a combination of a number of different algorithms which explored alternative tunings, certain rhythmic gestures, certain timbral patterns. Starting with that you begin with an absolute hubbub of sound. And then my role in the performance, and it was still an improvised performance, was to deconstruct it, so to gradually go back to the blank slate by stopping, twisting, and manipulating those algorithmic materials. It becomes a sort of deconstructed constructed performance, ending with no code at all. I've performed this piece several times now. Each time I hope that I manage to get more out, and what I mean by that is that I make several alterations to the ambience that have a much more profound aural consequence. When I played it last week at a concert in Cambridge I probably didn't do the best performance, maybe I just went through it too quickly. In Corfu, the weekend before, I managed to have a sort of deeper engagement with those musical and algorithmic materials. On average, the more times you perform a certain piece the more experience you have of that situation, and perhaps have more manoeuvres that you can make.

Because all the musical events of a performance take place in a here-and-now context, each is a distinctive form in which individuals come together precisely in order to explore a new angle on live improvised musics. This raises controversies about whether a particular real time performance brings with it a set of ascribed values, or whether the creativity involved is not a peculiar quality of the act, but a retrospective judgement on its product or form.

What are the creative values of such an individual performance act as distinct from collective improvisation creativity; and, indeed, to whom do we ascribe the role of 'creator' when the piece

---

[21] Term coined by Malloch and Trevarthen (2009) in a book of the same name.

[22] Bernstein (2010) terms these 'hierarchical knowledge structures', which are exemplified by the dominant knowledge position of computer science in Maton and Moore (pp. 106–7).

can be understood as the creative outcome of a uniquely specific combination of human and computer creativities? How then should we characterize the types of creativity realized by the composer-programmer? Live coding holds up well as a manifestation of a particular kind of 'computer creativity' which constitutes a pre-arranged code framework pre-built by humans who then modify the structures in live performance. The status of live coding, not necessarily just that by intellectual and industrial programming programmers, is gradually ascending, and will be crucial historically in the construction of further genres.[23]

Live coding involves distinctive tools that enable distinctive forms of computer creativity that occur within a distinctive type of supra-individual social arena, involving high levels of symbolic capital. Nick offers opinions about some of the ways of listening, of presentation and representation that are involved.

> *Nick*: So in terms of depth of engagement with algorithms, the interesting thing about live coding is that you could add a single character which fundamentally changes the musical landscape . . . it might be that just by substituting one variable for another you manage to sufficiently twist your running algorithms to take you into an entirely different territory. That is, particularly if you as the performer have anticipated that very change, an example of a quite profound understanding of algorithm and engagement with it in a concert situation. We have joked over the years in the live coding community that a lot of what we do, particularly if we haven't practised enough beforehand, is a bit too shallow. Sometimes it is just an equivalent of changing a number to change the amplitude. Not really getting into the true heart of the computer algorithms as musical representations.

The central tenet of live coding is the composer-programmer's execution of sophisticated algorithmic programming skills, musical knowledge and judgement, and the use of mathematical knowledge, experience, and practice to create virtuosic scripting languages and algorithmic techniques. Live coding involves a risky act of real time programming. It involves expertise in both fields of music and mathematics. But one wonders how live coding and its creativities are judged by audiences?

There has been some discussion of absolutes in relation to value judgements *for* live coding practices. Some have suggested that 'deeper' rather than 'surface' manipulation of algorithms refines our sensibilities and makes for better music, but what are the unique creativities manifest in live coding? Because we cannot produce absolutes about live coding does not mean that we cannot hold relatively objective, or at least non-arbitrary, reasons for thinking some live coded music creativities are distinctive.

> *Nick*: This is a contested point. My view is that it is not a very academic community although I am perfectly willing to accept that I am an institutionalized academic. Many other people who are involved are not. I would recommend you have a look at the TOPLAP website where there is a list of interested parties who have placed themselves under this umbrella organization.[24] I think you will find that most of them are more hackers than they are academics. [laughs] And people have approached live coding from different backgrounds, so you would find those who perhaps have some academic musical training who may find it interesting, I see myself falling there. You would also find computer scientists who also have a fascination for music and found their way into musical performance through live coding. And you may also find that not all live coding is about music, but perhaps about audiovisuals, or just visuals. So you will find visual artists who are fascinated with the ramifications of coding live. So it is a slightly

---

[23] For more discussion of how programming itself is becoming quite visible in modern life, see Ward and colleagues' (2004) TOPLAP epaper at www.toplap.org/index.php/Read_me_paper.

[24] TOPLAP stands for Transnational Organisation for the Proliferation of Live Audio Programming, a collective of programmers, composers, and performers exploring live programming to create music.

more diverse community perhaps. Because you have got people like me who have written academic papers about it, you could always see certain evidence of academic art I suppose . . . academics as butterfly characters tend to write about these things. Yet the community based around TOPLAP, the mailing list, has at least 300 members. I make no claims of it being a large community, but I think these days you would find live coding performances going on frequently around the world. And it is certainly an international community. . .

We conclude this discussion by making the following points about the projected live coding and creativity: (1) creativity acquires multiple meanings and values in the live coding practices of algorithmic composition and real time, improvised performance; (2) computer creativity provides the conditions and platforms for action, and offers choice of action and alternative values vested in the idea of creativity, as well as alternative sources of innovation and novelty; (3) the integration of improvisational, compositional, and performance creativities, and the algorithmic manifestations that arise from them, offer the dominant modes through which human creativity is expressed; and (4) the locus of programming choices made by the live coder can be understood as a uniquely specific combination of human and computer agency.[25]

Concluding remarks

This chapter concludes with a brief consideration of three ways in which improvisational creativities have played a central role in the real time performance practices of these five musicians. The first way, which lies at the centre of real time performance practice, concerns the symbolic relationship between community-genres, community practices, free and fixed medium performances, and human and computer creativity. The idea of a symbolic relationship[26] between musical improvised creativities is seen clearly in the mediation between musical 'domain' creativity, which is to say the types of creativity valued in musicians' accounts, and other types aligned to and arising from improvisation. It is also true that creativity is not neutral with respect to power/value. Some types of creativity are better aligned with practices that hold more power/value, whereas others are better aligned with practices that have less power/value. When viewed this way, any discussion of boundaries between musical domains and computer creativities must respect that these issues of power/value are implicated in our definitions, issues of concern, and the very conversation in which we are engaged throughout this book. It seems crucial that types of 'improvisational creativities' are not seen as synonymous with 'compositional creativity'.

The second is that the habitus of these musicians leads them to blur comfortable distinctions and shatter disciplinary boundaries, which strongly suggests multiple manifestations of improvisational creativities that are never construed and practised in just one dimension.

The third is that creativity plays an important part in the technology with which improvisers generate and allocate choices. Likewise, technology plays a central generative role in how certain types of creativity are recognized and valued. This aspect of creativity is closely related to a sense of what is new and what is novel, and what is at stake in the abiding value ascribed to programming activities endowed with creative significance.

....

[25] The conception of agency is bounded but enables musical and computer creativities to co-construct an endless series of exchanges, acts, the originality of which can consist in an unusual combination of the enabling structures in which they operate. A conception of the live coder as a creative, innovative agent is not deterministic but relational, bounded, and enabled by computer creativity.

[26] The idea of a symbolic relationship with the world was also taken up by Vygotsky and his followers with their concept of 'mediation' (Wertsch, 1993).

In earlier chapters we have seen DJs, songwriters, and bands fixate on recordings and sound quality, and the use of records as a material for creating music. Live coding emphasizes live processes instead of static art objects, text-based programming languages for computer music, real time scripting, and real time improvisation that is specific to a performance and to what counts as improvisational creativity. Improvisation is a mental approach and attitude normally associated with a way of working and playing. For some, it is synonymous with the creative process, whether it is applied to music or to any other form of human activity. Improvisation is also associated with taking big risks. Improvising with others is a test of one's ability to understand the temperament or style of another person in an instant. Improvisation is about acting without time for thinking, about receiving and transmitting instantaneously.

The controversies and debates we have examined in this chapter illustrate how live coders have abundant opportunities for renewal and growth. There is little doubt that our understanding of musical creativity and its nature and value in live coding performance practice will be the richer for having seriously explored these themes. As we examine the different meanings of creativity we find that it is closely related to a sense of what is new for people, and that it is contingent on who they are and where they are located in the field.

The relations between an improviser's creativities and a musician's habitus, which is informed by skills, knowledge, and self-conception as a 'laptop musician', are played out in the creative act itself. Categories of evaluation and judgement are contested. The focus is on the 'act', wherein the audience does not have to sit silent, nor do the musicians have to sit separated, or elevated. Rather, we have a sound-based live art performance, which takes many forms, from live coding to sound installations combining electronic, acoustic, and digital elements, with direct public consumption. What is at stake is the sound and its sound source, the degree of risk involved in the creative act, the communication of an experience that is code based and highly creative, and which is judged in the process of listening and looking at the algorithmic code display. In Bourdieu's terminology, we note particular technological skill sets—habitus—which position themselves, and are positioned in relation to aurality, sound, and sonic culture to create new, novel, unique, and original music and activate 'capitals',[27] giving rise to an interdisciplinary practice that fosters the manifestation of multiple creativities.

On the transformative power of sound and improvisation in live coding, we conclude this discussion by making the following points: (1) Musical creativity is about openness to creating new ideas; (2) even if the mind's own resources do not create all the ideas, and creativities co-exist between computer software and humans, it is digital creativity that provides the conditions platforms of action and offers choices of actions; (3) human creativity is a peculiar quality of the live act; (4) the locus of the situated choices made by the live coder in response to the computer can be understood as a uniquely specific combination of human and computer creativity; and (5) a revised definition of musical creativities, one which distinguishes between 'newness', 'novelty', and 'innovation', must take the laptop/computer and the type of musical creativities (improvisational creativity or compositional creativity) into account.

---

27 See Lareau and Horvat (1999), where they describe Bourdieu's tools metaphorically as: 'In a card game (the field of interaction), the players (individuals) are all dealt cards (capital). However, each card and each hand have different values. Moreover the values of each hand shifts according to the explicit rules of the game (the field of interaction) that is being played (as well as the way the game is being enacted). In other words, a good hand for blackjack may be a less valuable hand for gin rummy. In addition to having a different set of cards (capital), each player relies on a different set of skills (habitus) to play the cards (activate the capital)' (p. 39).

Key points

1. Real time live performance creativities emerge out of, and build on, improvisational modalities. It lies in the complementarity of the performance, guided by the moment-to-moment interaction of player and instrument, player and player(s), player and machine, player(s) and audience. Improvisational, exploratory, participatory, and empathic modalities spur musicians to play in the moment, allowing individual and collective interplay between fellow performers. The focus is more on sound in all its physicality, and the communicative musicality of real time performance, than on performances representing work.

2. The nature of improvisational creativity in live performance links to, and is illustrated by, multiply mediated activities, including the use of the computer as creative tool, and the new technologies that facilitate new creativities.

3. These live performance creativities embody myriad social forms and practices, which are bound up in the broader institutional and non-institutional forces that provide the basis for their cultural production and reproduction in the field of public and subsidized cultural institutions.

4. Live performance creativities have the following characteristics: (1) there is no single creativity for all real time, live performance musics; (2) live performance creativities involve practices developed by communities whose members allow them to learn, be shaped by, and understood as the scripting of social action; and (3) there are various kinds of live performance improvisation creativities. There is the category of 'collective creativity', illustrated by performers of traditional instruments and pitch-based genres (as exemplified in traditional folk fiddling and which, through free improvisation, gives rise to a sense of total belonging which, in turn, seems to be at the heart of gaining collective identity. There is also the genre of live coding, a subcategory of 'computer creativity', uniquely manifest in digital live coding, whereby the performance is a kind of 'live maths', making improvised music by scripted changes to an algorithmic program in front of a live audience. The computer is used as a creative tool and 'computer creativity' typifies distinct modalities that invoke interactive music processing systems in the context of real time performances by live coders who affirm the values of improvised musics.

Discussion questions

1. All music creativities are alike in important ways. All music creativities are different in important ways. Is one of these statements more important to understanding the nature and value of musical creativity than the other? Why?

2. Is there any possible distinction between sound, noise, and music? If so, is there any possible distinction between sonic creativity, noise creativity, and musical creativity? If so, how do we determine whether we are in fact making comparisons within the same musical creativity? In other words, is demarcating a distinction between one musical creative practice and another in some sense an arbitrary act that attributes greater unity to practices than may be warranted?

3. Do you believe it reasonable to claim that some musical creativities are better, or more creative, than others? If so, outline the criteria you feel might appropriately guide judgements and criterion building, demonstrating their application in two musical practices you feel clearly differ in value.

Chapter 8

Interactive audio design

This chapter explores another understanding of **collective** and **user-generated creativities**, now in relation to how audio designers work with musicians to bring together the ideas of teams, and coordinate the integration of these ideas into a unique product. Video games provide interaction with, and information for, the player, whose experience is strikingly similar to that of playing music. Each requires a high level of control over some physical instrument (such as a joystick or saxophone), involving recognizing where one is at each moment, and always relying on a combination of learned patterns and contextually appropriate improvisation. The music and sound tracks for audio and interactive applications are the work of audio designers.

Audio designers work with all aspects of audio software, including the programming, application, and production stages of interactive music projects. This work includes composition, sound effects, and the manipulation of musical elements—harmony, texture, melody, and rhythm and structure—to compose or augment existing music. They make innovative use of old technologies, and develop new ones to create unique audiovisual programs, and online audio tools offering timbral and textural combinations with the emphasis on sound effects and interactive music development. This requires the ability to use and write music to express intense emotion, evoke a sense of drama, and communicate a story.

In more detail, their work involves developing real time simulation-based programs and interactive products, such as 'chiptunes', which were composed for the microchip-based audio hardware of early home computers and gaming consoles. They design interactive audio content, 'to-picture' in video games, and 'to-objects' for musical instruments, and use music and sound to enhance and supplement graphics, text, and animation.

The accounts of two audio designers, who put together video game sound tracks and score the music for popular computer games, will show how many forms of creativity co-exist in their work, and its interplay between individual and social creativities. Their work can involve writing original music, creating briefs for other composers and managing/liaising with them, handling the creative side of the music licensing process, and implementing all of the music in the game. They work in very different ways on very different projects making the assets themselves or working with other sound designers and composers to achieve their audio vision for particular projects.

Introduction

Today, people are turning 'off' to the radio as we know it, and 'on' to the Internet, mobile phones, wireless and interactive technologies. According to a 2011 Yahoo! research report, just as Internet users watch 42% less television, radio listening has lost out to digital media, and music is heard more than ever before as an accompaniment to video games, commercials, films, software, and on television. Just as it takes approximately 10, 000 hours to learn to play a musical instrument skilfully, video game players spend about the same amount of time on video games, on average, by the age of 21 (Applegate, 2010; Leviton, 2008; Prensky, 2001). With the Internet, video games, television, email, instant messaging, social networks, and user groups, fans and consumers have far more options for discovering new music, for engaging with new kinds of programming, new modes of music participation, and many new forms of performance practice than ever before.

The making of video games is not only a cultural and sociological process, it is also an economic one. The video games industry generated £25 billion in revenue in 2010, and is arguably one of the most significant sources of entertainment today. Video games are a sensational phenomenon, particularly amongst young boys, who spend more time playing them than listening to radio, whilst creating a voracious market for new music.[1] Music's power to affect, disturb, disrupt, and evoke an emotional response allows it to be used to excellent effect for gaming. Much as in big screen movies, game music and game sound can communicate and move players. Game music is often dubbed 'adaptive' music because it is made to depend on the player's or character's actions; and this audio interactivity[2] helps to endow characters with emotions, adding depth of sentiment to the playing experience (Collins and d'Escrivan, 2007). Sound and sound effects are used to create and add to the tensions of the game playing experience in a console game, and can be a key component for orienting prospective attention. Most home games make use of light, non-threatening background music. For example, in the game *Sinister*, which features a character called Mario, the music changes when he jumps to the next level, but the same happy friendly style remains basically the same. In *Defender*, which is fraught with risk and uncertainty, sound is used to force errors. As in any sphere of activity, according to Bourdieu (1984a), 'an action, or a usage is legitimate when it is dominant and misrecognised as such, that is to say tacitly recognised' (p. 110). In other words, players are unconscious of the rules and principles of video gaming. These rules are played out in terms of forces of gain and loss, of purchasing power, of winners and losers, of supply and demand, of the 'products' of the field—the symbolic capital.

Certain types of games, which involve moving from level to level, are essentially repetitive. Most can be divided into three types: action (shooting, fighting, platforming, maze chase); adventure role playing, and puzzles (e.g. *Zelda*™, *World of Warcraft*®, *Tetris*®); and simulation, sports, and strategy (*e.g. SimCity, Gran Turismo*®, *Championship Manager, Warhammer*). Many of these use music that loops, is upbeat, and highly rhythmic. There are some highly successful commercial systems, such as Wii™, Xbox® 360, and PlayStation® 3, which simulate the playing of instruments (Electronic Arts™, 2007).[3] *Guitar Hero*® (RedOctane®, 2005) was inspired by the successful rhythm game *Dance Dance Revolution*® and, like *Rock Band*®, uses visual and musical cues to simulate playing the guitar. (Interestingly, you can now buy a real guitar with MIDI output to use with *Rock Band*® 3!)

Music and sound with image: natural partners

What are the forms, and what is the significance of 'music' in the video game industry? The concept of 'music' in video games has significance similar to that generally associated with films, and, in this sense, approach a universal social fact. Interestingly, video games are truly a postmodern expression, insofar as they are fast losing any cultural, ethnic, or national distinctions. Accounts of the

---

[1] For more discussion of the digital music revolution see Kusek and Leonhard (2005), who record that when the company Electronic Arts™ released its new *Madden* football videogame, each song on the game received over seven hundred million spins in the first six months. See also Landy (2007).

[2] For more discussion of sites and works involving interactive audio for the web, see www.vispo.com/misc/ia.htm.

[3] These games can link with specific bands and pieces of software created by third parties which run on them.

dynamic, communicative forms of 'music' and 'sound' necessary to a game development project, by composers who work as audio designers, focus on enhancing a game player's experience.

There are, broadly speaking, two ways of thinking about relationships between music and image, whether in films or games. First, when the music is perceived as belonging to the narrative space in which the image or animation takes place, it is called 'diegetic' as, for example, onscreen sound effects such as a door slamming, a pistol firing, a light switching. Second, when the music the composer creates is an accompaniment to run parallel with, or in synchrony with, the narrative of the image or animation (as with the direct 'painting of sound' in film (*Foley R*), it is called 'non-diegetic' or 'incidental' music. This latter definition remains somewhat ambiguous, because to 'run parallel' is an inevitability of a temporal medium, irrespective of the source of the music, and 'synchrony' does not intrinsically imply either diegetic or non-diegetic music. Non-diegetic music does not belong to, or emanate from the narrative space or world, but comes from beyond the 'fourth wall', that is, the 'orchestra pit'.[4] Films are associated with hit songs and sound track CDs, as are certain games. Sega® even started its own record label, Twitch Records, and has its own studio. It is no surprise therefore that both audio and sound designers typically and irreducibly weld sounds to visuals. Chion (1994) explains the nature of the relationship between visuals and sound in the narrative space of soundtracks as natural partners.[5] See, for example, Fig. 8.1: 'Laser Laser' 2011 for Apple iPhone is a generic retro space 'shoot-em-up' where to the enemy attacks are actually choreographed with the music. 'Sonus (One)' 2010 for the Apple iPhone is a spatial realization of aleatoric or randomly generated music (Fig. 8.2). Although not all of the music is left to chance, the player can intervene albeit in a seemingly haphazard manner.

Links between 'music' in the traditional sense and 'sound design', and the interchangeability of the terms 'audio design' and 'sound design' are strongly contested. 'Sound design' is certainly more focused on sound effects or, more specifically, on the use and creation of sound, whereas 'audio design' focuses on the use and creation of both sound *and* music. Studio composition and the manipulation of sounds can include *musique concrete*, and modern-day sampling techniques, as for instance on Amon Tobin's album *Foley Room*,[6] can blur the line between sound effects, sound design, and musical composition.

Who are these people who practise different forms of audio design?

All musical experience is interactive in the sense that when we play or listen to music we participate in its experience, whether actively or passively, consciously or unconsciously. As an audience member, mp3 file listener, or video game player—at both psychobiological and individual, and behavioural and social levels—a rhythm and sympathy of musical expression is experienced.

Audio designers are composers. They often work collaboratively with visual designers to create music for interactive projects; and also practise as ambient composers and sound artists who work in installations wherein the spatial positioning of sound sources, and psychoacoustic and acoustic manipulations are central aspects. New practices have been opened up by creative partnerships

---

[4] See Cottrell (2004) for an ethnomusicological account of London's classical music concert life that uniquely combines inside knowledge and ethnographic observation of creativity in musical performance, orchestras and the self (p. 103).

[5] A distinction between 'soundtracks' and 'music' is that sound track refer to the sounds of film or video that have no coherence separate from the image or game.

[6] *Foley Room* is the sixth studio album by Brazilian drum and bass artist Amon Tobin. It was released on 5 March 2007 by Ninja Tune.

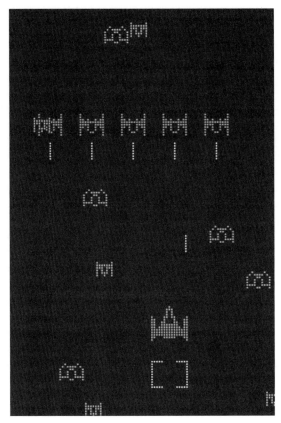

Fig. 8.1 'Laser Laser' 2011 for iPhone is a generic retro space 'shoot-em-up' where the enemy attacks are actually choreographed with the music.
Screenshot by Matthew C. Applegate. © Matthew C. Applegate, 2011.

between sound designers and composers. The company Tonehammer,[7] which no longer exists, was run[8] by a sound designer and a composer in partnership. The composer Troels Foreman is an award-winning artist, well known for his game, film, and television work. Tonehammer created sound worlds and virtual instruments that were very popular with media composers, and were often used in AAA games and Hollywood films, for example, much of the unique sound world of *Avatar*, and more recently, *Tron Legacy*. These virtual instruments were created by sampling the sounds made by objects, and by playing instruments in unusual ways—bamboo sticks, hitting a car with a crowbar, a waterphone, beer barrels, in addition to bowed pianos and sampled choirs. These 'instruments' were truly amazing feats of sound design that are very useful to composers. Another sound designer, virtual instrument company Native Instruments, has been releasing similar 'cinematic' packages for a while now. It is not surprising that companies like this are proliferating as technology evolves. This is a distinctive and changing form of creativity that has emerged from

[7] See http://www.tonehammer.com/th1.html for details about the distribution of Tonehammer and Microhammer products.

[8] In 2011 Tonehammer split into 2 different companies called SoundIron and 8Dio. However, the existing music libraries are still available from these new sources.

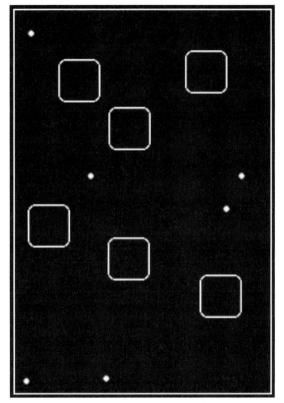

Fig. 8.2 'Sonus (One)' 2010 for iPhone is a spatial realization of aleatoric or randomly generated music. Although not all of the music is left to chance, the player can intervene, albeit in a seemingly haphazard manner.
Screenshot by Matthew C. Applegate. © Matthew C. Applegate, 2011.

the collaboration of a composer with a sound designer. There seems to have been a revolution in sound design that involves a shift from analogue to digital methods of recording and manipulating sight and sound. These are innovative practices being developed by 'sound' designers, not only for computer games but also for collective performance. That is, they are characterized not only in terms of sound and action, but also as interactions between music-makers.

Recently there has been a shift towards, and focus on, creative collaboration. Partnerships between sound designers and composers bring to light a number of examples of collaborative creativity wherein the end goal can be both entertainment and/or 'edutainment', that is, products with 'educational features' (Applegate, 2010).[9] Ultimately the forms creativity takes are increasingly the products of creative habits and the dispositions of individuals working in partnerships. We do not know we have capital until we enter a field wherein it is valued, wherein it buys into some idea or some thing. We see this demonstrated by Harry Gregson-Williams, a British composer, orchestrator, conductor, and music producer, who is best known for his film and game scores, of which he has composed over 60, using electronic music and orchestral pieces. He is also well known for his collaborations with director Tony Scott, having scored all Scott's films since the 1998 film *Enemy of the State*, and for, amongst others, *The Chronicles of Narnia*, *Sinbad*, *Shrek*,

---

[9] For a history of video game music see: gamespot.com/gamespot/features/video/vg_music.

Chicken Run, *Antz*, and *Domino*. His most recent project, the 2010 film *The Town*, directed by Ben Affleck, has received widespread acclaim and extraordinary reviews for both story and original score. In addition, he has composed video game music, such as that for *Metal Gear Video Games Saga*, for which his arrangement (with Nobuko Toda and others) of the original *Metal Gear Solid Main Themes* for *Metal Gear Solid* was one of many works that involved both orchestral and electronic textures. Soundtrack albums that feature vocal themes for the game are also released separately as part of the package.

Harry Gregson-Williams described himself in an interview as making 'music to order'[10]. He seems to question the known and the taken-for-granted, as well as being a person who likes experimenting with materials, ideas, action, and possibilities. This shows the real world context of media composers who move into the marketplace, creating music to order within an organizational framework, and innovating new products, new music, and new software that relies on the particular game player's skills, rendering creative (and innovative) processes wherein micro-level product development and macro-level organizational resources meet. This means engaging people, positioning ideas and products, influencing actions, potentially breaking the rules,[11] and iterating across the different types of actions and different phases of media production. Harry's composition, whether for film or game, entails finding 'plenty of room to express yourself' in an ongoing quest for new, all-pervasive communicative media musicality, and by adopting a way of working that is essentially collaborative, consultative, commercial, and entrepreneurial.

The practices featured in the present chapter vary according to the field in which products are set and move into the marketplace. These fields include entertainment and education. Both of these worlds are highly symbolic because they are based on values that arise from structured relations. These relations are multifarious and can be imagined as an interconnecting network that stretches from the individual to the macro level of society. The fields of entertainment and education are bounded spheres that are identifiable in terms of shared areas of activities, and which contain and connect with other fields at various levels. Each is lubricated by forms of knowledge that are only partially consciously known. Each have their own self-referential legitimacy, and, to a large extent, operate in a tacit manner. Such forms of knowledge inform particular creativities that conform to orthodox ways of creating music and working with sound, ways of viewing and being in the world as game players and video game developers. The creativities to which 'audio designers' give rise are in flux, forming and reforming themselves around individuals working in social space. In many ways, this chapter aims not only to extend our thinking about music's creativities but also about the overlapping fields of music, video gaming and the creative industries,[12] the dominant valued products of these fields, and how composers recognize and practise music creativities in situations where new technologies are the material of everyday life and experience.

My point here is that, for audio designers, capital is arbitrary, but accrues power through a game-hungry generation of game user's and content generators, willing to evaluate the communicative power of music and the scope of navigation with programmes. Users help shape and contribute to the design of the game.[13] The resource implications are significant as is the potential for organizational conflicts; and, from the standpoint of a 'media composer', being a team player

---

[10] For more information on Harry Gregson-Williams, see http://en.wikipedia.org/wiki/Harry_Gregson-Williams.

[11] Innovative practices of developing breakthrough new products are part of the start-up programmes developed by media organizations/cooperations.

[12] For a discussion of creativity in relation to the creative industries which makes sense of the contemporary dilemmas facing cultural producers and receivers, see Caves (2000) and Hartley (2005).

[13] For a discussion of online multiplayer adventure games such as *The Matrix Online*, which are controlled by the actions of the players not by a pre-existing or advance plot, see Blake (2007).

and playing out a type of collaborative creativity begets a studio-based compositional modality. This does not mean the silencing or suppression of individual artistic integrity, but rather that the individual becomes submerged in a product development practice, wherein the role of politics across diverse organizations cannot be underestimated. In the video game world, companies such as Media Molecule, a games development studio based in Guildford, UK, and Nintendo®, a multinational corporation located in Kyoto, Japan, make extensive use of 'user-generated content',[14] a process whereby user creativity has become central, ingrained, and part of a game's value. With user-generated content, companies provide tools for their users to comment on, respond to, and evaluate games as they are being developed.

I have discussed 'fan creativity'[15] in earlier chapters, but it is important to recognize that in the music and recording industries, finding creative ways to interact with and stimulate 'fan' type creativities has been described as manifesting a 'real world creative process'. For example, Imogen Heap, who is an outspoken advocate of new technology and the innovative use of fan creativity, interacts and collaborates with her fans to the extent that they contribute to her stage and recorded performances. In video game music and sound worlds, the creativity of 'audio interactivity' means the sound designer has to create many valid renditions from similar raw material. This 'live' interactive mode of consumption presents new challenges for composers and sound designers, as well as for the development of 'fan' or 'user-creativity'. Accepting that music in all cultures is characterized in terms of not only 'sound' and action, but also by interactions between musicians, then 'user-creativity' may be integral to sound design because it orientates attention and involves the coordination in time of performers' musical behaviours—whether simulated, virtual, or real—with those of others.

This gives rise to a number of questions. How are manifestations of music's creativities evidenced in the socio-generative work of audio designers as constituted in their practices? What are the rules which govern how the game is played? What ideas and (symbolic) values require them to possess certain capitals, and thus, by emphasizing certain practices, to step out of the automatic responses prompted by the generative dispositions, or habitus, of audio designers?

What follows is the narrative of Kenneth Young, the lead audio designer at Media Molecule, a games development studio based in Guildford, UK, who shares insights on how he brings together collaboratively created ideas, and speaks of his responsibilities for the audio experiences of the games they make (most recently the PlayStation® 3 title *LittleBigPlanet*™ and its sequel).

Introducing Kenneth Young

Kenneth was born in Edinburgh, Scotland, and lives in London, where he works as the lead audio designer at Media Molecule[16] where he is responsible for the audio experience in the

---

[14] The term 'user-generated content' entered mainstream usage during 2005 from web publishing and new media content production circles. Its use for a wide range of applications, including problem processing, news, gossip, and research, reflects the expansion of media production through new technologies that are accessible and affordable to the general public. All digital media technologies are included, such as question–answer databases, digital video, blogging, podcasting, forums, review-sites, social networking, mobile phone, and wikis. User-generated content may also employ a combination of open source, free software and flexible licensing, or related agreements to further reduce the barriers to collaboration, skill-building, and discovery. Player-generated content is the concept of video game content being created by the players of the game, as opposed to that created by a game's publisher or author.

[15] This term was first coined by Wikström (2009).

[16] Media Molecule (http://www.mediamolecule.com) is a British video game developer based in Guildford in Surrey. The studio was founded in January 2006 by former Lionhead Studios employees Mark Healey,

Fig. 8.3 *LittleBigPlanet*™ creators add music to their levels via a music object, represented here by the little ghetto-blaster. Music is triggered or, in the case of an interactive track, the mix adjusted when a person runs past a music object. This physical representation of the ethereal truly blurs any concrete notion of music as diegetic or non-diegetic. "LittleBigPlanet™", "Sackboy" and "Sackgirl" are trademarks or registered trademarks of Sony Computer Entertainment Europe Limited.

games they make, most recently the PlayStation® 3 title *LittleBigPlanet*™ (Fig. 8.3) and its sequel *LittleBigPlanet*™ *2*.[17] A strong sense of personal efficacy has had consequences for his career. His personal history stresses, over and over again, the importance of education and, at the same time, the need to successfully establish a career in the gaming world. The following account gives a clear sense that Kenneth has an appetite for, and disposition to, question the known, to experiment, to ponder over questions and possibilities, as well as the social resilience that is required of creative people, especially in the games industry.

> *Kenneth*: Well, my family is musical, my dad was a very keen semi-professional musician when he was younger and still loves to play. And my mum is from a musical family—her brother is a professional musician. I played the violin from the age of six or seven and had lessons practically every week until I was about 21. And then, when I finished high school, I knew that I was really into music, but I also knew that I didn't want to do performance. Because, well . . . I was good and people seemed to enjoy my playing but, I'm not sure, I haven't quite worked out why yet. I don't know, I'd hate to blame my parents and say it was purely parental pressure. Maybe I was just rebelling and doing the opposite of

---

Alex Evans, Dave Smith, and Kareem Ettouney. The studio's first game is the PlayStation® 3 title *LittleBigPlanet*™. Their plan was always to produce a chart-topping game, but to keep the size of the company as small as possible so as to maintain a tight rein on costs. Evans, in particular, was keen to avoid what he calls the 'cycle of debt'. It was chiefly this concern that led the founders to consider user generated content. *LittleBigPlanet*™'s best-selling point became its set of level-creation tools, and the ability to publish that content on the Internet. 'Every time you boot up there are more levels to play', says Evans. Media Molecule won the Studio of the Year award at the Spike Videogame Awards 2008. *LittleBigPlanet*™ scored a 95 on Metacritic. The game has also won numerous game of the year awards, leading to a 'Game Of The Year Edition' a year later.

[17] The sequel *LittleBigPlanet*™ *2* was released in January 2011, see http://www.littlebigplanet.com/en/2.

what they wanted, that might be one aspect of it. But I think also I just didn't get a lot out of it. I think part of it is that I'm a perfectionist and I was never happy with my playing. I don't think I was as good as I wanted to be, or as good as I knew I could be, although I probably didn't practise as much as I should have done . . . the trauma of failing my ABRSM advanced certificate has never left me. But later I knew I wanted to work in music, but I didn't honestly know how I could work with music without being a performer, because I didn't have any idea of how that was possible. I knew that you could be a composer . . . I ended up doing a degree in music technology, because that seemed to aptly combine my love of technology with my love of music.

Kenneth addresses here the professional identity (and habitus) of musicians, their expectations and the complexities of their career choices, and some key criteria concerning flexibility and versatility, habitus formation, and long-term career decision-making. He regards his career as a means to interpret the intrinsic and rational characteristics of his motivational changes and his 'perfectionism' as a music student.[18] Gardner (1993) concluded from biographical interviews, that 'the most notable creators almost always are perfectionists, who have worked out every detail of their conception painstakingly' (p. 211). The choices available to Kenneth show the interplay, not only between past and present, but also between the individual and the forces acting upon him; that is, how opportunity and aspiration are related. Kenneth also talked about his reasons for choosing a career within collaborative communities in the games industry rather than working independently as a professional performer. The fact that he returns to this decision demonstrates the significance of institutional influence, and how social origins infuse a powerful influence over personal history. He is clearly driven by goals that suit his interests and creative aspirations. Choices and decisions made at school level come into play again at the level of higher education, where, in a straightforward sense, he positions himself, and makes choices that are located within an established matrix of influences.

Kenneth: It was around 2001/2002 that I'd been thinking about and looking at obvious applications such as post-production work, film work, TV, and broadcasting. But that just seemed . . . I think the world of films certainly was very attractive to me, but I was clever enough to know that I had little chance of getting to work on, you know, the kind of films that I enjoyed at the time that, actually, in the UK that kind of work is less prevalent. And, you know, starting that gig you've got to work in Soho on a less than minimum wage whilst living in London! And it just didn't look very attractive, whereas in the games industry you're actually a full-time employee and you've got this salary coming in every month. And I obviously really enjoy games as well. I knew that I wasn't particularly employable when I finished my undergraduate degree. I didn't have any experience of sound to picture which, even though interactive audio doesn't work in exactly the same way as linear media, is still the bedrock where a lot of the theory and technique is based. And so that's why I did the Master's degree down in Bournemouth in sound design.

I basically spent that year just learning about all that side of things, as well as investing most of my free time finding out as much as I could about interactive audio, the collaborative process of making games, researching the games industry itself to see where all the companies are around the UK, who was making what, and getting my finger on the pulse of the job market. And I was lucky enough to get a job with Sony®'s London game development studio pretty much straight out of that Master's degree. And that was a junior position, which essentially means you do lots of menial tasks . . . I suppose it was an apprenticeship. I was very lucky actually, the people I was working with—probably because I was quite capable, but also partly because maybe they were just quite happy to let me get on with it, because it was less work for them—gave me an awful lot of responsibility early on in my job. I'm sure it was

---

[18] See Smilde (2009) for a discussion of professional identity and self-esteem amongst musicians, and how they learn.

only about three months into my job after I'd done a tiny little project that was only a few weeks' work that they gradually made me responsible for all the interactive audio in a very big project they were working on. And so it was a kind of baptism by fire, but also just a really great opportunity to just sort of get on and do stuff. And it's interesting, now that I'm a manager I've got a team of people I work with and am responsible for, if I think about the amount of responsibility that they gave me straight out of university I would never, ever [laughs] hire someone and give them that amount of responsibility. So I was just very lucky.

Kenneth's choices and his decision to pursue sound design, and acquire expertise and experience in designing innovative products within the collective enterprise of an organization, demanded a certain disposition (habitus), entrepreneurial thinking,[19] a clear values system, and a determined trajectory that together enabled his induction as an apprentice into the collaborative communities and competitive field of digital media. Capital attracts capital. He soon learned how teams create a novel emergent product, how to be responsive to a changing environment, how group creativity works, and how to successfully tap into and contribute to team collaboration in a company, wherein teams rely on diverse skills and expertise throughout a project cycle. His induction into this field required him to assume, within a relatively short time frame, the position of an apprentice working on high status activities, wherein the norms and value systems, the enterprise atmosphere, leadership styles and leadership principles[20] involved a homologous match between training and outcome. He soon learned that the distribution and aggregation of value or capital is a distinctive characteristic of this industry, and relates to the success and failure of new companies, corporate initiatives, and projects.[21]

Entrepreneurship in the video game industry

Kenneth makes the point that, through the mechanisms of apprenticeship, he learned the attitudes and values of this young and emerging field. Here we notice the value of conscientiously responding to franchised work demands and the dynamics of power, which infuses all aspects of the unmapped space where micro-level product development and macro-level organizational resources meet (Kanter, 2000).

The goal of creating effective game music involves a systems approach. Because all areas of the collective enterprise are often directly or indirectly involved, the result is a high degree of collaborative creativity. As Kenneth goes on to describe in this fascinating account of his work as an audio designer and developer of video games, individual processes and organization members are interconnected. The complexity of group creativity makes high demands:

> *Kenneth*: My job title is 'audio designer'. The reason I'm an 'audio' designer is because I'm in charge of both sound and music. There are a lot of people in my industry that are called 'sound designers', and they're primarily responsible for sound effects editing, dialogue editing, and their implementation. But my remit, partly because I work in a small company, is that I'm in charge of all the audio; everything you might hear is my responsibility. So, my role is to make sure that the game sounds good and supports and enhances the player experience. I'm not necessarily creating or implementing all the content myself, but it's my responsibility to make sure that all the different threads come together and the aural experience is as good as it possibly can be.

---

[19] The essence of entrepreneurial thinking, according to Volkmann et al. (2010) is, amongst other traits, hopeful thinking. It is action-oriented and team-oriented, and sees the potential feasibility of an opportunity.

[20] For more discussion of the significant role that enterprise culture plays, see Volkmann et al. (2010).

[21] For more discussion of these issues as they relate to the creative industry, see Caves (2000).

Environment is often cited as a component that is a very influential factor of a successful innovation and its realization and acceptance in the market place by target customers. Meeting the needs and demands of consumers means creating new and innovative ways of using both 'sound' and 'music' to enhance the experience of video games. This operates in two ways. First, it seems reasonable to suggest that a specific configuration of attitudes and habits, or video gaming capital, arises within this role, and is the product of expertise in developing new technologies and generative multi-media techniques—streaming high-quality sound and using sound creativity to enhance the experience of the game. Second, in the context of games, there is the expertise and aesthetics required to create 'adaptive' music, wherein the musical structure is selected depending on the player's actions. This means, as Kenneth explains, that the audio interactivity practice, or interactive audio, used in creating 'adaptive' music presents itself as cultural capital in a space of potential and active forces for the field of digital media and the mechanisms of change in video games practice.

Kenneth: For the most part, yes—it's recorded sound manipulated in real time. Sound synthesis is really in its infancy in computer games, there's not a lot of that going on. That's primarily because it's computationally expensive, and audio is not necessarily the most significant concern for processor cycles in an interactive entertainment experience. It's only with the current generation of games consoles and home PCs that we've had the kind of processing power available to even begin contemplating integrating and taking advantage of that kind of thing in any other than the most abstract or naïve ways. Essentially, we've not had to worry about it before, so we're kind of starting from scratch on that. But in terms of music, well there is quite an interesting historical development in computer games from where they came from, and how music was used in the past. In many respects the technology used to be more sophisticated. Games started out using analogue electronics so any sound or music had to be synthesized in real time. Then games moved to using note data-driven systems, such as MIDI, in the '80s and early '90s which triggered tiny, low quality sound samples or used synthesis techniques such as FM or wavetable, which makes sense when you consider that memory was an expensive luxury. Then all of a sudden CD audio came about, and so we went from having control over the individual notes, to all of a sudden just having these big fixed chunks of streaming audio. Which, of course, dramatically increased the audio quality, but we lost any ability to manipulate the music in real time at a fundamental level. But that approach is actually starting to make a come-back now, so all these things [that] people were doing 10+ years ago, are all of a sudden a lot more relevant. Why? Simply because the use of streaming audio, whilst the quality is better, it's a lot more limiting in terms of what you can do with, or to, it. And so, although we've devised techniques to allow the music to be manipulated in real time—for example, having parallel streams running at the same time which allows you to fade stems in and out in order to change the intensity of the music, to try and match the action that's happening on-screen in the game—these are actually pretty primitive. I mean, music's quite malleable and you can get away with that surprisingly well but, ultimately, you can't do anything particularly specific. You can't change the music in any really complex way by actually changing the notes themselves, and it's quite attractive to be able to do that. And so, on the authoring side of things when a composer is writing music, nowadays they can obviously do so much 'in the box' with virtual instruments. I guess the future plan is to be able to do some of that kind of authoring in real time using a note data driven system with high quality virtual instruments that are also running in real time on the console. I think for the most part, despite it being a new medium, games, like a lot of young art forms, beg, borrow, and steal from existing mediums and works as their 'safe' starting, or reference, point. But I think, certainly, game music has its own sound, partly because of the way it's used, but also because of the way the technology makes the music do things; it all gives it a certain sound, or a certain perceived experience. But I don't think the genre of the music, or the way it's generally conceived is necessarily particularly revolutionary. The only way it's obviously, identifiably unique is if you're writing for a complex interactive music system; that forces you to write in a certain way. If anything, it's restrictive. It's not empowering in the sense that a blank sheet of paper with a pencil [laughs] allows you to do whatever you want. I don't think games currently have that flexibility.

Here Kenneth distinguishes between product and process innovation. In the case of product innovation, he deals with what needs to be improved when new products and major developments of existing ones are a critical factor for future success. Process innovations are flagged as new or significantly improved manufacturing or process techniques, or methods of providing an improvement of the performance of the product. It is the capital of these improvements that Kenneth aspires to create.

Thirty years ago, the music that was possible in the early games was very primitive in terms of sound generation, with games composers being able to play only one or two voices simultaneously. Collins and d'Escrivan (2008) use the example of Space Invaders, now branded with a kind of cult status, to illustrate the quality of the sound and sound limitations. The 'creative dynamism' of the music is illustrated by Nintendo®'s Game Boy hand-held consoles, and the use of MIDI sequences and soundtracks (found in video games since the late 1980s) for high-quality audio, with the all-important innovation of 'live' interactivity. As we have seen, investing in breakthrough technology suggests that organizations implement and orient themselves to creating open, dialogical teams for anticipating/developing new musical responses and solutions from sound designers and composers. What Kenneth implies and acknowledges is the value-status or accrual of cultural capital from identified features, be they new renderings of musical combinations, remixed existing compositions, sampling and sequencing, or new forms that defy old compositional practices as licensed by the gaming field. We glimpse these various dimensions as Kenneth draws attention to the value of generative techniques in both video and audio, and the key message of the recognition they receive from those in the field who reconfigure and innovate mappings between sound and vision.

> *Kenneth*: The games industry kind of cannibalizes itself, and if one product is particularly successful then that can often set a benchmark . . . a benchmark which everyone else will either just emulate, or maybe try and improve on a little bit. So if that kind of benchmark product doesn't have anything particularly interesting going on with the audio, then it can be quite hard to actually persuade the powers that be to spend the time and resources required to develop new software to allow you to do things which will hopefully set the new or next benchmark that everyone else is going to aim for. So, a lot of the time game developers are reliant on the hardware platform holders, people like Sony®, Nintendo® and Microsoft® to develop software for the consoles, to allow them to do more interesting things. And that's just basically down to . . . you know, it comes down to time and money. It's a lot harder for an individual company to invest in this kind of thing, whereas it's a lot nicer if Sony® comes along and says 'Here . . . here's a tool we've spent lots of time and money creating. You can use this in your games now'. And of course that's within the console manufacturers' interests, because [it] means . . . their products then have an edge over their competitors by having better sounding games, or more interesting use of music. Now and again you get a game which does something a bit different and innovative. And it's often ahead of its time and everyone in the game audio community will react to something interesting and innovative like that. But you also know that there's no way you're going to be able to convince people in your company to invest in creating that kind of technology. But you know that it's possible and you know that one day some software will come along that you can just buy off the shelf that will allow you to do that.
>
> So, for example, there's a game that came out a couple of years ago called *Spore*, developed by Electronic Arts™' Maxis Studio. And, whilst it wasn't the first, it was certainly one of the most recent high-profile games to use a procedural element in its musical score. Maxis developed a proprietary version of Pure Data, an Open Source version of Max/MSP, which is a visual programming language for working with MIDI note data and real time digital signal processing of audio. It's most commonly used in quite academic explorations of sound and music, things like sonic art installations [and live coding]. Yeah, essentially it's friendly coding. So, rather than learning and typing text and numbers as in a text-based programming or scripting language, you can use cute little boxes and connect them up

via little patch cables to create quite powerful and complex processing systems. So, that's been around for years now outside of games, but *Spore* had that system running in real time in-game. Not so much as a system for end users to play with, although there was obviously an element of user interaction because that's what games are all about, but more so as an incredibly flexible development tool which empowered audio personnel on the project to do things in their game which nobody else is really doing or able to do without such a tool at their disposal.

I think that's a great example of something quite technologically innovative but it was also that rare kind of project where the team clearly had the time and the resources to do something a bit different on that front. I know that I am unlikely to be able to indulge in something quite so exotic in my own work, but I have faith that one day that kind of technology will be available to everyone. I guess the unknown factor is 'when'!

Importantly, the development of breakthrough techniques in the gaming field helps to constitute the field of power as a meaningful market in which it is worth investing one's energy. It is regarded as cultural capital: a recognition of the legitimacy of a creative idea that turns into an innovative practice, in this case, user-generated creativity. It defines a world endowed with value and status for the product and its developers. Enhanced capacity for recognizing potentially creative opportunities and the interactive cooperation of the different participants working in all areas of the enterprise culture is an active process, constituted by the logic of the field, and the unwritten rules of the game.

Kenneth: Some of the work that I did on my last project, *LittleBigPlanet*™, was a bit different. One of the main features of the game was that, although it was a traditional product in the sense that you buy it and you get to play the game, it also featured a built-in editor which allowed the people who'd bought the game to create their own games and then upload them for other people, who had the game, to play. And so that required that I think about how to empower the player to add sound and music to their own creations. Now, as a professional game developer, I spend all my time adding sound and music to the games that I'm working on. But I do that with quite technically complex, unintuitive, undocumented and buggy tools which, if we had released that kind of tool would have created a massive barrier to entry. So the goal was to make that process as simple and as accessible as possible, and although we're not the first game to allow people to do that, I think we were particularly successful in making that process simple and accessible. User-generated content is currently a buzzword or 'flavour of the month' in the industry. And *LittleBigPlanet*™ was, if you like, one of the games that contributed to the current interest surrounding that. Partly because it's been quite successful, but also because of this idea of making stuff accessible to the end-user. And that's been Media Molecule, the developer I work for, that's been our goal: to make creating games accessible to as many people as possible. But one of the wider reasons user generated content is attractive to the industry as a whole is that there is serious interest in having consumers that buy our product, holding on to that product.

So, it's the concept of trying to turn the product into a service, and that's obviously partly to do with monetizing the use of the product beyond the initial purchase . . . But with *LittleBigPlanet*™ user-generated content is the game's *raison d'être*, and there weren't many other games out there like that when we launched, all of which helped to make our product stand out in the marketplace. So, user-generated content has taken off and, you could say, become *de rigueur*. Maybe that's a warped exaggeration because I now have a keen interest in such projects, I don't know. But the movement is also closely tied into a lot of the social networking phenomena such as Facebook and Twitter that we're seeing just now on the Internet. That's certainly the direction that we are going in with our products.

For Kenneth, the value of working as an audio designer—the creativities that occur in complex collaborative and organizational settings such as this—is defined in terms of the values of the company, Media Molecule, which he works for. The company, collective in character, proclaims as its *raison d'être* that its workers adopt collaborative strategies to interact together as teams, performing a range of creative tasks. The sound and musical tasks are rendered by Kenneth but, as the music is bound up in the broader interplay of the sound and music's social, technological, and temporal dimensions, the product is developed and produced collaboratively in a world endowed with cultural capital, in which it is worth investing one's energy.

> *Kenneth*: I'm a full-time employee at Media Molecule, and I used to be the only audio person there but I'm now running a team. I've got one other full-time employee and then there's a contractor who I've brought in for eight months to help with the current project. Prior to that, like I say, I was the only person there, and that was very unusual to have just one member of audio personnel in a company working on a triple A game. Because you just . . . there's so much in a game now in terms of audio, that to have one person managing all that is actually crazy, and I certainly had to work very hard. Media Molecule is a small company, and the idea is to keep the company small; we're still under 40 people now. Your average triple A big game titles are generally made by anything from about 75 up to . . . you know, up to hundreds. There's some big concentrations of people in places like Canada where there are some massive companies with well over a thousand employees. They have the [ability] to throw huge [numbers] of people onto a project. The reason we're so small is partly because the kind of games we choose to make facilitate that. You know, we're not making a game which has absolutely massive amounts of content, which is where the resource drain is. If you can imagine creating lots of different art, animation, and models, essentially creating a whole world from scratch, you need a lot of people to do that. What we do is create a fair amount of assets, set the bar, and then give the assets and creative tools to our community, and they build the games for themselves. So we don't have that massive content creation bottleneck.

Innovation can be characterized by features that add something new, with the degree of novelty being important either for the collective enterprise itself, in terms of technology development, or in terms of application-specific aspects of the product. Then, of course, there is the added value and high importance of 'customer-centric thinking' (Volkmann et al., 2010, p. 106). Here Kenneth talks about the concept of innovation and how entrepreneurialism works in the game industry.

> *Kenneth*: If Sony® or another platform holder such as Microsoft® are developing some new technology, that's one aspect of innovation in the industry. And then where we as game developers can innovate is in the use of that technology. So we work with what we get given in terms of hardware or, increasingly these days, software. So much of it is software-based technology, of course, and the innovation that comes from us is in making interactive entertainment products built on top of that core innovation. So, you know, it's always exciting to be working on the next big thing in terms of the hardware you get given . . . But, ultimately, what we're trying to do is create something which people want to buy and have fun with, and enjoy. And tell their friends about and get them to buy it as well. And, ideally, try and have fun ourselves making and putting together that experience.

The role of innovation in new product development practices operates in two ways. On the one hand, it is a relation of conditions: the immanent necessity of the field (or of a hierarchy of intersecting fields) to position their products, to influence the field, to break rules, and create breakthrough projects and products. On the other, it is a relation of creativity and the construction of new technologies. The organizational habitus contributes to constituting the field of video game development as a meaningful company that is endowed with cultural capital, in which it is worth investing one's energy and money.

> *Kenneth*: And, yeah, certainly our last product was innovative and well received, so we've been the industry's darling the last couple of years. But whether we can continue to pull off that kind of innovation remains to be seen. I think we are contributing to our culture. I know there's still this stigma in much of society with playing video games, which other media like film or, perhaps to a lesser extent, television, have managed to rise above the initial criticisms of the medium. But the way they've done that is by actually being relevant and actually being entertaining and engaging with people in a meaningful way. And we're getting there, but I don't think we've necessarily reached that point where it's easy to

have a really good transparent discussion with, or argument against, people who say that games don't contribute much. Certainly, if you consider the number of people playing games there's absolutely no way that we can't be having an impact on people's lives. It's just not possible. But whether it's a positive contribution or not . . . I suppose that is where a lot of the debate is. And I just know from our last project . . . because it's a community-focused game, you know, that our game lives and dies by the number of people that are playing and using it, we get a lot of feedback from the community, and that's not actually that normal on a game.

Often you release a game, and because people just buy it and then, you know, sell it back to the shop, you don't necessarily get a lot of feedback from them. Certainly, with the Internet you can look at forums where people are talking about your game. But there is often not that direct link between the people that are making the game and the people that are playing it. Whereas we've got quite a strong link with our community, which we openly encourage, and we get sent a lot of e-mails from our fans, and people that have played the game and enjoyed it and want to interact with us. And through this you sometimes get a small insight into the ways that your game can touch people's lives. And so one example would be that *LittleBigPlanet*™ has been used by a paediatrician in the US to get really young kids to communicate how sick they're feeling when they're going through chemotherapy. These kids aren't so good at articulating themselves, particularly when it comes to describing their bodies. I mean, the English language has such a poor vocabulary here to the extent that even adults struggle to com- municate with doctors. But these kids can communicate through their little Sick Boy avatar in the game who is able to express emotions of happiness, sadness and fear at the click of a button. And they were using that as a really simple, accessible method of communicating with the kids in terms of how they were feeling before during and after their chemo. And there are so many examples of parents with autistic children who . . . you know, are completely obsessed with the game beyond anything else they've ever encountered. And it's the only thing they want to talk about, but because this is such a big part of their children's lives, and it gives them some common ground, they've found that it's a positive thing for their relationship and their child's development. That's one of the things which we honestly didn't really expect about the game when it came out. A really core part of our audience demographic is parents and children playing it together.

Kenneth regards *LittleBigPlanet*™ as more than a commercial success, for it has also brought about social innovations related to changes in communicative interaction. There is a relationship between media culture and the digital creativities within it in a large variety of forms and diverse contexts. Many children have access to console and video games (PlayStation® or Nintendo® Wii™). Research in the medical and scientific fields on the benefits of these multimodal activities, although relatively unexplored in accounts of media use in early childhood, suggests that, in developed countries, both children and parents are active users; and while patterns of interaction differ, many young children are competent users of technology from an early age. Parents feel that their children's creative participation develops a wide range of skills, knowledge, and understand- ing.[22] Importantly, individuals are differently positioned in relation to the value attributed to the creative process that leads to social innovations in digital media.

Kenneth's positioning of the product and the importance of user creativity

Kenneth's descriptions of his experiences give a potent sense of the relationship between pro- ducer and consumer. Clearly sound and music writing for digital media organizations generally,

[22] In J. Marsh et al. (2005), a survey of 1852 parents of children aged from birth to six in 10 local authorities in England is reported, in which young children's use of popular culture, media, and new technologies was identified (www.digitalbeginnings.shef.ac.uk/; see also J. Marsh (2006)).

and the gaming world in particular, has intentionality and interactivity at the heart of the creative process. There is 'a complex dynamic going on', embodied in a type of 'user-creativity'. The process involves 'focus testing' and 'peer review'.

> *Kenneth*: When we were working on the sequel to *LittleBigPlanet*™—*LittleBigPlanet*™ 2, obviously— we brought in 15 of the top creators from the game's community to come and check out our work in-progress, just to see what they would do with it. It was kind of focus testing, if you like, just to gauge if our game worked, and if people were able to use it. But we also get some PR out of that by showing the results of what they have done with it. Not what we've made, but actually what the community has been able to make with our game. And those people we call are hardcore creators, those are the ones who make games in our game, upload them and allow the hundreds of thousands of other people that are playing it to continue to play it, and enjoy it. And so the relationship we have with them is interesting, because on the one hand they're a consumer like anyone else that has played our game, you know, the audience of our game, but they are also creators within our game. So they've got this interesting position where they're not part of our company, but they're part of what we're doing. And so we are fans of their work as much as they are fans of our work. And the reason they are doing what they do is because they enjoy using the product, but they also enjoy the adulation that they get from other members of the *LittleBigPlanet*™ community who, when they play their levels, say, 'Oh that was great, I really enjoyed playing that. Please make more'.

There is a complex dynamic going on in this narrative. This is a particular practice associated with how innovators engage people in the community, and attempt to influence them in order to build a prototype/model that will influence their actions. What Kenneth describes are the mind-sets and actions used to gain acceptance and feedback on the company's products from outside and inside the organization. There is also a kind of positioning of the product that is enabled by gaining a profound understanding of customers' requirements and the technological possibilities of the product. The creative problem-solving skills required to address these challenges requires strategies for the incorporation of user-ideas and user-responses, and ways of facilitating creativity in the problem-solving process.

> *Kenneth*: It is, absolutely. I mean, we created the game to start with and we didn't really know if it was going to work or not. We had these ideas and we had these plans for what it was meant to be and what is was meant to do. But it's not until you actually get it out there and see what people do with it that you know whether it's achieving that ambition. And that's always completely separate to its commercial success; it's more a gauge of whether this thing you've been working on for several years does what you've been trying to make it do. And with *LittleBigPlanet*™, fortunately it did, which is great. The feedback comes in different ways. Feedback comes in the form of ideas, suggestions, restrictions they find themselves frustrated [with] because the game isn't doing one of the things they want it to do. There's a few ways that we read or gather this information. We get valuable feedback via emails and Internet forums. Sometimes when you read what someone's frustrated with, they've got their own idea about why they're frustrated. And if you follow that feedback directly you're not necessarily going [to] solve their problem, because the consumer isn't necessarily aware of what it is that's annoying them about the product. It's a lot more valuable to us to observe them using it.

Clearly product design and development is not just about creativity and the generation of ideas. It is also about the transformation of an invention into an innovative, marketable product.[23] Often concrete customer- or user-problems are recognized but technical or innovative opportunities for their solution are still lacking. User-generated content is important. One important challenge to audio design is how users respond to different ideas associated with uncertainty and risk.

---

[23] For discussion of entrepreneurship from a continental European perspective, see Volkmann et al. (2010).

Observations of how users in the target market respond to and engage with product innovations may be done in many different ways.

> *Kenneth*: There are a couple of ways that we use observation to help us improve a game; the first way we use observation is by conducting focus-testing during actual development. If you just watch someone you can see where they get stuck or frustrated straight away. This is important because it's really easy when you're making a game to make assumptions about what people's perception or experience of playing the game is going to be—in reality you're too close to the project to really have that fresh insight. But if someone's just got the product in front of them, then you're watching them and you thought you were communicating an idea effectively. But, all of a sudden, you can see that it just doesn't work and that you need to improve an aspect of your product. That's quite powerful, just watching what they create, seeing how fun it is to play the game and where it falls down, and how you can perhaps make it better.
>
> The second way we use observation is to actually release a finished game, and use the experience of seeing millions of people use it to learn from it, and apply this knowledge in updates or even future products. For example, in the first *LittleBigPlanet*™ everything's physical, and you can build things out of different materials, kind of like a virtual Meccano or Lego set. And then there are all the gadgets, which are things like pistons and motors that allow you to connect everything up and build massive Heath Robinson style creations. People then took that technology, or toolkit, and did unexpected things like building a calculator by creating lots of little binary circuits using physical logic gates. And, you know, we didn't put that functionality in the product, they constructed it in the product and then made something else with it. And so we can look at that and say 'This person has clearly spent a very long time building all these little circuits for themselves, why don't we add the functionality for people to be able to add circuit boards in the game with a suite of easy to use logic devices so that they might create even more insanely complex things with it'. And so that kind of observation of what the community are doing has immense value for us in how to improve and expand the product. In *LittleBigPlanet*™ 2 we're doing precisely that.
>
> We are simplifying and empowering the player to do that stuff a lot more quickly. The benefit of that isn't just for the hardcore creators, who are already able to do many of these things, albeit slowly and painfully, but for someone who doesn't have either the time or the knowledge to be able to do that, we've just given them a little gadget which does it all for them. So we've empowered the hardcore to do even more impressive things, but we've also empowered that tier of creators just below that who still want to create, but maybe don't have that same level of investment in the product. This creates a whole new level of weird and wonderful things that people can make in the game, and, naturally, this also benefits players who enjoy exploring other people's creations.

Here Kenneth reflects on the social determinants of game development. While most things seem to start from one person's vision, the game is constructed collectively, enlisting others to make it happen. To become enlisted, others need to see what the innovator sees. New product development is all about value to the business and social determinants. These social determinants are what create the market and produce reconfigurations. The potential of products is translated simply and straightforwardly into the direct evidence and insight displayed by the players. Considering the nature of how sounds and music communicate emotional meaning, and involving consumers in brainstorming and feedback at the front end of projects, are possibly two of the most important aspects of improvisational creativity for the audio designer.

> *Kenneth*: Yeah, but that's game development incarnate, to be honest. I mean that's obviously the process we have with our community. But when you work on a game it's not like a film where you have your script and then everything kind of flows from that, or you know that, because you've got so much experience of production how long it's gonna take you to shoot this particular film, or work much of it out up front and then just make it happen. You just need the money to do it. [laughs] Right? With a game you have this kind of core kernel of an idea, but no one's done what you're doing before. So you . . . well,

especially if it's an innovative title like *LittleBigPlanet*™, no one can look at that and say 'Right, it's gonna take x number of years to do this, because blah!' You just kind of have to start on it and see how far you get, and at that point that's when you've probably got some kind of prototype that you can show to a publisher and say, 'Look, this is our idea, it's nowhere near finished yet, but here's the core concept. Please give us some money to go and make it'. And then if they green light it, the way the development is then structured is in milestones, and so you kind of agree what you're going to deliver over a period of time. And that's a constant source of friction in the industry, because the publishers use milestones to measure how you're getting on, and you've got to meet your milestones because that's when you get paid your next chunk of money to carry on development.

But it's really hard at times to agree what you're going to deliver, because you've not made it yet. And, try as you might to think how long it will take you, you can never know for sure until you've made this piece of technology, or that asset, or that sound, or that piece of . . . Actually, music's probably a bad example, because you do . . . you can work out how long it's gonna take you to write a piece of music, roughly speaking. But it's knowing how that music is going to be used that is the challenging thing, because the game isn't finished when you're writing that piece of music.

Clearly, in the video games environment there are opportunities and risks in the application of specific technologies, which audio designers such as Kenneth cannot normally influence. The organization interacts with the external environment, and there are any number of forces operating on the company: budgets, investors, market forces, competitors, customers, local and global economies and the important challenge of anticipating what will happen in the future. When asked to reflect on the interplay between sonic and musical creativities, and what typically happens with the introduction of new technologies, particularly with the integration of customer views and technological aspirations, Kenneth describes a further aspect of collective improvisational creativity, where the members compete with one another, with each person's contributions inspiring the others to raise the bar and think of new ideas. It is a highly participatory process.

Kenneth: Well, there's a million and one ways to think about these things. I mean, for me, I don't view the audio as a separate part of the product, or of the project. Yet, I think audio's often viewed that way. I think as a specialist it's really easy to subcategorize all the stuff that you're doing, and think of it separate to everything else. But I think the key to it being successful is making sure that you've got a really clear idea of what it is you're trying to do. Not in terms of the audio, but in terms of what is the overall work you're creating or contributing towards. And so, for me, I take a lot of inspiration from the art direction simply because, well, I've never been in the position of working on a project in what I would call preproduction. When I worked at Sony® I was always brought in, I guess, not late, but certainly not in preproduction. So I didn't have any input into what the project was, or how the music would be used necessarily. When I came to Media Molecule to work on *LittleBigPlanet*™, the game had already been in development for just over a year. And at that point they had something to show, and they had some music in it, but they hadn't really thought much about the use of the music, or how it would be used. And so I took as my lead the art direction in the game, and what it was trying to look and feel like, and trying to reinforce that and work with that in terms of the music.

Then with our new project, *LittleBigPlanet*™ 2, I wouldn't say there was necessarily a significant preproduction on that because it's essentially a continuation of our work on *LittleBigPlanet*™ . . . But on our next project, whatever that is, it'll be interesting for me and for Media Molecule as a company that we'll be working on this new thing from scratch. Media Molecule started out with four people and its grown to just under 40, so it hasn't created a product from scratch with that full team, with all their opinions and ideas and creative-type-hissy-fits about how things should be done. So that's going to be interesting. But, generally, precisely when music starts to be thought about during the development of a video game is different for every project, and it depends a lot on the individual people that are involved.

Clearly the organization is a collective enterprise, and as players in the company acquire more capital, so they become more valued. But capital also exists in ever-changing configurations in relation to the field which generates it; and, the values of the gaming industry are constantly being renegotiated in implicit and explicit ways. In fact, consumers are also knowing collaborators in the process and practice of legitimizing a product, particularly in the ways that audio interactivity works, blending innovation in design and execution throughout the project lifecycle.

> *Kenneth*: The issue of who is responsible for defining how music is used in our work is important. Music is something which many people are really passionate about, even if they don't actually have much knowledge of it other than as a consumer. And I think that's where a lot of uses of music show themselves to be a bit weak. You quite often have someone who's quite senior on a project who's really into consuming music, and, precisely because they're in a senior position, they're able to dictate how music should and could be used in the project they're working on. And that can be awkward for the audio personnel, who you would hope would have more of an idea of how to use music.
>
> And so, for me, when I say I take my direction for the music from the art direction, I think that's a sensible way to do it, and ensures that rather than fighting against what you're perceiving when you're playing the game, that the music is actually a part of the experience, it enhances it. I don't think that's necessarily the way everyone does it, because the use of music in games is often quite naïve. We talk about wall-to-wall use of music, or wallpaper music. Unlike in a film where the music would be scoring the emotions in the scene or trying to heighten the drama in some way, for the most part during the 'gameplay' (where you're controlling a character or doing something), there's not generally any story involved there irrespective of whether it's a narrative game, so you don't have the same emotions that you would have in a film. You know, you're not dealing with sadness, you're maybe dealing with frustration, or you're dealing with the joy that someone gets out of completing a task . . . In a film the creator dictates the experience and says, 'This is how it is and you can take it or leave it. You can enjoy it or you can leave the cinema'. But in a game, because the audience is a part of the experience, because they are participating in it, they're controlling a character, or they are moving something about on screen. It's a lot harder to know what they are feeling, because their experience is less dictated, it's dictated in part by the players themselves.

This is a very hands-on practice. There are 'hard' influence actions and there are 'soft' influence actions. People are engaged in particular practices that have particular significance in terms of the iterative way in which they find solutions to technical, political and interactive problems.

Creative habits and dispositions required in being and becoming an audio designer

The limitations and successes of game sound and music can be identified by means of road-testing. They appear to be characterized by degrees of artistic freedom and commercial constraints. These may or may not balance, given that to produce a cultural artefact for the market requires intervention, guidance, collaboration, and consumer feedback. There is a reliance on the institutional networks that have been set in place, along with a need to accumulate capital acquired through being in a central position in the field in which creativities are realized. All of this relates to how the company positions itself within the field.

> *Kenneth*: Right, just now what we do is we make assumptions. We assume that the player is feeling a certain thing at a certain point in time, or we can dictate that we want them to be feeling that. And, to a certain extent, you can use music in that manipulative way that cinema does to, for example, make you cry. Even though it's maybe not quite sad enough to make you cry, the music can really get to you and push you over the edge. I don't think we are as successful at using music in that manipulative or emotive way, simply because we often don't know exactly what the player is feeling at a certain point in time. It's hard to go a little bit science-fictional and start thinking about how we could do that. Microsoft® have their Kinect system coming out soon, which is a camera-based sensor system. I'm not sure how good that would be for facial tracking, but that's certainly an obvious notion—trying to read

the emotional state of the player based on their face, pulse, all these kinds of things, which we'd use to tailor-make their experience.

Here we see an individual with social resilience, who cannot realize the musical creativity of a game product without collaborative agreement on judgements about the value and possibilities of music and sound. In other words, many of the rules and principles of audio design go on in a way that is not consciously known by those creating it in the same way as those playing it. Having an appetite for, possessing and activating the value of sound and music as capitals—as the value force of 'communicative musicality'[24]—is possibly the most important way in which people communicate and understand each other: through a direct sharing of actions, emotions, and intentions—symbolic capital. These judgments involve consideration of the human relationships and social processes through which a group of people have to realize a particular creation. This is a collaborative process involving a collective entity made up of multiple individuals. Even though the field is profoundly hierarchized, with dominant social agents and an institution having considerable power to determine what happens within it, there is still agency and change. Kenneth gives an indication of the relative power he holds and his agency in the organization (within the field of power).

> *Kenneth*: It is collaborative, I can't just dictate what the music is going to do without listening to anyone else's input, that would just cause frustration and make everyone unhappy. So I've developed processes which I think give me what I want and what I think is best for the project, whilst also giving the team the ability to have some input into the decisions that I'm making. Although, to be honest, with original music it's a bit harder because there's the creative brief I create for the composer, and not everyone can fathom how that might pan out without actually hearing the finished thing. I couldn't work in a situation where I've commissioned a piece of music, and I'm happy with it, but someone else in the team doesn't like it. I mean, I can't go back to the composer and say, 'Oh, there's some people in the team that don't like it, we're going to have to redo this'. As long as I'm happy, that just has to be the benchmark. You know, we're paying someone to do a task, and we can't exploit them by getting them to do endless iterations just to suit some people's particular tastes. So I do get to dictate that side of things, but I make sure I'm synched up with the other creative leads on the project so that I know we're working towards the same goal. It's a lot easier to talk about licensed music, where the piece of music is already existing. I can easily play a licensed track to the team and get their feedback.
>
> The process I've developed is that if anyone's got suggestions for a piece of music, I will always take that and consider whether it's suitable for the project or not. The way I like to think of individual pieces or sections of music is in terms of their role within the project—where is it used, how is it used, what are its requirements. Once I've identified this, I call it a 'slot'—this is also an important part of the budgeting and scheduling process. And so I will come up with two or three choices for that particular slot—what I've done is selected three bits of music which I think will work and, although I've got my favourite, I know that if the team picks my plan B or plan C, it's still going to work. So, I can hand that choice over to the team and say 'Okay, guys, which of these do people generally like the best, and more importantly why?' I'm not particularly interested in people saying 'I like that piece of music'. I'm a lot more interested in people saying 'I like this piece of music and I think it works because blah, blah, blah', because that lets me know if the music is working in the game rather than if they simply like the music in and of itself.

---

[24] 'Communicative musicality' is a term developed by Malloch and Trevarthen (2009), which refers to the power of musicality to facilitate and energize meaning in communication, and the vital role music plays in our biological-psychological make-up 'to know, think communicate, create new things and care for one another in movement' (p. 8).

It is worth emphasizing at this point that, as the mention of selecting licensed music, which is to say, existing pieces of music, implies, there are indeed royalty-free soundtracks and entertainment-industry-driven software that let you build musical arrangements that make use of pre-recorded audio files called 'loops' and 'one-shots'. Loops contain rhythmic patterns that you can extend to fill any amount of time, while one-shots contain sound effects and other non-repeating sounds. Combining and arranging sound effects and other non-repeating audio, when creatively reusing the music of the past and sound sources of the present, is part of standard digital music tools and applications such as Apple's GarageBand and Soundtrack programs.

> *Kenneth*: And so the benefit is that I essentially get what I want, and the team gets what they want, and we're both happy. And the project, or the work, doesn't suffer. The worst thing that can happen is that someone puts a piece of music into a game simply because they like the piece of music. The primary motivator's got to be that the piece of music works in the game, and not just based on a gut instinct, or an emotional response. I think you have to be able to articulate a reason for why a piece of music is there. So in *LittleBigPlanet*™ the story, if you could call it that, took the player on a journey around the world. And so we had different countries that you would visit on your journey. And I dictated that the licensed music in the game had to come from the particular country that you're in at that moment. It didn't make any sense to me if you're meant to be in Mexico that you hear music performed by a European band. People would say it doesn't matter as long as the music fits the game and we should just use it. But I think the problem there is that because people's enjoyment of music is so subjective you cannot be sure that everyone playing the game will enjoy that music in the way that you did. So the only thing you can rely on is having that concrete link, so that at least someone might think 'I don't like this track, but at least it makes sense'.
>
> And so, for me, that's how I approach the music—to always make sure that there's this kind of rationale. Certainly in the first *LittleBigPlanet*™ you find yourself in different countries and I wanted it to sound authentic. And that's actually quite hard to do! So, if I think of Mexico that suggests certain sounds. But I'm no expert and any knowledge I do have is no doubt based on years of watching TV and films and having these stereotypes thrown at me—it's not actually based on any real understanding of what Mexican music is like. So I try to back that up, if I don't have much of a real clue about what something sounds like, by doing research, listening to the different kinds of music that you get in Mexico, from traditional music to military music, culturally unique music, and just try and get a sense of how a particular culture sounds. Which is hard, because ultimately you're still trying to distil something that's quite complex, into one piece of music.

This shows a practice that is as much about creatively reusing music as it is about a journey into sound using digital technology, or about manifestations of music reflecting clubs and spaces anywhere in the world.

The role of new technologies in audio design

As mentioned earlier, the experience of playing a video game can be strikingly similar to that of playing music. Each requires a high level of control over some physical instrument (such as a joystick or saxophone), with reactions based or recognizing where one is in the moment. In each case the player relies on a combination of learned patterns and contextually appropriate improvisation for success.

Developing complex modern technologies such as the windows-and-mouse user interface technology[25] is not the work of a solitary individual but that of a team and its receptivity to reception through user feedback. It is as much about innovation in the technologies of, for instance, sound storage and diffusion, as it is about the conditions under which it is listened to and engages

---

25 For more discussion about team collaboration in innovative companies see Sawyer (2006b, pp. 41–8).

people, how it can or should be reproduced and reused, and about those breakthrough projects wherein team collaboration is an ingrained way of developing new technologies.

> *Kenneth*: There is a constant release of new technology, both in terms of hardware and software. And it's this constant race against that, and trying to maintain that, that means you don't actually have time to stop and really focus on perfecting what it is you're working with. It's like a technical race. It's not a race against the competition *per se*: that's not how it feels to me when I'm working on a project. You just know that because you're making a commercial product, and it's going to be out in an environment where there are other products which are trying to vie for people's time and money. So it's got to compete.
>
> I don't know how creative we are as human beings, but certainly in terms of the amount of time we spend on audio in a project—and this isn't just in games, but in film as well—there's much more time spent on the visual aspect of the project. It's not the focus of the project.
>
> People who are in creative control of a project tend not to have a background in sound, which is why the films that I admire for their sound invariably have someone, often the director, who is quite hands-on with the sound. And even if they're not a sound practitioner themselves, then they know about sound and how to use it effectively as a story-telling device. So, someone like Alfred Hitchcock, or perhaps a contemporary example would be the Coen Brothers, who work with awesome sound people as a collaborative effort. That's unusual in film, primarily because of the auteur model where the director often dictates what will happen even if they're not the best person to be making that call. And in games some projects or studios have that model where there's someone dictating how it's gotta be. And that's partly because, obviously, 'too many cooks spoil the broth' type scenarios and you've got to get decisions made. But, generally, I think games are more collaborative processes than films are. But I guess as someone who, despite my musical background, puts a lot of their passion and effort into working with sound, perhaps some of my bitterness has reared its head here in terms of feeling like a second-class citizen with regard to the kind of work I'm able to do. And, you know, you're never going to be a rock 'n' roll star as a sound artist! You've got to do it because you love it, which is obviously a good motivation for doing something. Record producers tend to deal with the sound of the music, perhaps more so than the music itself. And it's interesting that that is considered to be so important to the success of a piece of music that is primarily trying to create money more than it is trying to be a work of art.
>
> And I guess that's another aspect we haven't talked about, is that I'm conscious of the fact that I've spent a lot of time talking about the industry and the business side of things. That's probably something that you would not necessarily have encountered when talking to someone who is a sound artist.[26] I mean, especially if they've got a source of funding or patronage and they don't need to worry about making money. Maybe the work they're creating isn't designed to do that, and that's a different aspect of it as well. But one of the reasons that I obviously have an interest in, but also have been talking so much about that side of things, is that I work at a small company. There aren't layers and layers of management above me dealing with that side of things. It's like, there's my friend a few metres away [laughs] in the office who's making these decisions. And we talk about it and you learn about it, and you see the impact it has: that's not something most people are exposed to. I don't think most people you would talk to in the industry would necessarily be as interested in, or be able to talk about those things. But it's not just because I work at a small company. It's also of interest to me because the health

---

26 There is a hierarchy of composers and status of creativity associated with multi-media sound designers comparable with contemporary 'art' composers or sound artists. This was emphasized in my discussion with Vasco Hexel, a German film composer, who made this point when asked about the structure of the field and its values. He said 'Being a film composer or screen composer means you're not seen as a serious composer . . . Just because you work to a brief doesn't reduce the degree of accomplishment, virtuosity and desire to build on the techniques of the past masters. But the academy holds bourgeois values and doesn't like to have its artistic orthodoxies challenged'. For further discussion on film music, see R. Faulkner (2005).

of the industry, in terms of how well it's doing financially and how it is innovating, dictates what I can do in my job. And so, I think it's wise to keep your finger on the pulse, see what's happening, what's successful, and think about what might be round the corner.

Kenneth adopts a relational mode of thinking about his practice as a sound designer and the structural principles of the game industry. As lead audio designer, whose success lies in being able to tap into team collaboration, he moves between compositional and improvisational modes of creativity, and balances different kinds of thinking and opportunities and risks, surrounding himself with people who support his creativity. Whilst Kenneth implies that there are struggles for power in the subfields of media and digital cultures, he knows how to balance different kinds of thinking. He knows that creativity means thinking, acting, and producing in ways that often take a good deal of courage. Continuous, slow, and incremental developments are rare in a globalized world. Fast and dynamic changes prevail in the everyday life of the audio designer/entrepreneur as he or she faces constant challenges and pressures. The commercial or business aspects of the industry can be ideologically opposed to notions of 'culture' and 'aesthetics'. For Kenneth, working in video game audio design requires him to act as an intermediary in the relationship between aesthetics and industry. On the one hand, aesthetics values the power of music and, on the other, the industry sees music as a resource or a commodity. Audio designers use music consciously and actively in different situations at different levels of game-player engagement, so that listening contexts ultimately determine the value of the musical experience for listeners. The role and focus of music and sound in video games is neither passive nor taken for granted, but complex and sophisticated. On the one hand, video gaming acknowledges the importance of commodification by identifying the 'experience economy' as a potential source of income by explicitly engaging consumers in a personal and creative way, or, in other words, entertaining them. On the other hand, the music practices of the video gaming industry are being used to create values in other areas of life.

Creativity has a privileged place in the video gaming industry, and video gaming can be linked powerfully to teaching and learning. Many education systems are now struggling to shape a creative society and a work force that is adroit enough to exploit the opportunities of a new economy wherein innovation is seen as paramount. Musical creativity specifically, and creativity in general, are capacities that can be developed by all: creativity is not only possessed by the gifted and talented few.

The interplay of capitals, as with the new digital technologies and the voracious market for new games, is vital to the collective enterprise. Teams work collaboratively in the production of video games, as do their users, who contribute to the design of the game. The social values and status assigned to these capital-bearing products of entertainment and art are grounded in the use and reuse of existing materials. The capitals assigned go hand in hand with the construction of specific principles of perception and appreciation of the social world (with assets in the educational market, as will be described in the sections that follow). This represents a very significant shift in how video games are being redesigned to target players with new music and introduce new musical instruments to willing users. What it is to learn at the same time as playing a game is addressed in the following sections by Matthew, a sound designer and software programmer.

Introducing Matthew C. Applegate (alias 'Pixelh8')

Matthew was born in Ipswich, Suffolk, in the UK where he now lives with his partner, young family, and stepfather. As a child, he travelled a great deal and went to many different schools in many different countries, according to where his stepfather was needed by the military. Indeed, having recently completed a Master's at the Centre for Design Innovation, University Campus Suffolk, he now works as a multi-disciplinary artist, an award-winning 'chiptune composer'[27], and techno-anthropologist who programs some of the oldest and rarest computers in the world to create music and sound effects. Matthew is also an audiovisual programming guru, a Game Boy hacker, and, in combination with Nintendo®, developed interactive audio music software for the web, along with Music Tech for the Nintendo® Game Boy and the Pro-Performer for the Nintendo® Game Boy Advance, and Nintendo® DS, which turns both machines into real-time synthesizers. He is a patron of the Access to Music centre in Norwich, and a STEMNET ambassador, and teaches video game music and sound design in several universities. His latest work centres on the reuse of computers, which relates to his professional brand.

> *Matthew*: That came about by a combination of my lack of ability in creating 'user-friendly' graphics in my software, usually black and white or just text, also the sheer volume of machines I went through in the beginning, people thought I didn't like machines. I destroyed so many machines taking them apart learning how to make them make funny noises, several explosions later, several fires, and electric shocks, I have a better understanding and a name . . . I always describe what I do as 're-purposing', often taking what is potentially musical and focusing on making it primarily musical, anything can be made into a musical instrument, from cutlery to optical telescopes, badly wired light-bulbs to construction sites. Cubans will grab car parts to form a samba band, I take 'debris' from suburbia and make electronic music. I am simply doing what composers have always done, which is to mimic or to take the sounds from their environments, Bach and others took the birds tweeting in their garden, I don't have that, my life is full of the buzzing and beeping of technology, these sounds mean something to me and others like me, so I use them as instruments, to express myself.

Matthew represents a generation of musicians who do not come out of art schools, and whose earliest experiences and recollections of music training are vividly unpleasurable. With a background in electronic music, with enraptured tastes, preferences, and inclinations that do not draw on high culture, he challenges inherited notions of directly specified musical instruments. He describes his musical background.

> *Matthew*: I think I was both fortunate and unfortunate in my early years. I had a very unmusical family, no one played musical instruments, no one sang songs, I can't even remember being sung to. But that said it wasn't all bad, we had MTV™. I was one of the first kids in America to get it installed, and although limited in the number of videos it showed initially, it did put musicians in front of me.
>
> The second important factor was my stepfather. He had a huge '70s soul and funk collection on vinyl, the same albums that were being sampled and scratched in most of the early hip hop music of the time, so I had access to the same 'instruments' that the people I was listening to had. My stepfather was also in the American Air Force, which meant we travelled a lot. This was good and bad. Bad in the way long-term relationships with friends were pretty much impossible, but good in that I got experience of so many different cultures and musics from all over the world, not just the countries we were stationed [in] but from the other military families. I can remember that when I lived in Germany, I was always hanging out with the Puerto Ricans and Hawaiians and going to their family parties.
>
> I knew I wanted to be a part of music, listening to everything I could from Prince, KRS One, Patsy Cline, and John Williams, I wanted to be a part of [it] so bad, but I had no way in. My experiences at school with music were awful, I wasn't interested in playing 'old' music and I was very stubborn with

---

27 Chiptune composers use the reprogramming of old video games and computers to create new music; this is not a genre such as dance or funk, its newness is in the instrumentation. Most people think that it sounds like 1980s' video game music, and could be forgiven for doing so, but there is one very important difference: there is no game. The machines are highly limited, and are usually only capable of producing three tones simultaneously and a noise, usually for a drum track. It is a challenge to make new music under these tight constraints.

this, I can remember saying 'Why would I want to learn this old music, when I don't listen to it or enjoy it'. It was alien to me and in the end I was simply disciplined for not taking part in music.

My secondary school music experiences were no better. I was told the GCSE music class was 'full', and that I would have to choose something else. I think I had to do Business Studies. It was strange I was spending all my free time at home tinkering with electronics and music, and when I tried to formally learn about it I wasn't allowed, but in all fairness, it was this that spurred me on. This carried on until I left school. Ironically the first thing I did was get a part-time job to pay for my music theory tutor, a lovely lady who, despite being confused about why I would want to make electronic music, was keen to teach me. Weird isn't it: I leave school, only to earn money to pay for things I could have learnt in school.

I never wanted to 'play' music, I wanted to write it. I have a terrible sense of re-creating and performing rhythm, but it is these inaccuracies which inspire me, and this inability to play was perfect for me to form a relationship with computer-based music. I find it immensely empowering to be able to program a computer to perform the music that is in my head. I could never play multiple instruments live, but through another skill I have, programming, I can. Some people hear a tune and notate it. I hear a tune and code it. I don't see a difference: it is just using the technology of the time.

Several currents run together here. First, there is the excitement that technology ignites in Matthew, who attributes his creativity to computers and computation. Later, he elaborates on his acknowledgement of computer creativity as the source of whatever music he knows and produces. Second, there is his participation in music. His earliest recollections of music are through listening, rather than through producing or playing. He is not a performer, nor a product of the art music tradition, but a keen listener. His tastes, preferences and inclinations lean towards the positive exploration of 'musics from all over the world' (due to his travels, as part of a military family), and new worlds of sound that open up endless possibilities in computer-based and digital sound production. Third, there is the aspect of no two-way traffic between home and school music contexts, and the political implications of being denied access to music, of having 'no way in'. Matthew compares the culture that operates in schools and classrooms, and the process of enculturation that is slower than teaching or training but more long lasting. Having gained no educational credentials in music at school, having to play 'old music' at a school with an inflexible curriculum, and having to make his own arrangements for the services of a music teacher after leaving school, means that Matthew now supports a vision of schools and education which is more thoughtful, vastly more cooperative, greatly more compassionate, and a lot more creative.

Cultivating creativity

A great problem facing education is caused by the fragmentation of thinking and acting—a way of thinking that divides, and fails to see the interconnections and coherence that might result from new ways of working and thinking, and the application of new (and old) computer technologies. Composers such as Matthew work in collaboration to generate ways of re-programming old technology to create something new. How does this work in the field of audio design? Matthew describes himself on Wikipedia as 'a British chiptune composer'. Speaking of this kind of compositional creativity puts him in possession of a particular kind of Bourdieuian cultural capital. This is a kind of technological cultural capital which consists of familiarity with dominant culture but with an exceptional ability to understand and 're-purpose' technology. In the context of audio design, this means the ability to shift direction, even to redefine a more flexible approach to game technology in the face of the dominant view of the industry:

Matthew: Chiptune music is the re-programming or re-purposing of old video games and computers to create new functions and new music. It is not a genre like dance or funk: it is the instrumentation. Most people think that it sounds like '80s video game music, and would be forgiven for doing so; there is one very important difference, there is no game. It is taking highly limited machines usually, ones that can produce three tones simultaneously and a noise usually for a drum track, and make music out of that. It is those tight constraints that make it a challenge to make new things. I always find when you have a synth that can do everything, I get bored very quickly because there are too many options before an outcome, but if it can just produce a square wave, then you are going make a square wave and get on with the music . . . Chiptune composers use sequences and develop performance software for making sequencing files. There is a visual element and a performance element, but it involves much more than just hitting 'play'. But like video game machines, they should be played on. Other key figures in this field who are trying to help chiptune music grow and who are making software to help new artists get involved include 8Bit Weapon, Little Scale, Aleksi Eeben, and Paul Slocum from Tree Wave.

For me, personally, chiptune music is 50% music and 50% programming, although you don't have to be a programmer to make the music. Plenty of chiptune sequencers are out there, but you are then limited to using the sounds the programmers have made and run the risk of sounding like everyone else. An important thing to consider, especially when you think that these machines are already very limited in their range, is that the more of 'you' you can put in the more individual it will sound.

The irony of chiptune is that it was definitely inspired by '80s video games, and yet we spent years highlighting the difference between chiptune and video game music, and now chiptune composers are now being employed to write the new soundtracks of new video games, we have gone full circle. The second irony is that to do this kind of music you often have to hack the machines, something that the video game industry frowns on, but are now willing to forgive, as it helps make wonderful music for their retro-themed video games.

Given the use of such terms as capital, it is unsurprising that Matthew also refers to the differences between these two sets of compositional modes: chiptune and video game music. This helps explain differences in Matthew's responses to a variety of issues concerning how he understands the concept of creativity, and above all, just how his creativity happens in music. His experiments with technology are part of his personal history: he recycles technology. Old computers become the raw material for new creations. He is excited by the relevance of computers to musical creativity. Applications of the old technology are implemented by software rather than embodied in hardware. Combining familiar ideas in unfamiliar ways, he distinguishes novelty from radical originality. A novel idea is one which can be described and/or produced by the same set of generative rules as other more familiar ones. A radically original, or creative, idea is one which cannot. Matthew's radically original idea is that old technology becomes the subject and object of creative work when it is used as the raw material for a new creation. Its use enables the positive exploration of new worlds of sound and new applications.

Applications of new technology to art are often first inspired by existing aesthetic paradigms. New technology is frequently used to simplify or further develop existing procedures. Then new ideas emerge that more directly engage the technology itself. What is fascinating about Matthew's work as an audio designer of video games is that, as he recycles computers for the raw material of a new creation, he traces the radical inter-penetrations of entertainment and educational reappropriation. The two approach one another until, at their fringes, they become indistinguishable. This lack of distinction signals not a collapse, but the coming into being of a new cultural capital, whereby the experience of playing a video game becomes strikingly similar to that of playing music. When there are high levels of control over the physical and interactive aspects of a game, the player relies on a combination of learned patterns and contextually appropriate improvisation for success, thus combining entertainment and education. This type of innovation is brilliantly exemplified in Matthew's work, which links collaborative knowledge building to successful innovation in business environments:

> *Matthew*: My personal definition of an audio designer is music and sound effects, whereas a sound designer is just the sound effects, but this varies from project to project. Sometimes a sound designer

can be designing sounds to be used in a keyboard or sequencing software for someone to make music with. I do everything as it is all sounds to me. I prefer to work on my own on both the music and sound effects, as having an understanding of the ranges and the timbres, or 'sound palette' can create a 'smoother' sounding outcome; even if the outcome is to produce horrible unsettling noises, you still want it to have a consistency.

In terms of working with a team, especially on a game, I think it is really important to have meetings with the whole team at the same time, usually project the game or project on a big screen, to allow for everyone to see and hear it, and give feedback on it, on a level playing field if you like. I think of sound/audio designers as facilitators and as artists. They have the knowledge of generic conventions to achieve certain outcomes, sonically combined with the passion to create something wonderful for the project. There has to be give and take. You have to do a lot of listening to the game designers and programmers. I listen. You have to listen to the game designers. I have to get a feel for the project. I often find it beneficial to see it move, learn about the narrative. I make multiple versions of pieces of music and sound effects. We test them out and try and find the 'best' one for the project. I write the music and sound effects on my own, but allow for them to be scrutinized by everyone in the project, just like the coder will sit at his desk on his own and allow for us to comment on game play mechanics.

I have made several music instruments for the Nintendo® Game Boy Music Tech v1.0 and 2.0, Game Boy Advance, Music Tech Pro Performer and the Nintendo® DS Music Tech Master Stroke. These were video-game based musical instruments. They weren't games, but they made loads of game companies realize I could make game soundtracks. I made these on my own, writing the code and designing the sounds to be used in the software. It was probably down to my bad experience: trying to learn music that made me turn something that is already very much a part of children's life, a familiar device, into a musical instrument. Admittedly these were unofficial titles, using my programming skills from the '80s, but since then and talking to the various companies, I have decided to only do official development, primarily as it will allow me to reach a much larger audience and develop up-to-date hardware, making it more relevant to my goals.

I have since made musical software, Sonus 1 and Sonus 6, on the Apple iPhone to express the ideas of John Cage and Arnold Schönberg. Again these were solitary projects as they were, as I originally thought, only going to be of interest to a few people, but they have been downloaded several thousand times since their release in 2010.

I have done a lot of work for a lot of different companies, but in the past it has been under 'boilerplate non-disclosure agreements': horrible things which helped me learn about different aspects of sound and technology from musical instrument designs to operating systems.

I have only now started to make music and sound effects for video games publicly as 'Matthew C. Applegate/Pixelh8',[28] and amusingly enough they are all retro-styled games, utilizing my knowledge of the limitations of old computers, as well as the sounds of up-to-date machines like the Xbox® 360 and the iPhone. It is always amusing to me to hear the sound of a BBC Micro coming out of an Xbox® 360.

Applications of old technology to new video games are often first inspired by existing or developing procedures. Then new ideas emerge that more directly engage the technology itself. These arise as a product of use, accident, experiment or cross-fertilization, but always through hands-on interaction. New applications then feed back again into new uses of the old technologies and so on. This way of bringing together industrial and educational capitals has evolved from creative collaborations and the interweaving of social and individual processes in dynamic interactions that can drive aspects of both.

Matthew: So many games are being made today, and so many are so similar. A 'creative product' is not about reinventing the wheel. It is about spinning it in a new direction, taking something familiar, and

---

[28] All Matthew's music on iTunes can be found on his website: www.pixelh8.co.uk. His Apps can be found at the App Store.

make people go 'Woah, I wasn't expecting that'. There have been a few games recently that I really like, things like *Coma*, *Shift*, and *Angry Birds*. They are not ground-breaking ideas, but they are very interesting variations, executed very well.

Like everything in life, being 'you', copying others is fine, but it isn't 'you'. Some people stand out and it is usually because they are only concerned with making an interesting thing, not copying others. In music you can only fail to express yourself. Although it varies from project to project, the music and sound effects I am making for other people's software is fairly standard in terms of its goal. It is to provide sonic authentication of the game world, it is not the primary focus or drive of the game.

However, in my own software, music and sound is of primary importance. I want to see how these technologies could potentially help others get involved in making or performing music. I want to use the software to directly engage the users with the opportunity to perform, and to inspire them to also go outside of the game to learn additional things about music. That is the goal anyway.

I think breakthrough techniques and technology are important. However the most important element is the overall experience, and that can be through a standard control pad or a Microsoft® Kinect. It can be amazing 3D on the Nintendo® 3DS, or simple 2D on a mobile phone.

I am actually more interested in what users do, and 'hack', using these technologies, how the users create things based on products they are sold. Using the Microsoft® Kinect to assist doctors during surgery, speeding up the surgery because they don't have to scrub up again after handling photos, isn't just a cool use of technology, it is one of the first genuinely useful hacks I have seen; and I think it is because of this that companies like Sony® and Microsoft® are now looking at releasing development tools to the public.

Appropriating old technology to produce new forms of music-making is central to Matthew's integrative practice, in which he appropriates the experience of playing a video game to reproduce that of playing music. Thus, different patterns of collaborative creativity, as proposed by John-Steiner (2000), emphasize that there is no clear distinction between performance and composition, entertainment and education.

Concluding remarks

In this chapter we have shown that there is no singular form of musical creativity in digital media sound design and music composition. The way that musical creativity lies at the centre of digital media and audio design and practice for video games is an expression of the symbolic relationship between the worlds of human and computer creativity; that is, this viewpoint is social in origin. The idea of a symbolic relationship between music, sound and computer creativities is seen clearly in the mediation between individual and collaborative creativities in Kenneth's and Matthew's accounts.[29]

With the development of new digital technologies that lead to innovations in the field, new creativities arise which appear to be aligned with practices that gain capital or value. When viewed this way, any discussion of boundaries between musical and computer creativities, as with distinctions between sound artists and sound designers, must respect that these issues of power and value are implicated in our definitions and our issues of concern throughout this book.

The digital musicians' practices we have briefly surveyed here blur comfortable distinctions, shatter disciplinary boundaries, and are strongly suggestive of multiple, manifestations of collective and collaborative creativity, and user-generated creativities, as, for instance, construed and

---

[29] The idea of a symbolic relationship with the world was also taken up by Vygotsky and his followers with their concept of *mediation* (Wertsch, 1993).

practiced by the audio designer, Kenneth, and also by the other composers working in digital media who were interviewed as part of this project. Creativity is an important part of the digital technology with which digital media are produced. Some digital composers regard the notion of musical creativity as never having just *one* dimension. Likewise, digital projects incorporate understandings of music's social, technological, and temporal dimensions. The way the creative agency is distributed across time and space, and the way it forges relations between persons working on video game production, give rise to collective processes. Collective creativity's value is closely related to a sense of what is new, what is novel, and to the discourse of innovation. The highly capitalized culture industries, such as digital media, film and television, emphasize the interplay between individual and collective creativities; and the abiding source of value ascribed to digital media and its creativities are endowed with highly capitalized cultural and creative value.

The successful video games company has a market niche and customers who value its products. The security and growth of video game enterprises depend on **collective creativity**. Audio designers are embedded in an ecological, technological, economic, legal, and social environment with diverse relationships to different stakeholders: employees, colleagues, suppliers, capital providers, competitors, and customers. They see themselves as entrepreneurial musicians who wear several hats. They may be, at different times, composers, improvisers, songwriters, performers, inventors, designers, producers, engineers, entrepreneurs, innovators, and creative team players within a corporate system. They may be involved in collective problem-solving collective creativities. Audio designers rely heavily on, and develop, new and recycled technologies. This involves ever-changing configurations in the field (Applegate, 2010).

In the video game industry, user-creativity is central, ingrained, and part of a game's value. With user-generated content, companies provide tools for their users to comment on, respond to, and evaluate games as they are being developed. User-creativity[30] (by fans and consumers) provides feedback and verification of 'the space of possibles'[31]—what works and what does not. The validation of the game and the recognition of peers have the effect of increasing the right to the rarest possibilities, and, through this assurance, of increasing the audio designer's success and their capacity to realize this success. The ability of the audio designer to orient, affect, and maintain game players' attention with appropriate sound and music depends, in large part, on the possession of significant economic and symbolic capital. Positive or negative responses, what works and what doesn't, encouragement and approval of the game, all indicate to the audio designer the objective truth of the status of the game. The evaluations and verdicts of the users are central to the rapid prototyping that is part of the innovation process of the project cycle.

---

[30] 'User-creativity' is the social space, in which making and consuming are considered to be inseparable parts of the audio design preproduction and production cycle, with sets of evaluation and feedback phases. In the video game industry many companies are entirely based on user-generated content, but also in more traditional industries, such as news media, user-creativity is embedded practice. Today it is as common for online news media companies to provide tools for their readers to comment on news articles and to upload their own images as it is to have a header and a byline, see Wikström (2009).

[31] A term coined by Bourdieu (edited by Grenfell, 2008) and discussed in detail by Toynbee (2000).

Key points

1. A plurality of creativities are inscribed in interactive audio design and development for video game production, including improvisation and compositional modalities of creativity, entrepreneurial, collaborative, and collective creativities, and forms of user-creativity that are valued for the social attribution of meaning given by consumers and the creative power of collaboration.

2. The exchange of social and cultural capital is important not only in the making of game music and sound, but also—indeed, perhaps even more so—in the consumption of music. Chiptune culture has taken the term far beyond hardware synthesis, and to some extent gaming, with audio designers who possess sufficient (sub-) cultural capital to be able to foster a new musical genre, and to help constitute new audiences for this style of music to stand on its own. The Game Boy generation has brought the chiptune back to bear on a microchip, without losing the affordances of the tracker interface or the freedom of digital sampling. Even the most refined and technically elaborated chiptune music captivates a younger audience reared on PlayStations® and the Xbox®, with sound dimensions that focus on the rhythm and sympathy of musical expression and communication in unique ways.

3. Innovation is fully asserted as a cultural capital when it is able to constitute change in the field.

4. Audio interactivity involves innovative mappings between sound, music, and visuals, in which new forms of video gaming appear, and increasingly require new and repurposed technologies and programming to be developed. To this end, the computer as a technological creative agent offers an interactive musical environment that is endowed with musical creativity that does not necessarily depend on real-time human input to generate music. Software programmes generate both complex responses to the game player and subjective/technology interactions that arise from their own internal processes.

Discussion questions

1. Sound artists and audio designers are alike in important ways, yet their musical creativities are different. Explain. Is one part of this statement more important than the other for understanding the nature and value of musical creativity/ies? Why?

2. Are there any possible distinctions and values attached to music creativities and innovations arising from the creative agents who work in digital art and multi-media? If so, what are the possible distinctions? How, then, do we determine whether we are in fact making comparisons within the same musical creativity? In other words, is demarcating a distinction between one musical creativity and another in some sense an arbitrary act that imputes greater unity to practices than may be warranted?

3. Do you believe it reasonable to claim that some forms of musical creativity are better or more creative, than others? If so, outline the criteria you feel might appropriately guide some judgements and criterion building for demonstrating their application in two musical practices you feel clearly differ in value.

Part 3

The field of music in education

Chapter 9

A framework for understanding musical creativities

Introduction

In the previous chapters we have seen how different musical creativities generate practices that are unique in terms of their particular configurations. We have seen how some musical creativities resonate with some musicians' practices in some contexts and not in others. We have also seen that not all music, or musical creativities, are created equal. Performance creativities, wherein folk styles typically involve improvisation on a traditional tune, differ significantly from creating a new work in front of an audience using improvised algorithmic programming. A spectrum of hierarchies and values can be assigned, from on-the-spot improvisation through to formalized and notated composition, made by one individual and presented to an audience by another.[1]

Writing on the values of social interaction as scripted in improvisation, composition, and performance, Cook (forthcoming; see also C. Ford, 1995) deconstructs the different kinds of social interaction embodied in Western 'art' music and jazz improvisation, saying that 'both embody the same relational values: the need to play by ear—to communicate through the public medium of musical sound—means that everyone is open to everyone else, resulting in an ensemble that is egalitarian, or at least in which hierarchies are dynamic and negotiated'. (Cook, forthcoming, p. 8). The key point here is that the production of values is not only, or not simply, a matter of cultural authorship in terms of the construction of particular 'rules of art', but also the product of the field and forms of mediation that cannot be analysed independently of the characteristics of the individual as creator—that is, as the subject of his or her own creation.

Some musical creativities might be characterized quite differently, simply by stressing music's inextricable cultural 'situatedness', the affinities and diversification of musical creativities between different musics, and how the value of creativity to the musician extends deeply into the realm of the sociology of music. So it is important to bring together practices from different genres, and to identify how this spectrum of practices can lead to a logic for multiple musical creativities and a repertory of their authorship, modalities, and principles. My point here, as illustrated in previous chapters, is that musical creativities assume many forms, and serve many diverse functions, and are deeply embedded in the dynamic flux and mutation of a musician's personal and sociocultural life. We have seen how musicians' accounts link to individual histories, and how these lead to a recognition of creative practices in particular configurations as 'modus operandi', all of which are variably constituted within the field of music. We have seen how there is no single creativity that can stand for all music, everywhere, for all time.

Professional musicians who have a clear understanding of what they do and its value position themselves within the field(s) of social systems so as to accumulate particular forms of capital. Their affiliations and networks, and family and cultural heritage are all things that inform what

---

[1] See Allsup (2011) and Davidson and Coulam (2006) for a fascinating discussion of performance creativity in jazz and classical genres.

they do. Their dispositions (or habitus), acquired in their early stages of life, mediate between their social relations and what they think and do enabling them engage creatively in music in a particular way. What is possible is shaped by the field and the particular forms of capital musicians bring to it. Fields are shaped differently according to the rules, histories, legends, and lores that differentiate musical genres. The position and position-taking of these musicians, whether as originals band members, singer-songwriters, DJs, composers, improvisers, professional performers, or audio designers, and the field-to-field interactions of music, are enacted and driven by the logic of the field of music and the interrelationships between and within fields, which are themselves 'boundaried'[2] (see Fig. 9.1). Interrogating the ways in which musical creativities are operationalized by social agents (musicians and institutions), and understanding the social spaces in which musical creativities are valued, and in which they generate capitals as a product of the field of music, is an integral part of understanding musical creativities in the particular configurations of real world practice.

Rather than separating these practices into individual steps, I have described how musicians utilize particular forms of capital and treat them differently, and how the field depends on, and produces, more of that capital. It is the possession of a fertile imagination and an array of dispositional stances and entrepreneurial skills that enables musicians to utilize a variety of different forms of authorship and mediating modalities, which are then unified into a practical perspective (see Fig. 9.2). That is, all practices possess generative schemes, that are themselves both structured and structuring. These are acquired in the course of musicians' lives, and establish their long-term reputations, if not stardom, in the field of music.

In any event, individual professional musicians who work in the music industry, to a large extent, create music both inside and outside the system of commercial music. Their work can be funded by industry or government or both, and can be the result of combining art and commerce in the music.[3] The capacity of musicians to coordinate and sustain their diverse creative activities, whether self-employed or in corporate settings, affiliated with universities or other organizations, depends on their ability to achieve a sustainable practice. The reality of musicians' practices is related to: their potential roles within and outside of the cultural or creative industries; the musical networks in which they move; their awareness, as cultural entrepreneurs, of the need to continually review and develop their career goals and skills (S. Bennett, 2010); and their alliances to particular fields of musical production, as, for example, classical, folk, jazz, or popular music, or digital media or games industries.

Another important issue that arises from the interviewed musicians' descriptions and explanations of their practices concerns the assumptions that are made about their musical creativities when the practice of cultural production usually takes place within organizations and industries, with a focus on output, which is to say, delivering products that are commercially successful. In social psychologist Teresa Amabile's seminal research on individual creativity within organizations

---

[2] The significance of 'boundaried' in Bourdieu's explications of 'field' involves four semi-autonomous levels: the field of power, the broad field under consideration, the specific field, and social agents in the field as a field in themselves. For example, in the field of music, the discipline of music is a field, the musical genre or tradition is a field, and the industries of each genre are fields, within, for instance, the popular music industry.

[3] Frith (1996) has argued that there is no conflict between art and commerce, at least not in the music industry. Wikström (2009) goes further and argues that rock music was created inside the system of commercial music as a result of the integration of creativity and commerce. We see this particularly well illustrated by the opposition between 'major' verses 'indie' (or independent companies), the latter having a stronger focus on the text, the creativity, and the art than on commerce.

(e.g. 1996, 1998), when defining creativity in organizations, she focuses on output, since: 'A product or response will be judged as creative to the extent that (a) it is both a novel and appropriate, useful, correct or valuable response to the task at hand, and (b) the task is heuristic rather than algorithmic' (Amabile, 1996, p. 35). Thus, the relationship between art and commerce is best construed as comprising symbolic forms of power in a range of experiences and motivations, which can be either antagonistic or conducive to musical creation.

Clearly, real world practices are as diverse as the musical creativities, themselves being driven differently by different forms of authorship, mediating modalities, and principles of production. (This is the first main argument of this chapter.) These structures involve a 'complex conjunction of numerous structural determinants and conditions' that apply to the field of industries, whether they are small-scale or medium-sized enterprises.[4] So, the subtleties and complexities, dimensions, and principles that musicians acquire, as recounted in earlier chapters, specify the precise nature of multiple musical creativities, as they relate to the fields within the fields of power. Think, for example, about how cultural production attracts and selects artists with appropriate properties and dispositions within specific fields and field practices; and how, as Bourdieu argued, this depends on the habitus of the musician and the space of available 'possibilities' within the music industry, and the inter-field connections with other industries, and on what can be seen and said about how musicians plot field positions.[5]

Musical creativities and the music industry

Musicians work within the music industry. Whilst it goes beyond the remit of this book to go into the details of what constitutes the music industry,[6] it is generally thought to be rapidly becoming part of a generic entertainment industry wherein major corporations position themselves for expected market shares. Leyshon et al. (1998) present an interesting model of the music industry that features distinctive yet overlapping musical networks.[7] One such network is that of the creativity within which music is created, performed, and recorded. This network includes an army of stakeholders and brokers that work in the record industry with producers, sound engineers, recording companies, managers, lawyers, and the like. This is one of a multiplicity of musical networks in which musicians move and which are crucial in rendering musical creativities.

We have seen in the discourse of the musicians featured in this book that musicians move between tightly defined groups within well-defined fields of music (recordings, concerts, broadcasts, and so on). For example, as shown in Chapter 3, originals bands' musicians work towards getting signed by independent record labels so as to acquire a set of social, cultural, and economic capitals for the value of the symbolic currency that this can offer. Such symbolic value accrues

---

[4] See Wolff (1993). For further discussion of key theories and questions about agency, creativity, and structure, see McIntyre (2010) and other scholars who have shown how musicians working in the music industry, particularly in rock and other popular genres of music, are influenced by economic entities such as the recording, production, publishing and copyright industries.

[5] Bourdieu (1996) mapped positions of best-selling and recognized authors by looking at their dates of birth, stated profession, places of residence, prizes, decorations, and honours, and their publishers. He argued that in the field of art there were two opposing principles of hierarchization—that which meets commercial interests, and that which has no commercial value, or which is produced for its own sake; see also Bourdieu (1993c).

[6] For a detailed discussion of the logic and dynamics of the music industry and related industries and industry models, see Attali (1985), Engeström and Hallencreutz (2003), and Hesmondhalgh and Negus (2002).

[7] Leyshon et al. (1998) present four musical networks, one of which is the network of creativity.

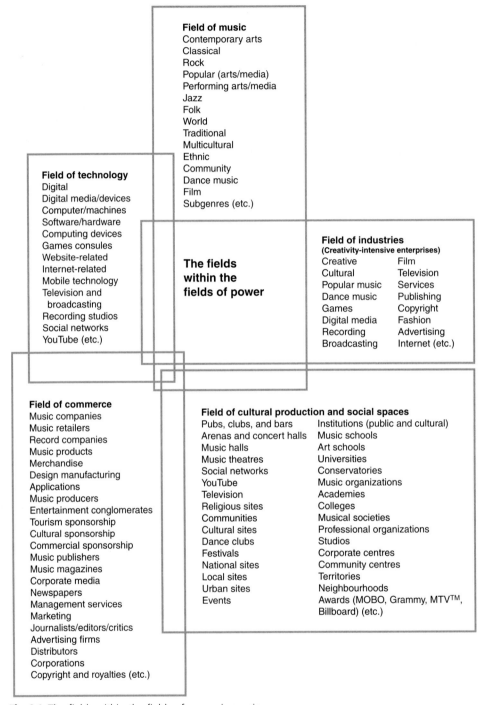

Field of music
Contemporary arts
Classical
Rock
Popular (arts/media)
Performing arts/media
Jazz
Folk
World
Traditional
Multicultural
Ethnic
Community
Dance music
Film
Subgenres (etc.)

Field of technology
Digital
Digital media/devices
Computer/machines
Software/hardware
Computing devices
Games consoles
Website-related
Internet-related
Mobile technology
Television and
  broadcasting
Recording studios
Social networks
YouTube (etc.)

**The fields
within the
fields of power**

Field of industries
(Creativity-intensive enterprises)
Creative   Film
Cultural   Television
Popular music   Services
Dance music   Publishing
Games   Copyright
Digital media   Fashion
Recording   Advertising
Broadcasting   Internet (etc.)

Field of commerce
Music companies
Music retailers
Record companies
Music products
Merchandise
Design manufacturing
Applications
Music producers
Entertainment conglomerates
Tourism sponsorship
Cultural sponsorship
Commercial sponsorship
Music publishers
Music magazines
Corporate media
Newspapers
Management services
Marketing
Journalists/editors/critics
Advertising firms
Distributors
Corporations
Copyright and royalties (etc.)

Field of cultural production and social spaces
Pubs, clubs, and bars   Institutions (public and cultural)
Arenas and concert halls   Music schools
Music halls   Art schools
Music theatres   Universities
Social networks   Conservatories
YouTube   Music organizations
Television   Academies
Religious sites   Colleges
Communities   Musical societies
Cultural sites   Professional organizations
Dance clubs   Studios
Festivals   Corporate centres
National sites   Community centres
Local sites   Territories
Urban sites   Neighbourhoods
Events   Awards (MOBO, Grammy, MTV™,
                             Billboard) (etc.)

Fig. 9.1 The fields within the fields of power in music.

only as a result of recognition from others. It legitimizes and consecrates the musicians' recordings as the outcome of collective creativity within the field.

The singer-songwriters featured in Chapter 4 showed that a similar process of legitimation takes place across the recording and broadcasting industries, the popular music industry, and the creative and cultural industries (Caves, 2000). The economic capital invested in the gaming industry, and in developing content for the global digital and networked infrastructure, causes creative individuals to be driven by commercial pressures to meet timelines and market demands for design innovation, and sits in opposition to the cultural capital associated with public and subsidized cultural institutions and digital art music. Each bears agency, each illustrates music's commodity forms, each demonstrates inventive aesthetics, each struggles for 'distinction'. This generates the paradox noted by Bourdieu (1996) that some art appears 'naturally more cultured' than others and, in a more general sense, generates criteria for judging one type of art to be 'higher' or 'lower' than another.

Musicians are constantly repositioning themselves across multiple fields. From the collective creativity of collaborative teams to the empathic creativity of improvised musics, we see musicians broaden their remit and locate their work across different industries. We see technology empowering musicians to communicate directly with their fans and audiences, using social networks and the digital distribution of music.

New industries overlap the music industry. The effect of this is to change how artists and audiences, DJs and crowds, audio designers, and consumers think about musical creativities, and how they cultivate distinguishing features based on 'in-group' identification and interaction. Think, for example, of the practices of DJ, producer, and remixer, reuser, de-composer, sound organizer, and 'scratcher'[8] examples of which were introduced in Chapter 5, and the sharers of music in digital formats, and consider 'the many ways in which existing music is recycled, remixed and repackaged' (Blake, 2007, p. 67). Here, in the midst of existing hierarchical social relations, the DJ imports ready-made material as a common and well-established practice. In contrast, the performance of live improvised musics draws on an array of unexpected sounds in the 'moment-to-moment interaction' of improvisation, since the aim here is 'to spur musicians to play genuinely in the moment, relying solely on their ingenuity and their instantaneous responses to the contributions of fellow performers' (Cox and Warner, 2009, p. 251). Or, again, consider live coding programmer-musicians working with algorithms. All these different techniques of performance involve unwritten 'rules of the game', but generate practices and attribute meanings in accordance with the values 'of a musical community in opposition to a music industry that solely values objects and commodities' (Cox and Warner, 2009, p. 251).

Arguments about 'high art' and 'low art' creativity proceed apace, as several chapters in this book have shown. We need to acknowledge the myriad of forms of multiply mediated musical creativities that arise in musical spaces and that these are deeply influenced by a series of complex factors: different communities of taste; the political economy of music; the way that musical creativities impact on the performance space itself; the open sourcing of recorded sound; the dialectic through which new musical sounds influence the development of tastes; digital technologies that influence the mobility and flexibility of music-making practices; the globalization of the music industry and local market forces; and the spread of new music-making and reproducing technologies.

---

[8] The term 'scratching' was coined to describe the practice of the real time manipulation of 12" discs on adapted turntables by DJs. See Cox and Warner (2009).

All of this is codified and commodified by 'the game of culture'[9] and by huge entertainment corporations.

What might be seen in one industry as being very creative indeed, and at the forefront of development, may not be valued in another. We know which music retains the power to fascinate audiences for centuries, and why some musical structures engage our creative capacities as listeners and others do not; but the boundaries of authorship have blurred, and we need to understand how musical creativities are understood and assigned meaning. The individual acquires, in the Bourdieuian sense, a 'feel for the game', a 'practical sense' (*sens practique*) that allows agents to act and react in specific situations in a manner that is not always calculated, and that is not simply a question of conscious obedience to rules. Rather, it is a set of dispositions linked to individual history (i.e. the musician's habitus) that generates practices and perceptions (R. Johnson, 1993).

If there really is 'no way out of the game' of culture, our best option is to understand the game, and work out the most appropriate and useful ways of playing it. Bourdieu's writings on the field of cultural production and tools of habitus and capital go some distance to help us understand the 'game', and conceptualize changing forms of musical creativities that involve new ways of viewing, conceiving, and approaching them as acts of creating music in the age of digital media.

Musical creativities and the rules of fields

This section offers a modest contribution to the growing literature on the social and political significance and economy of musical creativities (Cloonan, 2007; Leyshon et al., 1998; Sexton, 2007; Toynbee, 2000). Music sits at the centre of the performing and creative arts, of the cultural and creative industries and of the technological, commercial, and cultural production fields. We are witnessing a proliferation of aesthetic trends, of creative works that are made in a particular place and time, of the principles behind people's tastes, and of the meanings that are attached to these sorts of practices, particularly in relation to digital production and consumption. An expanded set of creative practices is emerging from: (1) the popular music industry, with the digital music revolution that has taken place in the past few decades;[10] (2) the games industry, with music and sound that has been 'scored' for, or adapted to, the rich multi-media environment of video games; and (3) the dance music industry. This makes it impossible, or at least inappropriate, to collapse various social groups and various social experiences into a single group, single experience, or single practice in the interests of arguing for a dominant field-specific logic. While the diversity of music matters, it does so in a way that is different from when creativities are the affective centre and agency of music. This raises a variety of issues relating to the old, narrowly construed and outmoded, formulations of musical creativity, which, no longer adequately describe practices in the digital world.

The multiplicity of musical creativities that we have identified enables us to understand what is distinctive about current practices, and how musicians position themselves within a particular field, making judgements to establish values for social, cultural, and economic capital. The musicians' accounts featured in this book show how the field of contemporary music and musicians

---

[9] Bourdieu (1984b) commenting on the meanings that are attached to the practices that constitute the field of cultural production, says: 'There is no way out of the game of culture; and one's only chance of objectifying the true nature of the game is to objectify as fully as possible the very operations which one is obliged to use in order to achieve that objectification' (p. 12).

[10] For a discussion of the record industry and the effect of the Internet and the digitization of music, see Born (1993) and Kusek and Leonhard (2005).

connects with other fields and, ultimately, the fields of technology, commerce, performance venues, and education (see Fig. 9.1).

Musical creativities and power

Because music is part of the field of power, the 'culturally arbitrary' ensures that things that are valued by dominant people, institutions and events are valued (at least in principle) by everyone, whether they like them, or use them, or not. The musician's habitus, in terms of what some sociologists describe as the 'specialization' or 'cultivation' of consciousness and the recognized mastery of a technique,[11] is supported by the values and discourses of the general social field, and the specific logic and history of the musical field. So the specific logic of the field of music, with its well-documented hierarchy and oppositions between genres of the field, can be understood in terms of Bourdieu's use of the term 'capital' and the symbolic value associated with and reflected by the intrinsic value of art works, and the capacity of those individuals regarded as having attained 'distinction' in the field to recognize and appreciate the cultural specifics of a domain.[12]

For example, in the popular music industry, the band that finds commercial success can be discredited if they are seen as compromising, negative, and 'vulgar' because of their quest for popularity, or they can be acclaimed for the prestige attached to stardom and popularity. It has been argued that musicians define their own status according to the different forms of capital associated with the different degrees of financial reward accruing from different performance events. Session players, or those who perform with well-established groups, earn more money than those who play in pubs, or give less frequent performances of free jazz, or live coders who play for boutique audiences.[13]

Bourdieu (1996a/1992) defines the field of power as 'the set of relations of force between agents or institutions having in common the possession of the capital necessary to occupy the dominant positions in different fields (notably economic or cultural)' (p. 215). This idea is important for explaining the distinctiveness and multiplicity of musical creativities, and how they belong to well-defined fields of music. For example, the DJ practices described in Chapter 5 illustrate an external function of music as a scene-making practice that operates either within the dance music industry or which can be used to support a prestigious corporate image and position within the more general field of power. The dynamic nature of these field interactions is further revealed by the 'self-making' that authorizes DJ identity, and contributes to 'place-making' and the normative conditions of a dance or club culture. DJs use field positioning to establish stylistic domination of the field: (1) in the production of new remixes; (2) in stardom associated with international guest appearances; (3) in the status associated with venues that are authorized to represent important sites for governing reputations; and (3) by a powerful set of pre-existing social conditions and material relations that regulate DJ work of international standing, the O2 arena for instance.

There is a mutual exchange of cultural and economic capital and instances of 'structured structuring' within the dance music and digital media industries, the commercial field of retailers and record companies, and the clubs and DJs who authorize what music is played. Commercial partnerships and sponsorships by business also influence the particular conditions in which creativities are constituted, the habitus of creators, positions taken in the music field, and in the field of power itself. Think, for example, about game audio designers who generate video game music in

---

[11] See 'Capital' discussed by Moore, 'Field' discussed by Thomson, and 'Habitus' discussed by Maton (2008, cited in Greenfell, 2008, pp. 49–67, 101).

[12] For more on 'particularities of genres' see Bourdieu (1984b).

[13] For further discussion of professional music-making, see Cottrell (2004).

collaborative teams, for whom the primary function of music is to motivate the player in game narratives, or to reflect the player's psychological state. Generally speaking, corporate entrepreneurship involves the recognition and exploitation of entrepreneurial ideas by collaborating teams. The future commercial success of the video lies in video game companies bringing together a group of people to create games for players who may not share an aesthetic disposition. Apart from their shared love of a particular game, video game players do not necessarily have much in common, but rather represent a multitude of people from diverse social origins for whom the function of the music in mediating the video gaming experience is all-important. The company has to learn from consumers, competitors, and other entrepreneurs, and from those seeking to elaborate an aesthetic for video game music and sound.[14] This latter group might be concerned about the extent to which a game did or did not conform to the conventions and rules of classic narratives. The company does this simply by noting (1) the things that are valued by dominant people, institutions (public schools, arenas, music theatres) and events (the Grammy Awards, MOBO Awards, MTV™ Immies,[15] Billboard Music Awards), and (2) the presence or absence of music at any point in the game, and its relevance to high and low art users. There are a multitude of positions, practices, logics, and values that form strong relationships between the fields of gaming, media, publishing, and music.

Bourdieu (1996a) clarifies the relationship between fields of power: 'It is a very general property of *fields* that the competition for what is at stake conceals collusion over the very principles of the game. The struggle for the monopoly of legitimacy helps to reinforce the legitimacy in the name of which it is waged' (p. 167, original emphasis). Think, for example, of the Olympic Games opening ceremony as a site for the exercise of social dominance. The practices that are followed use musical symbols, images, and discourses to shape the very rules of performance creativity. They are rendered visible in the opening ceremony by the country hosting the Olympic Games. As virtually any Olympic Games opening ceremony testifies, the attitudes and values of a society are expressed in performances that draw on past, present, and anticipated future musical practices and performance arts in general. All the music, musicians, and practices are instances of symbolic power and function in action.

This symbolic function and symbolic capital, especially that of creative products and the people who make them, is controlled by those 'gatekeepers' who are authorized to make judgements, such as an organizing committee or commissioning body. That is to say, the values underpinning the system of generative activity, or the type of creativity with which the music is constituted, are made to seem universally significant. These practices arise because they are important to dominant people and institutions, and because they come to be inscribed in the habitus and supported by the values and discourses of the field. In the case of the Olympic Games opening ceremony, this is executed by carefully selecting celebrity figures belonging to the 'establishment' and performing 'established' past masters.

There is a clear cultural and economic basis for choosing people from the field of artistic production according to the degree of recognized legitimacy bestowed on them, people who represent the field of music and who will best brand the event. The rules of musical production must be understood in terms of their sociocultural conditions of production, just as in aesthetic sense, the production of music is to be understood as essentially embedded within the structure of society. With the singer-songwriters featured at the Royal Buckingham Palace for the Queen, as discussed in Chapter 1, we see a perfect example of the dominant circles in which aesthetic judgements are

---

[14] For further discussion, see Sexton (2007).
[15] MTV™ Immies are held every year and aim to award the best talents in the Indian music industry.

made, and how celebrity musicians are products of a particular place and time, and of the gate-keepers who promote their personal interests—or, in Bourdieu-speak, of the dominant culture.

Figure 9.1 shows the fields within fields. It offers a static representation of a dynamic and ever-changing process. An individual musician, in terms of the structure of the field and the way it is mutually constituted, may struggle for position within any specific one, and within the fields within fields. The composers featured in Chapter 6 all work with contemporary ensembles, and depend on collaborative projects between musicians and media sponsors. The habitus of each contemporary ensemble is essentially distinct, and offers a potent configuration of social, cultural, and economic capital that can be used effectively to accelerate the ensemble's trajectory in the field of music and the industrial fields of the cultural, broadcasting, publishing, and recording industries. Audio designers working in the gaming industry come up with products that give consumers what they want, thereby driving revenues within the fields of commerce, technology, and industry. Both DJs and originals bands, as with singer-songwriters, are field participants in the field of popular music, as well as in the fields of technology and industry, and hence have accrued symbolic cultural capital which can be deployed within the artistic field itself. Audio designers help the companies in which they work to maintain a prestigious corporate image, and to position them strategically within the more general field of commerce.

Multiple musical creativities deployed within real world practice are dependent on key factors, such as whether they are based in popular media rather than in fine art, or have to do with personal politics rather than national politics, or are founded on the commercial enterprise that mediates the symbolic and economic capital ascribed to products arising from certain combinations of musical creativities. All these factors influence individual habitus, positions in the music field and the field of power itself. Distinctive attributes of musical creativities are found in real world practices in relation to particular types of performance spaces, concerts, and related events. Together they help constitute a particular genre. For instance, the traditional image of evening dress is considered appropriate for serious presentations of art music, compared with the more informal performances favoured by newer music by less familiar composers, or for live improvised musics, or situations wherein some of the conventional patterns of behaviour do not apply, such as popular music by an originals band, or a singer-songwriter performing esoteric genres at the fringes of culture, or DJs at a club.

Bourdieu argues that 'symbolic profit', which determines the specific hierarchy established among works and composers, songs and songwriters, club cultures and DJs, with these hierarchized categories corresponding to the social hierarchy of the respective audiences, actually constructs musical creativities by providing things and people with a specifically social being, by contributing to their public recognition.

> To the extent that the field progressively gains in autonomy and imposes its own logic, these genres also grow more distinct from each other, and more clearly so, according to the degree of intrinsically *symbolic credit* they possess and confer, this tending to vary in inverse relation to economic profit. In effect, the credit attached to any cultural practice tends to decrease with the numbers and especially the social spread of the audience, because the value of the credit of recognition ensured by consumption decreases when the specific competence recognized in the consumer decreases (and even tends to change sign when it descends below a certain threshold).

> (Bourdieu, 1996, p. 115, original emphasis)

Musicians, as well as companies, respond to distinctive taste patterns in the varied markets in which they work. This forms the basis of the 'pop charts', which translate into market forces via the consumption of records. New technologies are making the music industry larger, changing the relationships between record labels and artists, helping the spread of new music and the making of new music, as well as leading musicians down diverse paths as creators, producers, and performers.

Thus far we have talked about the field of music, the habitus of musicians, and the specific practices of musicians working in real world contexts. The correspondences between the ways in which musicians position themselves in the field and their myriad forms of authorship and mediations provides a coherent pattern of evidence for multiple musical creativities. How are these musical creativities differentiated, and how do they give rise to distinct practices?

Towards a framework (for the study) of multiple music creativities and the configurations of practice: a practice perspective of music creativities

Before moving on, let me sum up the arguments I have advanced so far concerning the essential differentiating features between musical creativities, and put forward a framework for understanding multiple music creativities in real world practice.

My understanding of multiple musical creativities has its roots in Csikszentmihalyi's three-pronged systems model of generic creativity, a model that has been embraced by other seminal thinkers about creativity (see, for example, Feldman et al., 1994). I do not question the importance and usefulness of highlighting interaction as an essential component of a three-pronged system 'composed of a culture (and micro-cultures or neo-tribes)[16] that contains symbolic rules, a person who brings novelty into the domain, and a field of experts who recognize and validate the innovation' (Csikszentmihalyi, 1988, 1990, 1996, 1999) (Fig. 9.2). However, I do take issue with the way in which these categories are used. As we have seen with the musicians featured in Part 2 of this book, the category of a 'domain' (cultures are sets of domains) does not arise in the same way in all areas of musical creation. The category is problematic in that it is not the only entity that influences and engages musicians' creative production. Besides this there are key relationships between artists and audiences, bands and their fans, DJs and dance crowds, and audio designers and users. Fans, dancers, and listeners all have varying degrees of input into the creative process; and so too do the fields of technology and industry, commerce, and cultural production. A field comprises those people who can affect the structure of a domain. It is also important to recognize, as Starko (2001) rightly points out, that 'it is possible for individuals to create works that are not accepted by the field at the time they are created' (pp. 62–3).

Bourdieu's work on the notion of 'field' (and 'capital' and 'habitus') is helpful for examining the relationship between individual subjects/actors, on the one hand, and social/ideological/economic structures, on the other, and for understanding how processes of subjectivity and identity are formed in particular fields of social production. Bourdieu (1993c) posits a considerably more complex view of the 'field' as consisting of a 'separate social universe having its own laws of functioning' (p. 162), wherein networks of positions are objectively held and constituted by the logic of the field, or rules of the game. A field constitutes specific forms of practices, and principles of both the practice and work produced within it. For music, the structure of the field influences the possibilities for having music published, broadcast, downloaded, and the principles behind people's tasks—why some people spend their time and energy in making cultural products, and the meaning attached to these practices by social groups. As shown in Fig. 9.1, many overlapping networks are constituted by a field at the time music is created. The fact that there are more people than just the individual creating a symbol system and cultural tradition affects the structure of a domain.

---

[16] Terms used by A. Bennett (1999) to describe the sociological study of the relationship between youth, music, style and identity.

In the field of music, there is no single, privileged cultural, social system of musical creativity but, as Born (2005) argues, there is 'perhaps the paradigmatic multiply-mediated, immaterial and material, fluid quasi-object, in which subjects and objects collide and intermingle . . . Music takes myriad social forms' (p. 7).

What distinguishes multiple music creativities is the diversity of actors in a field and its overlapping ones, along with a myriad social systems that become powerful modalities of action in communities. These modalities include social practices, social relations, and the social mediations that take place in social spaces. They are tied to historical practices, as well as new global and transnational, national, regional, and local practices. The gatekeepers may or may not have the breadth of knowledge required of them, and may be tied to singular and sedimented historical practices. They may, nonetheless, be called on to navigate a myriad of domains driven by technological and powerful modalities of temporal action that draw upon the digitization of music and art, and unprecedented shifts in the concept of musical work.

The systems model (see Fig. 9.2) encourages us to look beyond the dominant discourse, and to steer constantly back and forth between the circles/triangles of culture, person, and field. But, as Bourdieu (1990) argues, the relationship between people's practices and the contexts in which

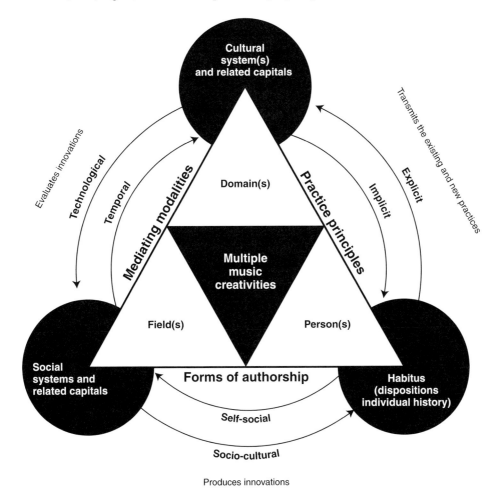

Fig. 9.2 A synthesized framework for understanding multiple musical creativities integrating the theories of Csikszentmihalyi (1999) and Bourdieu (1993c).

those practices occur are a consequence of 'schemes of action and perception, which, never having been constituted as explicit principles, can only produce an unwilled necessity, which is therefore necessarily imperfect but also a little miraculous' (p. 13). The practice of creativity, whether in the programming of live coding or the remixing of DJs, is the locus for diverse renderings of musical creativities. This chapter provides insights into how manifold forms of musical creativity are observable and are located as practices. The sites of practice featured in Part 3 include the school classroom, the community, cultural settings, arts partnership organizations and teacher education programmes. These sites of practice illustrate, as Bourdieu has argued, that the ideas, values, and beliefs by which a practice arises involve schemes of action and perception, situated in and governed by space and time. Figure 9.2 provides a schematic diagram of the forms of musical creativity inscribed in the practices reported in Part 2.

Csikszentmihalyi (1999) takes the position that creativity means 'the ability to add something new' to the 'culture'. Fig. 9.2 builds on his systems perspective. Individual creation, he says, must be 'sanctioned by some group entitled to make decisions as to what should or should not be included in the domain' (p. 317). Music is a multiply mediated discipline or 'domain', with rules and practices involving an interplay between symbol systems that emerge from and are influenced by the social system, or 'field' wherein gatekeepers, experts, and scholars have the right to choose the variations that can be preserved in that domain. Cultural forces and cultural institutions, therefore, produce deeply entrenched forms of cultural practices, which are not only tied to authorized domains, but are also linked to the ways in which music creativities are represented by different cultures and cultural systems.

Musical creativity is not a single object common to all cultures. There is no single cultural system but rather a myriad cultural systems represented by musicians in the field (see, for instance, Chapter 7, for discussions with folk musician Hazel Fairbairn, who participates in Irish, Scottish, and European styles of fiddle playing). Musical creativities also refer to real world activities that represent both sense-making and place-making activities (think for example about the DJ club cultures discussed in Chapter 5, and singer-songwriter Roshi's Iranian-Welsh sound-signature). Global media practices on the Internet make use of networked musical creativities (see, for example, networked improvisations such as Jam2Jam[17] or the collective production of many separate designers working collaboratively on different parts of a video game to realize new qualities or new production methods).

Bourdieu's notion of 'cultural capital' illustrates interdependence of access to cultural, economic, and political positions. Through their listening creativity, audiences are not passive consumers because cultural products are partly constructed by listeners contributing to the musical work (Wolff, 1993). Think, for example, how interactive audio designer Kenneth Young, in Chapter 8, promotes user interaction, and how originals band TFN, in Chapter 3, encourages fans to vote for their favourite tracks for inclusion on its next album. The potential for a democratized and collective creative practice is encapsulated in popular music's notion of the 'group', and the 'co-presence' of the record producer in the recordings of Zoey van Goey. These are cultural capitals at the heart of jazz or free improvisation. They include the interactional qualities of empathic creativity, folk music's community practices, which are imbued with collective memory, and the many musical landscapes of creative possibility across cultures and countries in which concepts of networked creativity are grounded less in notions of musical expert systems than in a shared wonder that requires new ways of thinking about virtual communities and new

---

[17] Jam2Jam is an application which generates music that you can control while it plays. Even better, you can connect via a network with others who have Jam2Jam to jointly control the music. You can jam just like a band, but without the need for complex instrumental skills.

musical hybridities. There are also multiple sub-cultures wherein music is created at the margins of fields. And this space is always necessarily inhabited by young people who live on these margins, and who attempt to reinvent themselves through sub-cultural musical narratives.[18]

For these reasons, expanding Csikszentmihalyi's 'systems model of creativity' (1999) from a heuristically promising approach to a point where it represents the myriad of multiply mediated music creativities must do justice to the practical logic of real world practice as well as to the objective structures within which such action takes place. Diverse practices were evident in the fluid roles between composer and performer in Robert's contemporary ensemble Topology, as discussed in Chapter 6, the DJ's culture and audiences in Chapter 5, and the practices of the live coders featured in Chapter 7, which constitute a specific social space of digital musicians. The point here is that the systems model is a heuristic which falls short on many counts. The details of the 'system', and how elements interact with each other within it, still needs to be clarified. There is a need to map the proliferation and diversification of musical creativities by professionals in the music industry, the mediating temporal and technological modalities, the forms of authorship, and the principles and production practices that characterize real world social groups. Combining Csikszentmihalyi's (1999) systems model with Bourdieu's (1993) ideas (Fig. 9.2) and real world production practices encourages us to look beyond the dominant discourse, to steer constantly back and forth between the circles/triangles of culture, person and field. As Bourdieu (1990) suggests, 'practice' is a consequence of 'schemes of action and perception, which, never having been constituted as explicit principles, can only produce an unwilled necessity that is therefore necessarily imperfect but also a little miraculous' (p. 13).

The significance of this framework is that it provides insight into how multiple musical creativities are observable and can be located in practice. The sites of practice featured in previous chapters include studios, performance venues, cultural settings, corporations, music festivals, institutions, and organizations. These sites of practice illustrate, as Bourdieu argued, that the ideas, values, and beliefs by which 'practice' engenders and mediates musical creativities depend on the conventions and legitimating frameworks of a specific activity situated in, and governed by, space and time.

Musical creativities and new forms of authorship

So far, I have rejected the simple linear conception of a single creativity for one super-genre, 'music', and proposed instead a multiplicity of musical creativities deriving from the complexity of the social world in which the musician is located. As shown in several chapters of this book, new musical creativities are being born, crossing territories, linking fields, and transgressing the boundaries of organizations, corporations and fields of commerce all the time. Certain practices and new technologies favour certain forms of authorship.

The traditional notion of 'the artist' or 'the author', seen from a sociological point of view, has been explored by many critical theorists and sociologists. Wolff (1993) moved away from the conception of the author as 'a fixed and monolithic originator of meanings' to a view that the author 'must be seen as constructed by social and ideological factors—and moreover, constantly re-constructed in this way—rather than as an entity above these factors, developing by some internal logic of its own' (p. 129). Toynbee (2000), on the other hand, speaks of ways of understanding authorship in popular music, as well as in the novel, in terms of 'social authorship'. He says:

> the social author stands at the centre of a radius of creativity, but the range and scale of voices available to her/him/them will always be strongly determined by the compass and position of the radius on

---

[18] For further discussion of youth music cultures, see Dillabough and Kennelly (2010).

the musical field. Perhaps the biggest advantage of treating popular music authorship in such a way is that it enables one to be sceptical about grand claims to creative inspiration (sometimes made by musicians themselves) without discarding the notion of agency, as voices in collective musical endeavour. (p. 46)

Toynbee also draws on Bourdieu's tools of habitus, fields, and capitals, and suggests that practices are generated by the habitus, for which the computer can act as a creative tool and partner in co-authoring musical creations. Blake (2007) goes further to say that,

a creative process which has been in many cases displaced from the body to the machine, and from the composer or performer to the DJ, producer and remixer . . . [in ways in which] . . . the music business has become increasingly jealous of its absolute 'rights' in the ownership of what it identifies as discrete pieces of music . . . by further new ways of making and distributing music. (p. 67)

Similar questions of composers' intentions and the 'authorial intention' have been addressed by the hermeneutics of music.[19]

Music arises not simply from individual composers' minds, but in constructions that reflect the tastes and fashions of social groups, social relations, and communities sharing common perspectives. The opposition of the individual to society has now been rejected, and evidence from this book and elsewhere reinforces the view that composers can only exist or be known as such through the social discourses and practices in which they are constituted. From the accounts of professional composers we see how the multilayered self is both enabled and understood in terms of itself and the social realms that capacitate these composers. Whilst the music studio may be one site where individual composers often take refuge, the embeddedness of their work in broader social and sociocultural relations negotiates the relationship of the self to the sociality of composing.

The forms of authorship identified in the real world practice of the musicians featured in this book emerge in two particular forms. The first are self-social forms of authorship involving the relational practices of personal (self-making), collaborative, and communal creativities, and the collective creativity bound up in the place and space that authorize the practice. This can also involve broader organizational or corporate forces in games, dance music, and popular music industries, or it can be tied directly to particular musical practices or subgenred forms, as with live coding. The second are sociocultural forms of authorship that are authorized to greater or lesser degrees by the various forms of cultural authorization that a spatial context provides, such as club cultures, folk traditions, ethnic styles, and other codified practices. To appreciate this we need to understand the rules and orientations of what Bourdieu (1999) has identified as the 'authorized language', whereby particular types of creativities emerge.[20] Forms of authorship can be cultural, intercultural, cross-cultural, multicultural, sub-cultural, ethnic, diasporic, fan-based, audience-based, crowd-based, or user-based. As an example, consider the kinds of intercultural forms featured in Chapter 4 with singer-songwriter Roshi, whose practices involve Iranian/Welsh cultural history expressed as a kind of an inward construct—like a silent attitude or insight.

---

[19] For an excellent discussion of authorial intention that represents diverse sides of the issue and discussion on the nature of disciplinary knowledge, see Iseminger (2006), Maton (2010a,b), and Maton and Moore (2010).

[20] We see territorial practices involving socio-spatial dimensions of place and space played out particularly in dance clubs by DJs. The 'authorized language' of DJs includes 'place-making' and 'self-making', allowing particular types of music creativity to emerge.

Musical creativities' temporal modalities

The concept of mediation occupies centre stage in the development of both critical musicology and the cultural studies of music. Born (2005) proposes mediation to be a concept that is 'from one perspective . . . the clue to transcending idealist ontologies of music; from a second, mediation [can be regarded] as diplomacy, as the negotiation between apparently incommensurable worlds' (p. 11). It is a useful concept in accounting for the dialectic between time and technology and their interrelations in music.

The concept of musical creativities emerges not only as a fluid entity but also as a relational practice representing temporal and technological mediations. Given that musical creativities concern explicitly what producers and listeners do, it is not surprising that the distinctions between improvising, composing and performing are far from clear. There are those who claim 'that the activities that we call "composing" and "performing" are essentially improvisational in nature' (Benson, 2003, p. 2), and that 'to improvise is not to compose' (Wolterstorff, 1994, p. 64). Stravinsky (1947) wrote about the work-based practice of composing a musical work as being 'the fruit of study, reasoning, and calculation that imply exactly the converse of improvisation' (p. 138). Whether the creation of music occurs during a performance, or in a notated composition, or is scored by one individual by hand or by another with a computer, the emphasis, as has been argued by Davidson and Coulam (2006), of 'this composition-performance spectrum depends on the cultural context' (p. 180). Creating a new work can be about performance creativity, that is, how a performer 'owns' the music through 'personal invention' by bringing into existence, as Cook (1998) argues, newly articulated interpretations and forms of expertise of musical production (Cook, 1998). Considerations of time are seen to be very important by Clifton (1983), an applied phenomenologist, who described music as being 'time in motion' and regards 'the unfolding of a piece of music' as 'an *act*' with time as a mediating concept (p. 81).

Music can be created in myriad ways. Its temporal mediations include compositional, improvisational, and performance creativities. These practices represent particular generative behaviours. For example, DJs engage in a kind of improvised performance, and extend and intensify the effect of rhythmic passages, combining them with other music to create new forms of live improvised music. DJs also engage in innovative practices of de-composition followed by re-composition, including sampling, mashups, dubbing, toasting, scratching, and isolating break-beats, and other bits of recorded sound and music, whereby music is remixed live with other sounds. For DJs certainly, but also for singer-songwriters, originals bands, and contemporary composers, the status of musical material becomes extraordinarily fluid. What might be a complete remix, song, track, or scripted musical work, including new material or reworkings of old, may subsequently be sourced for improvisatory inclusion in another work or another performance. Performance creativity can be repetition with a difference. Collaborative improvisation (e.g. Jam2Jam) can be achieved through digitized forms of music-making whereby the music is collectively generated and owned. Personal authorship and ownership in personal creativity can give way to a sense of communal authorship and ownership in communal creativity, when the musician's position in the chain of performer-creators (as with much live improvised musics) benefits from a personal contribution to the communal generation of the music.

Technological mediations constantly reconfigure musical creativities as practices that supersede the concept of a fixed, notated, musical work. Digital music media both extend and afford entirely new forms of authorship. For example, collaborative creativity can be networked, distributed, or relayed in the form of code, open to distribution via the Internet, allowing music to be de-composed and re-composed by a series of creative agents. This form of musical creativity, which has been coined 'relayed creativity',[21] uses digital operations to reconfigure and disperse musical creativities, giving rise to practices such as networked creativity involving a music-sharing or generative site, or the distributed creativity of gaming, whereby elements of sound and music are contributed by a teamworking on a game soundtrack, or relayed creativities when sound and music are distributed across the Internet and thus become continually and immanently open to de-composition and re-composition by any number of creative agents.

These practices, as have been described in previous chapters, are grounded in certain principles. They can operate at the centre or the borders of cultures, in spaces with 'authorized languages'[22] with particular modes of expression, and in performances which are authorized to greater or lesser degrees by various forms of music creativities that can take myriad forms of authorship and are multiply mediated. Each practice, however, can be identified, and contains within it sets of relations that operate in the context of other spatial relations and practices bound to social spaces wherein other fields of music are authorized. These fields are linked to fields of industry, commerce, and cultural production and are characterized by the defining structural logic of differentiation within the field, including its links with other fields. The temporal dimension of music also incorporates recorded, virtual, live, and sociospatial practices, whereby the audience might be a 'crowd', 'user', or 'fan', and where the roles of producer and audience/consumer overlap.

Musical creativities' technological mediations

We live in an increasingly technologically mediated world where our everyday lives are dominated by digital media. We make daily use of CDs, the Internet, mp3 players and iTunes. For teenagers, an iPod is both a status symbol and an object that shapes their everyday experience of the digital–audio–visual environments. The music that is chosen for an iPod's memory is particularly important since it represents identity and provides a powerful symbol of youth cultural practice (Dillabough and Kennelly, 2010). Such gadgets offer young people modes of musical participation, increased access to music, and tools for mediating their musical experience. Furthermore, these technologies can be adapted from professional studios to home environments, in which the practice of making, receiving, and creating music may change dramatically (Folkestad, 2006).

The notion of creativity being in relationship with, or emerging through, technology assumes we know where technology belongs and how it is embodied in accounts of creativity. Whilst some work has been published in this area (Brown and Dillon, 2007; T. Dillon, 2006; Ruthmann, 2007a; Savage, 2007; Seddon and O'Neill, 2006, 2003), our understanding of how this translates from art and industry to home and education is still imperfect.

Recent research has shown that new learning environments, such as the Internet, can facilitate the intersection of formal and informal educational settings (Webster and Hickey, 2006). The Internet, in particular, has shown itself to be a dynamic teaching tool for exploring, discovering, creating, communicating about, and playing in virtual music-making contexts. It provides a mechanism for connecting a network of places, spaces (both physical and symbolic), musical worlds, music-makers, generators, performances, and productions. In doing so, it enables participation across places and fields through multiple forms of expression. (For an example of the opportunities offered this kind of learning environment, see Futurelabs.[23])

---

[21] 'Relayed creativity' is a term coined by Born (2005).

[22] Bourdieu (1999) refers to 'authorised languages' as the particular forms of cultural authorization that provide legitimacy for certain practices within a particular space and place (p. 77).

[23] Futurelab is a non-governmental organization that develops creative and innovative approaches to education, teaching, and learning, particularly in the area of digital literacy and participation, learning spaces, play and computer games. See hwww.futurelab.org.uk.

The establishment of a community of engagement was implicit in the perspectives on nurturing creativity in a computer-mediated learning environment by teams involved in *Aspire*, *5x5x5=creativity* and *Beyond Current Horizons*, programmes to support futures thinking.[24] This initiative offered a combination of residential creativity labs (for 10–15-year-olds) and creativity fellowships with mentors and creative advisers (for 16–21-year-olds). The accounts of the 10–15-year-olds highlight their need to overcome fear of failure and feelings of self-consciousness (Burnard, 2006b). The kinds of challenges and dilemmas young people face, particularly when working creatively with technology, may affect how those who aspire to excel view themselves creatively in relation to the technology they use at school (Craft et al., 2008).

Globally spatialized Internet forms include digital and mobile music, their social networks, and the fluid roles in contemporary popular music between musicians, DJs, and audiences. For instance, the website 'ccmixter' declares itself to be 'a music sharing site featuring songs licensed under Creative Commons, where you can listen to, sample, mash-up or interact with music in whatever way you want . . . [and then] upload your version for others to . . . re-sample'[25] involving 185 voices from 12 countries which join a choir that spans the globe.) *Lux Aurumque*, which was composed and conducted by Eric Whitacre, and which merges hundreds of tracks individually recorded and posted to YouTube, is an astonishing illustration of how technology can connect us. Then again, YouTube is a means for pooling talent and downloading free audio feeds without having to call auditions locally and pay for professional talent to make a recording.

We all live technologically mediated lives. The easy use of the mobile phone, the games console, and the Internet has seen sound, vision, and information coalesce in a range of increasingly linked technological ways (Buckingham, 2005). It has led to the development of a new language to describe creating music as computer-generated, computer-mediated, software-based, hi-tech, low-tech, digital, digital-media-based—drawing on particular uses of programs and programming, using mobile technology and the Internet, and utilizing live, virtual, or recorded forms.

Earlier in this chapter I asked how the diversification of multiple musical creativities works in practice. I have just implicated six different ways in which musicians, strong in their particular competence as professionals and well-established in various musical practices, generate distinct musical creativities to produce certain types of music in certain types of social space which provide the basis for its production and reproduction. As shown in Fig. 9.3, these are:

(i)	self-social	and	(ii)	socio-cultural forms of authorship
(iii)	temporal	and	(iv)	technological mediating modalities
(v)	explicit	and	(vi)	implicit practice principles

(These are listed in detail in Appendix D, and were also elaborated earlier in this chapter.)

---

[24] *Aspire* is an approach to creative school transformation that offers a key role to students as researchers and ways of enacting educational futures at local level (http://education.exeter.ac.uk/aspire). 5x5x5=creativity is an independent, arts-based action research organization with charitable status supporting children and young people in developing creative skills for life. Artists, settings, and cultural centres collaborate to develop creative values, dispositions, relationships, and environments. It is an approach that puts the arts at the heart of educational futures (www.5x5x5creativity.org.uk). Beyond Current Horizons is the UK's strategic foresight project for education. It includes over 80 reviews of research and evidence in the area of socio-technological change and education (www.beyondcurrenthorizons.org.uk).

[25] See www.ccmixter.org; see also Eric Whitacre's Virtual Choir (www.ted.com/talks/a_choir_as_big_as_the_internet.html; filmed March 2010; posted April 2010).

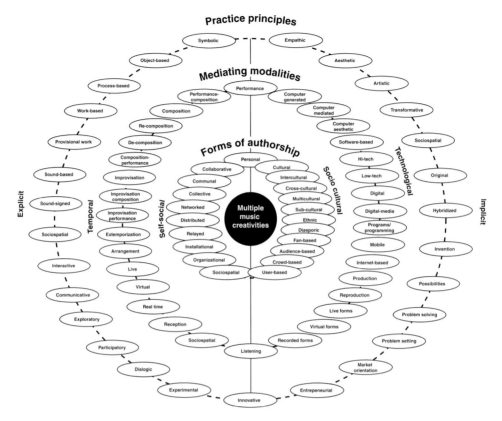

Fig. 9.3 Mapping the diversification of musical creativities in practice.

The attributes of a spectrum of practices of musical creativities

Musical creativities require the dynamic interaction of several dimensions. The final section of this chapter seeks to extract from this creative churn the specific characteristics of practice as evidenced within the musicians' narrative accounts featured in the previous chapters, and as articulated in the literature.

There is a myriad of dimensions expressed in the characterizations of musical creativities. Usually, attempts to capture the essence of musical creativities all share the idea of exploiting entrepreneurial opportunities. In particular, many of music's principles of production, whether explicit or implicit, are by their nature generalizations from practical experience, and are justified by their results, whether albums, concerts, or performances. Musicians have many ways in which they engage with these generalizations in the creation of music (Table 9.1).

Originals bands: a practice perspective

For originals bands, albums grow out of their 'collective musical endeavours' (Toynbee, 2000, p. 46). Fan-generated forms of authorship, or 'fans'' creativity' (Wikström, 2009, p. 177), provide an outlet for consumer creativity, which enables fans to play an active role and be part of their idols' and role models' creative process (A. Bennett, 2001). The role of fans in ascribing social meaning is crucial to an originals band's success. For TFN, with upcoming concerts and album construction, sharing their videos on YouTube and using blogs and Twitter has allowed the feedback to

Table 9.1 Configurations of musical creativities in real world practices

	Forms of authorship		Mediating modalities		Practice principles
	Self-social	Socio-cultural	Temporal	Technological	
Originals bands	Personal Collective Partnerships	Fan-generated Consumption creativity Sub-cultural-specific	Performance-composition	Applications simplify and develop (semi-)autonomous production	Entrepreneurial Sound-signature Band's trademarks Production
Singer-songwriters	Personal (constituting the self) Collaborative	Vesting of intercultural authority Inter-authorship Audience-mediated	Composition Song crafting Arrangement Song Performance	Participatory Song crafting	Vesting of intercultural authority Production
DJ cultures	Collective Distributed Networked Relayed	Crowd-generated Culture-specific	DJ re-composition	'Computer as creative partner' (Blake, 2007) Digital sampling Radactive Scratching Ripping Mixing Burning Vinyl records used as raw material of new creation	Sociospatial Transformative Entrepreneurial

(continued)

Table 9.1 (continued) Configurations of musical creativities in real world practices

	Forms of authorship		Mediating modalities		Practice principles
	Self-social	Socio-cultural	Temporal	Technological	
Composed music	Personal Collaborative	Culture-specific Audience-generated	Compositional techniques Performance elements Improvisational-compositional performance practices	Computer-mediated; wholly or partly abandoned mediating notation Individual recordings of compositions	Symbolic Aesthetic Experimental Work-based Products
Improvised music	Personal Communal Collaborative Virtual Live Recorded	Cultural-specific Cross-genre Collage of idioms and styles Audience-mediated	Improvisational Performance Networked	Cross-genre practices	Empathic Participatory Exploratory Interactive Cross-genre practices Dialogic
Interactive audio design	Personal Collaborative group culture Collective enterprise culture Consumption creativity	Cultural and global cultural text User-generated media	Studio compositional Chiptunes	Prominence of technological innovation, recycling technologies Computers serve as instruments	Interactive Communicative Entrepreneurial Market orientation

influence the band's decisions about certain tracks. Responding to fans' views, demands, and tastes engages their fanbase in personal and memorable ways. Originals bands are also bound up in the broader institutional forces that appear in the guise of performance-composition modalities, in which digital technologies enable bands to legitimately claim to be composers, producers, and performers. In addition to their skills in mixing songs, originals bands show all the imperatives of capital accumulation, often as trendsetters with an emerging imaginary aesthetic among musicians. As collective identity develops, so do attempts to exploit entrepreneurial opportunities. Creative musical practices are bound up with, and are demonstrated as, the 'collective identities'(A. Bennett, 2001, p. 151) forged by originals bands, which reflect the common youth practice of 'being in the know'—having insider-group knowledge which serves as a form of cultural power and the possession of 'sub-cultural capital'. This knowledge is tied to authorized special and social relations, though also linked to the ways in which spaces have been represented by musicians in the field, their symbolic power, and the local environment from which the group has emerged. Musical creativity is also bound up in the broader institutional forces that provide the basis of its production. Think, for example, of all three originals bands represented in Chapter 3, whose experiences become powerful modalities of action and representations of value and exchange that regulate the practice of their collective identities.

Singer-songwriters: a practice perspective

For singer-songwriters, albums grow out of personal and collaborative creativity. Songs are crafted and arranged, and are dependent to a large extent on the songwriter's performance culture. In the case of the musicians in Chapter 4, the singer-songwriters are infused with elements of Western and non-Western music. It seems that singer-songwriters are driven to creation for its own sake, regardless of whether the product will be received by good reviews or commercial success. Their personal creativity is valued for its art and cultural production rather than for its commercial value. The result is a distinctive fusion which quickly finds a wide appeal among populations in many different parts of the globe. Culturally related meanings are embedded within the life history of these songwriters and act as cultural layers. These layers are interdependent and help the singer-songwriters to identify themselves more strongly with intercultural expressions. Indeed, Roshi's resonance of the cultural politics of Iranian ethnic minority groups can lay claim to a new Iranian-Welsh 'voice'.

Intercultural creativity involves process, interaction, and mutuality. In Chapter 4, songwriters Roshi and Pippa display a particularly interesting approach to creativity as a culturally embedded practice through the breaking down of cultural barriers. Their practices give us privileged access to some of the cultural and intercultural values of various musical cultures and communities, and features acceptance, openness, and inclusion. These cultural influences act as a catalyst for something new. Drawing on Roshi's practice in particular, we see how creativity differs both in nature and content when it involves a process of reworking, combining, and breaking with some cultural elements to create new practices.

The practices of both singer-songwriters discussed in Chapter 4 are so highly differentiated that it becomes difficult to speak of a single, shared coherent practice. Rather, the cultural space created by them suggests they both locate themselves firmly in their contemporary urban surroundings, exploring and reflecting their personal beliefs and experiences, as well as their own creativity.

DJ cultures: a practice perspective

The most celebrated DJs and audiences favour the ongoing formation of collective identities created through their own particular brand of club event (A. Bennett, 2001). They make a display of celebratory or alternative identities, whilst strongly affecting and staying closely in touch with the crowd. DJs legitimately claim self- and crowd-generated authorship. DJs favour the use of a de-compositional procedure through the mixing and remixing of existing material, the outcomes of studio work, and the mediation of both a globally dispersed virtual community and a local one that participates in composition through the intimate interaction of DJ and crowd. Using real time manipulation of 12" vinyl discs on adapted turntables,[26] along with sampling, scratching, recycling, and remixing procedures, DJ's re-compose by assembling various bits and pieces of music. They remix parts of, or entire songs using digital sampling technology and scratching as two of many techniques. The way that DJs rip songs, mix music from an mp3 library and burn custom CDs has been coined 'radactive creativity'.[27] Existing recordings, hip hop, house and techno records in particular, are simultaneously the subject and object of their creative work: the record becomes the raw material for new creation. This transformative creativity involves the construction of place-based identities and individual and collective presence. 'Spatiality' is also one of the organizing principles of value, meaning, and practice within hip hop culture (Forman, 2004, p. 201).

Composed music: a practice perspective

Composed music constitutes a focus on authors—a cultural work is located in its ongoing social contexts. Cultural works are text-laden rather than context-determined; we may be remote from the context of a work's production but not cutoff from the product. When music is collaboratively authored, a new status and set of values is given to creators and creator-performers, as roles are not necessarily unified within a single person but rather within a performance ensemble. The meaning which audiences 'read' in composed music is partly constructed by them. The resultant 'inter-authorship' can provide a provocative counterpoint to the conventional understanding of 'tradition' as 'the act of handing down from generation to generation'.

Audience-generated practices bring together composers, performers, and listeners as partners in a dialogue. Not only can composed music change across performances, particularly in classical and experimental styles, but 'serious' composed works are now being replaced by personally manipulated versions. To identify the precise nature of creativity as a point on a continuum between behaviour modalities can involve: performance, performance-composition, composition, re-composition, de-composition, composition-performance, improvisation, improvisation-composition, improvisation-performance, and rearrangement.

Live improvised music: a practice perspective

Live improvised music is treated as a discrete art form; it may produce a heightened awareness of oneself, of sound and of space. There may be a sense of excitement, enjoyment, even an associated physical sensation. Trust is the essential element for there is a counterpoint between trust and control. An audience, whether passive or active, is a vital element within the performance space, and provides for a bidirectional exchange between players and audience. Live improvised music can constitute the self as well as communal practices involving cultural diversity. It can be a collage

---

[26] For further discussion, see Challis (2007), Cox and Warner (2009), and Dale (2010).

[27] 'Radactive creativity' is a term used in Hartley (2005, p. 166) to describe how DJs can 'snatch and sample sounds, remixing to create music that is both fresh and familiar'. Apple Computers describes the poetics of radactive creativity as the process of selecting and editing, of 'ripping, mixing and burning' as pivotal, because DJs embrace an open aesthetic that enables them to play with and remix the cultural materials at their disposal (Hartley, 2005, p. 166).

of idioms and styles without preparation or consideration, or it can be free from the influences of idiomatic norms and cultures. The music does not need to be notated, and there are no requirements to conform to the specifications of a musical style.

The use of laptops as instruments illustrates the prominence of digital technologies. Live coders are musicians who create music principally by improvised programming on laptops during a performance. Networked improvisation and free improvisation involve explorations and interactions between players and musical events. Improvisation entails empathic listening as much as individual creativity. Empathic creativity in creative musical interaction involves the ability to have emotional and experiential responses to another's responses and experiences—following someone else's nose (Cross et al., in press).

Interactive audio design: a practice perspective

In the design of video games, cultural and corporate practices ensure that diversity is achieved as an outcome of user-based consumption creativity. Audio design for video games is characteristically produced through studio composition, with prominence given to technological mediation, recycling technologies, and problem setting and solving by the computer. The trademark of the audio designer is the manner in which interactivity and communicative musicality is handled. Cultural diversity is important to the designers and managers of game companies because it implies that the product needs to respond to consumers worldwide. Managing corporate and technological innovations to meet market expectations, and the need for acceptance by society, makes significant demands on organizational resources. Games, after all, need players who enjoy the interaction.

Concluding thoughts

In this exploration of musical creativities we begin to grasp some of the most enduring assumptions that are built into our language and educational systems. We have considered the iconic status given to notated composition, a piece of music made by one individual and played by another, and the reigning focus of the great composers and composition-based music—whereas, in fact, most of the world's traditional musics, as well as the globally spatialized Internet forms,[28] have *not* originated through formal acts of 'composition', but are rather improvisational performances. We have identified how musical creativities are born of, and infused with, musical practices.

Six areas within the field of music have been described: creating in originals bands, creating as singer-songwriters, creating as DJs, creating composed musics, creating live improvised musics, and creating interactive audio designs within the gaming environment. Authorships, mediations, and principles have been grounded less in expert notions of social or cultural systems that divide up roles in terms of ends and means, or design and delivery, than in a shared wonder that demands new ways of thinking about and documenting musical creativities.

---

[28] Digital technologies afford and enhance dispersed and collaborative forms of creativities. Music can be scattered, flung via the internet in near-real time from any point of creation and departure to any number of points of destination.

Questions for reflection

1. What is the value of knowing about multiple musical creativities for musicians at a time when music seems so widely regarded as an entertaining indulgence, a non-academic diversion and irrelevant for many of the students in school music classrooms?

2. How does stressing differences and contrasts lead to important connections and relations, affinities and tendencies, patterns and trends in situations drawn from your own experiences?

3. Bourdieu says that practices are the result of what he calls 'an obscure and double relation' (Bourdieu and Wacquant, 1992, p. 126), or 'an unconscious relationship' between a habitus and a field (Bourdieu, 1993a, p. 76; Grenfell, 2008, p. 51). What are the features of your musical practice that result from relations between your dispositions (habitus) and position in the field (capital) within the current state of play in your particular social field?

Chapter 10

Pedagogy and learning with *musical creativities*

Introduction

The aim of teachers is to transform education—that is, to hold to values and practices that make radical improvements to its processes and outcomes. In the context of this book, the field of music in education, including schools, colleges, universities, and informal learning environments, needs to engender in a more complex understanding of *musical creativities*.[1] This entails developing new understandings, new practices, new pedagogies, and access to new forms of purposeful activity inspired by contemporary fields of music. It requires a shift from curricula of the past that have a narrowly specialized view of the 'subject' of music, to an orientation that champions contemporary practice. Doing so would have a profound effect on students as well as teachers. *musical creativities* could move into the spotlight and itself become subject to change.

The goal of all music teachers is to make music in education and education in music[2] more relevant, so as to give students faith in their own means of expression and provide them with the ability to distinguish between different kinds of *musical creativities*. Subjecting this proposition to closer scrutiny soon gives rise to larger questions. What are we trying to do as educators in schools, in further education, and higher educational institutions? What is the nature of the learning journeys in *musical creativities*? How should we plan for multiple *musical creativities*? How can we assess and differentiate *musical creativities*? Pedagogy and learning cannot be prescribed, but can follow certain educational values and principles arising from the nature of *musical creativities* itself. It is to these issues that I now turn.

In this chapter I will elaborate some of the educational applications of *musical creativities*—broadly construed as a composite of practices—showing how the three dimensions of authorship, mediation, and practice fundamentally change the way *musical creativities* can be used, and regularly refreshed, in the field of music in education. The challenge is to describe guidelines that have

---

[1] The plural conception of *musical creativities* is emphasized using italics so as to further exemplify how it functions itself as an expanded concept. See also Negus (1999).

[2] There is an important distinction between *music in education* and *education in music*. Music in education situates the field of music in the broadest context of the cultural practice known as 'education', wherein there are collectives (including classrooms, schools, etc.) and communities in which schools exist, set within larger cultural contexts; wherein pedagogy and learning emerges as a social practice involving curricular and cross-curricular community situated learning—which is to say the process of coming to know how to use participatory methods that stimulate and develop learning across multiple subjects. Education in music has a focus that is narrowly specialized and has a highly stratified type of learning which is institutionalized by the discipline of music itself. The guiding principles for a curriculum for the former (music in education) would focus on the multiple musical creativities that result from the interplay of areas of learning, and which are packed with opportunities for learners to find their strengths and engage in activities that can provide genuine challenges and prospects for multiple forms of music achievement. For further discussion, see McPherson (2006).

sufficient utility, yet resist the tendency to prescribe methods. Some of these educational practices will help to dispel myths (see the childhood myths discussed in Appendix D) and the outmoded misconception that there is one single type of creativity for all music. Other such guidelines will challenge other traditional conceptions of musical creativity and its representation in education within specific cultural and institutional contexts. All of this calls for changes in the cultural and creative practices that constitute the education of practices founded on the traditional belief in a single creativity for all music.[3] This is not to denigrate traditional teaching and learning practices but rather, to stimulate thinking about extending teaching practices in the light of contemporary music and new forms of musical creativity.

This chapter contains vignettes and narratives from the field of music in education to provide you with a brief glimpse of the journeys into the resourcefulness and reflectiveness of artist-musicians, as well as, and most importantly, the student and teacher experiences that lie behind a more complex understanding of multiple *musical creativities*. These vignettes and personal narratives provide examples of how *musical creativities*: (1) are revealed and distinguished in educational practice; (2) how they underpin educational practices as diverse as music itself; (3) how they are constituted by the logic (and rules) of the field of education in which they arise; and (5) how they have their own affiliations and capitals, and how this affects the way teachers and students can talk about the practices of *musical creativities* and the kinds of activities and discussions that are initiated.

From the perspective of the music industry and music in education, the challenge of teaching and assessing for *musical creativities* will be to meet the rigor demanded of practices followed in institutional communities and educational systems. In practice, this means that different paths can be taken to reach to the same place; and whilst there is a need to locate new ways of thinking and talking about *musical creativities* within certain scholarly and educational frameworks, there is no need to be a slave to them. But, as I often point out in this book, there is a need to claim a place for *musical creativities* as a critically important area of musical knowledge, musical learning, and pedagogical knowledge of a different type. *musical creativities* arise out of practices in which people have lived and learnt, and concerns what they explicitly and implicitly value about different forms of authorship, mediation, and principles of practice.

Previous chapters provided musicians' accounts of their differentiated and particular practices. For example, I discussed differences between the practices of collective composition in three originals bands' procedures and rehearsals, and the communal composition pervasive in some live improvised music, where the key features of authorship, mediation, and principles of practice are linked to the centrality and importance of empathizing, listening, communicating, and interacting. We saw how the nature of, for instance, live improvised performance practices performance creativities varies. Musical live coding is a form of practice that depends on social computing and algorithmic programming practised in real time. In folk fiddling,[4] the laws of functioning depend on the 'in-group' uniformity of collective improvisational performance knowledge and skills. It is

---

[3] For more discussion of the situated practice and definition of cultural education, see Campbell (1996, 2002), Cook (1990, 2006, in press), D. Faulkner et al. (2006), Ruthmann (2007b), Saether et al. (in press), Sefton-Green and Soep (2007), and Sumara and Davis (1997).

[4] Fiddle playing, or folk fiddling (also known as country, folk, Celtic or old time fiddling, old time music, or by cultural or regional names, e.g., Scottish, Cape Breton, Ukrainian-Canadian, French-Canadian, among others), based largely on British Isles models, was the principal medium of dance music in rural Canada. Changing performance contexts from dances to contests and concert performance have also affected many aspects of the music, as has the rise of formal instruction in recent years (www.thecanadianencyclopedia.com/index.cfm?PgNm=TCE&Params=U1ARTU0001206).

an ongoing challenge to show how these accounts of practice can be used to eradicate the stereotypical singular view of musical creativity and serve to define what *musical creativities* can be.

The following three vignettes illustrate ways of thinking about the 'taste cultures' of different kinds of *musical creativities*, and how teachers can teach *musical creativities* through (1) what they explicitly value and discuss with students; (2) the way in which they talk to groups and individuals about their own experiences; (3) how they themselves model *musical creativities*; (4) how they go about ascribing more or less value to the things that are learnt; and (5) above all else, perhaps, the way that they present themselves as listeners, fans, or music consumers—what kind of creativities they focus on in the diverse genres of Western art music, popular music, dance music, or contemporary digital arts music, as identified in Fig. 9.1.

Teachers do many things in order to create their own distinctive classroom learning culture, wherein 'taste cultures' are not innocently formed or experienced. 'Taste cultures' are formed by discourses on music and the role of musical creativity in reflecting on and building up concepts and so on. The three vignettes run through some of the ways in which creative practices in music can be explained and assigned to different fields: from one mega-seller Romantic composer, to a contemporary pop artist, to digitized art and sub-cultural forms. We look at the kinds of questions we ask ourselves, the kinds of formal and informal comments and evaluations we make, and the taken-for-granted assumptions that are brought to light from an unanticipated question.

Vignette 10.1 The *musical creativities* of popular music in the world of global entertainment

Imagine you have been asked to give an account of your first experience of the mega-seller contemporary pop artist, songwriter, performing and recording artist, actress, and entrepreneur Madonna in a live performance at one of her sell-out 1980s world tour concerts. The venue is a football stadium. This is a diva, who has built up the Madonna brand with dance tracks; whose iconic style perfects the industry's covert dream of creating a 'product' so cynically catchy that no one can resist its clever hooks, winning melodies, and smart lyrics; who has established a durable career; and made more money than can be imagined from promoting an image that illustrates how individual and collective identities are constructed and lived out. Your account details her brand, her singing and co-songwriting skills, and you reflect on her ability to constantly reinvent her persona, moving creatively and innovatively through several distinct images, a process which is a necessary part of ensuring her enduring star status. You reflect on the Madonna phenomenon of the 1980s, with her charismatic personality and captivating stage presence, her sexuality and creative character; on how Madonna 'wannabes' with peroxide hair, 1950s sunglasses, frilly pink dresses, and clutching Madonna posters were prominent among the 77,000-strong crowd at the London Wembley stadium: a scene which attracts a range of mainstream culture and sub-cultures, all of which express new ways of understanding and identifying the relationship between musical taste and identity. In dressing like her, the fans took on the success and glamour Madonna symbolizes, while identifying with her projected values of rebellion against parental authority. You wonder how the *studio* practice of collective composition, so pervasive in pop/rock music performance and recording, works for Madonna's collective production, and who these musicians are that associate with constructing a 'unique persona' like Madonna. You also wonder how much of Madonna's performance is offered up live, and about her openness to stylistic change, her portrayal of an alter ego, given the social message, sound production, and visceral spectacle supported by an army

> **Vignette 10.1 The *musical creativities* of popular music in the world of global entertainment** (*continued*)
>
> of professionals—a production that feels, at times, formulaic and aligned to market forces in the music and recording industries. Still you cannot help but admire the way she has continuously reinvented both her music and image, and retained a standard of autonomy within the recording industry. She is clearly a hard-headed entrepreneurial businesswoman. And yet the production is demonstrably a collective enterprise wherein promoters, record companies, organizations, designers, producers, and all the creative agents involved in it are subsumed within the cultural parameters of the domain and the social experiences of the field of popular music.

Vignette 10.2 The *musical creativities* of Western art music and the (mythical) lone genius

Imagine you have been asked to give an account of your first experience of attending a grand opera. Your account details a performance of an opera by the 'great composer-hero' Wagner— his final epic opera *Parsifal*, which invokes the 'total artwork' (*Gesamtkunstwerk)* and grand- ness of the poetic, visual, musical and dramatic arts, framed by time, space, and spectacle. You provide an 'idealized' description of the splendour of the costumes and the sets, the composi- tional expression of 'pure' music that brings more fulfilment than suffering, and you recall how the boxes were arranged primarily to allow you to view one another rather than the stage. All of this impressed you. You recall every detail about the set, its magnificence and complex layers of meaning, and what it was to be part of an audience in the opera house. You paid for a 'box' seat—historically, solely an aristocratic preserve and allocated strictly according to rank—and felt delirious with excitement, desiring only to listen with respectful attention: a listening attitude which is, of course, appropriate to 'serious' music, and which shows secular devotion towards the pose of the heroic individualism of the Romantic artist. You recollect how the canonical work of opera left you reeling from the valued traditions of such high-level creativity, itself a function of the Romantic legacy. You reflect on the extraordinary creativity of the composer and the cult of the musical genius. You ponder on the relationship of the composer to the wider community: the separation of the professional composer from the 'pas- sive' audience and the range of performance practices that have been legitimated by history. You think about the status of Wagner's works, the fixed roles of conductor, orchestra, diva and how they are all wedded to traditional beliefs underpinned by individualistic assumptions about musical creativity. You ascribe a lot of importance to your knowledge of opera. You speak of the laws of reason, the laws of musical creativity of the nineteenth century, and the diverse subjectivities that emerge from a complex fusion of art forms born and developed within an immutable cultural tradition.

Vignette 10.3 The *musical creativities* of contemporary dance culture and the collective aesthetics of club cultures

Imagine you've been asked to give an account of your first experiences of clubbing, club cul- ture, and the process of coming to know and create dance music as constituted by the interac- tive engagement, collective aesthetics, and 'vibes' created at a hardcore techno-house in a city-centre club in London. You retell the experience as one of feeling comfortable in this club

Vignette 10.3 The *musical creativities* of contemporary dance culture and the collective aesthetics of club cultures (*continued*)

space, of fitting in with the club culture in a venue that glows in the dark, with canvases of sur-real landscapes with rising suns and psychedelic snakes. The crowd looks pretty homogeneous. They are mostly dressed in a version of the acid house uniform of T-shirts, baggy jeans, and Kicker boots. You feel like you belong. You dance to a collage of hip hop, rap, and urban dance-music. It feels cool to dance to music that features repertoires that are (re)constructed from downloading and mixing Internet files, conceptualized, gained, shared, and evaluated within the social context in which they live musically. You encounter and interact with a prac-tice based around 'beats', that is, musical collages composed of brief segments of recorded sound and dialogue. You recognize cuts from unlikely records. It is the technologically informed, creative process of hip hop that takes place in a social context of sound reproduc-tion technology which makes an impression on you. You are transfixed by the complexity of interaction between DJ and crowd in the creation of a unique happening; the style-mixing involved in its production, made possible through technological mediation; the unique sound, the originality and aura; and the strongly held values of most DJs. You engage with a variety of different musical moods by moving between different rooms or floors. The club stages a number of parallel events, and as a frequent club-goer you feel free to move between these events as you please. This makes 'clubbing' less of a singularly definable activity and more of a series of fragmented, temporal experiences. Different music plays on different floors. Different DJs construct different sound-signatures. There is a café room which plays hip hop and jazz, and another room in which people sing house music; then there is the techno music with a sort of trance techno played upstairs. It feels entirely new, or at least different. Perhaps this is the guise of a sociospatial creativity that orchestrates the crowd. There is a centrality of musical taste which is shared. You love this music and call it 'ragga-hip-hop-jungle'. It involves digital record-ing and sound storage, multi-track studio de-composition and practices of re-composition, utilizing the downloading of mp3 files sampled from the Internet, and the means by which people happily distribute and mutually tune into each other's music. This is how the club scene offers up a critical space for you as a consumer. You can make choices in terms of what kinds of music is appropriated, how the music is lived out, and what it stands for. It is the collective authorship, the technological mediation and mutual tuning in of de- and re-compositional assemblages, of break-beats and other bits of recorded sound and music that combine with sounds remixed live with other sounds in which the collectivist aesthetics of the production and consumption of music are observed (see C. Ford, 2010).

The three scenarios of scripting *musical creativities* I have given (or as Nicholas Cook would say 'scripting social interaction'[5]), although some might consider them educationally purposeless, can be understood as conceiving and framing the social phenomenon of *musical creativities* in a way that presumes its meaningfulness and coherence to young people. *musical creativities* illus-trates the 'taste cultures' and 'collective aesthetics' brought together at dance clubs, where DJs flex their awesomely efficient *musical creativities* for pumping up and fuelling a dance floor; epic operas that invoke the Romantic legacy of the cult of composer; and performances where pop divas render the idealized image of mainstream music industries. They show how social interaction blurs

---

[5] Nicholas Cook's (forthcoming) chapter on scripting social interaction characterizes the sociality of music-making in terms of the embeddedness of social processes as exemplified by jazz and freely improvised music.

the traces and boundaries of individual and collective authorship. The main point here is how the reification of an outmoded 'musical creativity' offers us only one explanation, when musicians' real world practices, and students who fail to learn, or those who just give up on music in education, give material form to legitimate many practices.

At the opera, new light is shed on the classical music industry, and how people learn to identify the hero-genius composer as a 'lone artist', through the dominant cult of genius.[6] In the constellation of mainstream popular practices, and the publicity given to the pop star's latest album, what there is to hear determines what people want to hear, and what people want to hear determines what there is to hear; all of which exemplify and contribute to the composite creative practices. These different practices are all differently produced in the intimate interactions of the tradition of the genre, the artist and the audience, the performer and the crowd. How the music derives from a continuous circuit of mediations, translations, and interactions is what renders it creative.

In education, these different types of *musical creativities* provide us with a range of fresh tools that we can see are already making substantial changes to all aspects of musicians' real world practices. In terms of pedagogy and learning, what are the educational implications for developing *musical creativities*? Do artists see themselves as potential recipients of the opportunities for learning afforded by partnerships with teachers? What happens when teachers and artists work together to develop pedagogic practices to support multiple *musical creativities*? Are industrial practices useful models? What the ways teachers respond to artists' conscious habits, if any, of the practice of *musical creativities*?

Building *musical creativities* in collaborative pedagogic partnership contexts

Pedagogy can be thought of as an act grounded in disciplinary achievement (as, for instance, the acquisition of subject knowledge), and as ways of teaching bodies of pedagogical knowledge. Pedagogy can also, as argued by Ward et al (2004) and Alexander (2008, 2009), constitute performance, based on acts and thought, beliefs and theories of teaching. There are pedagogies that focus on learning as an event (Atkinson, 2002), on what it is to learn (Kress, 2003) and on clearly defined outputs (Bernstein, 1996), among others. Drawing together the connectedness between the music industry and education, how do artists and teachers make visible their pedagogy and learning in building *musical creativities*?

In the previous chapter, three categories or dimensions of *musical creativities* were discussed in detail: authorship, mediation, and practice principles. A key feature of this framework (see Fig. 9.2) is the notion that real world practices arise out of an interplay between these dimensions, as seen in Csikszentmihalyi's (1999) systems model, involving domains, fields and person, and Bourdieu's (1993c) expanded idea of the field of music in education as consisting of a 'separate social universe having its own laws of function' (p. 162). So, what are the practices which are valued, and which therefore constitute capital and exert power over other practices in the field of music in education within which teacher-artists' pedagogic practices can be understood.

Teachers often concretize their taken-for-granted assumptions about *musical creativities* that are implied in the practices and knowledge children and students are expected to acquire and demonstrate by the end of specific periods of teaching and learning (these periods may end at

---

[6] At the risk of generalizing hugely and possibly offending a lot of people in the jazz, world, folk, classical, and pop/rock industries, I apologize in advance. I am merely making the point that people are forced to make falsely narrow and arbitrary choices, to think about what constitutes their chosen musical field, in a learning career that requires openness at the margins and middle of the 'mainstream' against which they measure their alternative worth. See Westerlund (2008) for further discussion on values.

ages 7, 11, 14 and 16, and are called 'Key Stages' in England). It is instructive to consider the language of music curricula to see what types of *musical creativities* are being promoted. It is also instructive to see how the pedagogy for building *musical creativities* is framed. Is there an emphasis upon critical and reflective awareness of music so that children and students can acquire a broader understanding of their own musical practices in relation to the diverse practices of others and different cultural traditions of music? Are there contrasts in terms of activity that encourage exploring, producing, designing, experimenting, taking decisions, solving problems, making choices alone or doing things together, or is the emphasis on interactional qualities, or performance practices, or how variant versions are relayed and transformed across time, space, and persons?

There is a long history of collaboration between teachers and professional artists in participatory arts activities, both in schools and communities.[7] Pedagogic practice in partnerships between artists and teachers varies considerably. When teachers and artists collaborate, they often prefer working within the classroom according to different organizational parameters of space, material, and time. The visiting artist typically uses a more improvisational, open-ended approach, whereas the classroom teacher typically uses a more structured compositional style. Thus, these artist-teacher partnerships provide us with an opportunity to see how building *musical creativities* operates in educational action. How do these dyads balance the more unpredictable, improvisational approach of the visiting artist with the more compositional and performative style of the teacher? What would take them from teaching together, independently and side by side, to co-constructing an emergent pedagogy?

In this chapter, I will move beyond these divisive stereotypes of teacher and artist, and feature two examples of collaborative partnerships. Each of these examples of a teacher and an artist teaching collaboratively demonstrates how they create 'spaces for teaching', giving rise to clearly differentiated *musical creativities* in a way that promotes conditions conducive to student creativity, such as risk-taking and allowing for not knowing what might happen next.

The following narratives of practice relating to *musical creativities* illustrates to us the many possibilities about different practices of teaching and learning music in education.

Narrative 10.1[8]

In this narrative Dot, an artist, talks about her principles of practice. She describes the shared space of her pedagogic practice, which provides an example of the dialogic improvisation of teaching.

Dot: I'm interested in the idea of holistic creative education. I work from the understanding that there isn't a right or wrong outcome or even one answer. I want to support young people's creativity rather than drive it. I normally start with activities which open up and explore possibilities and communicate an openness to ideas in the ways we model collaborative action and a passion for the exploration of our own creative learning and teaching . . . Everything evolves organically. I don't run to a detailed plan but I do hold long planning sessions with the teacher . . . And, I like to spend quite a bit of time before starting a project observing the classroom practice of the teachers involved . . . we conduct mutual observation. This influences how I work . . . I prioritize students' ideas and work to engage students, to have them question and embark on a process of enquiry. I try to promote a kind of fluid reflective practice which is a bit like researching your own practice. I encourage risk-taking and play, and expect students to take responsibility for what they do. That is crucial. I get them to work in a participatory way where exchanging ideas and experiences is expected also of the teachers. I'm not there to teach but share. I do a lot of talking with the teacher during the sessions and engaging collaboratively . . . it helps to share the burdens and pressures . . . prior to and during the gig. I spend a lot of time after

---

7 For further discussion on artistic partnerships in educational and community settings see Burnard and Maddock (2007). Also see Burnard and White (2008), Colley et al. (in press), Lapidaki et al. (in press), and Pringle (2008).

8 For a detailed discussion of this partnership project, see Burnard and Swann (2010).

sessions talking through what was working and what wasn't working. I also have a lot of extended conversations long before and immediate after sessions, and I make a big deal of shared dialogue during sessions with the teachers . . . I like [us] to explore each other's pedagogic territories . . . to share the space of learning and teaching. I think learners gain a lot of understanding through this collaboration but through these exchanges and with students working along teachers. The key, for me, is that it's all about engaging in and reflecting on the making process and in reflecting on this process, encouraging both teachers and students to articulate their ideas, and play together, the space opens up, it promotes teachers' learning from the children and each other . . . it opens boundaries that form bridges . . . and becomes more open-ended and supportive.

As found in other studies that report artists' accounts of their own artistic practices and pedagogy, this artist felt that what made the partnership work was the tuning-in and sustained dialogue between teachers and students, along with: giving space and time to think, and extend ideas; offering precise feedback; and extending rather than trying to force the children to accept the Romantic principle that musical invention depends on the self-expression of the individual composer-genius who must refuse to follow established rules (the work-based practice). Other common elements in these practices include allowing students authorship, choice, and forms of mediation, and, most importantly, modelling creative action within a genuine partnership.

John, the teacher, reflects on the mediation of time and task as a transaction taking place not only between the artist and students within the classroom but between the artist and teacher.

John: To me, working with artists is about several things. One important thing for me is to look at and try to model their different ways of working; I've learned so much more from doing their tasks alongside the students . . . rather than expecting them to come in and deliver and then go away again . . . I see, in the course of a lesson and across a series of lessons, how they get students to explore their own ideas before going on to decide on the tasks and activities to be undertaken, and about the particular tasks which move to imaginative playful spontaneous stuff, then move to create something in response, working with them in different ways to create safe spaces for risk-taking. And another important thing is with the students. What I am trying to do here is to be a person who responds to ideas, just like the students; to come up with ideas and to bring our own reflections to share. But [it] is the giving up of control which I struggle most with. It's like learning to teach all over again . . . Standing back and just letting the students play and go about their work without jumping in and dictating further instructions of how best to approach or 'the right' way more spontaneously to do something . . . The students reflect on their learning and themselves as learners. So do I, but as their teacher I bring my own practice to the surface and share it with more spontaneity with the artist. I've learned to work from the understanding that there isn't a right or wrong outcome or even one answer. I've learned more responsive ways to support young people's creativity. Just like Dot, I start with warm-up and release activities which open up and explore possibilities and communicate an openness to ideas. Unlike Dot, I do run to a detailed plan because of the continued tensions of target setting and testing but what I've learnt from Dot is how best to liberate myself, balance my scripted and unscripted teaching, and my students needs by minimizing the worst elements of this regime and engaging my students in regular artistic ventures where they don't have to feel fearful of 'being wrong'.

What emerges here is that artists tend to define themselves and the nature of *musical creativities* differently, and, at times, in opposition to teachers (Pringle, 2008). Artists often resist describing their practice as teaching. In contrast, they often describe their pedagogic practice in the language of building *musical creativities*, as a dance between dialogical improvisation and the fixed plans, repertoires, and routines yielding to high levels of real time decision-making. It is not uncommon for both teachers and artists to go through periods of uncertainty and discomfort as they negotiate this tension between different conceptions of the use of time, space, and resources in relation to how classroom and school procedures normally operate.

Narrative 10.2

This narrative illustrates a different conception of *musical creativities* wherein there is deep commitment and concern for individual expression and enquiry. The pedagogy takes on different forms of authorship, mediation, and practice principles. One artist, talking about one of the productive tensions he experienced working in a school, when interviewed at the end of an artist-led project involving 10 workshops across a term (Triantafyllaki and Burnard, 2010), had this to say about the tensions between the two competing agendas—high-stakes testing and the importance of giving students' authorship choice:

An important thing for me is my art-making demands: risk-taking, questioning, challenging the status quo, bending and breaking the rules, speculation, disturbance, conflict, discomfort, and shock. These principles overlay my pedagogic practice in schools. There are tensions and clearly risks attached for those engaged in the fluid nature of art-making processes. The consequence of reflection, putting in breathing spaces and still points, and reflecting critically on what, why, and how we learn, and how we work in partnership with teachers and students in schools can be really tricky. The effect of encouraging students to pursue a line of thinking may cause them to question or challenge the values and practices of their own teachers, and that the school can be seen as subversive. But I don't have a problem with this kind of subversive creativity. You have to walk a fine line, and this concern shouldn't but often does lead me to compromise my professional work and educational partnerships. It's a tight-rope walk with competing priorities that mean the inroads that I may have made can easily be lost . . . Sometimes you just have to invite students to find the space and take the time to sit and think about it, to be experimental and exploratory, to explore the relations between different compositional and improvisational practices, and try and reduce the perceived risk by the offer to think and encourage thinking together about alternative ways rather than just pursue one way to go about it. It's important to recognize the role played by having a taste for Mozart, for Cage, for Bach and Stockhausen; for awareness of trends in musical tastes across history, and even to the roles of amateur and music-lovers in history as seriously as those of significant composers and professional musicians . . . I'm never shy of sharing my views and experiences with the students. But this doesn't go over that well with all teachers. Some just can't move away from didactic teaching and it just becomes impossible to navigate a way through or negotiate the dynamics of each other's ideology. So, they become the provider of information, or the police person or worse, just stress the potential of amateur practices.

The collaborating teacher in this partnership was used to a deeply disciplined and scripted pedagogy; she even compared her own practice to 'a fully orchestrated score'. When she worked with this artist, she noted:

There were definite tensions. We didn't have time to build up any kind of relationship. They very loosely guided the students on a very different, quite unspecified, learning journey to me . . . they used a very different kind of planning model to me and used—well—actually . . . wasted time over conversations which I felt were unnecessary . . . and that brought about tensions and burdens which some pupils found [themselves] very challenged by. There just isn't that kind of time to sit for hours and talk. They don't seem to have any sense of how a classroom, curriculum, and its structures work. There just isn't the time or curriculum opportunity to give oneself the freedom to let go and work at such an emotionally charged level as this. I watched from the sidelines rather than participated . . . I don't like being put on the spot with all eyes on me and besides, I have to be on the ready to regain control and police behaviour . . . I know why a few of the students get upset. It can be very destabilizing for some students . . . Confidences can take a real knock when tasks are high on ambiguity and therefore perceived as very risky. I just had to help out some students by showing specifically how to do things so they could achieve the set criteria that we are all used to . . . but this upset the artists who made it perfectly clear these differences were not going to be resolved . . . there wasn't time to talk it through, to adjust to them, and I didn't feel like being very collegial anyway. They had all the talent but none of the critical elements that, for me, define teaching for creativity, for me, like being in control and which, for me, should play out like a fully orchestrated score. In the end I didn't have the time nor energy to work it through with them.

The pedagogy and learning that arise in the partnership between artists and teachers can be complex, and can give rise to a clash of confidence and power struggles (in relationships based on power) with, in some cases, control being relinquished to whose opinions count. Artists can hold strong views about going with the flow, whereas teachers often see themselves cast in the role of a didact or policeman. Pringle (2008) and Burnard, 2011a make similar points: that artists can adopt creative and experimental pedagogic modes because, generally, they are free from curriculum constraints, whereas teachers are not. Thus putting *musical creativities* into action is not a seven-day wonder, a quick fix, or a miracle cure for all ills and difficulties in the field of music in education. It is potentially a long journey that starts with a few small steps, and which is capable of fundamentally shifting the way music teachers think about how they teach creativity in music and conceptualize *musical creativities*.

In sum, ways of enabling improvisational and performative forms of creativity in pedagogic partnerships include:

◆ providing time to reflect critically on emerging pedagogic practices and the interactional, participatory, exploratory, experimental, entrepreneurial qualities (principles of practice) that embody *musical creativities*;

◆ allowing for a high proportion of pupil talk, much of it occurring between pupils, teachers, and artists, and reflecting on different constellations of *musical creativities*, for example, improvised performance and technological mediation, the focus of classroom discourse;

◆ modelling the use of a variety of *musical creativities* to communicate both teachers' and artists' ideas to pupils;

◆ allowing time for extended planning sessions that reflect on the content to be taught and how it is organized around a limited set of powerful ideas;

◆ modelling the ways in which the classroom ethos encourages teachers, artists, and pupils to offer speculative answers to challenging questions without fearing failure;

◆ developing pedagogic practices that invite and build *musical creativities*, including flexible thinking, risk taking, multivocality, professional innovation, and illustrating inherent freedoms that characterize improvisatory forms of creativity.

Building *musical creativities* with digital technology[9]

Imagine a one-size-fits-all form of pedagogy[10] in music education that builds on assumptions about creativity and the instrumental use of technology expressed as separate, unrelated concepts. There are no expectations about the usefulness of integrating creativity and technology; in fact, the essence of each is to be not-the-other. Creativity is viewed as an internal strategy, and technology as an external strategy for acquiring musical knowledge, skills, and understanding that teachers use at different instructional levels.

---

[9] 'Technology' is a term that is seen as encompassing the use of new technologies, digital tools, and the Internet, as well as computer-based technology in the music classroom.

[10] 'Pedagogy' is seen as encompassing appropriate and finely grained professional judgements about how teaching is undertaken and learning nurtured.

Now, imagine instead a music pedagogy that assumes multiple forms, where creativity, like inspiration, comes from outside-in *and* inside-out, as a process inseparable from technology, playing into and recruiting from these different forms. A gradual but perceptible process of pedagogical evolution takes place, with music educators developing new strategies that go beyond making new tools 'fit in' to current ways of working. Instead, the 'deeper' object of musical learning arises inseparably from creativity and technology as interrelated tools. Both teachers and learners use these tools to manage their own learning, creating opportunities for the making, reception, consumption and production of music. In this scenario, learning goals concerns how pupils would like to work musically and what resources they would like to use; e-learning tasks and e-communication are expected ways of promoting creativity in the music classroom. Various models of artistic engagement are negotiated, with collaborative opportunities for media-rich choices in adaptive learning environments. These are richly resourced to both provoke and support shared reflection and interaction between participants. Interaction takes place through diversified networks that support worldwide access at home and at school.

Clearly, there are many approaches to pedagogy and learning that reside on a spectrum between the simple dichotomies at either end. However, the dichotomies emphasize the significance of assumptions about the mutuality of creativity and technology inherent in pedagogy. New possibilities for engaging with *musical creativities* and developing practices of differentiation highlight the opportunity for networked real time improvisation using digital instruments connected via electronic networks and a broad range of school and community applications. New pedagogies and learning opportunities, feature novel interactional types of *musical creativities*, which use, for instance, networked computers and the Jam2Jam software such as that developed by Brown et al. (2002). These interactional types of *musical creativities* link to industrial standard generative tools and programs which create an accompaniment for live performances using acoustic/electric instruments, offering tools that create forms of transformative creativity. Just as DJs (as described in Chapter 5) are artists in the construction of the 'scene', 'buzz', 'vibe', or 'atmosphere' created in the interaction of DJ and crowd, new technologies (including both hardware and software-based music systems) are capable of overlapping practices and methods for constructing cultural and sub-cultural youth practices, similar to the deconstructive and reconstructive practices and development of the DJ industry (see Brown and Dillon, 2007, in press; Finney and Burnard, 2007).

Moving on, we see that *musical creativities* and technology are not autonomous, nor are they competing or irrelevant to each other. Understandings and assumptions that underpin the need for enhancing opportunities for 'creative teaching' in the field of music in education bring the notion of pedagogy and pedagogic change into unprecedented focus. Music in education and technology are not always comfortable bedfellows for teachers (Cain, 2004; Mellor, 2001; Savage, 2002). As music teachers, we all struggle to keep up with the pace of change in music technology. At the same time, the pupils we teach mediate their musical worlds through technology—for example, downloading music, sharing files, and making music on their home computers with easily available commercial software. This presents challenges for teachers wishing to use music technology: (1) how to engage with the way young people use music and technology; (2) how to get a grip on understanding the processes of teaching and learning with digital technologies from both the pupils' and their own perspectives; (c) how to develop creative approaches to teaching music through the use of technology; and (d) how to develop a mutually stimulating learning environment, rich with possibilities, at the same time as meeting the drive for measurable standards.

Mike Challis is a freelance composer and educator who utilizes technology to enable composition in a variety of situations. He works in schools, prisons, and with community groups. Mike has written extensively on the DJ factor as an alternative approach to composition, one that acknowledges the strong identification with DJ culture felt by many young people (as shown, in particular, by case studies of boys).[11] He has a lot to say about the collaborative forms of authorship, the mode of performance-composition, utilizing technological mediations, sounds that are remixed live, based on practice principles that are object-based, and innovative practices of re-composition in schools.

Narrative 10.3

Running DJing for full secondary classes is always going to be difficult as it really is a one-person hands-on at a time thing to do in workshop situations. I am fortunate in that I work with one, two, or three pupils in the pupil referral unit I work in, and I have other activities that can happen at the same time as I have a small studio off the side with a Mac for making tracks or chatting in studio conditions. I have worked on projects in prison and elsewhere with a couple of DJs, most recently Mikey Matala. He is absolutely brilliant and manages to work with larger groups, teaching beat matching and scratch techniques. Here is my take on it. Sound bleed is always a problem in school environments, as to do turntables effectively you must both hear the live sound and be able to cue on headphones, and DJs like it loud. I use a small classroom (6 m by 6 m) well away from others. It is possible for a DJ to listen to the cue in headphones but the students don't really get it. I run sessions with two turntables fed into a DJ mixer and then out to powered speakers. I also have the ability to bring in a third channel which is useful for playing tracks from a CD deck or computer into the mix. Good turntables are essential, you get what you pay for. Belt drive decks are a real no-no. They need to be direct drive. A good pair will be at least £600 and then the mixer will be an additional £100–200 plus headphones, speakers and some vinyl (about £6 each). Good sources of vinyl are Red Eye Records, Juno Records, and Hard to Find Records. The last two are also good sources of equipment and have catalogues you can browse online. I use real vinyl at the PRU, Mikey uses a system called Serato Scratch which allows him to use any track on his computer controlled by timecode vinyls on the decks. The latter is very flexible and teaches beat-matching in a visual way. I have found the book *How to DJ [Properly]* (Broughton and Brewster, 2002) to be useful when teaching decks. I usually lend this to the students that become really enthused about learning more. They often have friends that can teach them more tricks, the key thing though, as with all instruments, is to have time to practice and hone your skills. In that respect it is probably necessary to treat learning to DJ the way they would someone who wanted to learn to be a percussionist from the point of view of allowing lots of access to those who are keen (often obsessively so) to become proficient.

Several factors may have an impact on transforming teacher practice. Many studies have pointed to school-level and teacher-level barriers, along with practical constraints in the workplace (see Challis, 2007; P. Webster, 2006). Developing effective pedagogy and learning around technology-based and creativity-integrated activity involves people at all levels of experimentation, boundary-crossing, collaborative negotiation, and *musical creativities* opportunism. Along with the demands of curriculum coverage and assessment, if music teachers are to become flexible learning leaders they need to be researching how effective teaching and learning happens in their own digital-rich music classrooms. These are issues in which researcher-practitioner-musicians are playing a crucial part. The integration of *musical creativities* with knowledge generation through a cyclical process of experimentation, evaluation, and refinement are providing us with policy-driven prototypes of innovation in music (see more of Mike Challis's work in Finney and Burnard, 2007; see also the innovative Musical Futures programme, now well-established in English schools and theoretically justified in Green's (2008, 2010) groundbreaking research on informal learning).

---

[11] For more discussion see Burnard (2007) and Challis (2007).

Research has also shown that technology is deeply embedded in the contemporary lexicon of young people's musical lives (Folkestad, 2006). The Internet, for example, is their new playground and creates different social rooms for them. In addition, many young people are already high-end, or consumption-bound, users and consumers of music technology, mass media, and production technologies. They are often motivated by out-of-school experiences of digital musical cultures.[12] What they bring to school from their home and community offers new challenges to teachers. On the one hand, technologically mediated creativities can shake the most cherished practices of classroom music teachers, but, on the other, it can generate the desire, and ways in which, to diversify the nature of *musical creativities* in practice.

The wide range of online multi-media resources, and the changing nature of *musical creativities* are redefining how teachers use digital technologies in their teaching. The interrelationship between multiple *musical creativities* and technological mediations across formal and informal learning contexts changes what is perceived as cultural and social capitals. These practices are authorized in particular spatial locations and through sub-cultural affiliations, yet shaped by the narratives of young people, whether expressed from the hard edge of sub-cultural practice or the blunt edge of individualism in school cultures.

We know that underachievement, dropping-out, and negative attitudes to music have been advanced to explain the contested nature of music education. We know that teachers are pressured to accept that they do not know everything, nor are they the purveyors of all musical knowledge (Pitts, 2005). We also know that the challenge of technology includes finding ways to: (1) develop knowledge about digital music brought from home to school; (2) move technology from being an 'add-on' to being embedded in the secondary music curriculum; (3) employ technology synonymously with creativity to do more than merely 'serve' tradition; and (4) enable technology to bring 'real world' experience into the classroom. All of these issues underscore the changing nature of school music specifically, and schooling generally. Where we have less understanding, and need more substantial research, is in how to identify and theorize the interrelationship between *musical creativities* and new technologies. We need pedagogies that uncover new ways of thinking about practice, and that have the potential to fuel change in teacher professionalism. (See, for example, Webster (2006) for a comprehensive review, and the practitioner research featured in Finney and Burnard (2007).)

At the interface between home and school, teenagers experience a changing sense of place and belonging. The application of new technologies for music learning and teaching at school, and the way in which students use technology at home is a major concern for teachers in their thinking about what should be included in the curriculum, how it should be delivered, and the confluent questions of why, when, and where in the curriculum it should be positioned. The particular ways in which new technologies and creativity are promoted, perceived, and practised continue to underscore key reports and promotions of resource materials. Several questions arise: Where should we place technology in relation to the curriculum? Should it be at the centre? Or is it better to have technology-as-subject or music-technology-as-subject or technologically-mediated *musical creativities* at the centre? When and how do we use technology appropriately in order to develop a DJ turntablist and MC practices?

---

[12] This is not an empirically researched claim. We need to be wary of labelling a generation. From my own experience of teaching in schools and universities, just because students use iPods and mobiles does not mean they can all make creative use of sound using technology beyond a kind of surface interaction.

Narrative 10.4

Teacher-musician-researcher Peter Dale[13] offers his innovative practice using DJ desks that gives material form to legitimating DJing as an educational practice. His narrative on pedagogy and learning with DJing turntables focuses on ways that transform pedagogy and learning in music classroom.

Peter: The ambivalent-about-school-music learners face only one problem: they lack musical ability. Or is it that they just lack motivation? Either way, eight years using (occasionally) DJ decks for teaching music has shown me that 'the dex' get young people (especially disaffected young people) highly motivated. This motivation is not simply to listen to the particular type of dance music found on the discs they use for mixing. I find that DJing impacts on the learners overall motivation for getting to grips with various fundamental aspects of music. In my PhD, I explored the question as to whether, in music, 'anyone can do it'. Being a DJ or MC is a good example of something which, on the face of it, anyone can do. Having said that, as I showed in my PhD research, we tend, as cultural consumers/actors, to search for people who can do things well; and in music education, I have found that DJing and MCing well is, for whatever reason, something in which the disaffected and otherwise 'failing' pupils can demonstrate great ability. We can say, perhaps, that this form of classroom music-making brings a certain justice into play, even if only for a moment. I would suggest that the first step towards using DJing turntables in a classroom is to forget this word 'composition'.

An experienced DJ will plan a set, perhaps lasting 20 or 30 minutes, and when this set is accompanied by improvising MCs (as often happens in my classroom), it is fair to call it a composition of sorts, that said. But, in terms of 'first steps', I would suggest that performance rather than composition is the best thing to keep in mind. Get the two turntables (or CD players, which I'm told are also easy to use) and discuss the basic terms: why is there a groove? How many grooves are there? (Two—one on each side—is the correct answer, by the way!) What do we call this thing which sits in the groove? And so on. I find that, from the moment the needle falls in to the groove, and I start sliding it back and forth ('scratching'), the learners are usually transfixed by the remarkable sound. Get a volunteer or two to experiment with scratching (I normally use the solo vocal and guitar breaks from Queen's 'I Want to Break Free' or Ozzy singing acapella on Black Sabbath's 'War Pigs', simply because the solo sound should make it easier for learners to understand that they are actually hearing a sound backwards and forwards (also, hearing Sabbath helps to get attention of the 'goth' and 'metaller' pupils, some of whom might complain about hating dance music).

Moving on to the mixer, again pupil demonstration can work wonders for exploring the possibilities for sonic combination (e.g. Ozzy singing over the top of some hardcore dance track—easy enough to pull off, even for the novice DJ). If there are some enthusiasts of hardcore MC-orientated dance music (which is likely, in the contemporary inner-city UK school at least, I contend), you might be able to get someone to MC over a dance record, or get someone to perform a mix. A potential problem, of course, is that all this presumes that you have DJ decks and some suitable vinyl to hand. The former is easily purchasable from contemporary educational catalogues; that said, asking the pupils for tips (if you have enthusiasts) and then ordering online is probably the best method for acquiring suitable vinyl.

As to what we can [do] from bringing this music and the musical equipment in to the classroom, I would say we gain a very valuable lesson: that, in some contexts, the pupils know more about music than we do. Admitting this fact is valuable because, in that moment when the pupils realize some individuals amongst their number can DJ much better than the teacher, the learning climate is transformed for the better: the

13 This narrative is based on an email discussion with Peter Dale on DJing, MCing and the value of the 'dex' for low-achieving and disaffected boys. Pete has been head of music for many years at a challenging inner-city school in the north east of England. Before taking up teaching, Peter performed in numerous punk underground bands, gaining generous support from several of the most significant 'alternative rock' groups of the 1990s (Sonic Youth, At the Drive-In, Fugazi, and others). He also ran the influential DIY record label Slampt during the same period. He has an MA and has recently completed a PhD entitled 'Anyone Can Do It: Traditions of Punk and the Politics of Empowerment' from Newcastle University (2010).

music classroom becomes a dangerous place where, as I have just stated, the possibility for a feeling of justice appears for just a moment, perhaps. I am drawing here, as I did in my PhD, on Derrida's conception of justice: a possibility (or impossibility which, nevertheless, must be) contingent upon 'aporia' (and thus necessarily requiring a decision). 'Perhaps', in other words, is the condition of justice, for Derrida. Justice, in his view, does not follow from some 'equality' or perfect mutuality being made present, for justice cannot have full presence. In my PhD, I suggest that music can sometimes encourage the appearance of a feeling which, perhaps, is a glimpse of something like the justice about which Derrida theorizes. When the learners take control of my classroom, and when I learn from them how to DJ or I learn about how they put together their MC raps, perhaps there is a flash of justice, I would suggest. It would be naive, or at least it would be contrary to the theories of Derrida, to think that justice can be fixed or made into law, however; and I would argue, therefore, that it is as much the relations within the classroom as it is the decks or the musical content of 'DJ music' which makes this form of musicking valuable in a school environment.

Clearly, understanding how effective learning should happen in school music and further or higher education institutions requires a realignment of both learner and teacher creativities. Institutionalized pedagogy and learning needs to reflect real world practice by looking to the fields in which they operate.

If we seek to take account of new thinking about pedagogy—how the establishment of a community of engagement conforms to the needs of the learner, and the links between local communities and the global community—then we need to reframe the expanding classroom environment. We have evidence of 'how' pupils, teachers, and artists learn collaboratively. We also have evidence of 'when' and in 'what' contexts technology and pedagogy can be coupled and made an implicit part of *musical creativities*.

Educational environments, as exemplified in music classrooms, differ from those of earlier decades. The integrated, pervasive networks that support innovations in teaching, have been well documented and theorized (see Loi and Dillon, 2006). In music education, research studies have been published on the possibility of using media-rich sources of musical information (S. Dillon, 2006), on the opportunities for interaction and collaboration with people who otherwise would be inaccessible (Seddon, 2007), and on the use of digital networked technologies in adaptive educational environments, where these facilitate creative musical activities (Ruthmann, 2007a).

We have seen that technology frees time for creative development through automation. Somekh (2000, 2007) maintain that digital technologies offer the opportunity to extend spaces for creativity by bringing communities together, for example, in collaborative partnerships between schools and other learning sites at the level of individual artists, arts organizations, and schools and universities. Composers, performers, audiences, and artists offer teachers new kinds of interactivity and extend the spaces available for interaction and exhibition. This makes it possible to experiment, be innovative, take risks, and close the traditional gap between the 'inside' and 'outside' of school communities of learning. (See Ledgard, (2006) for a discussion of the work of the Teacher Artist Partnerships (TAP) consortium.)

The potential of the Internet as a new learning environment has resulted in several organizations developing technology-enhanced learning. The Associated Board, for example, recently launched an innovative free website: www.soundjunction.org. SoundJunction comprises a set of dynamic tools for exploring, discovering and creating music. The site offers opportunities to link creativity with technology, and claims to break the boundaries of conventional musical practices. Another learning environment for stimulating creativity with innovative technological practice is Sonic Postcards.[14] This national education programme devised and delivered by Sonic Arts Network, which

---

[14] Sonic Postcards is used in schools throughout the UK, encouraging pupils to engage with their sound environment and be creative with ICT. The website (http://soundandmusic.org/projects/sonic-postcards) contains Sonic

promotes and explores the art of sound via the Internet (www.sonicartsnetwork.org). Sonic Arts Network has recently been awarded The New Statesman New Media Award 2006 for making the most significant contribution to education through the use of new media technology. Sonic Postcards won the award for helping children learn about new media technology by developing a fun and educational experience. The way Sonic Postcards works is through enabling pupils from across the UK to explore and compare their local sound environment by the composition and exchange of sound postcards with other schools via the Internet. It illustrates how the impact of digital technologies intersecting with civic life, can affect a small community, or an entire nation. This is a promising use of technology that extends rather than reinforces traditional models.

Students appropriate and learn music's diverse forms, as illustrated by new participatory styles of creativity such as that generated by style mixing, an outcome of the fluid roles between DJs and audience at urban dance clubs, and modalities of *musical creativities*, as illustrated by the compositional/ improvisational and performance styles of creativities, for their own purpose. They learn how to subvert conventions and structures and to irritate the guardians of musical canons——that is, the old relationships of power and patronage which value the sedimented, established, and entrenched singular category of 'musical creativity' which has been more taken for granted than explicitly questioned. The social dimensions of creativity, particularly in the use of the Internet, encourage the blurring of traditional boundaries, and confront claims to being the route to judging what constitutes creativity, and the application of a single, unified, or universalizing set of criteria for evaluating individual pieces and performances. With style mixing we see music's production and consumption merge in the blatant appropriation and re-assembling of stylistically diffuse hooks, riffs, and melodic phrases contingent on the dance, the bodies, and the sensibilities of dancegoers. Similarly, in digital experimental art music, where digital musicians specialize in algorithmic composition,[15] as we saw in Chapter 7 with the genre called 'live coding', the status of the musical material becomes extraordinarily fluid, reappearing as a sample source for improvisatory inclusion in another work.

We also see music circulate through the Internet to be newly 'realized' and 'remixed' in local club performances through the sampling practices of DJs. The use of the Internet is gradually making its way into schools. There is a slow change in orientation to the technology, away from the information-retrieval stance to one that can promote and stimulate the realization of meaning and a genuine response; a rethinking of the relationship to internet technology and an attempt to address the lack of congruence between youth, style, and musical taste. Sharing and shifting of expertise needs to be recognized as a characteristic feature of digital technology creativities. For this to happen, the issue central to building *musical creativities* is to challenge existing pedagogical practice. If technology is to be used effectively in collaboration with other Internet users and artists/ practitioners there are many decisions to be made. For instance:

◆ What should the level of resources and collaboration be? Should it include collaboration in course design, teaching in teams, the joint development of resources and sharing of resources available for students to allow technologies to play a central role in building *musical creativities*? Should it engage in learning comparable to parallel invention in mainstream music industries?

....

Postcards created by the pupils alongside their accompanying work, such as films, images of art work and creative writing, as well as other information such as project details, teacher resources, press, and partner information.

[15] Algorithmic composition or musical 'live coding' makes creative use of technology, particularly digital technology, by exploring tool development for abstract compositional modes using laptops. For further discussion of how musical live coding and other music education technology can transform pedagogy and learning as developed by Professor Alex Ruthmann, University of Massachusetts, see www.alexruthmann. com/blog1/

◆ What is the nature of the learning tasks that build *musical creativities* with technology? How do we plan for *musical creativities* experiences which incorporate understandings of music's self-social, technological, and temporal dimensions effectively?

◆ How do the boundaries of individual, collaborative and collective authorship shift with technological mediations, and change the nature of the teacher's role?

◆ How should courses and the organization of teaching change to make better use and mediation of both a globally dispersed, virtual community, and a localized, co-present public through the use of digitized music and the Internet.

◆ How does digital technology change the nature of the assessment of *musical creativities*? Does *musical creativities* make it possible to change assessment practices radically?

Building *musical creativities* within children's learning cultures: forms of authorship in composition

Here I introduce a study of children's accounts of the experience of composing, and what composing came to mean to a group of 12-year-old children who, as members of a weekly lunchtime 'Music Creators' Soundings Club, were watched, listened to, and invited to reflect on their understanding and negotiated meanings as part of a social community. A phenomenological approach to analysis was used to make sense of the final interviews (see Appendix A), data to which we now turn. It was found that the children composed in qualitatively different ways. Of the 18 participants, four illustrative cases are presented. From observation and analysis of compositions, composition was thematized as:

◆ a fluid integration of action and thought emphasizing the sociality of authorship;

◆ a time-based piece including a spectrum of activities ranging from improvisation during a performance through to formalized and partially notated composition changed in performance;

◆ a formative defining act or form using principles of 'object-based', 'sound-based', and 'process-based' practices.

However, as seen elsewhere (M.S. Barrett, 2003; Espeland, 2003), the diversity and complexity of the composing experience is more salient when children are focused on their own perceptions of the experience of composing. These phenomenological accounts, drawn from the final interviews, which took one hour each, resulted in over 100 pages of material. This provided information for the researcher about the significant events of composing, the individual and socially imposed rules of engagement, aspects of their creative functioning, and their perceptions relating to the making of their own meanings and the meanings of their musical worlds as composers. The findings show that those children who composed individually had their own instrument and were accustomed to routine schedules of between 30 minutes to three hours of composing their own music each week. Paired or trio collaborations resulted in the players spending extended periods of out-of-session time working together, to the extent of regular 'sleepovers' or recruiting a new member as a performance facilitator. For these children, the compositional experience seemed to be defined by temporal parameters—'Having time to think'. This meant that time became a function of the act itself, as can be seen in the following narratives.

Narrative 10.5

Tim composes 'proper pieces' demonstrating personal authorship with emphasis on performance-composition. Tim had completed five years of formal instrumental tuition on piano and reached Grade 5 piano, Grade 4 theory and Grade 3 violin. For Tim, composing meant 'playing around' until he 'found a chord' he liked and began 'working with it'. He would then assign a chord as a signpost 'to mark the point where I return to the first section'. Then he would 'fix' these 'bits' into sections. This involved 'fixing' what was good and 'marking it out' into sections and 'binning the bits that weren't good or were too hard to play or remember'. For remembering the order of each section, he used a strategy of signposting certain time points which 'mark the end of each section'. The strategy of envisioning 'sections' allowed him to move around and back-and-forth playing through and thinking 'back to the beginning idea'. This process involved the construction of a frame, some aspects of which were notated, which evolved as the piece was built up and assembled in bits. As Tim metaphorically suggests: 'It's something like when you do a puzzle, you do a bit and you can't do anymore so you go away and then you come back and you've found some more ideas for fixing and finalizing'. Tim committed these 'proper pieces' to memory using a recursive pathway that involved looking back, orbiting around, and moving back-and-forth between phases of exploration ('finding'), selection ('focusing'), aural testing ('fixing'), revision and editing ('finalizing') on evolving drafts in musical memory.

Narrative 10.6

Lia composes 'quick pieces' demonstrating communal authorship with emphasis on improvisation-performance. Lia had played the guitar since the age of seven. When she 'made her own pieces' they were always on guitar. She'd spend most of her time 'mucking around with ideas'. Unlike Tim, Lia was less inclined to revise or select ideas for reworking. Instead, composing was directly linked to her love of performing and the having of, and playing with, ideas. All of her compositions were referred to as 'pieces I play', as is illustrated in the following comments: 'For me, a made-up piece is just like . . . a quick piece you like to play now' and often did play in front of friends and family. 'You can even make mistakes and you just gear up and include them . . . Whenever you play it again, it comes out different anyway so its never really the same thing or set in your memory.' Her intention was to make pieces afresh. Ideas were edited to what was playable through physical action and memorable as ideas revisited. 'You just put your mind to it . . . by mucking around with some ideas you find from things you know . . . it's a musical search . . . I like to reuse ideas . . . then you anchor these ideas while you play through without stopping.' Lia intentionally composed 'quick pieces'. She moved between sensory and motor processes in a way she described as 'being like an intersection', whereby 'ideas come from all directions and from different places'. She would 'find' and 'anchor' musical ideas that were both sensory-directed and patterns of physical action: the actions of a body well attuned to its needs, goals, and interests, rendered possible through the body's interaction with an experience-shaping 'musical search'. There were moments of sensory immersion 'in my own world', while at other moments her bodily hardware, whether innate or acquired, 'would go a little bit crazy and do whatever comes out first'. Lia emphasized the role of body and action specific to 'being a guitarist', in which the relation between sound and body was evident, embedded and constituted in her constructed meaning of 'quick pieces'.

Narrative 10.7

This narrative is about collaborations of 'pieces you don't play and forget', demonstrating collaborative authorship with emphasis on composition-performance. Of the eight pairs of players who exclusively co-constructed pieces, Chloe and Sorcha both thought that friendship-pairing enabled them to extend their individual capabilities as well as offer some protection from the judgement of others. Chloe emphasized the value of collaboration in her commentary about co-composing several 6–10 minute pieces, one of which was called 'The Life Cycle of a Flower'. She said: 'Our pieces were made and played together . . . when we performed it sounded like an actual piece. It's not like you're in music where you must have this and this and this. We could do what we wanted and it was ours. It's because it wasn't like a little piece that you play and forget, it was like doing our best stuff in it. It wasn't like "we better do this and that" because it's easy.' For Chloe and Sorcha, composing a piece gave them the exclusive right to play their own music, whereupon each piece became endowed with a meaning that was understood in relation to children's musical purposes, and which involved an exclusive collaborative partnership in the making of 'a piece we play'. This was made possible by assembling sections according to a form-defined plan that was decided prior to starting work on the piece. 'I really enjoyed having all that time, like all day, to work on it . . . It was like the biggest thing I've done, except for doing exams and playing flute and stuff. It got the best of both of us . . . This really was my piece.' The pursuit of memorability and playability meant that 'playing it again and again is different to playing it just once'.

Similarly for Maria, always partnered with Sidin, the boundary between imagining and forming wholes meant: 'I figure out a couple of ideas first. Then I play them and Sidin makes something up and then we stop and talk. We keep starting and stopping, and then going back over and over parts, and then playing the whole thing through loads of times.' The planning is made explicit by a process Sidin described as 'confirming' whereby they played and then purposively stop to share with each other feedback on the worthiness of an idea. As a revisionist strategy, 'confirming' appeared to be central to the socially mediated meanings of collaborative creativity.

Narrative 10.8

Ashton, Adrian, and Dion are three boys who work as a collective with emphasis on de- and re-composition and re-mixing known songs. For some children, arrangement and interpretation appear to be indistinguishable and yet the relation to composition was evident in the collaboration of Ashton, Adrian, and Dion, who deliberately reworked and reassembled versions of an existing pop song, R. Kelly's 'I Believe I Can Fly'. The first presentation of the song was introduced by Adrian who said: 'We know the songs and we've put them together. We've changed some bits, merged others, though'. In the next session the song was rearranged to incorporate a third voice, plus congas, and a dance routine. The next presentation involved a remix. Each successive version was reworked, reauthored, and presented anew. None of these performances highlighted aspects of the adult model which relates composition as a process involving planning, use of sketches (Sloboda, 1985), and other staged-based notions (Wallas, 1926), or as an original product separated in time from performance, or an exactly specified product. These reauthorings of 'our piece', as described by Dion, showed deliberate manipulation and remixing of musical elements of known songs that they all owned and identified with. Theirs was a song that was re-composed, wherein the music is formative, creating a sense of collective identity and collective authorship.

The multivoicedness of children as composers

The discussion that follows explores the significance of *musical creativities* in terms of the different types of creativities children utilize as composers and the ways in which they ascribe meaning differently.[16] The differences are conveyed through the use of an image-based research tool called 'talk-and-draw', utilized during the final interview. Here, I invited the children to think back over their experiences of composing over six months, to draw an image to convey what it is to compose, and to tell me about what they had drawn (see Burnard, 2000a,b, 2004, 2006b,c). Table 10.1 shows a small sample and summary of children's meanings most characteristically conveyed and explored.

Musical creativities emerge that shape how children composed in qualitatively different ways. These *musical creativities* are bound to larger questions concerning the nature of the representations

---

[16] For further discussion of examples in which children's composing approaches are conveyed through the use of the image-based research tool called 'talk-and-draw', utilized during the final interview, see Burnard (2006b).

Table 10.1 Summary and sample of children's accounts of *musical creativities*

Authorships	Modality	Accounts	Practice principles
Personal	Performance-composition	My own journey . . . my own path . . . my own musical search . . . to find, fix, and fuse ideas . . . while you play through without stopping; to make proper pieces	Recursive, individual production of a piece as a temporal imaginary. A performative constructive process using cued elicitations, looking back, orbiting around; time-mapped fixed pieces
Communal	Improvisation-performance	I combine a lot of different people's ideas in my music; and combine ideas with other music to create quick pieces	A performance results from ideas meeting and colliding in a process of inherited cultural knowledge. A process of retelling by playing through, and deliberately salvaging and anchoring ideas in real time pieces
Collaborative	Composition-performance	Together we make something up and then we stop and talk . . . keep starting and stopping . . . confirming . . . going back over and over . . . we make lasting pieces together that we don't play and forget	A mutual encounter of collaborative appropriation of material; required joint remembering based on co-authoring and authorized ideas of pre-performance
			Composing using weaving and spinning feedback, 'confirming' as a reinforcing device for time-testing ideas varied in performance
Collective	Re-composition	We got some tracks and other sounds to use . . . we added new bits . . . we remade beats . . . added new lines . . . redid loops	Successive re-creations, low-tech bricolages afforded by reworking, reauthoring, and remixing song elements

that young people both see and interpret as self-social practices which take place in this space. What these metaphors suggest about composition is that meaning is multi-dimensional and multi-layered. In the course of describing and explaining how they composed, the children gave descriptions and explanations that constituted their views on composing, underscored by their assumptions about themselves as composers: particular perspectives arising out of the musical community of which they were a member. In recognizing and synthesizing these complexities, a consolidated thematic overview is offered (see Fig. 10.1) which attempts to portray children's experience of *musical creativities* in terms of a phenomenological characterization into temporal, spatial, relational, and bodily themes.

For these children, composition was essentially a meaning-making activity. It was constructed and negotiated between them, as participants within a community called 'The Creators Club'. This involved an interplay between the intentions underlying their creative process, to create a time-tested, time-based, time-bound and time-free activity using pieces which ranged from those that were relived 'over and over' in order to make a 'proper' piece to ones 'you don't play and forget'.

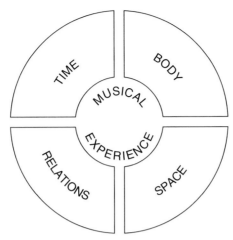

Fig. 10.1 Experiential dimensions of *musical creativities.*

Composing depended upon the 'knowing' body to draw on prior experience and knowledge as tools for reflecting within a time frame when the past was experienced as achievement. Rules for creating and acting together of pieces newly created, re-created anew or re-authored during performance were broadly understood, not only as formal and explicit but also as unwritten or tacit routines for 'anchoring' or 'confirming' the worthiness of ideas. The role of rehearsal, or 'playing back over', as a reflective, recursive process was a common aspect in time-bound and time-tested pieces, constructed in collaboration with others or individually with others in mind. The use of feedback was a common characteristic of collaborative compositional settings to articulate their developing ideas. The composing process did not follow a straight path but rather took a more cyclical or recursive shape, based on assembling parts to forming a structured whole.

The children played out a range of relationships with compositions in ways which demonstrated a strong correlation between the degree of structuring of a composition and the identity attributed to it. For example, there was an 'ideas piece', a 'quick piece', a 'proper piece', a piece 'you don't just play and forget' and an 'actual piece'. Often the *raison d'être* for composition was to create an identifiable piece that required the child/children to critically and consciously create an intended object. The compositional map often contained definitive structural signposts that acted as temporal markers to facilitate memory. Thus, the lived space of composing a piece was in a sense an object of involvement that was defined as an artefact of their musical biography or past experience.

We have plenty of research evidence to show how teachers have for many years been aware of the need to give children space to be creative in music, and to create music that matters to them, and which records how they have been excited by the times when children have produced music that has a real sense of authorial voice and a powerful set of meanings. But there has been no explicit meta-musical-language[17] available to most teachers to give children explicit feedback on their work, and to help them develop this sense of voice and ability with which to convey their personal and collective meanings more powerfully. In part, this comes from the traditional privileging of

---

[17] 'Meta-musical-language' is a term used for the specialist and general vocabulary used to discuss music's diverse creativities—literally, a language about musical creativities. So it might include relatively familiar terms such as composing, improvising, and genre, as well as more specialist terms such as remixing, sampling, re-assembling, and style mixing.

notated compositions over improvised real time performing and sound-based forms of creativity. Since most music teachers have not been, and are not, composers or improvisers they have little personal experience to draw on, which exacerbates the lack of explicit protocols for teaching and assessment.

Assessment and student engagement in *musical creativities*

The early work on creativity from 1950 to 1970, used psychometric approaches, such as the Torrance Tests of Creative Thinking, to measure creativity. These relied on paper and pencil assessments that tested divergent thinking, cognitive fluency, flexibility, and originality, and were widely used to identify children who were 'creative'. Since that time the emphasis has shifted to the study of people's capacity to think creatively, which has resulted in a very large body of literature. In the UK, the seminal report of the National Advisory Committee on Creative and Cultural Education (NACCCE, 1999) uses a definition of creativity that reflects this shift, namely that creativity is 'imaginative activity fashioned so as to produce outcomes that are both original and of value' (p. 30). However, the subsequent elision between 'creativity' and 'creative learning', and what they might look like in relation to *musical creativities*, has led to ambiguity in the application of these terms in different educational contexts; and lack of clarity concerning what development in *musical creativities* is, how it can be supported, and what purposes it might serve. We have yet to find ways to assess effectively and make clear distinctions between differentiated *Musical creativities* within the accountability parameters that value certain kinds of creativity and knowledge across key stages of school curricula.[18]

A uniform assessment framework needs to be developed that incorporates consistent judgements about assessable product outcomes and evidence of achievement in *musical creativities*, as for example, creative outcomes concerning both 'originality' and 'value' creativity constructs, and commonly agreed indicators of change in the progression of *musical creativities*. But there are important questions to consider concerning how progression in differentiated *musical creativities* might take place? What changes have occurred over time in terms of what students know, understand and can do to 'progress' in *musical creativities*? How does this influence pedagogy? Not having answers to these questions has made it difficult to construct assessment rating processes that translate contemporary assessment theory into viable classroom practices, particularly when they are required to fit different contexts and purposes whilst maintaining internal consistency and coherence.

A limited start was made by Craft et al. (2006), in a small study of progression in creative learning that examined musical and written compositions by primary and secondary school pupils. A reanalysis of this study took matters a stage further (Burnard, 2008), by inventing product outcomes linked to pupils' perceptions of creative qualities. From this analysis, development in creative learning became apparent in terms of how pupils evaluated the product outcome. There are ways of conceptualizing distinct creativities, as examined in general descriptive research studies that characterize elements of pedagogy and learning generally and those specific to music.[19] But although there

---

[18] For further discussion of some of the most enduring challenges in educational practice on the assessment of creativity in general, and in relation to music/arts education specifically, see Black and Wiliam (2006), Burnard (2011a,b), Hennessey and Amabile (1999) and Leong et al. (in press).

[19] Other descriptive research studies have placed emphasis upon reflection on the characteristics of the creative learning process as well as the product outcome. These studies, including the Arts-PROPEL project (Burnard, 2011c; Burnard and Lavicza, 2010b,c; Burnard and Younker, 2002; Burnard and Wyse, 2002; Burnard et al., 2007, 2010a,b; Burt-Perkins, 2009; Byrne et al. 2002), report on the centrality of teachers' constructs of creativity. A further problem arises from the setting in which creativity assessment

is evidence that teachers can make judgements about what they are assessing, the way in which teachers of different subject domains judge, or capture and report formatively and summatively, the multiplicity of *musical creativities* and the creative learning processes or the creative product outcomes, still remains unclear. The key themes that emerge from the research are therefore concerned with:

◆ how the theoretically derived constructs of multiple creativities in music and creative learning relate to those of various participants (teachers, pupils, artists, etc.) within the genres articulated in the field of music and music in education (see Fig. 9.1);

◆ how different genres record, evaluate, and assess understanding and progress in and across multiple creativities in music;

◆ how teachers make judgements, and whether these take account students' own self-assessments about *musical creativities* and creative learning in music.

The point being made here is that assessment practices need to differentiate multiple creativities in music and acknowledge students' own self-assessments, and provide a range of assessment practices that fit different contexts and purposes, whilst maintaining internal consistency and coherence.

Culturally specific aspects of performance creativity and the role of individuality and personal style in musical multiple creativities are key concerns regarding assessment, along with the differing purposes of formative and summative assessment with regard to *musical creativities*. We are concerned, specifically, with the notion that true formative assessment can often be replaced by ongoing summative assessment:

> there is an assumption that all assessment by teachers is formative, adding to the blurring of the distinction between formative and summative purposes and to teachers changing their own on-going assessment into a series of 'mini' assessments each of which is essentially summative in character.

> (Harlen and James, 1997, p. 365)

Clearly we need formative assessment to develop *musical creativities* itself, and summative assessment to chart their progress. Knowing appropriate assessment criteria for the latter are more likely to help teachers formulate appropriate formative interventions in pupils' work. We also need to remember that the formative use of summative assessment is, in most international school systems, a common modality in today's schools.

There have been a number of attempts to develop detailed, practice-based work on creativity assessment.[20] There are also accumulating reports of successful models, based on Amabile's (1983) 'consensual assessment technique' (CAT). These have been used in visual art, composing music (Hickey, 2000), poetry and story writing. CAT has also been used for assessing creativity in products (Murphy and Espeland, 2008), for open tasks, and for artists to judge the drawings of primary school children (Hennessey and Amabile, 1988). It would seem from research into teacher's practices incorporating CAT that they do have the ability to correctly identify varying levels of creativity as evidenced in the creative products of children.

A recent study of the assessment of outcomes other than those conventionally assessed (Daugherty et al., 2008) explored the foundations of a valid assessment, meaning one which aligns curriculum and pedagogy in a symbiotic relationship that is not linear or cyclic, but a moving mosaic, responding to pupil's perceptions, needs and circumstances. Spruce (1996) argues that validity is

---

takes place across curricula areas. Collectively, these authors have gleaned their knowledge of assessment practices across a wide range of programme settings and subject domains.

[20] However, for reasons of space these are not discussed here. Nonetheless they are good examples of steps along the route towards creativity assessment.

the key and overarching issue in all assessment studies. The notion of 'construct validity' is therefore central to how 'creativities' are both perceived and applied in the curriculum/assessment relationship and in the day-to-day practice of music teachers and pupils.[21] This raises useful questions. Where does creativity reside in assessment for different *musical creativities*? What constructs are teachers actually assessing? How do teachers of different subjects judge something to be creative?

Two studies provide evidence that teachers can make judgements about creativity specifically and within this mix, and that they know how multiple creativities are present in arts learning. The DELTA (Development of Learning and Teaching in the Arts) research project, conducted by Hargreaves et al. (1996), reported substantial agreement between primary school teachers. Whilst teachers appeared to use similar criteria in their evaluations, it was less clear on how they arrived at their judgements. Building on this earlier work, Burnard and Lavicza (2010a,b) used interviews, contextual observations, analysis of practice and assessment artefacts and an online survey to link teacher–pupil creativity constructs with assessment practice. In this Creativity Assessment Practice in the Arts (CAPA) project, key constructs used in practice include risk-taking, skill components, and the originality of the product outcome.

These discussions concerning theory and practice, and putting theory into practice, lead naturally to questions of how teachers view creativity generally and, in terms of the multiple creativities in music, how these creativities are evidenced in the product outcomes of creative learning in music. This leads us to refine the earlier questions.

- What is the distinction between multiple creativities in music as outcomes and processes? What are the criteria on which teachers base their qualitative evaluations? For example, are they based on forms of authorship (collaborative creativity, communal creativity, collective creativity), or temporal modalities of performance creativities, such as improvisation-performance (creating a new work during a performance) or composition-performance (creativity in the performance of a notated composition)?

- Do constructs along the spectrum of *musical creativities* differ between teacher, pupil, and artists? How and in what ways are they seen as differentiated forms of expertise, highlighting the mental, and physical skills involved in articulating and expressing music from the mind, through the body, on and out of the instrument?

- How do teachers make summative and formative judgements? How are these judgements different from what music industries measure? Are there forms of assessment and a framework of progression that recognize individual development in *musical creativities*, and that can: (1) discriminate between different levels; (2) make meaningful comparisons; and (3) measure change in pupils' development of *musical creativities* between assessments?

- What is the role of peer assessment in assessing a spectrum of *musical creativities*?

Which *musical creativities* are most versatile and appropriate for teaching? What are the appropriate competencies for creativity in music, and how do they differ from tradition to tradition, field to field? What can we learn from existing music education initiatives intended to broaden the concept of musical creativity? What *musical creativities* are amenable to evaluation and why do the music and education fields have very different approaches to evaluation?

---

[21] For further discussion of ways of documenting moments of significant creativity in music and understanding how these evolve, develop, and change among children and young people, see Burnard (1995), Craft et al. (2007, 2008), Crow (2006, 2008), and Csikszentmihalyi and Wolfe (2002).

The ways that professional musicians tune in to teachers and learners provides an important clue as to how teachers can better negotiate the spectrum of *musical creativities* that is bound up in the broader institutional forces which provide the basis of musical production and reproduction. In the same way that string instruments are tuned on the basis of tension, so the success of pedagogy and learning in *musical creativities* depends on the tension between pedagogy and professional practice being maintained in balance. On the one hand, as we open up the spectrum of *musical creativities*, effective learning environments will be those that are attuned to diverse ways of working, and which create new ways to enhance *musical creativities* in education.

Ways of enabling a spectrum of *musical creativities* include:

◆ reflecting critically on the specific and deliberately chosen creative elements, forms and modalities of the task, and the degree of invention that makes one musical creativity different to another;

◆ allowing time for a high proportion of pupil talk, much of it occurring between pupils and pupils, pupils and teachers, and with musicians reflecting on industrial approaches to developing diverse forms of creativity in music;

◆ modelling the use of multiple *musical creativities* and documenting the cognitive facts that constitute the substance of the understandings gained in the modelling process;

◆ exploring different skills and performance behaviours and behaviour modalities that communicate culture-specific aspects and awareness of community cultural development, and engagement along a spectrum of *musical creativities*;

◆ enabling the inclusion of career education and industrial experience in practices of *musical creativities* in the curriculum areas in which educational change can be vigorously pursued;

◆ developing pedagogic practices that embrace industrial experience and practices.

One of the most immediate problems facing teachers and researchers is to agree on a satisfactory definition of the term '*musical creativities*'. A satisfactory definition must embrace the spectrum of creativities that songwriters, DJs, composers, artists, musicians, producers, music teachers, and learners presently engage in. What these real world practices contribute to our understanding of the nature of *musical creativities* is the understanding that a single creativity in music is not enough. We need to develop a language for talking about *musical creativities* that serves the needs of musicians, producers, composers, teachers, and listeners alike. We need to assert our own belief in the importance of *musical creativities* and the way it pervades every aspect of our musical lives and society. We need to reflect on the underlying 'rules' and strategies of the fields of music in which we work and play, in a similar way to that of Bourdieu in *The Rules of Art*. Of course we must make sense of our own engagement in music and the modalities that guide our creativities as composers, improvisers, songwriters, and DJs. For this, we need to rethink how we experience multiple creativities in music. Our discussion in this chapter has sought to show that across different sites within the field of music and music in education, music rules in the way that it does because of the rules which govern its creative practices. It remains to be seen whether the innovative, entrepreneurial practices being pursued by contemporary musicians, and the issues raised in this book will sharpen the challenges of *musical creativities* that confront all of us working in educational and industrial settings. The crucial issue is to find what sustains the necessity of diverse creativities in music and our capacity to value multiple creativities in music in personally relevant and culturally significant ways. We need to explore the extent to which teachers may participate in this process as both subjects and agents and, in so doing, enhance their professionalism.

Discussion questions

1. While most of us in education have general notions of what collaborative creativity is about, such notions often diverge significantly from what those in creative industries understand them to be. This divergence of views is known all too well by musicians in relation to their own field. So what are empathic and intercultural creativities, and what might be the mistaken assumptions here? What assumptions form the basis for your own personal views?

2. How should people be trained in distinctive *musical creativities*? Do distinctive *musical creativities* characteristically aspire to something more ambitious and considerably more substantial than they represent? If so, why?

3. How can we promote and develop distinctive forms of *musical creativities* in music education that aspire to something more ambitious than the rhetorical and political, and that presume to be based on something more substantial than mere assertion?

4. How can personal and collaborative creativities in music be developed and assessed in education?

5. What are the challenges that teachers face in the practice and assessment of multiple *musical creativities*? What if the route which is taken for assessment depends on one further question: what (or whom) is the assessment for? What distinguishes your view and grounds for belief and action, and your commitment to critical reflection?

6. Is the songwriter's silence, their putting down of the pen, an act of performance?

Appendix A

Methodology and methods

This section outlines the rationale for organizing the book according to narratives of practice, and presents a rationale for the investigation of how multiple musical creativities inhere in the practices of musicians. Following this introduction, the aim of the study, research questions, case study methodology, sampling criteria, and design will be discussed, and its adequacy and applicability considered.

The sociologist Bourdieu (1993c) and phenomenologist Van Manen (1990) have defined the relationship of objective and subjective worlds from a perspective in which the criteria of rationality itself are already value-laden. These values are attributed to the meanings that we derive from the 'things' and events of the world. In accepting subjectivity and objectivity as inseparable, we emphasize the social nature of research and the researched. As Van Manen (1990) noted:

> Human science is rationalistic in that it operates on the assumption that human life may be made intelligible, accessible to human *logos* or reason, in a broad or full embodied sense. To be a rationalist is to believe in the power of thinking, insight and dialogue ... It is a naïve rationalism that believes that the phenomena of life can be made intellectually crystal clear or theoretically perfectly transparent. That is why a human science that tries to do justice to the full range of human experience cannot operate with a concept of rationality that is restricted to a formal intellectualist interpretation of human reason. Likewise, the language of thinking cannot be censured to permit only a form of discourse that tries to capture human experience in deadening abstract concepts, and in logical systems that flatten rather than deepen our understanding of human life. (pp. 16–17)

Given the principal aim of the present research, which is to explore the nature of, and extent to which, multiple creativities in music can be understood to involve different kinds of practices, it would be inappropriate to set out to test hypotheses about these creativities or to work with a closed set of analytic categories which would reduce data to quantification and statistical analysis. But rather, as was made clear by Merleau-Ponty (1962), experimental intervention should be replaced by experiential situations and constructivist, context-bound knowledge, rather than the testing of universal assumptions. The experiences of the participating musicians are to be interpreted within the contexts wherein they create. The constructivist stance strives to understand the subjective human experience, and to grasp meanings from within. Similarly, the musicians' perceptions and reflections in this study come from the inside, not the outside, of creative practice.

Selecting the musicians

The 19 musicians who are featured in the book are aged between 22 and 62 years, and form part of a sample drawn from a larger multi-dimensional study involving 47 participants, all of whom are known and visible members of musical communities which are recognized by the wider society. Drawn from diverse sites and settings, these musicians were considered to be engaged with diverse creative practices. All agreed to be interviewed about their practices.

The sampling criteria included: (1) being employed as professional composers and teaching composition in higher degree institutions; (2) having their music performed regularly; and (3) negotiating multiple selves that shift between creator, performer, and musician. I have also drawn on further sets of interview data from research studies carried out between 1999 and 2011. These focus on cohorts of students, teachers, and artists working in arts partnerships in UK settings, and include phenomenological accounts of 18 children aged 12 years. Several closely related studies of young people, teachers, and artists-in-schools are included. These interviews, which concern musicians, creativity and the making of meanings and the meanings of their practices, are drawn from a number of previous studies carried out over 15 years.

I include musicians from dramatically varying communities, cultures, and societies, such as Australia, Taiwan, England, Scotland, Wales Ireland, USA, Canada, Iran, and China, and from different musical and social backgrounds, and ethnic and class identities. As writers, including Bourdieu, have argued, a community is not natural or inevitable. Rather, it is constructed by a series of discourses about 'society'; and its boundaries are established arbitrarily as the result of (often) centuries of tradition, a community emerging only as the result of a series of societal practices.

Conducting interviews

Van Manen (1990) identified interviews as recorded conversations that serve 'as a resource for developing a richer and deeper understanding of a human phenomenon' (p. 66). To encourage deep conversations about the ever-expanding practices used by musicians, to advance our understanding of who they are, what they do, and what they know and can tell us about musical creativities, interviewing needs to designed 'to aid us in gaining access to the conceptual world in which our subjects live' (Geertz, 1973, p. 24).

The drawbacks, as argued by Graue and Walsh (1998) concern time limitations, gaining access, and sufficient time to be able to confirm the depth and breadth of artistic practices, and to illustrate the variety of ways that ideas are given form and how projects are planned and executed. The data contained a significant number of interviews (a total of 40 interviews were conducted, of which 19 included here) over a prolonged period of time (six months) in conjunction with some observations and examination of artefacts. The depth of data collected in the present study was considered to be sufficient to support any findings.

Conducting individual semi-structured interviews, given sufficient time (two hours) and follow-up sessions (further two hours) enabled participants to reflect deeply on their real world practices of creating music, whether as a consequence of the different creativities that inhere in regulated and unregulated spaces, with particular modes of self-expression and performance modes, and authorized to greater or lesser degrees by various institutional and cultural capitals and positional statuses.

Whether these spaces represent sites and forms of recording, of performance, for collaboration, as fluid or fixed kinds of mediation, was considered important. It was also important for the researcher to: (1) acknowledge previous experience and relationships with music; (2) establish rapport; (3) help build a relationship on a one-to-one basis; and (4) provide time for reflection on vital aspects of their musical orientation and practice (Creswell, 1998). In some cases a second and third interview was sought to explore: (1) aspects of practice needing further elaboration; and (2) the nature and relationship between distinctive musical creativities.

The initial two-hour interview served not only as a means of encouraging each musician to reflect on their own experiences of creating music but also as a way of collecting specific details of their musical biography. In the initial interview it was decided to include the constructivist elicitation technique developed by Denicolo and M. Pope (1990), which is based on the principles of Personal Construct Psychology (see Burnard and Triantafyllaki, forthcoming; G.A. Kelly, 1955).

It was considered important to provide the musicians an opportunity to give voice to the attitudes and orientations implicit to their musical worlds. Thus, the tool of critical incident charting was used to encourage a reflective conversational style of engagement, whereby musicians would be asked to reflect on their prior musical experiences and recall a specific instance, situation, person, or event that they considered to be of special musical significance. The ensuing accounts of their creative experiences were charted in the form of a winding river, where each bend represented an influential incident and a manifestation of their formative experiences in music.

Dilemmas

One of the most problematic methodological dilemmas that emerged was the difficulty that comes from reductive categories for distinguishing one musician from another, one practice from another, and one musical genre from another. The practice of dividing music into one tradition over another is as problematic as simply labelling Duke Ellington's practice as 'composer'. Whilst he was described as a pathfinder into new realms, and one of the first jazz musicians to be labelled a 'composer'—a Western tradition which promotes the office of the composer—he was also a first-rate jazz pianist, a performer, and a big band and orchestral leader. To label him as a 'composer' suggests qualitatively distinct and irrelevant connotations.

It is no accident then, with the ever-accelerating pace of technological innovations, that firm lines cannot be easily drawn between being 'a composer' and being a specialized 'performer'. Specializations may exist, either because certain types of music, associated with special activities are the prerogative of particular groups, or because exceptional musical talent makes itself felt. More often, however, musicians cultivate multiple specializations, build broad-ranging vocations, and practise in a variety of genres, the boundaries of which are established arbitrarily. Composers may also cross several professional roles as artistic collaborators, record producers, authors, curators, narrators, critics, and theorists.

So I was not content to delimit chapters exclusively by style, using boundaries that are established as firmly as classical, jazz, or popular, or as arbitrarily as many sub-cultures of rap, hip hop, and fusions of electroacoustic music and electronic styles. The idea that musicians can be classified by type (laptop musician, digital musician, rock musician), or by an identifiable group that is homogeneous, coherent, and possesses common marks of identity and societal practices, in the forms of shared traditions, identical language, or institutional affiliations and so on, was less important than to establish authorized values of the various fields that constitute them. Hence categories of practice were established as constituted and authorized values of the various fields of music: originals band album writing and production, singer-songwriting and song performance, DJ cultures, composed and improvised musics, and interactive audio design.

Musicians often maximize their potential and strength by drawing on institutional specialization in a potent mix of performance artists, programmers, creative, producers, academics, teachers, sound mixers/engineers, authors, and researchers. However, they often resent narrowly categorical labels. Musicians are understood here not, or not simply, in terms of the construction of a career profile. How best to label musicians whose careers embody a labyrinthine development of multiple specializations, and who have many roles and promote several personas, serves to confound the logic of the field. The linguistic issues, and the rationale for categories to structure Part 2 was a problem not easily solved.

Anyone can confirm that even if they do not now play an instrument they once learnt, they are able to remember something of that learning. They will know that when you try to play something, or even sing a song from childhood, the memory seems to be traced by the fingers themselves or the vocal cords, which know what to do without being consciously directed. The division between roles of musician and performer, (performer and composer being the most common roles shared by musicians), is something which is easier to understand by clarifying purposes and practices.

Researching practice

Practices are things we do and develop. They concern the means by which we adopt particular cultural ideas and routines to govern ourselves (Atkinson, 2002). For Foucault, discourses are 'practices which form the objects of which they speak' (Foucault, 1972, p. 49). Discourse constructs the topic. Discourse influences how ideas are put into practice. Discourses *are* practices.

Bourdieu's (1990b) understanding of 'practice' in the sense of 'experience' by no means implies merely passive taken-for-granted ('doxic') knowledge. It allows us to understand how social imperatives prompt individual position-taking in a manner which, avoiding a mechanistic model of determined action, appeals to an order based on 'feeling'. Bourdieu's theory of practice thus operates on the same principle as works of art themselves, that is to say, they unify a multiplicity of discrete objects, harmonizing imperatives based on biological needs with social imperatives. Furthermore, although practice is actually experienced as 'unwilled necessity', it is neither the consequence of mere mechanical reproduction, and neither is it the working out of the seed of inspiration. In an unrecognized act of understated subversion, Bourdieu (1990a) has made artists' actions the model of all normal skilled practices accomplished in everyday life.

> The coherence without apparent intention and the unity without an immediate, visible, unifying principle of all the cultural realities that are informed by a quasi-natural logic (is this not what makes the 'eternal charm of Greek art' that Marx refers to?) are the product of the age-old application of the same schemes of action and perception, which, never having been constituted as explicit principles, can only produce an unwilled necessity which is therefore necessarily imperfect but also a little miraculous and very close in this respect to a work of art. (p. 13)

Practices orient people towards who, where, and when they are, and there are certain dimensions to acting as a person, as with a music teacher and learner, which must be constructed in practice, such that people can function as people. However, whilst people can only be people within these necessary, culturally provided orientations, there is a variety of possible ways in which these orientations can be elaborated in terms of thinking about what it is to be creative in music. Similarly, the values and meanings associated with musical creativities all index a reconstruction of 'how' one 'is' creative in music, relative to 'when' and 'where' one is in relation to 'who' is judging 'what'.

An understanding of practice describes the way creativities in music are framed, encountered, and critiqued on the basis of insights. There are at least four ways of understanding practices that are parts of the theoretical framework for conceptualizing 'practice' that I am using here. First, practices are transformative, meaning that creativity in music is recursive, and constantly undergoes change as new experiences 'talk back' through the process of creating music. Second, practices are constructivist in the sense that they are produced as a consequence of integrating theory and practice, which results in descriptive awareness, explanatory insight, and powerful understanding. Third practice is conceptual. Musical creativities use knowledge of the field that is available through personal and culturally accessible domains. Fourth, practice is contextual insofar as musicians enter into communities that bring together diverse personal, education, social, and cultural perspectives. These features of practice are by no means definitive, and each owes a legacy to paradigms of theory and practice that, under certain circumstances, may be used as explanatory systems, interpretive frameworks, or imaginative forms.

In conducting an enquiry that seeks to understand accounts of practices, I work with Bourdieu's concept of 'habitus' and his recognition that individuals contain within themselves their past and present position in the social structure 'at all times and in all places, in the forms of dispositions' (Bourdieu, 1999, p. 82). Unlike rational action theory which underplays cultural contexts, the concept of habitus emphasizes the enduring influence of a range of contexts, familial, peer group, institutional and class cultural, and their subtle, often indirect, but still pervasive influence on choices. It foregrounds the power of implicit and tacit expectations, affective responses, along with aspects of cultural capital, such as confidence and entitlement.

The idea of a narrative description of practice is described by Van Manen (1990) in this way:

> Phenomenological text is descriptive in the sense that it names something. And in this naming it points to something and it aims at letting something show itself. And phenomenological text is interpretive in the sense that it mediates. Etymologically 'interpretation' means explaining in the sense of mediating between two parties. It mediates between interpreted meaning sand the thing toward which the interpretation points. (pp. 26–7)

Alongside these theoretical concepts, Ricoeur (1981, 1991, 1992) defined historical and narrative understanding as 'interpretation in the precise sense of understanding the expressions of life fixed by writing' (1991, p. 64). Within hermeneutic thinking, the 'true meaning' of a narrative can lie in its creation, or in the subsequent moments in which it comes into the hands of successive interpreters. In interviews with these musicians, one often had the sense that what was said turned towards the real point of reference, towards that 'about which' they were speaking, whilst at other times what was said seemed to refer to an ideal sense of what it is to compose a song or an orchestral piece. Sometimes, as in any interview, one party cannot really *see* the other unless the other can see him or her in turn. So, I was seeking to understand the meaning of the thinking and doing—the practices—of musicians in diverse settings, rather than to understand what it means to be a musician in a certain setting in time. The specific shift from interpretation to promoting understanding is important, and informed by Heidegger (1962). For him, understanding is something primary which is constantly operating in us, whereas 'interpretation consists in merely cultivating this primal understanding' (p. 101).

Csikszentmihalyi's (1999) systems model provides further concepts of 'domain', 'field' and 'person', nested within the parameters of an interpretive-constructivist paradigm; and underpinned by a hermeneutic phenomenological perspective, provides a descriptive analytical focus that allows one to 'see through' existing data, texts, and contexts so as to be open to alternative conceptions, and to provide an imaginative opening through which to retrieve pasts, regardless of place or time.

It has also been important to use a notion of 'practices' as narratives, not only as maps of creative practices arising in particular social settings wherein they take place, but also to explore the social positioning in which music is created. This method lets us attend to the particularities of musical creativities. Thus a musician's habitus is acquired in the family as the product of early childhood experiences, along with schooling. It provides a general disposition, within which creative practices and narratives exteriorize themselves as subtle descriptions, which involves unwritten 'rules of the game' (the range of possibilities inscribed in the field), and which can be analysed independently of the characteristics of their occupants.

Bringing together sociological and phenomenological readings of musical creativities represents an attempt to understand the logics of practices generated by musicians whose real world practices offer a wide, essentially hermeneutic, repertoire for understanding new creativities in music, and makes connections between the macro and micro forces of changing forms. Thus, an understanding of how musicians struggle to hold together the creative identities they construct for themselves and others as they navigate complex creative terrains is also particularly important here.

Analytic procedures

The interviews employed semi-structured protocols based on the authors' previous work and the literature, along with more open-ended questions, to encourage descriptions and stories of the network of connections that bind composers together. Following the interviews, the transcript material was reduced by eliminating the words of the interviewer, and replacing them with italicized words that changed each question into a statement. This was done to preserve the meaning and flow of the exchanges while, at the same time, indicating that these words came from the question posed by the interviewer. Next, a structural approach was used to produce a shorter, synthesized narrative account with sequential and non-repetitive language. Then these condensed stories were written in the third person to illustrate the presence of the researcher in the account. The synthesized narratives were examined further to elicit common and more conceptual themes across the narratives, using an adapted version of constant comparison inquiry, as shown in Appendix Figure A.1.

Criteria for judging research quality

As with many narrative researchers who use interviewees as their prime way of eliciting data, I did not attempt to 'live the story' (Clandinin and Connelly, 2000) of musicians, because I did not gather or record detailed observation or field notes. However, other available documents, artefacts produced from the Internet, and Facebook and YouTube recordings were analysed. Some time was spent, when possible, becoming familiar with each participant's context to observe their work as musical creators and performers. Past, present, and future aspects of their work as musicians were included so as to emphasize relational and contextual dimensions.

Charmaz (2005) suggests five major criteria for judging the quality of inquiry and for understanding practices. These are displayed in Appendix Table A.1, along with the specific features of this project.

Narrative inquiry

Narrative inquiry is grounded in an interpretive epistemology, and recognizes the relationships between telling a story, analysing a narrative to construct meaning, and narration as a mode of learning and knowing (Clandinin, 2007; L. Webster and Mertova, 2007). The objective of narrative inquiry is to shift investigation towards the figures or people involved in the phenomenon under study. Narrative inquiry has the potential to provide a means for understanding not only how musical creativity is constructed and what it means, but also to understand what guides the purposes of the undertaking, what influences its delivery, how decisions are made and problems solved, the contexts of the activity, and responses to outcomes. In this way, narrative inquiry provides a new understanding of multiple musical creativities.

Chase (2005) suggests several approaches to narrative inquiry that are closely aligned with fields of research. These are the approaches of: narrative psychologists, who examine how stories affect people's lives; narrative sociologists, who examine the content and process of storytelling and identity construction; other sociologists, who use intensive interviewing to examine how interviewees use language to construct meaning and make sense of their personal lives; anthropologists, who merge life history approaches with tradition; and the more critical practices of ethnography. In this study, I develop the narrative sociologists' approach to understanding, and illustrate how practices intersect as iterative and continuous aspects of creativities in music.

The focus of the research centres on musicians themselves and their practices. The researcher's task was to gather, process, and organize the data, which allowed participants to explore, respond,

Phase 1 (P1): Open coding analysis

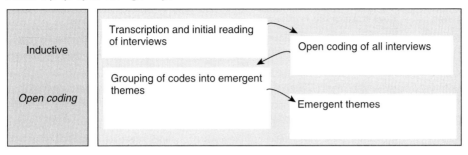

Phase 2 (P2): Inductive and deductive coding analysis

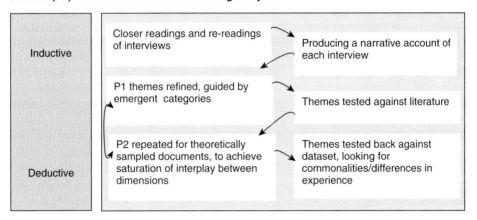

Phase 3 (P3): Whole-text reanalysis and saturation

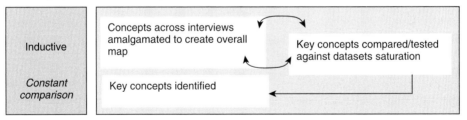

Appendix Fig. A.1 The analytical process.

and reflect on their practice, their beliefs, and experiences of musical creativities. At the same time it is acknowledged that research such as this can only be defined by the perceptions and interactions of those who participate in that particular social reality (Pring, 2000).

While I have written this book for a global audience, many of the examples, data samples, and examples are taken from English, Scottish, Welsh, Australian, Taiwanese, Irish and US-American sources. This is not just because it is convenient to do so, but also because these are the national contexts with which I am most familiar. I feel that this familiarly allows me to make more confident claims about how certain practices work as exemplars of wider global trends.

I do not pull these musicians' accounts of good practice neatly together in order to give stakeholders a formula for taking instant action. To collapse the complexity of multiple musical creativities would be as unhelpful as insisting on their mystery. Instead, I map what is going on, and why we

Appendix Table A.1 Five criteria for judging the quality of research inquiry

Criterion	Ways in which this is achieved	Where this is achieved
Credibility/ trustworthiness	Findings were developed over a range of interviews, across a range of settings and sites	There is sufficient field text material and summaries of analyses to support and elucidate the claims of the work
Originality	The categories are grounded and insightful The analysis provides a conceptual interpretation and the work makes a contribution	Literature on the topic is reviewed, and education implications identified
Resonance	The richness and completeness of the research links micro understandings to wider macro ones, and interpretations make sense and contribute to participant understanding	Respondent validation was gained at various points in the research with several readings by the participants sought
Usefulness	Readers can make use of the work in their own lives, and the analysis shows the links to potential action and social change with contributions that initiate further research	Interpretations of the findings were made available to respondents, and a section on the educational implications of our work is included
The nature of the writing	The text is reflexive and resonates with the real world	Participants' own words are used to ground the research in the real world

need to pay attention to new musical creativities as significant practices, and show the implications of this spectrum of musical creativities for the working lives of musicians. What each of these musicians makes clear is that musical creativities can be understood and effectively implemented in the contemporary context of the music curriculum and pedagogy generally. Recognizing, researching, and reflecting on practice is primary in this process. It is imperative if we are to develop a comprehensive view and champion multiple musical creativities. Furthermore, it is fundamental to innovative pedagogy and learning in music for successive generations of musicians.

Appendix B

Theory—understanding the thinking tools of Pierre Bourdieu

Pierre Bourdieu's work provides a context for exploring the nature of multiple creativities in music and their orientations in different kinds of practice. His model draws attention to how we encounter the rules of the game for key players in particular social settings, such as a record company, a sponsor, a patron, a classroom, or a workplace. He defines what constitutes musical creativities; how the field attracts and selects artists; and how key players in art establishments represent musical creativities differently. He identifies on what the presumed value of capital, its possession, and activation is based; the importance of social networks and value accorded displays of capital in these particular settings; the importance ascribed to the social and cultural resources of individual members of the society; and the general property of fields that the competition for what is at stake conceals.

Bourdieu argues that individuals belonging to different social locations are socialized differently. This socialization provides children, and later adults, with a sense of what is comfortable or what is natural, which he terms 'habitus'. These background experiences also shape the amount and forms of resources, in his terms, 'capital', that individuals inherit and draw on as they confront various institutional arrangements of 'fields' of the social world.

Bourdieu is also attuned to power, and the field of power as the domination of powerful groups over scare resources. For example, composers work hard to become established, and to occupy dominant positions as cultural producers in the field of contemporary arts and the culture industries, which has become a leading sector of capital in recent years. Here the key factors include individual artistic and commercial enterprise, the value of interaction between the fields of media, publishing and music, and grants and commissions from patrons, sponsors, fine art institutions within the contemporary arts field, and the broader social space. The field bestows recognition and success. Success is important for the field positioning of these individuals, as is the establishment of field networks, mutually beneficial field relations, and successful associations with key figures in the field, success proposed in association with key institutions and venues, such as major concert halls, by performing groups known within the field, and who know the rules of the game. I return to this notion of 'the game' later.

Commercial partnerships, media sponsorships, prizes, and awards, such as the MOBO and Grammy awards, also influence their individual musician habitus and their positions in the field. For DJs and popular musicians, including originals bands and singer-songwriters who can have very differently constituted habitus, working in the recording industry, as with audio designers working in the games industry, their collaborative and collective projects rely for success on wide distribution and commercial success in the broader social space.[1] It is in this context that the concept of 'field' becomes crucial. 'Field' encompasses some of the same dynamics as 'market' (the music industry) or 'social institution' (corporations and educational institutions wherein

---

[1] This discussion recalls the references to 'high art' and 'low art' as perceived by such writers as Toynbee (2000); various authors address similar issues (see R. Wright, 2010; Negus and Pickering, 2004; McIntyre, 2010).

practices can be institutionalized or not, and boundaries well established or not). In this respect, Bourdieu's idea of the field is much broader than Csikszentmihalyi's. The former is interested in the power of individuals to define not only what constitutes a highly valued activity, but also in the reasons why particular practices are valued more highly than others. Csikszentmihalyi's work suggests the importance of studying the strategies individuals use to maintain or improve their social position. Status, privilege, and similar social rewards are allegedly 'earned' by individuals. That is, they are perceived as resulting from creativity, intelligence, talent, effort, and other strategically displayed skills.

Bourdieu, in showing how cultural capital is acquired and used in daily life, makes clear that individuals' social position is not the result of personal attributes, such as effort, giftedness, or academic success. In particular, he argues that individuals in privileged social locations are advantaged in ways that are not a result of the intrinsic merit of their cultural experiences. Rather, cultural training in the home, the investment of time by parents and other family members or hired professionals to sensitize the child to cultural distinctions, are awarded unequal value in dominant institutions because of the close compatibility between the standards of child-rearing in privileged homes and the standards proposed by these institutions. The key factor in this book here, and what Toynbee (2000) describes as 'the most salient characteristic of the music industry' (p. 3), concerns the accumulation of capital. For an originals band, for example, cultural capital encompasses a broad array of participation in high status activities: the building of a 'catalogue' of widely distributed innovative albums, the acquisition of status through high-volume record sales, successful world tours, and entrepreneurship in image building and forms of collective authorship. The key issue, for musicians at the forefront of improvised musics, is 'live' performance and the significance of social authorship.[2]

Bourdieu clearly intends 'habitus' to be understood as a set of internalized dispositions that operate in a large number of social spheres. He uses the word to refer to what people think and do, their preferences in food and furniture, music and makeup, books and movies. In this book, the key aspect of musicians' habitus is the way it disposes people to play, to perform, to create and make music, to record and produce music in a particular way. Bourdieu calls this orientation a 'strategy', which is a semi-conscious but characteristic way of doing things. For musicians working in the field of classical music, habitus can be expressed as a principle of invention. For example, a group from Sheffield called the Arctic Monkeys released a single entitled 'I bet you look good on the dancefloor' in January 2006, that sold more than 120,000 copies on the first day and 363,000 copies in the first week. In this example, 'habitus' means how they made their music and found an audience. When the Arctic Monkeys were ready to record, the group did not go to an established multinational such as EMI or Warner but to a small independent company called Domino, which was founded as a one-man, one-woman enterprise in a South London flat in 1993. Next, the group studiously avoided the usual route of demonstration disc, manager, and record company in favour of the Internet. Their first music downloads were available for free and encouraged fans to exchange tracks. Whatever the Arctic Monkeys may have foregone in royalties, the group made up many times over by creating a very large and loyal following who flocked to their concerts. This means that the Arctic Monkeys' habitus—that is, what the group's members thought and did—their practice, was, according to Bourdieu (1993) to establish:

> the configuration, at the moment, and at the various critical turning-points in each career, of the space of possibilities (in particular, the economic and symbolic hierarchy of the genres, schools, styles, manners,

[2] Toynbee's (2000) model of 'social authorship' implies that 'there must be recognizable traditions which the social author can work with' (p. 160).

subjects etc.), the social value attached to each of them, and also the meaning and value they received for the different agents or classes of agents in terms of the socially constituted categories of perception and appreciation they applied to them. (p. 65)

The musician's habitus, the group's habitus, the institutional habitus are the dispositive centres of musical creativities for which the operative principle is linked to individual history, different ways of talking, eating, thinking, acting, and knowing one's place and sense of the place of others operating within 'the rules of the game'. Habitus generates the creative capital that, alongside cultural capital and social capital, constitutes advantage and disadvantage in society.

The analogy of a card game is often given. Lareau and Horvat put it this way (1999):

> In a card game (the field of interaction), the players (individuals) are all dealt cards (capital). However, each card and each hand have different values. Moreover, the value of each hand shifts according to the explicit rules of the game (the field of interaction) that is being played (as well as the way the game is being enacted). In other words, a good hand for blackjack may be a less valuable hand for gin rummy. In addition to having a different set of cards (capital), each player relies on a different set of skills (habitus) to play the cards (activate the capital). By folding the hand, a player may not activate his or her capital or may play the cards (activate the capital) expertly according to the rules of the given game. In another game, the same player may be dealt the same hand, yet because of a lack of knowledge of the rules of the game play the hand poorly. Thus, in analysing social settings, researchers must attend to the capital that each individual in a given field has, as well as each individual's ability and skill in activating the capital. (p. 39)

In this book, Bourdieu's concepts of 'habitus', 'capital', and 'field' provide the main conceptual tools for making sense of the data. I have used 'a light touch' analysis so as to look through the lens of Bourdieu's theoretical framework, illustrating how habitus and capital provide a way of understanding the sets of positions occupied by musicians in diverse settings, and for identifying the point at which habitus, with its accompanying capitals (musical knowledge, background, opportunities), intersects with field, determining what renders multiple forms of musical creativities and the ways in which they arise in the ever-expanding powerful practices used by musicians. Drawing on research into the creative practices of musicians, children, teachers, and teacher-artists, I argue that musical creativities are multiple, and advance a way of understanding their distinctive features and the propensity to identify them as manifestations of practice.

Appendix C

Supporting material

1. Featured musicians

Appendix Table A.2 Featured musicians

Chapter	Practice	Musician	Country/Group	Websites and downloads
3	Originals bands	Steve Mackay Fans: Joanne Joshua Jack	Australia; 'Twelve Foot Ninja' (TFN)	www.twelvefootninja.com www.myspace.com/twelvefootninja www.facebook.com/twelvefootninja http://en.wikipedia.org/wiki/Twelve_Foot_Ninja
		Leah Kardos	England; 'Helzuki', 'My Lithium and Me' (MLM), and 'Spider & I'	www.leahkardos.com www.helzuki.co.uk http://bigoandtwigetti.bandcamp.com/album/feather-hammer
		Adam Scott	Scotland; 'Zoey Van Goey' (ZVG)	www.zoeyvangoey.com http://www.chemikal.co.uk/artists/zoey-van-goey/
4	Singer-songwriters	Pippa Andrew	England; 'Mobile Jazz Cafe'	www.malaikasproject.com www.myspace.com/mobilejazzcafe www.thevoicecollective.co.uk
		Roshi Nasehi	Wales/Iran; Pars Radio	www.rifmountain.com/shop.html www.myspace.com/roshisongs
5	DJs	Jazzie B— Soul II Soul	UK	www.soul2soul.co.uk/ www.myspace.com/officialjazzieb www.redbullmusicacademy.com/video.../jazzie_b_funki_dred_OBE/ www.djhistory.com/interviews/jazzie-b
		Rob Paterson	USA (New York)	www.myspace.com/robpatersonmusic www.examiner.com/djs-in-new-york/interview http://soundcloud.com/redlightmusic http://en.wikipedia.org/wiki/Rob_Patterson

Appendix Table A.2 (continued) Featured musicians

Chapter	Practice	Musician	Country/Group	Websites and downloads
		DJ XUAN	Taiwan	www.djXUAN.com
		Shiuan Liu		www.facebook.com/i.am.XUAN.liu
		GT—Groove Terminator	USA (Los Angeles)/ Australia	www.myspace.com/grooveterminator
		Simon Lewicki		http://en.wikipedia.org/wiki/Groove_ Terminator
6	**Composed musics**	Donnacha Dennehy	Ireland	www.donnachadennehy.com
			(The Crash Ensemble)	www.crashensemble.com
		Liza Lim	England	www.australianmusiccentre.com.au/ artist/lim-liza
			(ELISION Ensemble)	www.elision.org.au
		Robert Davidson	Australia	www.topologymusic.com
			(Topology)	www.australianmusiccentre.com.au/ artist/davidson-robert
7	**Improvised musics**	David Toop	England	www.davidtoop.com
				www.myspace.com/davidtoop
		Rod Paton	England	www.rodpaton.com
			LifeMusic	www.lifemusic.org
		Hazel Fairbairn	England	www.worldfiddle.biz
		Andrew Brown	Australia	www.explodingart.com
		Nick Collins	England	www.cogs.susx.ac.uk/users/nc81
8	**Interactive audio designers**	Kenneth Young	Scotland	www.gamesound.org
		Matthew Applegate	England	www.pixelh8.co.uk
				http://en.wikipedia.org/wiki/Pixelh8

Multiple musical creativities thematized

Forms of authorship

(a) Self-social

individual
collaborative
communal
collective
networked
distributed
relayed
installational
organizational
sociospatial

(b) Sociocultural

cultural
intercultural
cross-cultural
multicultural
sub-cultural
ethnic
diasporic
fan-based
audience-based
crowd-based
user-based

Mediating modalities

(a) Temporal

performance
performance-composition
composition
re-composition
de-composition
composition-performance
improvisation
improvisation-composition
improvisation-performance
extemporization
arrangement
live
recorded
virtual
real-time
listening
reception
sociospatial

(b) Technological

computer-generated
computer-mediated
computer's aesthetic
software-based
hi-tech
low-tech
digital
digital-media
programs/programming
mobile
Internet
sound (re-)processing/production

music (re-)processing/production
reproduction
live forms
virtual forms
recorded forms

Practice principles

(a) Explicit

symbolic
object-based
process-based
work-based
provisional work
sound-based
sound-signed
sociospatial
interactive
communicative
exploratory
participatory
experimental
innovative
entrepreneurial
problem-setting
problem-solving

(b) Implicit

empathic
aesthetic
artistic
transformative
sociospatial
original
hybridic
invention
possibilities

Appendix D

Top ten myths about children's music creativities

Creativity myths have been widely exploded by several authors whose interests lie in professional music making. Here, the intention is to provide readers with information that goes well beyond many adult preconceptions and simplified definitions of what constitutes children's musical creativities. The idea is to list specific myths about children's music creativities, and where to turn to literature which dispel them and show the complexity and sophistication of children's practices (see Cook, 1998; Cottrell, 2004; Sawyer, 2006a,b; Small, 1998; Weisberg, 1993 for related discussion on creativity myths).

Myth 1: That there is only one type of children's musical creativity

A wealth of literature generated in the past 10–15 years has revolutionized the ways in which we can study, define, and debate the narrowly scoped concept of 'musical creativity', which often falls far short of admitting to the multiple creativities inscribed in children's music play and practices. Different descriptions of children's musical creativities can be found and illuminated in early childhood musical play, creative thought, and activity, numerous studies of which promote contemporary children's musical creativities in the early years, and are relevant to young children who might become professional musicians in the future. It is not helpful to collapse being creative in music into whether we can compose (see Burnard et al., 2006; Campbell, 1991a, 1998; Harwood, 1998; K. Marsh 2008; S. Wright, 2010 for research evidence to support the claims made about children's multiple creative abilities).

Myth 2: Music creativities are an attribute of a privileged genetic elite of children who are born to be musicians

We are not condemned to thinking of musical creativities as the possession of the gifted and talented few. There are many more 'creatives' than Mozart. The perpetuation of high art orthodoxies of Western art music continues to valorize the myth of the Great Composers and with it, the nineteenth-century Romantic-era belief that only child prodigies commit themselves to, and foster a capacity for, music creation. Musical creativities do not simply gush forth from some mysterious place for a few select individual children, nor do they do so despite the prevailing social conditions. We have plenty of evidence that children develop creative skills through participatory music-making in contexts involving personal, collaborative, communal, collective, empathic, and intercultural creativities. Encompassing informal learning and non-formal learning contexts, the social systems in which children's creative endeavours in music-making are nurtured and developed are significant (see Burnard, in press; and chapters by Colley et al., Cross et al., Lapidaki et al., Leong et al., and Saether et al. in McPherson and Welch, in press).

Myth 3: Young children do not begin to realize their own music creativities until they are in their teens

Gardner (1982) talks of the 'preschool years . . . as a golden age of creativity, a time when every child sparkles with artistry' (p. 86). In early childhood, children's musical creativities are characterized within a wide variety of contexts, which may involve spontaneous song-making, singing, dancing, and playing together, and improvising with instruments and performing on any number of instruments in any number of ways. From there, the development of children's multiple musical creativities continues throughout their life, just as the infinite varieties of musical expression in infancy are given life by the intrinsically musical nature of human interaction (see Malloch and Trevarthen (2010) for compelling research that credits infants with complex skills and creative mental abilities).

Myth 4: Children's original music-making lacks coherent structure and fluency until they can use the repertoire of genre-specific languages

Children manifest and liberate themselves in their use and function of music creativities in ways that defy traditional psychological definitions. How children shape their own development is evidenced from infancy through adolescence, with much evidence to support the saliency of the social dimension of musical creativities, shaped largely by those people who surround them, like their parents, carers, family, and friends. What comes across most strongly from studies of young children is the sense of primacy of relationships and interactions between child and adult, social contexts that are shaped largely by family circumstances. Taking time to reflect on how children, from early childhood through to adolescence, constitute their own forms and genres of musical creativities, and musical culture making is as necessary as for adults to reflect on their constructions of what musical creativities are (see Burnard, 2006a,b, 2008, 2010, in press; K. Marsh, 2008; Young, 2003, amongst others).

Myth 5: Children need advanced years of formal training to engage successfully in the performative act of musical improvisation

In the context of playgrounds, researchers provide us with compelling perspectives from which children's musical creative development may be viewed, such as their improvisation and variations on playground chants. Children effortlessly discover, explore, and negotiate polyrhythms and syncopations in highly sophisticated social music-making through many empirically informed ways (see J. Marsh 1995, 1997, K. Marsh, 2008, Harwood, 1998; Davies, 1986; amongst others).

Myth 6: Children simply do not have the skills to compose proper pieces

So many assumptions are embodied in this myth concerning a spectrum of activities ranging from improvisation during a performance through to formalized and notated composition made by one individual that is presented to an audience by another. While some children prefer to work alone to author creative products, others prefer to engage collaboratively, communally, collectively, technologically networked, whereupon being a group member responsible for jointly authoring a piece that can be replayed across time, space, and persons. Assumptions about compositions being fixed end-products do not resonate with contemporary digital art music, the status of which material becomes extraordinarily fluid when performers redefine, de-compose and re-compose musics, as with DJs who rapidly proliferate variant versions. 'Proper pieces' conveys Goehr's seminal critique of the concept of the musical work. Compositions are always being changed through performance creativity, as, for example, with composers' own reinterpretations of theirs and other's pieces. The practice of privileging certain creativities (compositional creativity being just one) is a practice of privileging history. Empirically informed ways that children engage as composers and performer of their own music within a framework of personal and social invention offer evidence of new kinds of musical creativities that challenge ideas about 'work-based practices' centred on the belief that composed works should be perfectly formed, finished, and transcend any particular performance (see Goehr, 1992).

Myth 7: Children cannot say much about their own musical creativities

We now have persuasive empirical evidence about how children take great satisfaction in talking about their own practice of musical creativity, and how they establish multiple performance practices and conceptualize their own distinctive creativities in music. Research makes clear that we need to take very seriously what children can tell us about their experience of creating musics, and how they feel empowered to create something or to cover, rework, or create new forms along a continuum of improvised and composed performance practices. The pioneering work of Jean Rudduck (1999) on the concept of 'student voice' highlights the importance of student perspectives, their having things to say about their processes of creativity, having opinions that matter about music cultures, and how variable discourses can be part of the sub-cultures that they belong too (see Burnard and Björk, 2010; Burnard et al., 2011; Finney, 2011 amongst others).

Myth 8: Children do not learn much about composing from computers

No matter how children's musical creativities and technology have been investigated from the various methodologies or different theories, research findings make clear what counts in the digital age can be understood as ultimately divested in children's practice from their own intentions to represent their own cultural and sub-cultural meanings. Children love to tell us about the ways in which they use technology as a vehicle for their creative explorations, how they come to shape collective identities through the discovery of technology, how they position themselves through technology, and to talk about their technical sophistication, their early engagement with and fluid roles in contemporary popular musics, their contribution to developing new musical hybridities, their creative capacities in virtual communities, and their ease of access and propensity to engage interactively with gaming technologies that offer them liberation and immersion as young digital musicians (see for example, Finney and Burnard, 2007).

Myth 9: Children's creativity in music is just for toddlers' growth and development

In educational circles, there has long been a strong advocacy of creative expression as the key to optimal social and emotional development. And there is no doubt about the value of aesthetic learning for young children. But this makes for problems. The fact that creativity is so closely identified with early years' music and arts education makes it difficult to take children's music creativities seriously after primary school. This myth flies in the face of all the evidence that we have about the lifelong and life-wide value of creativities in music. Creativity is now being acknowledged as an observable and valuable component of all social and economic enterprise from cradle to grave (see S. Wright, 2010, amongst others).

Myth 10: Children do not create distinct music cultures with distinctive musical creativities

This is another one of those myths that prevail about children's musical creativities that invariably follows from an idea of the arts as the 'cute and flabby' side of an arts/science binary. In this way music education collapses into remedial mess-making for children at risk, or as a means to re-engage those kids who are either school drop-outs or at risk of becoming so, rather than recognizing and developing the creativity and cultural innovation of childhood's musical creativity. Yet, children's cultures, their creative activities and the creative environments that support the music they make should be valued as dynamic dimensions of children's activities and socialization that emerge through interactions with society. Children are members of the 'super-culture' such as 'children', several 'sub-cultures', such as family members or Caribbean or Asian children, boys or girls, and 'intercultures' such as players, collectors or listeners to particular types of music, classrooms, groups, or clubs in or out-of-school. What is common across research reports is the extent to which findings uncover new ways of thinking about children's distinct music cultures and distinctive musical creative practices. Children's engagement in music making plays a prominent role as a real life theme of children's lives. Children engage as performers, composers, producers, and listeners, whether at the margin of urban centres or at the centre of city and country communities, finding and defining themselves, giving voice to their own ways of transmitting cultures and operating creatively in music. More often, with specific reference to West African singing games, young children's creative undertakings are connected to their membership of numerous socio-cultural groups as learning environments in which the child is immersed. Children draw socially and culturally on many musical worlds as they give voice to their own creative practices (see Addo, 1997; Burnard, 2006; Campbell, 2004; Schippers, 2010; Wade, 2004).

References

Addo, A.O. (1997) Children's idiomatic expressions of cultural knowledge. *International Journal of Music Education,* **30**, 15–25.

Adorno, T. (1976) *Introduction to the Sociology of Music.* Translated by E. Ashton, New York, NY: International Publishing Group.

Alexander, R. (2008) *Essays on Pedagogy.* Abingdon, Oxon: Routledge.

Alexander, R. (2009) Pedagogy, culture and the power of comparison. In H. Daniels, L. Hugh, and J. Porter (eds) *Educational Theories, Cultures and Learning: A Critical Perspective,* pp.10–26. London: Routledge.

Allsup, R. (2011) Popular music and classical musicians: Strategies and perspectives. *Music Educators Journal,* **97**(3), 30–4.

Alperson, P. (1984) On music improvisation. *Journal of Aesthetics and Art Criticism,* **43**(1), 17–30.

Alperson, P. (1985) Improvisation: music for an occasion. *British Journal of Music Education,* **2**(2), 177–86.

Amabile, T. (1983) *The Social Psychology of Creativity.* New York, NY: Springer-Verlag.

Amabile, T. (1996) *Creativity in Context: Update to the Social Psychology of Creativity.* Colorado: Westview.

Anon. Live algorithm programming and a temporary organisation for its promotion. Available at: www.toplap.org.

Applegate, M.C. (2010) Cultural perceptions, ownership and interaction with re-purposed musical instruments. *Journal of Music, Technology and Education,* **3**(2/3), 93–106.

Aranosian, C.M. (1981) Musical creativity: the stream of consciousness in composition, improvisation, and education. *Imagination, Cognition and Personality,* **1**(1), 67–88.

Aronowitz, S. (1994) *Dead Artists, Live Theories and Other Cultural Problems.* London: Routledge.

Atau Tanaka, A., Tokui, N., and Momeni, A. (2005) 'Facilitating Collective Musical Creativity'. *Association for Computing Machinery: Multimedia Conference Proceedings,* pp. 191–8. 6–11 November. New York, NY: ACM Press.

Atkinson, D. (2002) *Art in Education: Identity and Practice.* Dordrecht, Netherlands: Kluwer Academic Publishers.

Attali, J. (1985) *Noise: The Political Economy of Music.* Minneapolis, MN: University of Minnesota Press.

Azzara, C. (2002) Improvisation. In R. Colwell and C. Richardson (eds) *The New Handbook of Research on Music Teaching and Learning: A Project of the Music Educators National Conference,* pp. 171–88. Oxford: Oxford University Press.

Back, L. (1996) *New Ethnicities and Urban Culture: Racisim and Multiculture in Young Lives.* London: UCL Press.

Bahn, C.R. (1997) Composition, improvisation and meta-composition (string bass, jazz, performance). *Dissertation Abstracts International,* DAI-A, 4116.

Bailey, D. (1992) *Improvisation: Its Nature and Practice in Music.* New York, NY: Da Capo Press.

Baily, J. (1985) Music structure and human movement. In P. Howell, I. Cross, and R. West (eds) *Musical Structure and Cognition,* pp. 237–58. London: Academic Press.

Baily, J. (1991) Some cognitive aspects of motor planning in musical performance. *Psychological-Belgica,* **31**(2), 147–62.

Banaji, S., Burn, A., and Buckingham, D. (2006) *The Rhetorics of Creativity: A Review of the Literature.* London: Arts Council England.

Barrett, E. and Bolt, B. (eds) (2010) *Practice as Research: Approaches to Creative Arts Enquiry*. London: I.B. Tauris.

Barrett, M. (2005a) Children's communities of musical practice; some socio-cultural implications of a systems view of creativity in music education. In D.J. Elliott (ed.) *Praxial Music Education: Reflections and Dialogues*, pp. 177–95. New York, NY: Oxford University Press.

Barrett, M. (2005b) Musical communication and children's communities of musical practice. In D. Miell, R. MacDonald and D. Hargreaves (eds) *Musical Communication*, pp. 117–42. New York, NY: Oxford University Press.

Barrett, M.S. (2003) Meme engineers: Children as producers of musical culture. *International Journal of Early Years Education*, **11**(3), 195–212.

Barrett, M.S. (2006) 'Creative collaboration': an 'eminence' study of teaching and learning in music composition. *Psychology of Music*, **34**(2): 195–218.

Barrett, M.S. and Gromko, J.E. (2007) Provoking the muse: a case study of teaching and learning in music composition. *Psychology of Music*, **35**(2), 213–30.

Bayton, M. (1993) Feminist musical practice: Problems and contradictions. In T. Bennett, S. Frith, L. Grossber, J. Shepherd, and G. Turner (eds) *Rock and Popular Music*, pp. 177–92. New York, NY: Routledge.

Becker, H. (1963) *Outsiders: Studies in the Sociology of Deviance*. New York, NY: Free Press.

Becker, H (1984) *Art Worlds*. Berkeley, CA: University of California Press.

Becker, H., Faulkner, R., and Kirshenblatt-Gimblett, B. (2006) *Art from Start to Finish: Jazz, Painting, Writing and other Improvisations*. Chicago, IL: University of Chicago Press.

Bennett, A. (1980) *On Becoming a Rock Musician*. Amherst, MA: University of Massachusetts Press.

Bennett, A. (1999) Subcultures or Neo-tribes? Rethinking the relationship between youth, style and musical taste. *Sociology*, **33**(3), 599–617.

Bennett, A. (2000) *Popular Music and Youth Culture: Music, Identity and Place*. Basingstoke: Palgrave Macmillan.

Bennett, A. (2001) *Cultures of Popular Music*. Buckingham: Open University Press.

Bennett, D. (2008) *Understanding the Classical Music Profession: The Past, the Present and Strategies for the Future*. Aldershot, Hampshire: Ashgate.

Bennett, S. (1976) The process of musical creation: interviews with eight composers. *Journal of Research in Music Education*, **24**(1), 3–13.

Bennett S. (2010) *Understanding the Classical Music Profession*. Aldershot, Hampshire: Ashgate.

Bennett, T., Frith, S., Grossberg, L., Shepherd, J., and Turner, G. (1993) *Rock and Popular Music: Politics, Policies and Institutions*. London: Routledge.

Benson, B.E. (2003) *The Improvisation of Musical Dialogue: A Phenomenology of Music*. Cambridge: Cambridge University Press.

Berendt, J.E. (1992) *The Jazz Book: From Ragtime to Fusion and Beyond,* revised edn. Translated by H.B. Bredigkeit, D. Morgenstern and T. Nevill, pp. 161–2. Westport, CT: Lawrence Hill.

Berleant, A. (1987) Musical de-composition. In Alperson, P. (ed.) *What is Music? An Introduction to the Philosophy of Music*, pp. 239–54. Pennsylvania, PA: Pennsylvania State University Press.

Berliner, P. (1994). *Thinking in Jazz: The Infinite Art of Improvisation*. Chicago, IL: University of Chicago Press.

Berliner, P. (2006) Grasping Shona musical works: a case study of Mbira Music. In H. Becker, R. Faulkner, and B. Kirshenblatt-Gimblett (eds) *Art from Start to Finish: Jazz, Painting, Writing and other Improvisations*, pp. 126–34. Chicago, IL: University of Chicago Press.

Bernstein, B. (1990) *Class, Codes and Control, Volume IV: The Structuring of Pedagogic Discourse*. London: Routledge

Bernstein, B. (1996) *Pedagogy, Symbolic Control and Identity*. New York, NY: Rowman and Littlefield.

Black, P. and Wiliam, D. (2006) Assessment for learning in the classroom. In J. Gardner (ed.) *Assessment and Learning*, pp. 9–25. London: Sage.

Blacking, J. (1955) *Music, Culture, and Experience*. Chicago, IL: University of Chicago Press.

Blacking, J. (1967) *Venda Children's Songs*. Chicago, IL: University of Chicago Press.

Blacking, J. (1973) *How Musical Is Man?* Seattle, WA: University of Washington.

Blake, A. (2007) *Popular Music: The Age of Multimedia*. London: Middlesex Publishing Press.

Blanning, T. (2002) *The Culture of Power and the Power of Culture*. Oxford: Oxford University Press.

Blanning, T. (2008) *The Triumph of Music: Composers, Musicians and their Audiences*. London: Penguin Books.

Boden, M. (2005) *The Creative Mind: Myths and Mechanisms*. London: Routledge.

Born, G. (1993) Afterword: Music policy aesthetic and social difference. In T. Bennett, Frith, S., Grossberg, L., Shepherd, J., and Turner, G. (eds) *Rock and Popular Music*, pp. 266–92. New York, NY: Routledge.

Born, G. (2005) On musical mediation: Ontology, technology and creativity. *Twentieth-century Music*, **2**(1), 7–36.

Born, G. and Hesmondhalgh, D. (2000) *Western Music and Its Others: Difference, Representation and Appropriation Music*. Berkeley, CA: University of California Press.

Bourdieu, P. (1973) Cultural reproduction and social reproduction. In R. Brown (ed.) *Knowledge, Education and Cultural Change*, pp. 71–112. London: Tavistock.

Bourdieu, P. (1977) *Outline of a Theory of Practice*. Translated by R. Nice. Cambridge: Cambridge University Press.

Bourdieu, P. (1977b) Cultural reproduction and social reproduction. In J. Karabel and A.H. Halsey (eds) *Power and Ideology in Education*, pp. 487–511. New York, NY: Oxford University Press.

Bourdieu, P. (1984a) *Distinction: A Social Critique of the Judgement of Taste*. Translated by R. Nice. Cambridge, MA: Harvard University Press.

Bourdieu, P. (1984b) *Homo Academicus*. (English edn 1988a). Translated by P. Collier. Cambridge, UK: Polity Press.

Bourdieu, P. (1988) Vive la Crise! for heterodoxy in social science. *Theory and Society*, **19**(5), 773–88.

Bourdieu, P. (1990a) *In Other Words: Essays Towards a Reflexive Sociology*. Cambridge, UK: Polity Press.

Bourdieu, P. (1990b) *The Logic of Practice*. Translated by R. Nice. Cambridge, UK: Polity Press.

Bourdieu, P. (1993a) *Sociology in Question*. London: Sage.

Bourdieu, P. (1993b) The market of symbolic goods. In *The Field of Cultural Production*. Cambridge: Polity Press.

Bourdieu, P. (1993c) *The Field of Cultural Production: Essays on Art and Literature*. Edited and introduced by R. Johnson. Cambridge, UK: Polity Press.

Bourdieu, P. (1993d) Some properties of fields. In *Sociology in Question*, pp. 72–7. London: Sage.

Bourdieu, P. (1996). *The Rules of Art: Genesis and Structure of the Literary Field*. Cambridge, UK: Polity Press.

Bourdieu, P. (1999) [1993] *The Weight of the World: Social Suffering in Contemporary Society*. Translated by P. Parkhurst Ferguson, S. Emanuel, J. Johnson & S. T. Waryn. Cambridge, UK: Polity Press. [Originally published as 'La misere du monde' (Paris: Seuil)].

Bourdieu, P. and Wacquant, L.J.D. (1992) *An Invitation to Reflexive Sociology*. Chicago, IL: University of Chicago Press.

Bowman, W. (2004) 'Pop' goes? Taking popular music seriously. In C.X. Rodriguez (ed.) *Bridging the Gap: Popular Music and Music Education*, pp. 29–49. Reston, VA: MENC: The National Association for Music Education.

Brinner, B. (1995) *Knowing Music, Making Music: Javanese Gamelan and the Theory of Musical Competence and Interaction*. Chicago, IL: University of Chicago Press.

Broughton, F. and Brewster, B. (2002) *How to DJ [Properly]: The Art and Science of Playing Records*. London: Transworld Publishers.

Brown, A.R. (2001). *Modes of Compositional Engagement Mikropolyphonie, Volume 6*. http://farben.latrobe. edu.au/mikropol/volume6/brown_a/brown_a.html. Available at: http://eprints.qut.edu.au/ archive/00000168/and (archived at http://pandora.nla.gov.au/tep/10054).

Brown, A.R. and Dillon, S.C. (2007) Networked improvisational musical environments: Learning through online collaborative music making. In Finney, J. and Burnard, P. (eds) *Music Education with Digital Technology*, pp. 96–106. London: Continuum Press.

Brown, A.R. and Dillon, S.C. (in press) Collaborative digital media performance with generative music systems. In G. Macpherson and G. Welch (eds) *The Oxford Handbook of Music Education*. New York, NY: Oxford University Press.

Brown, A.R. and Sorensen, A. (2009) Interacting with generative music through live coding. *Contemporary Music Review*, **28**(1): 17–29.

Brown, A.R., Sorensen, A., and Dillon, S. (2002). Jam2Jam (Version 1) [Interactive Generative Music-Making Software]. Brisbane: Exploding Art Music Productions.

Buckingham, D. (2005) *Schooling the Digital Generation: Popular Culture, the New Media and the Future of Education*. London: IoE, University of London.

Burnard, P. (1995). Task design and experience in composition. *Research Studies in Music Education*, **5**, 32–46.

Burnard, P. (1999) Bodily intention in children's improvisation and composition. *Psychology of Music*, **27**(2), 159–74.

Burnard, P. (2000a) How children ascribe meaning to improvisation and composition: rethinking pedagogy in music education. *Music Education Research*, **2**(1), 7–23.

Burnard, P. (2000b) Examining experiential differences between improvisation and composition in children's music making. *British Journal of Music Education*, **17**(3), 227–45.

Burnard, P. (2002) Investigating children's meaning making and the emergence of musical interaction in group improvisation. *British Journal of Music Education,* **19**(2), 157–72.

Burnard, P. (2004) Reflecting on music learning and rethinking contexts. In Bartel, L. (ed.) *Questioning the Music Education Paradigm,* pp. 244–57. Alberta: Canadian Educator's Association.

Burnard, P. (2005) What matters in general music? In Elliott, D. (ed.) *Praxial Music Education: Reflections and Dialogues*, pp. 267–71. New York, NY: Oxford University Press.

Burnard, P. (2006a) Reflecting on the creativity agenda in education. *Cambridge Journal of Education*, **36**(3), 313–18.

Burnard, P. (2006b) The individual and social worlds of children's musical creativity. In G. McPherson (ed.) *The Child as Musician: A Handbook of Musical Development*, pp. 353–74. Oxford: Oxford University Press.

Burnard, P. (2006c) Understanding children's meaning-making as composers. In I. Deliège and G. Wiggins (eds) *Musical Creativity: Multidisciplinary Research in Theory and Practice*, pp. 146–67. New York, NY: Psychology Press, Taylor and Francis.

Burnard, P. (2007) Creativity and technology: Critical agents of change in the work and live of music teachers. In J. Finney and P. Burnard (eds) *Music Education with Digital Technology*, pp. 196–206. London: Continuum Press.

Burnard, P. (2008) Creative learning and progression in the arts. In M. Rouhete (ed.) *Evaluating the Impact of Arts and Cultural Education: A European and International Research Symposium*, pp. 161–72. Paris: La Documentation Francaise, Centre Pompidou.

Burnard, P. (2011a) Creativity, pedagogic partnerships, and the improvisatory space of teaching. In K. Sawyer (ed.) *Structure and Improvisation in Creative Teaching*, pp. 51–72. New York, NY: Cambridge University Press.

Burnard, P. (2011b) Rethinking musical creativity. In O. Odena (ed.) *Musical Creativity: Insights From Music Education Research*, pp. 5–28. Aldershot: Ashgate.

Burnard, P. (2011c) Constructing assessment for creative learning. In J. Sefton-Green, P. Thomson, L. Bresler, and K. Jones (eds) *The Routledge International Handbook of Creative Learning*, pp. 140–9. London: Routledge/Falmer.

Burnard, P. (in press) The multiple creativities of music: Expanding discourses for change in music education. In G. Welch and G. McPherson (eds) *The Oxford Handbook of Music Education.* New York: Oxford University Press.

Burnard, P. and Björk, C. (2010) Using student voice research to understand and improve musical learning. In C. Harrison and J. Finney (eds) *Finding The Student Voice*. pp. 24–33. Matlock, Derbyshire: National Association of Music Educators (NAME).

Burnard, P. and Lavicza, Z. (2010a) Teachers' conceptions and practices of assessing creativity. Paper presented at the BERA 2010 Conference, Warwick, UK, Creativity SIG, 2 September.

Burnard, P. and Lavicza, Z. (2010b) *Primary and Secondary Music and Visual Arts Teachers' Conceptions and Practices of Assessing Creativity in the Arts (ACA): Developing the ACA Questionnaire.* Research Note for the International Research Commission, 25–30 July, Northeast Normal University, Changchun, China, July. Available at: http://www.isme.org.

Burnard, P. and Lavicza, Z. (2010c) *Primary and Secondary Teachers' Conceptions and Practices of Assessing Creativity in the Arts.* International Research Commission Conference Proceedings. Changchun, China: International Society of Music Education.

Burnard, P. and Maddock, M. (2007) Pupil and teacher perceptions of artist pedagogy: an exploratory study. In *Proceedings of the British Educational Research Association Annual Conference*, London, September (CD Rom).

Burnard, P. and Swann, M. (2010) Pupil perceptions of learning with artists: a new order of experience? *Thinking Skills and Creativity*, **5**(2), 70–83.

Burnard, P. and Triantafyllaki, A. (forthcoming) Exploring where the self and the social meet in contemporary composers' fields of production in music using narrative enquiry. In S.O. Neill (ed.) *Personhood and Music Learning: Multidisciplinary Perspectives and Narrative Voices.* Canada: CMEA/ACME Biennial Book Series, Research to Practice.

Burnard, P. and White, J. (2008) Creativity and performativity: counterpoints in British and Australian education. *British Educational Research Journal, Special Issue on 'Creativity and Performativity in Teaching and Learning'*, **34**(5), 667–82.

Burnard, P. and Wyse, D. (2009) Creativity in the primary curriculum: Reconciling disconnections between policy, theory, research and practice. Paper presented at the British Education Research Association (BERA) Conference, September, Manchester, 3–5 September.

Burnard, P. and Younker, B.A. (2002) Mapping pathways: Fostering creativity in composition. *Music Education Research*, **4**(2), 245–61.

Burnard, P. and Younker, B.A. (2004) Creativity and individual composing pathways: perspectives within a cross-cultural framework. *International Journal of Music Education*, **22**(1), 59–76.

Burnard, P. and Younker, B.A. (2008) Investigating children's musical interactions within the activities systems of group composing and arranging: an application of Engestrom's Activity Theory. *International Journal of Educational Research*, **47**(1), 60–74.

Burnard, P. and Younker, B.A. (2010) Towards a broader conception of creativity in the music classroom: A case for using Engström's Activity Theory as a bases for researching and characterising group music-making practices. In R. Wright (ed.) *Sociology of Music Education*, pp. 165–91. Aldershot, Hampshire: Ashgate.

Burnard, P., Grainger, T., and Craft, A. (2006) Documenting possibility thinking: A journey of collaborative enquiry. *International Journal of Early Years Education, Special Issue on Creativity and Cultural Innovation in Early Childhood Education*, **14**(3), 243–62.

Burnard, P., Craft, A., Cremin, T., and Chappell, K. (2007) Creative learning and progression through composing music. Paper presented at The 4th International Conference of Research in Music Education, University of Exeter, 11–14 April, CDROM

Burnard, P., Fautley, M., and Savage, J. (2010a) *Assessing Creativity in the Secondary School Classroom: Exploring Variations in Teachers' Conceptions and Practices.* Full Paper Conference Proceedings of the 29th ISME World Conference, Beijing, 1–6 August (CD Rom).

Burnard, P., Kelly, E., and Biddulph, J. (2010b) Mapping the creative journeying in practitioner research. In M. Khine and I. Saleh (eds) *Practitioner Research: Teachers' Investigations in Classroom Teaching*, pp. 1–15. Hauppage, NY: Nova Science Publishers.

Burt-Perkins, R. (2009) The learning cultures of performance: applying a cultural theory of learning to conservatoire research. In A. Williamson, S. Pretty, and R. Buck (eds) *Proceedings of the International Symposium on Performance Science*, pp. 249–54. European Association of Conservatoires (AEC). Available at: www.legacyweb.rcm.ac.uk/ISPS/ISPS2009/Proceedings.

Byrne, C., MacDonald, R., and Carlton, L. (2002) Assessing creativity in musical compositions: flow as an assessment tool. *British Journal of Music Education*, **20**(3), 277–90.

Cain, T. (2004) Theory, technology and the music curriculum. *British Journal of Music Education*, **21**(3), 215–21.

Campbell, P. (1991a) The child-song genre: A comparison of songs by and for children. *International Journal of Music Education*, **17**, 14–23.

Campbell, P. (1991b) Unveiling the mysteries of musical spontaneity. *Music Educators Journal*, December, 21–4.

Campbell, P. (1996) *Music in Cultural Context: Eight Views on World Music Education*. Reston, VA: Music Educators National Conference.

Campbell, P. (1998) *Songs in Their Heads: Music and its Meaning in Children's Lives*. New York, NY: Oxford University Press.

Campbell, P.S. (2002) The musical cultures of children. In L. Bresler and C.M. Thompson (eds) *The Arts in Children's' Lives: Context, culture and Curriculum*, pp. 57–69. Dordrecht: Kluwer Academic Publishers.

Campbell, P. (2004) *Teaching Music Globally: Experiencing Music, Expressing Culture*. New York, NY: Oxford University Press.

Campbell, P. and Teicher, J. (1997) Themes and variations on the creative process: tales of three cultures. *Research Studies in Music Education*, **8**, 29–41.

Caves, R. (2000) *Creative Industries: Contracts Between Art and Commerce*. Cambridge, MA: Harvard University Press.

Challis, M. (2007) The DJ factor: teaching performance and composition from back to front. In J. Finney and P. Burnard (eds) *Music Education with Digital Technology*, pp. 65–74. London: Continuum Press.

Chanan, M. (1994) *Musica Practica: The Social Practice of Western Music from Gregorian Chant to Postmodernism*. London: Verso.

Charmaz, K. (2005) Grounded theory for the 21st Century. In N.K. Denzin and Y.S. Lincoln (eds) *The Sage Handbook of Qualitative Research*, 3rd edn, pp. 507–35. Thousand Oaks, CA: Sage.

Chase, S.E. (2005) Narrative inquiry: Multiple lenses, approaches, voices. In N.K. Denzin and Y.S. Lincoln (eds) *The Sage Handbook of Qualitative Research*, pp. 651–80. Thousand Oaks, CA: Sage.

Chion, M. (1994) *Audio-Vision: Sound on Screen*. Translated and edited by C. Gorbman. New York, NY: Columbia University Press.

Clandinin, D.J. (ed.) (2007) *Handbook of Narrative Inquiry*. Thousand Oaks, CA: Sage.

Clandinin, D.J. and Connelly, F.M. (2000) *Narrative inquiry: Experience and Story in Qualitative Research*. San Francisco, CA: Jossey-Bass Publishers.

Clifton, T. (1983) *Music as Heard: A Study in Applied Phenomenology*. New Haven, NJ: Yale University.

Cloonan, M. (2005) What is popular music studies? Some observations. *British Journal of Music Education*, **22**(1), 77–93.

Cloonan, M. (2007) *Popular Music and the State in the UK: Culture, Trade or Industry?* Ashgate Popular and Folk Music Series. Ashgate: Aldershot.

Cloonan, M. and Johnson, B. (2006) Killing me softly with his song: an initial investigation into the use of popular music as a tool of oppression. *Popular Music*, **21**(1), 27–39.

Cohen, S. (1991) *Rock culture in Liverpool: popular music in the making*. Oxford: Oxford University Press.

Colley, B., Eidsaa, R.M., Kenny, A., and Leung, B.W. (in press) Collaborative creativity in partnership practices. In G. Welch and G. McPherson (eds) *The Oxford Handbook of Music Education*. New York, NY: Oxford University Press.

Collins, N. (2008) Live electronic music. In N. Collins and J. d'Escrivan (eds) *The Cambridge Companion to Electronic Music*, pp. 38–54. Cambridge: Cambridge University Press.

Colwell, R. (ed.) (2002) *Handbook of Research in Music Teaching and Learning. A Project of the Music Educators National Conference*. New York, NY: Schirmer.

Cook, N. (1990) *Music, Imagination and Culture*. Oxford: Clarendon Press.

Cook, N. (1998) *Music: A Very Short Introduction*. Oxford: Oxford University Press.

Cook, N. (2006) Playing God: creativity, analysis and aesthetic inclusion. In I. Deliège and G.A.E. Wiggins (eds) *Musical Creativity: Multidisciplinary Research in Theory and Practice*, pp. 9–24. New York, NY: Taylor and Francis.

Cook, N. (forthcoming) Scripting social interaction: Improvisation, performance, and Western 'art' music. In G. Born., E. Lewis, and W. Straw (ed.) *Improvisation and Social Aesthetics*. Hanover, NH: Wesleyan University Press.

Cook, N. (in press) Against reproduction. In E. Sheinberg (ed.) *Music Semiotics: A Network of Significations—In Honor of Raymond Monelle*. Farnham: Ashgate.

Cottrell, S. (2004) *Professional Music-Making in London: Ethnography and Experience*. Aldershot, Hampshire: Ashgate.

Cox, C. and Warner, D. (2009) *Audio Culture: Readings in Modern Music*. London: Continuum Press.

Craft, A., Burnard, P., Grainger, T., and Chappell, K. (2006) *Progression in Creative Learning*. London: Arts Council England, Creative Partnerships.

Craft, A., Cremin, T., Burnard, P., and Chappell, K. (2007) Teacher stance in creative learning: A study of progression. *Thinking Skills and Creativity*, **2**(1), 136–47.

Craft, A., Cremin, T., and Burnard, P. (eds) (2008) *Creative Learning 3–11 and How We Document It: What, How and Why?* Stoke-on-Trent: Trentham.

Creswell, J. (1998). *Qualitative Inquiry and Research Design: Choosing among Five Traditions*. London: Sage.

Cross, I. and Woodruff, G.E. (2009) Music as a communicative medium. In R. Both and C. Knight (eds) *The Prehistory of Language*, pp.77–99. Oxford: Oxford University Press.

Cross, I., Laurence, F., and Rabinovitch, T. (in press) Empathy and creativity in group musical practices: towards a concept of empathic creativity. In G. Welch and G. McPherson (eds) *The Oxford Handbook of Music Education*. New York, NY: Oxford University Press.

Crow, B. (2006) Musical creativity and the new technology. *Music Education Research*, **8**(1), 121–30.

Crow, B. (2008) Changing conceptions of educational creativity: a study of student teachers' experience of musical creativity. *Music Education Research*, **10**(3), 373–88.

Csikszentmihalyi, M. (1988) Society, culture and person: A systems view of creativity. In R.J. Sternberg (ed.), *The Nature of Creativity*, pp. 325–39. New York, NY: Cambridge University Press.

Csikszentmihalyi, M. (1990) The domain of creativity. In M.A. Runco and R.S. Albert (eds), *Theories of Creativity*, pp. 190–212. Newbury Park, CA: Sage.

Csikszentmihalyi, M. (1996) *Creativity: Flow and the Psychology of Discovery and Invention*. New York, NY: Harper Collins.

Csikszentmihalyi, M. (1999) Implications of a systems perspective for the study of creativity. In R. Sternberg (ed.) *Handbook of Creativity*, pp. 313–35. New York, NY: Cambridge University Press.

Csikszentmihalyi, M. and Wolfe, R. (2002) New conceptions and research approaches to creativity: Implications of a systems perspective for creativity in education. In K.A. Heller, F.J. Monks, R.J. Sternberg, and R.F. Subotnik (eds) *International Handbook of Giftedness and Talent*, 2nd edn, pp. 81–93. Oxford: Elsevier.

Dale, P. (2010) Anyone can do it: traditions of punk and the politics of empowerment, PhD dissertation, Newcastle University.

Dalhaus, C. (1983) *Foundations of Music History*. Translated by J.B. Robinson. London: Cambridge University Press.

Daugherty, R., Black, P., Ecclestone, K., James, M., and Newton, P. (2008) Alternative perspectives on learning outcomes: challenges for assessment. *Curriculum Journal*, **19**(4), 243–54.

Davidson, J. and Coulam, A. (2006) Exploring jazz and classical solo singing performance behaviours: A preliminary step towards understanding performer creativity. In I. Deliège and G.A.E. Wiggins (eds) *Musical Creativity: Multidisciplinary Research in Theory and Practice*, pp. 181–200. New York, NY: Taylor and Francis.

Davies, C. (1986) Say it till a song comes (reflections on songs invented by children 3–13. *British Journal of Music Education*, **3**(30), 270–93.

de Certeau, M. (1984) *The Practice of Everyday Life*. Berkeley, CA: University of California Press.

DeCurtis, A. (1999) *Lost in the Supermarket: Myth and Commerce* in *the Music Business*. In K. Kelly and E. McDonnell (eds) *Stars Don't Stand Still in the Sky: Music and Myth*, pp. 31–5. London: Routledge.

DeCurtis, A. (2005) *In Other Words: Artists Talk About Life and Work*. Milwaukee, WI: Hal Leonard Corporation.

Deliège, I. and Richelle, M. (2006) Prelude: The spectrum of musical creativity. In I. Deliège and G.A.E. Wiggins (eds) *Musical Creativity: Multidisciplinary Research in Theory and Practice*, pp. 1–6. New York, NY: Taylor and Francis.

Deliège, I. and Wiggins, G.A.E. (eds) (2006) *Musical Creativity: Multidisciplinary Research in Theory and Practice*. New York, NY: Taylor and Francis.

Denicolo, P. and Pope, M. (1990) Adults learning—teachers thinking. In C. Day, M. Pope, and P. Denicolo (eds) *Insight into Teachers Thinking and Practice*, pp. 155–69. Basingstoke: Falmer.

DeNora, T. (1995). *Beethoven and the Construction of Genius: Musical Politics in Vienna, 1792–1803*. Berkeley, CA: University of California Press.

DeNora, T. (1999) Music as a technology of the self. *Poetics*, **27**, 31–56.

DeNora, T. (2000) *Music in Everyday Life*. Cambridge, UK: Cambridge University Press.

DeNora, T. (2003) *After Adorno: Rethinking Music Sociology*. Cambridge: Cambridge University Press.

Dillabough, J. and Kennelly, J. (2010) *Lost Youth in the Global City: Class, Culture and the Urban Imaginary*. New York, NY: Routledge.

Dillon, S. (2006) Before the eyes glaze over. *Music Forum: Music Council of Australia*, **13**, 32–33.

Dillon, T. (2006) *Exploring young people's collaborative and creative processes using keyboard and computer-based music technologies in formal and non-formal settings*. PhD thesis, Department of Psychology, The Open University.

Dillon, T. (2007) Current and future practices: embedding collaborative music technologies in secondary schools. In J. Finney and P. Burnard (eds) *Music Education Digital Technology*, pp. 117–31. London: Continuum.

Dobbins, B. (1980) Improvisation: an essential element of musical proficiency. *Music Educators Journal*, January, 36–41.

Duckworth, W. (1995) *Talking Music: Conversations with John Cage, Philip Glass, Laurie Anderson, and Five Generations of American Experimental Composers*. New York, NY: Schirmer Books.

Dumais, S.A. (2002) Cultural capital, gender and school success: the role of habitus. *Sociology of Education*, **75**, 44–68.

Einstein, A. (1945) *Mozart: His Character and His Work*. London: Oxford.

Emmerson, S. (1989) Composing strategies and pedagogy. *Contemporary Music Review*, **3**, 133–44.

Engström, A. and Hallencreutz, D. (2003). *Från A-dur till bokslut - Hårda fakta om en mjuk industri*. IUC Musik & Upplevelseindustri. December 2003.

Espeland, M. (2003) The African drum: The compositional process as discourse and interaction in a school context. In M. Hickey (ed.) *Why and How to Teach Music Composition: A New Horizon for Music Education*, pp.167–92. Reston, VA: MENC, The National Association for Music Education.

Fairbairn, H. (1993) *Group Playing in Traditional Irish Music*. Cambridge: Cambridge University Press.

Fairbairn, H. (1994) Changing contexts for traditional dance music in Ireland: The rise of group performance practice. *Folk Music Journal*, **6**(5), 66–99.

Farber, J. (2011) (Chapter 2) 'Britney Spears' 'Femme Fatale' review: Dr. Luke and Max Martin Take Over Brand and Steal it. Available at: http://articles.nydailynews.com/2011-03-29/entertainment/29375832_1_luke-and-max-martin-britney-brand-2007-s-blackout

Faulkner, R. (2005) *Music on Demand: Composers and Careers in the Hollywood Film Industry*. New Brunswick, NJ: Transaction Publishers.

Faulkner, D., Coates, E., Craft, A., and Duffy, B. (2006) Creativity and cultural innovation in early childhood education. *International Journal of Early Years Education*, **14**(3), 191–9.

Feldman, D.H., Csikszentmihalyi, M., and Gardner, H. (eds) (1994) *Changing the World: A Framework for the Study of Creativity*. Westport, CT: Praeger.

Finnegan, R. (1989) *The Hidden Musicians: Music-Making in an English Town*. Cambridge: Cambridge University Press.

Finney, J. (2011) *Music Education in England, 1950–2010: The Child-centred Progressive Tradition.* Aldershot, Hampshire: Ashgate.

Finney, J. and Burnard, P. (eds) (2007) *Music Education with Digital Technology.* London: Continuum Press.

Folkestad, G. (1998) Musical learning as cultural practice as exemplified in computer-based creative music-making. In B. Sundin, G.E. McPherson, and G. Folkestad (eds) *Children Composing*, pp. 97–134. Sweden: Lund University.

Folkestad, G. (2006) Formal and informal learning situations or practices vs. formal and informal ways of learning'. *British Journal of Music Education*, **23**(2), 135–46.

Ford, A. (1993) *Composer to Composer: Conversations about Contemporary Music.* St. Leonards, NSW: Allen and Unwin.

Ford, C. (1995) Free collective improvisation in higher education. *British Journal of Music Education*, **12**(2), 103–12.

Ford, C. (2010) Musical presence: towards a new philosophy of music. *Contemporary Aesthetics*, **8**. Available at: http://www.contempaesthetics.org/newvolume/pages/journal.php.

Forman, M. (2004) Represent: race, space and place in rap music. In M. Forman and M.A. Neal (eds) *That's the Joint! The Hip-Hop Studies Reader*, p. 201. London: Routledge.

Fornäs, J., Lindberg, U., and Sernhade, O. (1995) *In Garageland: Rock, Youth and Modernity.* London: Routledge.

Foucault, M. (1972) *The Archaeology of Knowledge.* London: Tavistock Publications.

Foucault, M. (1977) What is an author? In D.F. Bouchard (ed. and translator) *Language, Countermemory Practice*, pp. 113–38. Ithaca. NY: Cornell University Press.

Foucault, M. (1980) *Power/Knowledge: Selected Interview and Other Writings.* Edited by C. Gordon. Brighton: Harvester.

Frith, S. (1983) *Sound Effects: Youth Leisure, and the Politics Rock.* London: Constable.

Frith, S. (1988) *Music for Pleasure: Essays in the Sociology of Pop.* Cambridge, UK: Polity Press.

Frith, S. (1996) *Performing Rites: Evaluating Popular Music.* Oxford: Oxford University Press.

Frith, S., Straw, W., and Street, J. (2001) *The Cambridge Companion to Pop and Rock.* Cambridge: Cambridge University Press.

Fuller, D. (1989) The Performer as Composer. In H.M. Brown and S. Sadie (eds) *Performance Practice Vol. II*, pp. 117–18. London: MacMillan Publishers.

Gardner, H. (1982) *Art, Mind and Brain: A Cognitive Approach to Creativity.* New York, NY: Basic Books.

Gardner, H. (1993) *Creating Minds: An Anatomy of Creativity Seen Through the Lives of Freud, Einstein, Picasso, Stravinsky, Eliot, Graham, and Gandhi.* New York, NY: Basic Books.

Gardner, H. (1998) *Extraordinary Minds: Portraits of Exceptional Individuals and an Examination of our Extraordinariness.* New York, NY: Basic Books.

Geertz, C. (1973) *The Interpretation of Cultures: Selected Essays.* New York, NY: Basic Books.

Gell, A. (1998) *Art and Agency: An Anthropological Theory.* Oxford: Clarendon Press.

Ghiselin, B. (ed.) (1952) *The Creative Process: A Symposium.* Berkeley, CA: University of California Press.

Goehr, L. (1992) *The Imaginary Museum of Musical Works: An Essay in the Philosophy of Music.* Oxford: Clarendon Press.

Gordon, E. (1987) *The Nature, Description, Measurement, and Evaluation of Music Aptitudes.* Chicago, IL: G.I.A. Publications.

Gracyk, T. (1996) *Rhythm and Noise: An Aesthetics of Rock.* London: I.B. Tauris.

Graue, M. and Walsh, D. (1998) *Studying Children in Context: Theories Methods and Ethics.* London: Sage.

Green, L. (1988) *Music on Deaf Ears: Musical Meaning, Ideology and Education.* Manchester: Manchester University Press.

Green, L. (2001) *How Popular Musicians Learn: A Way Ahead For Music Education.* London: Ashgate.

Green, L. (2002) *How Popular Musicians Learn.* Aldershot: Ashgate (first published in 2001).

Green, L. (2008) *Music, Informal Learning and the School: A New Classroom Pedagogy.* Aldershot: Ashgate.

Green, L. (2010) Research in the sociology of music education: some introductory concepts. In R. Wright (ed.) *Sociology and Music Education*, pp. 21–34. Farnham, Surrey: Ashgate.

Grenfell, M. (2008) (ed.) *Pierre Bourdieu: Key Concepts.* Durham: Acuman Publishing.

Grenfell, M. and Hardy, C. (2007) *Art Rules: Pierre Bourdieu and the Visual Arts.* Oxford: Berg.

Grenfell, M. and James, D. (1998) *Bourdieu and Education: Acts of Practical Theory.* London: Falmer Press.

Grove, G. (2004) *Beethoven and His Nine Symphonies.* Whitefish, MT: Kessinger Publishing Co. (first published in 1896).

Haddon, E. (2006) *Making Music in Britain: Interviews with Those Behind the Notes.* Aldershot: Ashgate.

Hargreaves, D.J., Galton, M.J. and Robinson, S. (1996) Teachers' assessments of primary children's classroom work in the creative arts. *Education Research*, **38**(2), 199–211.

Harlen, W. and James, M. (1997) Assessment and learning: differences and relationships between formative and summative assessment. *Assessment in Education: Principles, Policy and Practice*, **4**(3), 365–79.

Hartley, J. (ed.) (2005) *Creative Industries.* Oxford: Blackwell.

Harwood, E. (1998) Go on Girl! Improvisation in African-American girls' singing games. In B. Nettl and M. Rusell (eds) *In the Course of Performance: Studies in the World of Musical Improvisation*, pp. 113–25. Chicago, IL: University of Chicago Press.

Hass, R.W., Weisberg, R.W., and Choi, J. (2010) Quantitative case studies in musical composition: The development of creativity in popular-songwriting teams. *Psychology of Music*, **38**, 463–79.

Heidegger, M. (1962) *Being and Time.* Translated by John Macquarrie and Edward Robinson. New York, NY: Harper & Row.

Hennessey, B. and Amabile, T. (1988) The conditions of creativity. In R. Sternberg (ed.) *The Nature of Creativity: Contemporary Psychological Perspectives*, pp. 11–38. Cambridge: Cambridge University Press.

Hennessey, B.A. and Amabile, T.M. (1999) Consensual assessment. In M.A. Runco and S.R. Pritzker (eds) *Encyclopedia of Creativity, Volume* **1**, pp. 346–59. San Diego, CA: Academic Press.

Hesmondhalgh, D. and Negus, K. (eds) (2002) *Popular Music Studies.* London: Arnold.

Holden, S. (1992) The evolution of the singer-songwriter. In DeCurtis, A., Henke, J., and George-Warren, H. (eds) *The Rolling Stone Illustrated History of Rock & Roll*, pp. 299–308. London: Straight Arrow.

Hickey, M. (2002) The use of consensual assessment in the evaluation of children's music compositions. In C. Woods, G. Luck, R. Brochard, F. Seddon, and J.A. Sloboda (eds) *Proceedings from the Sixth International Conference on Music Perception and Cognition.* Keele, UK: Keele University (CD-Rom).

Homan, S. (2006) *Access all Eras: Tribute Bands and Global Pop Culture.* Berkshire: Open University Press.

Huizinga, J. (1970) *Homo Ludens: A Study of the Play Element in Culture.* London: Maurice Temple Smith.

Iseminger, G. (ed.) (2006) *Intention and Interpretation.* Philadelphia, PA: Temple University Press.

Jameson, F. (1991) *Postmodernism or the Cultural Logic of Late Capitalism.* Durham: Duke University Press.

Johnson, R. (1993) Editor's Introduction: Pierre Bourdieu on Art, Literature and Culture. In P. Bourdieu. *The Field of Cultural Production: Essays on Art and Literature. Edited and Introduced by Randal Johnson*, pp. 1–29. Cambridge, UK: Polity Press.

John-Steiner, V. (2000) *Creative Collaboration.* New York, NY: Oxford University Press.

Jones, C.W. (2008) *The Rock Canon: Canonical Values in the Reception of Rock Albums.* Aldershot, Hampshire: Ashgate.

Kahn, D. (2001) *Noise, Water, Meat: A History of Sound in the Arts.* Cambridge, MA: MIT Press.

Kanellopoulos, P. (1999) Children's conception and practice of musical improvisation. *Psychology of Music*, **27**(2), 175–91.

Kanter, R.M. (2000) When a thousand flowers bloom: Structural, collective and social conditions for innovation in organization. In R. Swedberg (ed.) *Entrepreneurship: The Social Science View*, pp. 167–210. New York, NY: Oxford University Press.

Kelly, G.A. (1955) *The Psychology of Personal Constructs, Volume 1 and 2.* New York, NY: W.W. Norton and Co.

Kelly, K. and McDonnell, E. (eds) (1999) *Stars Don't Stand Still in the Sky: Music and Myth.* London: Routledge.

Kenny, B.J. and Gellrich, M. (2002) Improvisation. In R. Parncutt and G. McPherson (eds) *The Science and Psychology of Music Performance: Creative Strategies for Teaching and Learning*, pp. 117–34. Oxford: Oxford University Press.

Kress, G.R. (2003) *Literacy in the New Media Age*. London: Routledge Falmer.

Kurkela, V. and Väkevä, L. (eds) (2009) *Decanonizing Music History*. Newcastle upon Tyne: Cambridge Scholars Publishing.

Kusek, D. and Leonhard, G. (2005) *The Future of Music: Manifesto from the Digital Music Revolution*. Boston, MA: Berklee Press.

Landy, L. (2007) *Understanding the Art of Sound Organization*. Cambridge, MA: Massachusetts Institute of Technology.

Lang, P.H. (1941) *Music in Western Civilization*. New York, NY: Norton.

Langer, S.K. (1953) *Feeling and Form: A Theory of Art*. New York, NY: Scribner.

Lapidaki, E., Rokus de Groot, R., and Stagkos, P. (in press) Communal creativity as socio-musical practice. In G. Welch and G. McPherson (eds) *The Oxford Handbook of Music Education*. New York, NY: Oxford University Press.

Lareau, A. (1987) Social class differences in family-school relationships: the importance of cultural capital. *Sociology of Education*, **60**(2), 73–85.

Lareau, A. and Horvat, E.M. (1999) Moments of social inclusion and exclusion: race, class and cultural capital in family-school relationships. *Sociology of Education*, **72**(1), 37–53.

Ledgard, A. (2006) Fair exchange: shared professional development and reflective action. In P. Burnard and S. Hennessey (eds) *Reflective Practice in Arts Education*, pp. 169–82. Dordrecht: Springer.

Leong, S., Burnard, P., Jeannert, N., Leung, B., and Waugh, C. (in press) Assessing creativity in music: international perspectives and practices. In G. Welch and G. McPherson (eds) *The Oxford Handbook of Music Education*. New York, NY: Oxford University Press.

Levitin, D. (2008) *The World in Six Songs*. London: Penguin Books.

Leyshon, A., Matless, D., and Revill, G. (1998) *The Place of Music*. New York, NY: Guilford Press.

Loi, D. and Dillon, P. (2006) Adaptive educational environments as creative spaces. *Cambridge Journal of Education*, **36**(3), 363–82.

Longhurst, B. (2007) *Popular Music and Society*. Cambridge, UK: Polity Press.

Malloch, S. and Trevarthen, C. (eds) (2009) *Communicative Musicality: Exploring the Basis for Human Companionship*. Oxford: Oxford University Press.

Margolis, J. (1977) *Philosophy Looks at the Arts*. Philadelphia, PA: Temple University Press.

Marsh, J. (1995) Children's singing games: Composition in the playground? *Research Studies in Music Education*, **4**, 2–11.

Marsh, J. (1997) Variation and transmission processes in children's singing games in an Australian playground. PhD thesis, University of Sydney.

Marsh, J. (2006) Emergent media literacy: Digital animation in early childhood. *Language and Education*, **20**(6), 493–506.

Marsh, J., Brooks, G., Hughes, J., Ritchie, L., Roberts, S., and Wright, K. (2005) *Digital Beginnings: Young Children use of Popular Culture, Media and New Technologies*. Sheffield: University of Sheffield.

Marsh, K. (2008) *The Musical Playground: Global Tradition and Change in Children's Songs and Games*. Oxford University Press.

Maton, K. (2008) Habitus. In M. Grenfell (ed.), *Pierre Bourdieu: Key Concepts*. Durham: Acuman Publishing.

Maton, K. (2010a) Analyzing knowledge claims and practices: languages of legitimation. In K. Maton and R. Moore (eds) *Social Realism, Knowledge and the Sociology of Education: Coalitions of the Mind*, pp. 35–60. London: Continuum Press.

Maton, K. (2010b) Canons and progress in the arts and humanities: Knowers and Gazes. In K. Maton and R. Moore (eds) *Social Realism, Knowledge and the Sociology of Education: Coalitions of the Mind*, pp. 154–79. London: Continuum.

Maton, K. and Moore, R. (eds) (2010) *Social Realism, Knowledge and the Sociology of Education: Coalitions of the Mind*. London: Continuum.

McCutchan, A. (1999) *The Muse That Sings: Composers Speak about the Creative Process*. New York, NY: Oxford University Press.

McKinlay, A. and Smith, C. (eds) (2009) *Creative Labour: Working in the Creative Industries*. Basingstoke: Palgrave MacMillan.

McIntyre, P. (2010) Songwriting, creativity and the music industry. In R. Sickels (ed.) *The Business of Entertainment, The Music Industry: Volume 2*, pp. 1–20. Westport, CT: Praeger.

McIntyre, P. (2011) Rethinking the creative process: The systems model of creativity applied to popular songwriting. *Journal of Music, Technology and Education*, **4**(1), 77–90.

McIntyre, P. (2012) *Creativity and Cultural Production: Issues for Media Practice*. London: Palgrave McMillan.

McMillan, R. (1996) A terrible honesty: the development of a personal voice in musical improvisation. PhD dissertation, University of Melbourne.

McPherson, G. (1994) Improvisation: past, present and future. In *Proceedings of the 21st World Conference of the International Society for Music Education*, pp. 154–62. Tampa, Florida.

McPherson, G. (2006) *The Child as Musician: A Handbook of Musical Development*. Oxford: Oxford University Press.

McPherson, G. and Welch, G. (eds) (in press) *Oxford Handbook of Music Education*. New York, NY: Oxford University Press.

McWilliam, E. (2008) *The Creative Workforce: How to Launch Young People into High-Flying Futures*. Sydney: University of New South Wales Press.

Mellor, L. (2001) Welcome to the dance machine: entertainment, edutainment, education? An investigation of children's composition responses using the CD rom dance *eJay*. *National Association of Music Educators Magazine (NAME)*, **7**, 25–9.

Merker, B (2006) Layered constraints on the multiple creativities of music. In I. Deliège and G.A.E. Wiggins (eds) *Musical Creativity: Multidisciplinary Research in Theory and Practice*, pp. 25–42. New York, NY: Taylor and Francis.

Merleau-Ponty, M. (1962) *Phenomenology of Perception*. London: Routledge and Kegan Paul.

Moore, R. (2010) Knowledge structures and the Canon: A preference for judgements. In K. Maton and R. Moore (eds) *Social Realism, Knowledge and the Sociology of Education: Coalitions of the Mind*, pp. 131–79. London: Continuum.

Mozart, W.A. (1952). A letter. In B. Ghiselin (ed.) *The Creative Process*. Berkeley, CA: University of California Press.

Murphy, R. and Espeland, M. (2006–2008) *Upbeat (Teachers' Resource Books, Pupils' Books and CDs to Support Music in Primary Schools*. Dublin: Carroll Education.

Nardone, P.L. (1996) The experience of improvisation in music: a phenomenological psychological analysis. PhD dissertation, Saybrook Institute, University of Michigan

National Advisory Committee on Creative and Cultural Education (NACCCE) (1999) *All Our Futures: Creativity, Culture and Education*. London: Department for Education and Employment.

Negus, K. (1999) *Music Genres and Corporate Cultures*. London: Routledge.

Negus, K. and Pickering, M. (2004) *Creativity, Communication and Cultural Value*. London: Sage.

Nettl, B. (1974) Thoughts on improvisation: a comparative approach. *Musical Quarterly*, **60**(1), 1–19.

Neuman, D. (1980) *The Life of Music in North India*. Detroit, IL: Wayne State University Press.

Nilson, C. (2007) Live coding practice. In *Proceedings of the 2007 International Conference on New Interfaces for Musical Expression*, pp. 112–17. New York, NY: Association for Computing Machinery.

Odena, O. and Welch, G. (2009) A generative model of teachers' thinking on musical creativity. *Psychology of Music*, **37**(4), 416–42.

Pasler, J. (2008) *Writing through Music: Essay on Music, Culture and Politics*. Oxford: Oxford University Press.

Paton, R. (2010) *Living Music: Improvisation Guidelines for Teachers and Community Musicians*. Chichester: West Sussex County Council.

Perkins, R. (2012) The construction of 'learning cultures': an ethnographically-informed case study of a UK conservatoire. PhD dissertation, University of Cambridge.

Pitts, S. (2005) *Valuing Musical Participation.* Aldershot, Hampshire: Ashgate.

Pope, R. (2005) *Creativity: Theory, History, Practice.* London: Routledge.

Prensky, M.R. (2010) *Teaching Digital Natives: Partnering for Real Learning.* London: SAGE.

Pressing, J. (1984) Cognitive process in improvisation. In W.R. Crozier. and A.J. Chapman. (eds), *Cognitive Processes in the Perception of Art*, pp. 345–64. Amsterdam: Elsevier Science Publishing.

Prévost, E. (1995) *No Sound is Innocent: AMM and the Practice of Self-Invention.* Harlow, Essex: Copula and Matchless Recordings and Publishings.

Pring, R. (2000) *Philosophy of Educational Research.* London: Continuum Press.

Pringle, E. (2008) Artists' perspectives on art practice and pedagogy. In J. Sefton-Green (ed.) *Creative Learning*, pp. 41–50. England: Arts Council.

Rabinowitch, T., Cross, I., and Burnard, P. (in press) Between consciousnesses: embodied musical intersubjectivity. In D. Reynolds and M. Reason (eds) *Kinesthetic Empathy in Creative and Cultural Practices.* Bristol: Intellect Press.

Reay, D. (1995) 'They employ cleaners to do that': habitus in the primary classroom. *British Journal of Sociology Education*, **16**, 353–71.

Reay, D. (1998) 'Always knowing' and 'Never being sure': Institutional and familial habituses and higher education choice. *Journal of Education Policy*, **13**(4), 519–29.

Reay, D. (2004) 'It's all becoming a habitus': Beyond the habitual use of habitus in educational research. *Special Issue of British Journal of Sociology Education on Pierre Bourdieu*, **25**(4), 431–44.

Reay, D., David, M., and Ball, S. (2005) *Degrees of Choice: Class, Race, Gender and Higher Education.* Stoke-on-Trent: Trentham Books.

Reddington, H. (2007) *The Lost Women of Rock Music: Female Musicians of the Punk Era.* Aldershot: Ashgate.

Ricoeur, P. (1981) *Hermeneutics and the Human Sciences.* Cambridge: Cambridge University Press.

Ricoeur, P. (1991) *From Text to Action: Essays in Hermeneutics.* London: Athlone Press.

Ricoeur, P. (1992) *Oneself as Another.* Chicago, IL: University of Chicago Press.

Rudduck, J. (1999) Teacher practice and the student voice. In M. Lang, J. Olson, H. Hansen, and W. Bunder (eds) *Changing Schools/Changing Practices: Perspectives on Educational Reform and Teacher Professionalism*, pp. 41–54. Louvain: Garant.

Ruthmann, S.A. (2007a) Strategies for supporting music learning through online collaborative technologies. In J. Finney and P. Burnard (eds) *Music Education with Digital Technology*, pp. 131–42. London: Continuum Press.

Ruthmann, S.A. (2007b) The composers' workshop: An emergent approach to composing in the classroom. *Music Educators Journal*, **93**(4), 38–44.

Saether, E., Mbye, A., and Shayesteh, R. (in press) Intercultural creativity: Using cultural meetings as a prompting force for creative learning and change. In G. Welch and G. McPherson (eds) *The Oxford Handbook of Music Education.* New York, NY: Oxford University Press.

Savage, J. (2002) New models for creative practice for music technologies. In D. Harris (ed.) *How are You Doing? Learning and Assessment in Music*, pp. 38–44. Derbyshire: National Association of Music Educators.

Savage, J. (2007) Pedagogical strategies for change. In J. Finney and P. Burnard (eds) *Music Education Digital Technology*, pp. 142–56. London: Continuum.

Sawyer, K. (1997) (ed.) *Creativity in Performance.* Greenwich, CT: Ablex Publishing Corporation.

Sawyer, K. (2003) *Group Creativity: Music Theatre, Collaboration.* Mahwah, NJ: Lawrence Erlbaum Associates.

Sawyer, K. (2006a) *Explaining Creativity: The Science of Human Innovation.* Oxford: Oxford University Press.

Sawyer, K. (2006b) Educating for innovation. *Thinking Skills and Creativity*, **1**(1), 41–8.

Schauffler, R.H. (1946) *Beethoven: The Man who Freed Music.* New York, NY: Tudor.

Schippers, H. (2010) *Facing the Music: Shaping Music Education from A Global Perspective.* New York, NY: Oxford University Press.

Seddon, F. (2007) Music e-learning environments: Young people, composing and the internet. In J. Finney and P. Burnard (eds.) *Music Education with Digital Technology*, pp. 107–17. London: Continuum.

Seddon, F.A. and O'Neill, S.A. (2003) Creative thinking processes in adolescent computer-based composition: an analysis of strategies adopted and the influence of instrumental training. *Music Education Research*, **5**(2), 125–37.

Seddon, F.A. and O'Neill, S.A. (2006) How does formal instrumental music tuition (FIMT) impact on self- and teacher-evaluations of adolescents' computer-based compositions? *Psychology of Music*, **34**(1), 27–45.

Sefton-Green, J. and Soep, L. (2007) Creative media cultures: making and learning beyond the school. In L. Bresler (ed.) *International Handbook of Research in Arts Education*, pp. 835–54. Dordrecht: Springer.

Sexton, J. (2007) *Music, Sound and Multimedia: From the Live to the Virtual*. Edinburgh: Edinburgh University Press.

Shuker, R. (1994) *Understanding Popular Music*, 2nd edn. London: Routledge.

Skeggs, B. (2004) Exchange, value and affect: Bourdieu and the self. *Sociological Review*, **52**, 75–95.

Sloboda, J.A. (1985) *The Musical Mind*. New York, NY: Oxford University Press.

Sloboda, J. (2005) *Exploring the Musical Mind: Cognition, Emotion, Ability, Function*. Oxford: Oxford University Press.

Small, C. (1998) *Musicking: The Meanings of Performing and Listening*. Wesleyan: University Press of New England, Hanover.

Smilde, R. (2009) *Musicians as Lifelong Learners: Discovery Through Biography*. Ontwerpen: Eburon Delft Academic Publishers.

Smith, G.D. (2010) 'I Drum, Therefore I Am?' A study of kit drummers' identities, practices and learning. PhD dissertation, Institute of Education, University of London.

Solomon, L. (1986) Improvisation II. *Perspectives in New Music*, **24**, 224–35.

Solomon, M. (1980) On Beethoven's creative process: a two-part invention. *Music and Letters*, **61**, 271–83.

Somekh, B. (2000) New technology and learning: Policy and practice in the UK, 1980–2019. *Education and Information Technologies*, **5**(1), 19–37.

Spruce, G. (1999) Assessment in the arts: issues of objectivity. In G. Spruce (ed.) *Teaching Music*, pp. 168–85. London: Routledge.

Somekh, B. (2007) *Pedagogy and Learning with ICT: Researching the Art of Innovation*. London: Routledge.

Spruce, G. (1996) Assessment in the arts: issues of objectivity. In G. Spruce (ed.) *Teaching Music*, pp. 168–74. London: Routledge.

Starko, A. (2001) *Creativity in the Classroom*. London: Lawrence Erlbaum Associates.

Stauffer, S. (2001) Composing with computers: Meg makes music. *Bulletin of the Council for Research in Music Education*, **150**, 1–20.

Stauffer, S. (2002) Connections between the musical and life experiences of young composes and their compositions. *Journal of Research in Music Education*, **50**(4), 301–22.

Storr, A. (1991) *The Dynamics of Creation*. London: Secker and Warburg.

Stravinsky, I. (1947) *Poetics of Music in the Form of Six Lessons*. Cambridge, MA: Harvard University Press.

Sumara, D.J. and Davis, B. (1997) Enactivist theory and community learning: toward a complexified understanding of action research. *Educational Action Research*, **5**(3), 403–22.

Swanwick, K. and Tillman, J. (1986) The sequence of musical development: a study of children's compositions. *British Journal of Music Education*, **3**, 305–39.

Thornton, S. (1995) *Club Cultures: Music, Media and Subcultural Capital*. Cambridge, UK: Polity Press.

Toop, D. (1984, 1991, 2000) *Rap Attack*. London: Profile Books.

Toop, D. (1995) *Ocean of Sound*. London: Profile Books.

Toop, D. (1999) *Exotica: Fabricated Soundscapes in a Real World*. London: Profile Books.

Toop, D. (2004a) *Haunted Weather: Music, Silence and Memory*. London: Serpent's Tail.

Toop, D. (2004b) Uptown throwdown. In M. Forman and M. Neil (eds) *That's the Joint! The Hip-Hop Studies Reader*, pp. 233–46. London: Routledge.

Toynbee, J. (2000) *Making Popular Music: Musicians, Creativity and Institutions*. London: Hodder.

Triantafyllaki, A. (2008) Instrumental music teachers' professional identity and practice in a Greek University music department and a conservatoire workplace. PhD dissertation, University of Cambridge.

Triantafyllaki, A. (2010) 'Workplace landscapes' and the construction of performance teachers' identity: the case of advanced music training institutions in Greece. *British Journal of Music Education*, **27**, 185–201.

Triantafyllaki, A. and Burnard, P. (2010) Creativity and arts-based knowledge creation in diverse educational partnership practices: Lessons from two case studies in rethinking traditional spaces for learning. *UNESCO Observatory E-Journal, Multi-Disciplinary Research in the Arts*, **1**(5), http://www.abp.unimelb.edu.au/unesco/ejournal/pdf/burnard-paper.pdf.

Väkevä, L. (2010) Garage band or GarageBand? Remixing musical futures. *British Journal of Music Education*, **27**, 59–70.

Van Manen, M. (1990) *Researching Lived Experience: Human Science for an Action Sensitive Pedagogy*. Canada: Althouse.

Volkmann, C.K., Tokarski, K.O., and Grunhagen, M. (2010) *Entrepreneurship: Concepts for the Creation and Growth of New Ventures*. Berlin: Gabler.

Vygotsky, L.S. (1971) *The Psychology of Art*. Cambridge, MA: IT Press.

Wade, B.C. (2004) *Teaching Music Globally: Experiencing Music, Expressing Culture and Thinking Musically*. New York, NY: Oxford University Press.

Wallas, G. (1926) *The Art of Thought*. London: Watts.

Ward, A., Rohrhuber, J., Olofsson, F., McLean, A., Griffiths, D., Collins, N., and Alexander, A. (2004) Live Algorithm Programming and a Temporary Organisation for its Promotion. Available at: http://toplap.org/index.php/Read_me_paper.

Webster, L. and Mertova, P. (2007) *Using Narrative Inquiry as a Research Method: An Introduction to using Critical Event Narrative Analysis in Research*. London: Routledge.

Webster, P. (1990) Creativity as creative thinking. *Music Educators Journal*, **76**(9), 22–8.

Webster, P. (2006) Computer-based technology and music teaching and learning: 2000–2005. In L. Bresler (ed.) *International Handbook of Research in Arts Education*, pp. 1311–28. Dordrecht: Springer.

Weisberg, R.W. (1993) *Creativity: Genius and Other Myths*. Oxford: Freeman.

Wenger, E. (1998) *Communities of Practice: Learning, Meaning and Identity*. New York, NY: Cambridge University Press.

Wertsch, J.V. (ed.) (1993) *Culture, Communication and Cognition: Vygotskian Perspectives*, 2nd edn. Cambridge: Cambridge University Press.

Westerlund, H. (2008) Justifying music education. A view from the here and now value experience, *Philosophy of Music Education Review*, **16**(1), 79–95.

Wiggins, J. (2002) Creative process as meaningful musical thinking. In T. Sullivan and L. Willingham (eds) *Research to Practice: A Biennial Series*, pp. 78–88. Toronto, Canada: Canadian Music Educators Association.

Wikström, P. (2009) *The Music Industry: Music in the Cloud (DMS—Digital Media and Society)*. Cambridge, UK: Polity Press.

Williamon, A., Thompson, S., Lisboa, T., and Wiffen, C. (2006) Creativity, originality and value in music performance. In I. Deliège and G.A.E. Wiggins (eds) *Musical Creativity: Multidisciplinary Research in Theory and Practice*, pp. 161–81. New York, NY: Taylor and Francis.

Willis, P., Jones, S., Canaan, J., and Hurd, G. (1990) *Common Culture: Symbolic Work at Play in the Everyday Cultures of the Young*. Milton Keynes: Open University Press.

Wolff, J. (1992) *Aesthetics and the Sociology of Art*, 2nd edn. Ann Arbor, MI: University of Michigan Press.

Wolff, J. (1993) *The Social Production of Art*, 2nd edn. London: MacMillan Publishers.

Wolterstorff, N. (1994) The work of making a work of music. In P. Alperson (ed.) *What is Music? An Introduction to the Philosophy of Music*, pp. 101–29. Pennsylvania, PA: Pennsylvania State University Press.

Wright, R. (ed.) (2010) *Sociology and Music Education*. Surrey: Ashgate.

Young, S. (2003) Time-space structuring in spontaneous play on educational percussion instruments among three-and four-year-olds. *British Journal of Music Education*, **20**, 45–60.

Zolberg, V. (1990) *Constructing a Sociology of the Arts*. Cambridge: Cambridge University Press.

Author Index

Note: 'n.' after a page reference indicates the number of a note on that page.

Subject Index

Note: 'n.' after a page reference indicates the number of a note on that page.